D0854938

This Day In Religion

by Ernie Gross

Published by Neal-Schuman Publishers, Inc.
23 Leonard Street
New York, NY 10013

Printed and bound in the United States of America

ISBN 1-55570-045-4

CONTENTS

PREFACE

An increasing number of Americans are reading such religious books as inspirational nonfiction and fiction with a religious theme. Theologians and clergy, of course, read scholarly works on religion. For these groups, *This Day in Religion* will provide a convenient, up-to-date, one-volume source for checking names, dates, and places, for cross-referencing people and their ideas. Who founded the American Catholic parochial school system? When did the Mormons end polygamy? When was the Order of St. Patrick established in Ireland?

There are also many people who consider themselves religious but confine their religious reading largely to the Bible. They are missing out on a wealth of events that have occurred since the biblical texts were written. For them, *This Day in Religion* offers a starting point from which to explore the exciting world of the development of Western religion and the often heroic lives of the saints, reformers, and other key figures.

This book is devoted primarily to Christianity, with lesser emphasis on Judaism and Eastern religions. It does not pretend to be a theological work and does not have any denominational leanings. It is strictly a book of facts.

Compiled from religious encyclopedias, dictionaries, and biographies, this work contains, in almanac form, a synopsis of the people and events that shaped contemporary religion. To cover as wide an area as possible, we have kept each entry brief. We have included a glossary to avoid sprinkling the pages of the text with learned footnotes. Each word or phrase that requires an explanation has an asterisk leading the reader to the glossary. There is also a bibliography of books for further consultation and an index, referenced by date.

The author hopes that *This Day in Religion* will not only arouse the interest and curiosity of readers and lead to additional study, but that it will also serve as a useful research, planning, and teaching tool for laity and clergy alike.

Ernie Gross

JANUARY 1

Feast of the Circumcision, commemorating the circumcision of Jesus eight days after his birth as required by Hebrew law.

379 St. Basil the Great, one of three Cappadocian Fathers* of the Catholic Church, died at about 49; was bishop of Caesarea in Cappadocia (now central Turkey); wrote "Rules," which make the Scriptures the norm of all monastic doctrine and practices, "Hexameron" and "The Morals;" developed the structure and spirit of Eastern monasticism; also observed as his feast day in the Orthodox Church.

391 St. Telemachus (or Alamachius), Eastern monk, was killed by spectators while trying to stop Roman gladiatorial show; as a result, Emperor Honorius halted the games; also observed as his feast day.

533 St. Fulgentius of Ruspe, North African bishop (508-533), died at 68; considered a Father* of the Church; also observed as his feast day.

1049 St. Odilo, fifth Abbot of Cluny (monastery near Macon in France), died at 87; inaugurated local observance of All Souls Day, which spread throughout the church; canonized 1063.

1431 Alexander VI, pope from 1492 to 1503, was born in Jativa, Spain as Rodrigo Lanzol Borgia; a nephew of Pope Calixtus III, he was considered one of the worst Renaissance popes.

1484 Huldreich Zwingli, the most important figure in the Swiss Reformation, was born near Zurich; began preaching "true divine Scriptures" in 1520, helped stir revolts against fasting and clerical celibacy; like Luther, he accepted the supreme authority of Scriptures but applied it more vigorously and comprehensively (died 1531).

1502 Gregory XIII, pope from 1572 to 1585, was born in Bologna, Italy as Ugo Buonocompagni.

1583 Simon (Bishop) Episcopius, Dutch theologian was born in Amsterdam; systematized, headed Arminian* movement after 1609; wrote Arminian confession of faith (died 1643).

1705 Charles Chauncy, Congregational clergyman, was born in Boston, the great grandson of Charles Chauncy (1592-1672); pastor of First Church, Boston for 60 years; opposed George Whitefield revival movement and attempts to impose on the colonies the Church of England service and system (died 1787).

1713 Blessed Joseph Tommassi died at 64; called the "prince of liturgists;" elevated to cardinal (1700) by Pope Clement XI, whom he served as confessor.

1750 Frederick A. C. Muhlenberg, Lutheran clergyman, was born in Trappe, Pa.; served in the Continental Congress (1779-80) and House of Representatives (1789-97), where he was the first Speaker (died 1801).

1779 Universalist Church of America was organized in Gloucester, Mass. with the dedication of the church on Water St.

1782 Juan Crespi, Spanish Franciscan missionary, died at 61; accompanied explorers Junipero Serra and Francisco Palou in the West; built a church in Tilaco, which still stands.

1786 John Early, Methodist prelate was born in Bedford County, Va.; a founder, board chairman, Randolph Macon College; one of the founders of the Methodist Episcopal Church, South, serving as a bishop (1854-66) (died 1883).

1819 Philip Schaff, religious scholar, was born in Chur, Switzerland; professor, Mercersburg (Pa.) Seminary, co-founding the "Mercersburg Theology" (1844-63); with Union Theological Seminary (1870-93); founder, American Society of Church History (1888); translated Herzog's religious encyclopedia into English; author (Creeds of Christendom, History of the Christian Church) (died 1893).

1826 Robert Rainy, Scottish Presbyterian leader, was born in Glasgow; principal, Free Church College, Edinburgh (1874-1901); played leading role in union of Free Church and United Presbyterian Church (1900), serving as first moderator (died 1906).

1836 The first Jewish congregation in Missouri held a service in St. Louis.

1842 Samuel D. Ferguson, Liberian Episcopal prelate, was born in Charleston, S. C.; missionary bishop of West Africa (1885-1916), the first Black elevated to an Episcopal bishopric (died 1916).

1855 Garrett Theological Seminary in Evanston, Ill. held its first classes; endowed by Eliza Garrett, widow of the Chicago mayor.

1856 Frank W. Gunsaulus, eloquent Congregational clergyman, was born in Chesterville, Ohio; served Plymouth Congregational and Independent Churches in Chicago (1887-1919); his appeal led Philip D. Armour to endow Armour Institute of Technology, of which Gunsaulus was president (1893-1921) (died 1921).

1874 Joseph E. Van Roey, Archbishop of Belgium (1926-61), was born in Vorselaar, Belgium; elevated to cardinal 1927 (died 1961).

1875 The *Canadian Methodist Magazine* began publication.

1884 Canon Alfred Barry was consecrated Bishop of Sydney and Metropolitan of Australia.

1888 Pope Leo XIII observed his 50th anniversary as a priest with 48 cardinals, 238 archbishops and bishops on hand in Rome: called for the independence of the church.

1934 The Church Union was formed by joining the English Church Union and the Anglo-Catholic Congress; dedicated to the defense of Anglo-Catholics.

1961 The merger of the American Lutheran Church, Evangelical Lutheran Church, and United Evangelical Lutheran Church went into effect; resulted in a church of nearly 2,500,000 members.

1966 Pope Paul VI called on the United States, Soviet Russia, Communist China and North and South Vietnam to work for an early end to the Vietnam War.

1967 Pope Paul VI issued the apostolic constitution, "Indulgentiarum doctrina," presenting a doctrine of indulgences as the church's official way of supporting the penance of its members; an indulgence taking effect only when a penitent is ready to advance his repentance by a greater love of God.

1968 The Canada Conference of the Evangelical United Brethren Church and the United Church of Canada merged.

1977 Rev. Jacqueline Means became the first woman to be ordained an Episcopal priest in ceremonies at All Saints Church, Indianapolis, with Bishop Donald J. Davis officiating.

1977 Fourteen Orthodox churches began preparations for the Great and Holy Synod, the first council in 1200 years.

1986 The Evangelical Lutheran Church in Canada began operations following the merger of the Evangelical Lutheran Church of Canada and the Canadian section of the Lutheran Church of America.

1988 The Evangelical Lutheran Church in America began functioning as the nation's fourth largest Protestant denomination; the 5.3 million member body was created by the merger of the Lutheran Church in America, the American Lutheran Church, and the Association of Evangelical Lutheran Churches.

JANUARY 2

Feast of the Martyrs for the Holy Scriptures, commemorating those who refused to surrender New Testament books as ordered by Diocletian; especially true in Litchfield, England, where almost the entire population was exterminated for its refusal (Jan 2, 303).

Feast day in the Catholic Church of St. Basil the Great, a Father* of the Church; had previously been observed June 14.

533 John II, born Mercutius, was consecrated as pope; served until 535; most important event of his pontificate was settlement of the Theopaschite* controversy; deposed an adulterous bishop, the first such jurisdictional act by a pope.

827 St. Adalhard (or Adelard), Abbot of Corbie (10 miles east of Amiens, France), died at 73; famed for setting up diocesan colleges; also observed as his feast day.

936 Leo VII was consecrated as pope, serving until 939; sought to install monastic reforms.

1784 William Allen, Congregational clergyman, was born in Pittsfield, Mass.; president, Dartmouth U. (1817-19), Bowdoin (1819-31, 1833-38); compiled "American Biographical and

Historical Dictionary," first work in America of its kind (died 1868).

1792 Edward Perronet, Anglican hymn writer, died at 71; best known hymn was "All hail the power of Jesus name."

1794 John Dempster, Methodist theologian, was born in Florida, N.Y.; founded Wesley Theological Institute, Newbury, Vt. (1845), the first American Methodist seminary; later became Boston U. Divinity School (died 1863).

1820 Isaac Errett, religious editor, was born in New York City; editor, *The Christian Standard*, official newspaper of Disciples of Christ Church (1866-88) (died 1888).

1822 Bernhard Felsenthal, rabbi, was born in Münchweiler, Germany; served Chicago synagogue (1864-87); a leader in Reformed Judaism and Zionist movements (died 1908).

1828 Jeremiah E. Rankin, Congregational clergyman and educator, was born in Thornton, N.H.; president, Howard U. (1889-1903); wrote the hymn, "God be with you till we meet again" (died 1904).

1833 St. Seraphim of Sarov, a famed Russian Orthodox mystic, died; also observed as his feast day in the Russian Orthodox Church.

1836 St. Caspar del Bufalo, founder of the Missioners of the Precious Blood, died at 61; canonized 1954; also observed as his feast day.

1853 George A. Gordon, Congregational clergyman, was born near Aberdeen, Scotland; pastor, Old South Church (1884-1929) (died 1929).

1856 Wilfrid P. Ward, Catholic author and apologist, was born in Old Hale, Ware, England; wrote biographies of Cardinals Wiseman and Newman and two-volume work on the role of his father (William G. Ward) in the ideological upheaval at Oxford (died 1916).

1873 St. Therese de Lisieux, Carmelite nun, was born in France; known as the "Little Flower of Jesus;" one of the most popular saints; canonized 1925 (died 1897).

1887 The Jewish Theological Seminary of America was founded in New York City by Alexander Kohut and Sabato Morais.

1945 The appointment of Geoffrey F. Fisher as Archbishop of Canterbury was announced.

1964 Pope Paul VI began three-day visit to the Holy Land, the first visit there since St. Peter.

1979 Worldwide Church of God, founded by Herbert W. Armstrong, was placed in temporary receivership after California officials accused church officers of "pilfering" its assets.

1980 Hans Kung, Swiss theologian who was suspended by the Vatican, was ordered to leave the theology department of Tubingen University in Bonn, West Germany.

JANUARY 3

236 St. Anterus (or Antherus), pope from Nov 21, 235, died; suffered martyrdom for authorizing the collection of acts of martyrdom by notaries, specially appointed persons to verify the truth of deeds or writings.

512 St. Genevieve, patron saint of Paris, died; reputed to have saved the city (451) from the Huns by her prayers; also observed as her feast day.

1521 Martin Luther was excommunicated by the issuance of a papal bull, "Decet Romanum pontificem."

1694 St. Paul of the Cross, congregations founder, was born in Ovado, Italy as Paul Francis Danei; founded the Congregation of the Discalced (barefooted) Clerks of the Most Holy Cross, the Congregation of Passion of Our Lord Jesus Christ (the Passionists), and the Institute of Passionate Nuns; canonized 1867 (died 1775).

1763 Joseph Fesch, French cardinal, was born in Corsica; an uncle of Napoleon, he was Archbishop of Lyon (1802-03), ambassador to the Vatican (1803-07), where he arranged the crowning of Napoleon as emperor by the Pope; later opposed Napoleon's policies and was banished to Rome (died 1839).

1793 Lucretia C. Mott, Quaker minister, was born in Nantucket, Mass.; active in anti-slavery movement with husband, James, and in women's rights activities (died 1880).

1802 Felix A. P. Dupanloup, Catholic prelate, was born in St. Felix, France; as Bishop of Orleans (1849-78), he instituted method of teaching children known as the "catechism of St. Sulpice;" became a foremost Catholic educator (died 1878).

1816 Anne Ayres, first woman in the United States to become a Protestant sister, was born in London; she was an original member of the Sisterhood of the Holy Communion (died 1896).

1825 First American secular utopian society was founded in New Harmony, Ind., by Robert Owen, Welsh socialist and philanthropist; lasted only a few years; Owen started others in Great Britain and United States, none of which succeeded.

1836 Young John Allen, Methodist missionary to China, was born in Burke County, Ga.; served in Shanghai (1860-1907), pioneer of Christian journalism in the Far East; founder, Anglo-Chinese College (died 1907).

1857 Catholic Archbishop Sibour of Paris was assassinated by a priest, Verger.

1884 E. Stanley Jones, Methodist missionary, was born in Clerksville, Md.; missionary to India and Far East (from 1907); crusaded for Christian unity through federal union (died 1973).

1915 Cardinal Desire J. Mercier of Belgium was arrested by Germans after he wrote pastoral letter to be read in all churches calling on Belgians to show their patriotism and endurance.

1963 Siberian Evangelical Christians, claiming religious persecution, were denied asylum in the American embassy in Moscow on the grounds that the matter was an internal Soviet problem.

1975 The Vatican issued a statement on ways to improve Catholic-Jewish relations, reasserted its condemnation of anti-Semitism, and called for eliminating all forms of discrimination against Jews.

1979 Spain and the Vatican signed agreements abrogating the 1953 concordat and redefined the status of the Catholic Church in Spain.

JANUARY 4

Feast day in the Catholic Church of St. Elizabeth Ann Seton, the first native of North America to be canonized.

275 St. Eutychianus became pope, served until 283.

1581 James Ussher, Archbishop of Armagh and primate of Ireland (1625-40), was born in Dublin; defeated attempts to make doctrinal standards of Irish church duplicate those of England; so great was his reputation for scholarship, tolerance, and sincerity, that on his death (1656), he was given a state funeral at Westminster Abbey by Oliver Cromwell.

1660 James Pierpont, clergyman and educator, was born in Roxbury, Mass.; pastor in New Haven (1685-1714); a founder and original trustee of Yale U. (died 1714).

1672 Hugh Boulter, Archbishop of Armagh and primate of Ireland (1724-42), was born in London; Bishop of Bristol (1719-24); virtual ruler of Ireland during Protestant ascendancy; helped reform Irish Anglican Church (died 1742).

1716 Aaron Burr, Presbyterian clergyman and educator, was born in Fairfield, Conn.; pastor, First Church, Newark, N.J. (1736-57); second president, College of New Jersey (later Princeton) (1748-57); father of Vice President Aaron Burr (died 1757).

1804 Samuel M. Isaacs, leading American orthodox rabbi, was born in Leeuwarden, Netherlands; rabbi in New York (1838-79); founder, editor, *Jewish Messenger* (1857-78); a founder, Mt. Sinai Hospital, Hebrew Free School Assn., and United Hebrew Charities (died 1878).

1893 President Benjamin Harrison proclaimed amnesty for past offenses against the newly-enacted Anti-Polygamy Law.

1956 Queen Elizabeth approved the appointment of Arthur Michael Ramsey, Bishop of Durham, as Archbishop of York.

1964 Pope Paul VI, beginning a three-day pilgrimage to the Holy Land, was surrounded by large crowds near the Damascus Gate to Jerusalem.

1985 Shemuda III returned to Cairo and resumed his duties as patriarch of Egypt's Coptic Church; he had been exiled in 1981.

JANUARY 5

Feast day in the Catholic Church of St. Simeon Stylites, who spent his time (433-459) atop a pillar, occasionally preaching to those gathered below; the first of the Stylite ascetics.

Feast day in the Catholic Church of St. Telesphorus, martyred pope, who served from about 125 to 136.

Feast day of St. Convoyan, founder (about 831) and abbott of the monastery of St. Saviour.

Feast day of St. Dorotheus the Younger, 11th Century founder and head of monastery at Khiliokomos.

269 St. Felix I was elected pope, served until 274.

1066 St. Edward the Confessor, English king (1042-66), died at 63; founder of Westminster Abbey; canonized 1161.

1548 Francisco Suarez, Jesuit leader, was born in Granada, Spain; considered the greatest Jesuit theologian (died 1617).

1782 Robert Morrison, Presbyterian missionary, was born near Newcastle, England; first Protestant missionary to China (1807); translated Bible into Chinese, wrote a Chinese dictionary, grammar; established the Anglo-Chinese College at Malacca (1820) (died 1834).

1811 Cyrus Hamlin, Congregational missionary, was born in Waterford, Me.; founded, headed, Robert College, Turkey (1863-77); president, Middlebury (Vt.) College (1881-87) (died 1900).

1835 Olympia Brown, first woman ordained minister, was born in Prairie Ronde, Mich.; first to be ordained in a regularly-constituted church (Universalist) in United States; president, Wisconsin Women's Suffrage Assn. (1887-1917) (died 1926).

1844 Albert E. Dunning, Congregational clergyman and editor, was born in Brookfield, Conn.; general secretary, Congregational Sunday School and Publishing Society (1880-89); editor, *The Congregationalist* (1889-1911) (died 1923).

1860 Edgar Y. Mullins, Baptist clergyman and theologian, was born in Franklin County, Miss.; secretary, Board of Foreign Missions, Southern Baptist Convention; president, Southern Baptist Theological Seminary, Louisville (died 1928).

1862 Christopher G. LaFarge, church architect, was born in Newport, R. I.; with partner, responsible for original design of Cathedral of St. John the Divine in New York City and many other cathedrals (died 1938).

1877 Henry Sloane Coffin, Presbyterian clergyman and theologian, was born in New York City; pastor, Madison Ave. Church, New York City (1905-26); president, Union Theological Seminary (1926-45); moderator of Presbyterian Church (1943-44) (died 1954).

1913 Pierre Veuillot, Archbishop of Paris (1966-68), was born in Paris; elevated to cardinal 1967 (died 1968).

1963 The first all-African Christian youth assembly closed a week's session in Nairobi, Kenya, with Protestant, Anglican, and Orthodox representatives from 35 nations in attendance.

1964 Pope Paul VI and Athenagoras I, ecumenical patriarch of Constantinople, met on the Mount of Olives in Jerusalem in the first meeting of leaders of the Roman Catholic and Orthodox churches since 1439.

1982 An Arkansas federal judge struck down an Arkansas law requiring the teaching of creation science, a theory of creation based on the Bible, in schools in which the theory of evolution was taught; the court ruled that creation science teaching violated the constitutional separation of church and state.

JANUARY 6

Feast of the Epiphany, commemorating the moment when it was perceived that Jesus Christ was the savior of all mankind.

Feast day of St. Wiltrudis (died about 986), founder and first abbess (about 976) of an abbey of Benedictine nuns, which became famous as Bergen (Baring) bei Neuberg.

1088 Berengar of Tours, French ecclesiastic, died at 90; attacked dogmas of transubstantiation* and the real presence; condemned for heresy, later recanted and spent the rest of his life as an ascetic; significance lies in assertion of the rights of dialectic* in theology.

1214 Archbishop of Canterbury and the barons presented their demands for reform to King John, who deferred his answer until June 15, 1215 (the Magna Carta).

1256 St. Gertrude, German mystic, was born; described her mystical experiences in "Revelations of Divine Love," a classic of mystical theology; one of the first exponents of devotion to the Sacred Heart (died 1311).

1275 St. Raymond of Penafort, Spanish monk and theologian, died; co-founder (1222) of Order of Our Lady of Mercy for the Redemption of Captives (the Mercedarians); called to Rome (1230) to codify canon law, served as general of the Dominicans (1238-40); canonized 1601.

1406 Roger Walden, Archbishop of Canterbury (1397-1405), died.

1412 Joan of Arc, was born in Domremy, France; at 13, she believed she heard voices from angels of God, telling her to aid the Dauphin (Charles) by raising the English siege of Orleans (1428); Charles consented and with a small force, Joan forced the English to withdraw; captured (1430) by Burgundians, who sold her to the English; charged with witchcraft and heresy; tried, found guilty by French clergy, burned at the stake (1431); canonized 1920.

1509 Melchor Cano, theologian, was born in Tarancon, Spain; provincial of the Dominican Order (1559-60); represented Spain at the Council of Trent; wrote "De locis theologias," an important statement of Thomistic* philosophy; a bitter opponent of Jesuits (died 1560).

1525 Casper Peucer, German reform leader, was born near Dresden; son-in-law of Philipp Melancthon; imprisoned (1574-86) for activity in secret Calvinist movement (died 1602).

1736 John and Charles Wesley arrived in Georgia at the invitation of General James Oglethorpe for what John Wesley was later to describe as the "second rise of Methodism."

1740 John Fawcett, Baptist clergyman, was born near Bradford, England; wrote hymn, "Blest be the tie that binds" (died 1817).

1811 Owen Lovejoy, Congregational clergyman and Maine legislator, was born in Albion, Me.; served in House (1854-64) and was one of first to urge Lincoln to lead the new party (Republican) (died 1864).

1821 Jakob Frohschammer, Catholic priest, was born in Germany; excommunicated (1871) for his radical views, holding that the human soul is created from unliving matter in the act of begetting (died 1893).

1842 Walter H. R. Elliott, educator and editor, was born in Detroit; founder (1896) of *The Missionary*, official organ of the Catholic Missionary Union; co-founder, Apostolic Mission House in Washington, for training missionaries (died 1928).

1890 Pope Leo XIII issued an encyclical letter on the moral duties of Catholics, which were being neglected.

1895 Pope Leo XIII issued the encyclical, "Longinqua oceani." warning against considering the American separation of church and state as ideal.

1924 The French Government granted legal status to the Catholic Church, with the right to occupy former property, after agreement with Pope Pius XI.

1928 Pope Pius XI issued the encyclical, "Mortalium animos," forbidding Catholics from taking part in reunion movements such as "Faith and Order."

1941 President Franklin D. Roosevelt, in his annual message to Congress, defined his goals for world peace in the "Four Freedoms" - Freedom of Speech, Freedom of Worship, Freedom from Want, Freedom from Fear.

1973 More than 140 church groups in the United States and Canada began "Key 73," a drive said to be the biggest evangelical campaign ever undertaken ecumenically.

JANUARY 7

Feast day of St. Cedd (or Cedda), bishop of the East Saxons who founded many churches and monasteries.

Feast day of St. Raymond of Penafort, Spanish canonist and co-founder of the Mercedarians.

312 St. Lucian, Catholic theologian regarded as the founder of the Antioch theological school, martyred; also observed as his feast day in the Catholic Church.

1566 St. Pius V was named pope, served until 1572; his main task was the detection and destruction of heresy; banished luxury in his court, raised the standard of morality in Rome, enforced the discipline of the Council of Trent; revised the Roman Breviary (1568), the Missal (1570).

1655 Innocent X, pope from 1644 to 1655, died.

1805 David Whitmer, Mormon leader, was born in Pennsylvania; brought Joseph Smith to his father's farm near Palmyra, N.Y., where the golden plates which Smith had uncovered were translated into the Book of Mormon (1830); Whitmer was privileged to examine the plates; later the two disagreed and Whitmer was excommunicated (1838) (died 1888).

1844 St. Bernadette of Lourdes was born as the peasant girl, Bernadette Soubirous, in Lourdes, France; had vision of Our Lady of Lourdes, who told her to make known the healing power of the waters; led to formation of Shrine of Lourdes; canonized 1933 (died 1879).

1880 Giacomo L. Copello, chancellor of the Catholic Church (1959-67), was born in San Isidro, Argentina; Archbishop of Buenos Aires (1932-59), elevated to cardinal 1935 (died 1967).

1890 A Brazilian decree proclaimed the separation of church and state.

1898 Hryhorij Osijchuk, primate of the Ukrainian Orthodox Autocephalous Church of the United States (1971-85), was born in Volliva, Russia (died 1985).

1934 Evangelist Billy Sunday began an intensive two-week revival campaign in Calvary Baptist Church, New York City; this was his first visit to New York City since 1917.

1967 The Methodist Church in Kenya became autonomous.

JANUARY 8

Feast day of Atticus, patriarch of Constantinople (404-425), who is venerated as a saint in the Orthodox Church; esteemed for his charity and piety.

Feast day of St. Apollonaris, Bishop of Hierapolis in Phrygia (Asian part of modern Turkey); a famous Christian teacher of the Second Century.

482 St. Severinus, who preached Christianity in what is now Austria, died; known as the "apostle of Austria;" also observed as his feast day.

1198 Celestine III, pope from 1191, died at 92.

1198 Innocent III, born Giovanni Lotaris de Conti, was named pope; served until 1216; his papacy marked the climax of medieval papacy; he was the first to use the title of "Vicar of Christ;" thought of his office in a semi-divine light "set in the midst between God and man, below God but above man;" urged the Fourth Crusade, which resulted in the capture of Constantinople and the establishment of the Latin Empire; presided at the Fourth Lateran Council (1215).

1438 Council of Ferrara-Florence opened, designed to reunite the Orthodox and Roman Catholic churches as a prelude to an effective alliance to save Constantinople from the Ottoman Turks; temporary union worked (1439) but Constantinople fell (1453), ending the Byzantine Empire; council ended 1445.

1440 Felix V was elected antipope by the Council of Basel; won only minimal allegiance; accepted terms of rightful pope, Nicholas V, and abdicated 1449.

1664 Moïse Amyraut, French-born Calvinist theologian, died at 68; his liberal form of Calvinism (Amyraldism) had many followers in colonial New England.

1735 John Carroll, first American Catholic bishop, was born in Upper Marlboro, Md.; became bishop in 1790, serving until 1808, when he became Archbishop of Baltimore, serving until his death (1815); founded (1791) what is now Georgetown U.

1792 Lowell Mason, hymn composer, was born in Medfield, Mass.; wrote many well-known hymns (Nearer, My God, to Thee; From Greenland's icy mountain; My faith looks up to Thee; Blessed be the tie that binds) (died 1872).

1900 Arthur Lichtenberger, presiding bishop of the American Episcopal Church (1958-64), was born in Oshkosh, Wis. (died 1988).

1962 Theoclitos, Greek Orthodox Archbishop of Athens and primate of Greece (1957-62), died at 72.

1966 Stefan Wyszynski, Catholic primate of Poland, was barred by the Polish Government from attending the Vatican celebration of the 1000th anniversary of Christianity in Poland.

1967 Pope Paul VI registered his disapproval of legislative moves to permit civil divorce in Italy.

1972 Dr. John C. McQuaid, Archbishop of Dublin and Primate of the Irish Republic Catholics, resigned at 76; he was succeeded by the Rev. Dermott Ryan.

1985 Rev. Lawrence Jenco, Catholic priest, was kidnapped in Beirut, Lebanon; released July 26, 1986.

JANUARY 9

Feast day of Claudius Apollonarius, Second Century Christian apologist; among his writings was "Defence of the Faith."

1554 Gregory XV, pope from 1621 to 1623, was born in Bologna, Italy as Alessandro Ludovisi (died 1623).

1626 Armand Jean Rance, French monk, was born in Paris; founder of the Trappist branch of the Cistercian Order (1664), abbot of LaTrappe monastery (1664-95) (died 1700).

1765 Pope Clement XIII issued the bull, "Apostolicum pascendi munus," defending the Jesuits against widespread attacks.

1807 Edwin F. Hatfield, Presbyterian clergyman and educator, was born in Elizabethtown, N.J.; pastor of Presbyterian churches in New York City and St. Louis (1832-63); served on administrative staff, Union Theological Seminary (1846-74) (died 1883).

1866 The Polish Government took over all church property.

1873 Rev. Henry Ward Beecher, most popular clergyman of his time, was charged with adultery by Theodore Tilton, alleging alienation of his wife's affection; Beecher was later acquitted.

1978 The missing 500-year old statue of Buddha was found in a Maxwell St., Chicago, flea market; it had disappeared while being flown from Thailand to a Denver temple.

JANUARY 10

Feast day in Orthodox Church of St. Gregory of Nyassa, one of the leading intellectuals of the Fourth Century; brother of St. Basil the Great; influenced the mystical tradition of the Eastern Church; a Father* of the Church and Bishop of Nyassa (371-396).

Feast day of St. Marcian, who built or restored a number of churches in Constantinople and was famous for his miracles.

236 St. Fabian was elected pope, serving until 250, when he became the first martyr victim under Decius.

681 St. Agatho, pope from 678 to 681, died; said to have been over 100 years old when named pope; furthered spread of Roman liturgy in England; highlight of his reign was the Sixth Ecumenical Council in Constantinople; also observed as his feast day.

1276 Blessed Gregory X, pope from 1271 to 1276, died; also observed as his feast day.

1479 Johannes Cochlaeus, Catholic controversialist, was born in Wendelstein, Germany; was a prominent opponent of Martin Luther (died 1552).

1607 St. Isaac Jogues, Jesuit missionary, was born in Orleans, France; served as missionary to Indians in Great Lakes area; slain in 1646; canonized along with six other North American martyrs in 1930.

1645 William Laud, Archbishop of Canterbury (1633-45), was beheaded.

1840 Louis N. Begin, Canadian Catholic prelate, was born in Quebec; Archbishop of Quebec (1898-1925); elevated to cardinal 1914; led a campaign of social action (died 1925).

1867 William P. Merrill, Presbyterian clergyman and hymn writer, was born in Orange, N.J.; served Sixth Church, Chicago (1895-1911), Brick Church, New York City (1911-38); wrote several hymns (Rise up, O men of God; Not alone for mighty empire) (died 1954).

1876 The new Catholic University in Paris was inaugurated.

1984 The United States and Vatican City restored full diplomatic relations after an interruption which began in 1867.

JANUARY 11

Feast day of St. Hyginus, pope from about 138 to about 142.

314 St. Miltiades, pope from 311 to 314, died.

705 John VI, pope from 701 to 705, died.

1696 Charles Albanel, French Jesuit missionary, died at 80; while serving in Quebec, he reached Hudson Bay (1672) by land, probably the first white man there.

1759 The first American life insurance company was incorporated in Philadelphia — the "Corporation of Poor and Distressed Presbyterian Ministers and of the Poor and Distressed Widows and Children of Presbyterian Ministers."

1791 William Williams, Welsh Calvinistic Methodist clergyman and hymnist, died at 74; among his hymns was "Guide me, O Thou Great Jehovah."

1810 Johann L. Krapf, German missionary and philologist, was born near Tübingen; missionary to East Africa, where he was co-discoverer of Mts. Kilimanjaro and Kenya (1848-49); introduced many Ethiopian manuscripts into Germany and England (died 1881).

1827 George Q. Cannon, Mormon leader, was born in Liverpool, England; an apostle of the Mormon Church (1857-1901); first counselor (1880-1901); delegate, House of Representatives (1873-81); imprisoned, fined for polygamy (1888); missionary to Hawaii and translated Mormon works into Hawaiian (died 1901).

1842 William James, psychologist and philosopher, was born in New York City; one of the founders of pragmatism; although not a church member, wrote of his own beliefs in "The Varieties of Religious Experience" (died 1910).

1843 Henry Y. Satterlee, Episcopal prelate, was born in New York City; while Bishop of Washington (D.C.) (1896-1908), he planned, started Washington Cathedral (died 1908).

1864 Thomas Dixon, Baptist clergyman, was born in Shelby, N.C.; best known for his novel, "The Clansman," which later became the movie, "The Birth of a Nation," for which he wrote the screenplay (died 1946).

1867 Sergius, patriarch of Moscow and all Russia, was born; served as primate of Russia (1943-44), achieving recognition (1943) of the Russian Orthodox Church by the Soviet Government (died 1944).

1869 Rev. Kelly Lowe organized the first Black Sunday School in the United States in the Springfield Baptist Church in Augusta, Ga.

1877 The legislature of New Mexico passed an act incorporating the Jesuit Fathers over the governor's veto; Congress annulled the act Feb 4, 1879.

1930 Pope Pius XI issued an encyclical declaring that the education of the young is pre-eminently a function of the Church.

1961 Halford Luccock, American clergyman who wrote a column under the name of "Simeon Stylites" in the *Christian Century* (1949-61), died in New Haven at about 75.

1968 Mosheh Zevi Segal, head of the Bible Department at Hebrew University (1926-68) and a pioneer in the study of Hebrew phonetics, died in Kfar Sava, Israel at 92.

JANUARY 12

690 St. Benedict Biscop (originally Biscop Baducing), English Benedictine abbot and builder of monasteries, died at 42; introduced the stone-built church and the art of glassmaking into England; teacher of St. Bede the Venerable; also observed as his feast day.

1167 St. Aelred (or Ailred), spiritual writer and contemporary of St. Bernard of Clairvaux, died at 58; sometimes called the English St. Bernard; canonized 1191; also observed as his feast day.

1632 Lazarists, or Congregation of Priests of the Mission, was founded.

1723 Samuel Langdon, Congregational clergyman and educator, was born in Boston; pastor, North Church, Portsmouth, N.H. (1747-74); president Harvard U. (1774-80) (died 1797).

1781 Richard Challoner, English Catholic leader, died at 90; led movement to revitalize Catholicism in 18th Century England and administered Catholic activities in ten countries and British North America.

1825 Brooke Foss Westcott, Anglican prelate and theologian, was born near Birmingham, England; divinity professor, Cambridge U. (1870-90), Canon of Westminster (1883-90), Bishop of Durham (1890-1901); co-author with F.J.A. Hort of a Greek text of the New Testament (died 1901).

1863 Vivekananda, Hindu saint and religious leader, was born in Calcutta; founded the Ramakrishna Order, represented Hinduism at World's Parliament of Religions in Chicago (1893) preaching the oneness of existence, the divinity of the soul, and the harmony of religions; inaugurated the Vedanta* movement in the United States (died 1902).

1953 Pope Pius XII elevated to cardinal Paul L. Leger, Archbishop of Montreal, and James F. McIntyre, Archbishop of Los Angeles.

1960 Charles M. (Daddy) Grace, evangelist who founded the House of Prayer for All People (1926), died in Los Angeles at about 79.

1972 The South Dakota Episcopal Diocese consecrated Rev. Harold S. Jones a suffragan bishop; a Sioux, he became the first Native American bishop in the Episcopal Church.

1972 The Salvation Army announced that Commander Edward Carey, head of the American Salvation Army, would retire January 28 to be succeeded by Commander Paul J. Carlson.

1974 Bishop Seraphim was chosen Archbishop of the Greek Orthodox Church; he was enthroned January 16 in the Athens Cathedral.

1982 The U. S. Supreme Court ruled 5-4 to bar a suit by the Americans United for Separation of Church and State which charged that a federal gift of property in Valley Forge, Pa. to the Forge Christian College violated the constitutional church/state separation.

JANUARY 13

367 St. Hilary of Poitiers, French bishop (353-367), died at about 52; a Doctor* and Father* of the Church, he was the most respected Latin theologian of his time; also observed as his feast day.

533 St. Remy (or Remi or Remigius), "Apostle of the Franks," died; was Bishop of Reims, reputedly converted Frankish King Clovis to Christianity.

603 St. Kentigern (or St. Mungo), first Bishop of Glasgow and its patron saint, died at about 85; evangelist in southwestern Scotland; founded the monastery at St. Asaph's in Wales, where he had been driven to take refuge (553-573).

1378 Calixtus III, pope from 1455 to 1458, was born in Valencia, Spain as Alfonso de Borgia.

1616 Antoinette Bourignon, Flemish religious reformer and self-proclaimed visionary, was born in Lille, France; claimed to have received direct revelations from Christ, who expressed dissatisfaction with current churches; formed a quietist theology based on internal and supernatural impulse; unsuccessful in founding a new ascetic order; ideas were condemned by many Protestant churches and all her works were on the Catholic index of forbidden books; had many followers in Scotland and renunciation of these beliefs is still required at ordination in the Established Church of Scotland (died 1680).

1635 Philipp J. Spener, Lutheran clergyman was born in Rappoltsweiler, Germany (now France); founder of pietism* which advocated personal piety rather than dogmatic beliefs (died 1705).

1691 George Fox, English-born founder of the Religious Society of Friends (Quakers), died at 67; began (1647) teaching that the truth is to be found in the inner voice of God speaking to the soul; about 1650, he formed "Friends of the Truth;" a magnetic personality of great spiritual power, selfless devotion, and patience in persecution; a remarkable organizer.

1817 John Henry A. Bomberger, German Reformed clergyman, was born in Lancaster, Pa.; pastor, Old Race St. Church, Philadelphia (1854-70), a leader of the anti-Mercersburg forces; founder, first president, Ursinus College, Collegeville, Pa. (1869-90) (died 1890).

1832 Horatio Alger, Unitarian clergyman, was born in Revere, Mass.; best known for his 100 popular books for boys stressing pluck, honesty, and hard work (died 1899).

JANUARY 14

Feast day in the Serbian Church of St. Sava, organizer and first archbishop of the independent Serbian Church (1219-36).

Feast day of St. Kentigern (or St. Mungo), first Bishop of Glasgow and its patron saint.

Former feast day of St. Hilary of Poitiers; now observed January 13.

346 St. Barba'shmin (or Barbasymas), Persian martyr, died; also observed as his feast day.

1477 Hermann of Wied, elector and Archbishop of Cologne (1515-46), was born in Germany; originally opposed Martin Luther, then instituted reforms in his diocese, moving closer to Protestant cause; reforms failed and he was excommunicated by Pope Paul III, (1546), deposed as elector (died 1552).

1505 Pope Julius II issued a constitution, "De fratrum nostrorum," which declared that any pontifical election procured by simony* was null and void.

1615 John Biddle, father of English Unitarianism, was baptized; wrote "Twelve Arguments," which denied the Holy Trinity; imprisoned and later (1655) banished by Oliver Cromwell to Scilly Islands to save his life; returned and died in London prison (1662).

1745 Gershon M. Seixas, patriot and rabbi, was born in New York City; rabbi, Spanish and Portuguese Synagogue, New York City (1766-76); closed rather than continue under British rule; led successful fight to remove Pennsylvania constitutional ban on Jews holding public office (died 1816).

1847 Borden Parker Bowne, Methodist liberal, was born in Leanderville, N.J.; author of "Personalism," which expounded the doctrine that ultimate reality consists of a plurality of spiritual beings or independent persons (died 1910).

1847 Wilson Carlile, English founder (1882) of the Church Army to help the poor, was born near London; called the "archbishop of the gutter" (died 1942).

1875 Albert Schweitzer, medical missionary and musicologist, was born in Alsace; founder (1913), head of hospital at Lambarene, Africa; author (The Quest for the Historical Jesus); awarded 1952 Nobel Peace Prize (died 1965).

1880 Pierre Gerlin, Archbishop of Lyon (1937-65), was born in Versailles, France; elevated to cardinal 1938 (died 1965).

1892 Martin Niemöller, German Protestant clergyman, was born; founder of the German Confessional Church; imprisoned (1938-45) for anti-Nazi stand and opposition to state control of Lutheran Church; a president, World Council of Churches (1961-68) (died 1984).

1893 Pope Leo XIII established an apostolic delegation in Washington, D.C. with Archbishop Francisco Satolli as the first delegate.

1902 The Chinese Government issued an edict protecting missionaries and native Christians.

JANUARY 15

Feast day of St. Macarius the Elder (about 300-391), a desert monk; founded a colony of monks in the desert of Scetis (west of the Nile River), one of the chief centers of Egyptian monasticism.

Former feast day of St. Paul of Thebes, called the founder of monasticism and probably the first desert hermit monk; said to have lived 113 years in the desert of Upper Egypt; the teacher of St. Anthony; observance of his feast day was discontinued in 1969.

708 Sissinius was elected pope; served only until February 4.

1549 Acts of Uniformity were issued by Parliament and King Edward VI, declaring that the order of worship drawn up by Archbishop Cranmer and others "with the aid of the Holy Ghost" should be the only one used after May 20; penalties included fines and imprisonment; repealed 1554, re-enacted 1559.

1803 Nathan Marcus Adler, rabbi, was born in Hanover, Germany; chief rabbi of Great Britain (1844), suggested the Uniform Synagogue Act (died 1890).

1809 Cornelia Connelly, religious order founder, was born in Philadelphia; founder, first superior, Society of the Holy Child Jesus (1847-79) (died 1879).

1841 Charles A. Briggs, scholar and theologian, was born in New York City; a foremost Old Testament scholar and vigorous exponent of "higher criticism;" suspended by Presbyterian General Assembly following a heresy trial for neglecting to take strict doctrine of inerrancy as the starting point for scholarship (1893); Union Theological Seminary broke with the Presbyterian Church as a result, becoming independent and undenominational; he was ordained by Episcopal Church (1900) (died 1913).

1848 Arnold B. Ehrlich, theologian, was born in Wlodawa, Poland; came to the United States in 1878, made important contributions to Old Testament scholarship (died 1919).

1854 The first Protestant church in New Mexico (Baptist) was dedicated in Santa Fe.

1859 William H. P. Faunce, Baptist clergyman and educator, was born in Worcester, Mass.; served churches in Springfield, Mass. and New York City (Fifth Ave. Church); president, Brown U. (1899-1929); author (What Does Christianity Mean?) (died 1930).

1866 Nathan Söderblom, Lutheran archbishop, was born in Trönö, Sweden; primate of Sweden (1914-31); organized first World Conference on Life and Work (1925), which eventually led to the formation of the World Council of Churches; awarded 1930 Nobel Peace Prize (died 1931).

1902 David J. Mathew, Catholic bishop auxiliary of Westminster (1938-45), was born in Lyme Regis, England; apostolic visitor to Ethiopia and other African missions (died 1975).

1906 Gustave Weigel, theology teacher at Catholic U. of Chile (1937-48), was born in Buffalo, N.Y.; consultant to the Secretariat for the Promotion of Christian Unity (1960-62), participant in Second Vatican Council (1962-64) (died 1964).

1920 John J. O'Connor, Catholic Archbishop of New York (1984-), was born in Philadelphia.

1929 Martin Luther King Jr., pastor and civil rights leader, was born in Atlanta, Ga.; founder, president, Southern Christian Leadership Conference; led numerous marches, sit-ins; awarded 1964 Nobel Peace Prize; assassinated in Memphis, Tenn. 1968.

1973 Israeli Premier Golda Meir and Pope Paul VI met in the Vatican, the first meeting of a pope and an Israeli Government official.

1977 A new church body, Anglicans United, was formed by dissident Episcopalians opposed to women priests.

JANUARY 16

Feast day of St. Fursey, Seventh Century Irish monk, noteworthy for his visions; writings considered inspiration for Dante's Divine Comedy.

309 St. Marcellus I, pope in 308-309, died in exile.

1756 Isaac Backus, champion of religious liberty, founded a new Baptist church in Middleborough, R.I.; served as its pastor for 50 years.

1786 Virginia adopted a statute of religious freedom, which had been drafted in 1779 by Thomas Jefferson; he ranked its authorship as one of his three great achievements - the others being the Declaration of Independence and the founding of the University of Virginia.

1813 Georges Darboy, third Archbishop of Paris (1863-71), was born in Fayl-Billot, France; consecrated newly-restored Cathedral of Notre Dame; shot to death as prisoner during Franco-Prussian War in 1871.

1853 Vladimir S. Solovyov, mystic and philosopher, was born in Moscow; strong advocate of reconciliation between the Russian Orthodox and Catholic churches; author (The Crisis of Western Philosophy, Russia and the Universal Church, History of Materialism, History of Ethics) (died 1900).

1929 Commissioner E. J. Higgins was elected General of the Salvation Army.

1953 Pope Pius XII issued the apostolic constitution, "Christus dominus," which standardized the relaxations in the Eucharistic Fast introduced during World War II.

1982 The Vatican and the United Kingdom established full diplomatic relations after a 450-year estrangement.

JANUARY 17

356 St. Anthony (Antony) of Egypt, an early Christian desert monk, died; some times called the founder of Christian monasticism; also observed as his feast day.

1463 Antoine Duprat, French cardinal (1527) and chancellor, was born in Issoire, France; negotiated the Concordat of Bologna (1516) with Pope Leo X by which the French crown gained greater control over church appointments in France (died 1535).

1484 Georg Spalatin, German Lutheran leader, was born near Nuremberg; associated with Martin Luther in advancing the Protestant Reformation; translated Latin writings of Luther, Philipp Melancthon, and Erasmus (died 1545).

1504 St. Pius V, pope from 1566 to 1572, was born near Turin, Italy as Michele Ghislere.

1694 Bishop St. Vallier of Quebec denounced all comedies and tragedies and prohibited all persons from attending a performance of Moliere's "Tartuffe."

1733 Devereux Jarratt, colonial Episcopal clergyman and missionary, was born in Kent County, Va.; rector of Bath Parish, Dinwiddie County, Va. (1763-92), serving an area of nearly 600 miles in Virginia and North Carolina (died 1801).

1789 Johann A. W. Neander, Protestant historian and theologian, was born in Öttingen, Germany; wrote numerous ecclesiastical histories; professor of church history, U. of Berlin (1813-50) (died 1850).

1829 Catherine Booth, known as the "mother of the Salvation Army," was born in Ashbourne, England; wife of William Booth, Army founder, she designed the Salvation Army flag and famous poke bonnet; helped introduce Army in United States, Australia, Europe, India, and Japan (died 1890).

1832 Henry M. Baird, Presbyterian clergyman and educator, was born in Philadelphia; wrote authoritative history of the Huguenots (died 1906).

1834 Cyrus D. Foss, Methodist prelate, was born in Kingston, N.Y.; served bishoprics in Minneapolis (1880-88), Philadelphia (1888-1910); president, Wesleyan U. (1875-80); president, Methodist Board of Church Extension (1888-1906) (died 1910).

1961 Archbishop of Canterbury Geoffrey F. Fisher announced his resignation.

1965 The heads of five Eastern Non-Chalcedonian churches began meeting in Addis Ababa, Ethiopia to discuss unity in the first common meeting since 451.

JANUARY 18

Feast of St. Peter's Chair in Rome, commemorating the occasion when St. Peter ascended the throne as Bishop of Rome, becoming the first pope.

336 Marcus was elected pope, serving until October 7.

1095 St. Wulfstan (or Wolstan), last English bishop named by a Saxon king, died; served as Bishop of Worcester (1062-95); canonized 1203.

1460 Pope Pius II issued the bull, "Execrabilis," which banned appeals from papal actions to a council, a complete reversal of his pre-papal position.

1562 The Council of Trent opened its third session after a lapse of 10 years; drew to a final close Dec. 4, 1563.

1778 Joseph Tuckerman, Unitarian clergyman, was born in Boston; founded (1812) Boston Society for the Religious and Moral Improvement of Seamen, the first sailor's aid society in the United States (died 1840).

1815 Konstantin von Tischendorf, biblical critic, was born near Leipzig, Germany; remembered for discovering, deciphering the important "Codex Sinaiticus," a Fifth Century manuscript of the epistles of St. Paul (died 1874).

1836 The Union Theological Seminary was founded in New York City, opening for instruction Dec. 5, 1836.

1880 Alfredo I. Schuster, Catholic cardinal, was born in Italy; Archbishop of Milan (1929-54); his most noted works were his nine-volume liturgical commentary, "Liber Sacrementorum" and his book on St. Benedict (died 1954).

1901 Pope Leo XIII issued the encyclical, "Graves de Communi," which dealt with Christian democracy.

1924 Pope Pius XI in an encyclical letter sanctioned a statute for organization of diocesan associations in France, allowing the French church to become legal owner of money required for church maintenance and the priesthood.

1970 David O. McKay, head of the Mormon Church, died at 96; five days later, he was succeeded by 93-year old Joseph Fielding Smith, grand nephew of the church founder.

JANUARY 19

Feast day of St. Wulfstan (or Wolstan), Bishop of Worcester for 32 years; canonized 1203.

Feast day in Sweden of St. Henry of Upsala, martyred bishop and patron saint of Finland.

Feast day of Blessed Margaret Bourgeoys (1620-1700), French-born founder (1676) of the Congregation of Notre Dame of Montreal; beatified 1960.

1563 The Heidelberg Catechism was completed; designed to pacify and unify conflicting Protestant ideologies; moderately Calvinistic in doctrine, it was meant to serve as both a catechism for youth and a confession of faith; it is the most ecumenical of Protestant catechisms and is still in use in some Dutch and German Reformed churches.

1565 Diego Laines (or Lainez or Laynes), Jesuit leader, died at 53; a founder of the Society of Jesus (Jesuits) with St. Ignatius Loyola; second general of the Jesuits (1558-65); his reign notable for the success and expansion of the order; emphasized the importance of education designed to influence the young for the good of the church.

1686 Hakuin, Japanese monk, was born in Hara, Japan; successfully revitalized the Rinzai sect and trained a body of skilled disciples; considered one of the great Zen masters (died 1769).

1774 Thomas Gillespie, founder of the Relief Church of Scotland, died at 68; deposed by Scottish Presbyterian Church for refusing to help install a pastor opposed by the congregation; preached on the open highway for six years before founding (1761) the Relief Church.

1798 Samuel A. Worcester, Congregational missionary, was born in Worcester, Mass.; worked among Cherokee Indians in Georgia, published newspaper and other documents in Cherokee language; imprisoned two years by the state, then moved his operation to an Oklahoma mission (died 1859).

1815 Abel Stevens, Methodist clergyman, was born in Philadelphia; historian of Methodism in the United States (died 1897).

1847 Josiah Strong, Congregational clergyman, was born in Naperville, Ill.; published two popular tracts - "Our Country," which emphasized evils and dangers in our social and economic life, and "The New Era," which defined the functions of the Christian Church on earth; founded League (later American Institute) for Social Service to carry on Christian work (died 1916).

1856 George E. Horr, Baptist educator, was born in Boston; president, Newton Theological Institute (1908-27) (died 1927).

1888 Ernesto Ruffini, conservative Archbishop of Palermo, Sicily, (1945-67), was born in San Benedetto, Italy; elevated to cardinal (died 1967).

1901 Ernest C. Colwell, Methodist educator and theologian, was born in Hallstead, Pa.; with University of Chicago Divinity School - professor of New Testament (1930-44), dean (1938-45), president (1945-51) (died 1974).

1961 Arthur M. Ramsey, Archbishop of York, was nominated to succeed Geoffrey F. Fisher as the 100th Archbishop of Canterbury.

1965 The Central Committee of the World Council of Churches authorized a regular exchange of meetings with representatives of the Catholic Church.

JANUARY 20

Feast day in Finland of St. Henry of Upsala, English bishop and patron of Finland, who was martyred about 1156.

Feast day of St. Sebastian, who was martyred in Rome during the reign of Emperor Diocletian about 354; he was a soldier who made many converts and refused an order to stop converting.

250 St. Fabian, pope from 236 to 250, died; martyred as the first victim during the persecution under Decius; pontificate marked by rapid development of the church; also observed as his feast day.

473 St. Euthymius the Great died; Armenian-born monk who exercised great influence on Palestine monasticism; also observed as his feast day.

1045 Sylvester III, Bishop of Sabina (suburban Rome), became pope; served less than two months.

1541 A popular meeting in Geneva ratified a plan of John Calvin to set up a church court to maintain discipline - a weekly consistory to judge all church evildoers.

1569 Miles Coverdale, English prelate and biblical scholar, died at 81; produced the first English version of the entire Bible (1539), edited the second Great Bible (called Cranmer's Bible) (1540); left England on the fall of Oliver Cromwell (1542); returned to become Bishop of Exeter (1551-53).

1724 Isaac Backus, Baptist clergyman, was born in Norwich, Conn.; pastor, First Baptist Church, Middleborough, Mass. (1756-1806); champion of religious liberty (died 1806).

1874 Karl Heim, Protestant theologian, was born in Germany; professor of systematic theology at various universities; his major work was the six-volume "Evangelical Faith and the Thought of the Present" (died 1959).

1884 John J. Mitty, Archbishop of San Francisco (1935-61), was born in New York City (died 1961).

1891 Dr. Charles A. Briggs delivered an address at Union Theological Seminary, New York City, on "The Authority of the Scriptures," which resulted in his heresy trial; the New York Presbytery dismissed the charge of heresy (Nov 4) but referred matter to the church's General Assembly, which eventually found him guilty.

JANUARY 21

Feast day of St. Agnes, one of the most celebrated Roman martyrs; burned at the stake (about 304) for refusing to renounce her faith and marry the prefect's son; patron saint of young girls, who formerly observed St. Agnes' Eve (Jan. 20-21) with rites intended to reveal their future husbands.

Feast day in Orthodox Church of St. Maximus the Confessor, Byzantine monk and spiritual writer.

259 St. Fructuosus, Bishop of Tarragona (southwest of Barcelona, Spain), was burned at the stake for refusing to offer pagan sacrifices; also observed as his feast day.

1276 Blessed Innocent V, born Pierre de Champagni, was named pope, the first Dominican pope; died in about six months; in short reign, he managed to bring peace to warring cities of Italy; beatified 1898.

1525 Konrad Grebel, Swiss religious leader, along with Felix Manz and George Blaurock, founded the first German Anabaptist* church and performed the first adult baptism in modern history.

1619 Claude Dablon, Jesuit missionary, was born in Dieppe, France; served as superior of Canadian missions (1671-80, 1686-93); assigned Jacques Marquette to accompany Joliet in his exploration (died 1697).

1621 Pilgrims aboard the Mayflower gathered on shore at Plymouth, Mass. for their first religious service in America.

1773 Klemens A. von Droste zu Vischering, German prelate, was born in Munster; Archbishop of Cologne (1835-42), imprisoned (1837-39) following a dispute with the Prussian Government over mixed marriages (died 1845).

1797 Edward Mote, Baptist clergyman and hymn writer, was born in London; best known for hymns "My hope is built" and "No earth nor hell my soul can move" (died 1874).

1800 Theodor Fliedner, German Protestant theologian, was born; founder of housing for nursing deaconesses at Kaiserswerth and elsewhere; founded first German prison society (1826), refuge for female convicts (1833), infant school (1835) (died 1864).

1858 Joseph Krauskopf, a leader in American Reformed Judaism, was born in Ostrowo, Poland; served Philadelphia synagogue (1887-1923); founded National Farm School in Doylestown, Pa., a nonsectarian agricultural institution (died 1923).

1862 George D. Herron, Congregational theologian and socialist, was born in Montezuma, Ind.; professor of applied Christianity, Grinnell (Iowa) College (1893-99); joined Socialist Party (1899); with Mrs. E. D. Rand organized the Rand School of Social Sciences, New York City (1906) (died 1925).

1874 Frederick M. Smith, Mormon leader, was born in Plano, Ill., grandson of Joseph Smith, Mormon Church founder; succeeded father as president of the Reorganized Church of Jesus of Latter-Day Saints (1915-46) (died 1946).

1874 Samuel H. Hooke, religious editor and writer, was born in Cirencester, England; editor for 23 years of *Palestine Exploration Quarterly;* translated Bible into Basic English; wrote 14 books on the Christian faith and the Old Testament (died 1968).

1967 The Methodist Church in Sierra Leone became autonomous.

1982 Leaders of the American Lutheran Church, the Lutheran Church in America, and the Association of Evangelical Lutheran Churches announced they hope to complete formation of a new Lutheran church by 1987.

JANUARY 22

Feast day in Orthodox and Syrian churches of St. Timothy, companion of Paul.

304 St. Vincent of Saragossa (northern Spain), patron of the wine industry, died; martyred in Spain; also observed as his feast day.

1832 William S. Perry, Episcopal prelate and historian, was born in Providence, R. I.; Bishop of Iowa (1876-98); historian of Episcopal Church (1868-98) (died 1898).

1843 Francis L. Patton, educator and theologian, was born in Bermuda; professor, Princeton Theological Seminary (1881-88), president (1902-13); professor, Princeton U. (1884-1913), president (1888-1902) (died 1932).

1850 St. Vincent Pallotti died at 55; founder of the Society of Catholic Apostolate (Pallotine Fathers); also observed as his feast day.

1896 Norman T. Gilroy, first Australian Catholic cardinal, was born in Sydney; Archbishop of Sydney (1940-71) (died 1977).

1899 Pope Leo XIII issued the encyclical, "Testem benevolentiae," condemning as "Americanism" certain proposals by some churchmen that the church modify its doctrine to suit modern civilization, grant more individual freedom, and eliminate vows in religious life.

1900 Superior and 11 monks of the Assumptionist Fathers in France were charged with belonging to an illegal association and with issuing propaganda against the government; community dissolved and the persons were fined.

1901 Associations bill was passed by the French Chamber of Deputies, legislating against unauthorized religious tutelage and communities; promulgated July 1; about half the 16,500 religious establishments filed for authorization under the act but the Jesuits, Passionists, Assumptionists, Benedictines, and some others left France.

1922 Benedict XV, pope from 1914 to 1922, died at 68.

1972 The Swiss Government announced it would revoke the 124-year-old ban on the Society of Jesus (Jesuits) and the constitutional ban on the construction of new monasteries and convents.

1978 A special study group of the 2,600,000 member United Presbyterian Church in the U.S.A. recommended the church adopt a policy permitting the ordination of practicing homosexuals who otherwise meet the requirements for the clergy; recommendation was disapproved by the General Assembly in May.

JANUARY 23

Former feast day of St. Raymond of Penafort, Spanish Dominican friar who compiled (1230) medieval papal statutes and rulings; canonized 1601; now observed Jan. 7.

1167 Abraham ben Meir Ibn Ezra, Spanish Jewish scholar, died at 75; translated into Hebrew the work of Jewish philologists and philosophers who had written in Arabic, opening a wealth of literature; wrote many books on various sciences; also known for commentaries on the Bible; was the inspiration for Robert Browning's "Rabbi Ben Ezra."

1295 Boniface VIII was crowned pope, served until 1303.

1572 St. Jane Frances de Chantal, French nun, was born in Dijon; founder with St. Francis de Sales and superior of the Congregation of the Visitation of Our Lady (Visitation Nuns) at Annecy (1610); canonized 1767 (died 1641).

1789 The first American Catholic college (Georgetown) was founded in Washington, D.C.; opened in 1791.

1790 Samuel H. Turner, Episcopal clergyman and educator, was born in Philadelphia; professor, General Theological Seminary, New York City (1818-61); author of a series of commentaries on books of the Bible (died 1861).

1813 Franz Delitsch, German biblical scholar, was born in Leipzig; one of the foremost interpreters of the Old Testament; sought to combat anti-Semitism and foster conversion of the Jews (died 1890).

1814 Rome, which had become part of the Kingdom of Italy, was returned to the Pope.

1853 Charles Gore, Anglican prelate and theologian, was born near London; Bishop of Birmingham and Oxford; author (The Church and the Ministry, Lux Mundi); regarded as leader of the Anglo-Catholic movement (died 1932).

1891 Cardinal John Simor, Archbishop of Grau and primate of Hungary, died; succeeded by Arch-Abbot Claude Vaszara.

1941 John Oxenham, English author, died at about 85; remembered for hymn,"In Christ, there is no East or West."

1970 Joseph Fielding Smith, great nephew of Joseph Smith, the church founder, was named the 10th president of the Mormon Church.

1972 Archbishop of Canterbury Arthur M. Ramsey preached in St. Patrick's Cathedral, New York City, the first time any head of the worldwide Anglican communion occupied the pulpit of the Catholic cathedral.

JANUARY 24

Feast day in the Catholic Church of St. Babylas, Bishop of Antioch (about 240-250), who once refused to admit an emperor to church because of an unrepented crime.

Former feast day in the Catholic Church of St. Timothy, companion of the Apostle Paul, who called him "my son in the Lord;" now observed January 26.

772 Stephen III, pope from 768 to 772, died.

817 Stephen IV, pope from 816 to 817, died.

1059 Nicholas II, former Bishop Gerard of Florence, was enthroned as pope; served until 1061.

1118 Gelasius II, born Giovanni de Gaeta, was elected pope; served until 1119; persecuted and driven out of Rome; died in the convent of Cluny, France.

1519 A papal bull made Julian Garces, a Dominican, Bishop of Cozumel Island, Mexico.

1722 Edward Wigglesworth was named the first Thomas Hollis Professor of Divinity at Harvard University, probably the first American divinity professor.

1814 John W. Colenso, Bishop of Natal (1853-63), was born in Cornwall, England; compiled dictionary, grammar of Zulu language; translated Bible into Zulu; provoked controversy with his liberal views; championed natives against Boer oppression (died 1883).

1818 John M. Neale, Anglican clergyman and hymnist, was born in London; established the Sisterhood of St. Margaret (1854); known for his translation into English of Greek and Latin Christian hymns and wrote many hymns (O happy band of pilgrims, Art thou weary?); author of a five-volume history of the Orthodox Church (died 1866).

1827 John A. Broadus, Baptist clergyman and educator, was born in Culpeper County, Va.; professor, president, Southern Baptist Theological Seminary, Greenville, S.C. (later Louisville, Ky) (died 1895).

1899 Catholic Bishop Denis O'Connor was named Archbishop of Toronto.

1902 Ephraim A. Speiser, professor of Semitics and Hebrew and Semitic language and literature (U. of Pennsylvania 1931-65), was born in Skalat, Poland (died 1965).

1918 Oral Roberts, evangelist, was born in Ada, Okla.; built up his Pentecostal Church to millions of members through personal and television evangelism.

1975 The Most Rev. Frederick Donald Coggan was enthroned as Archbishop of Canterbury.

JANUARY 25

Feast day of St. Ananias of Damascus, who brought St. Paul into the Church; after conversion, Paul continued, blinded, to Damascus where Ananias restored his sight; also the feast day of St. Paul's conversion from Saul of Tarsus to Paul the Apostle, the greatest Christian missionary.

Feast day in the Orthodox Church of St. Gregory of Nazianzus (in Cappadocia, eastern Asia Minor); a Doctor* of the Church and one of the Cappadocian Fathers; one of the greatest champions of orthodoxy against Arianism*; served as Bishop of Constantinople (380-389).

817 Paschal I was consecrated as pope, served until 824; received a document from Louis I confirming the rights and possessions of the church; a devoted supporter of monasticism.

844 Gregory IV, pope from 827 to 844, died.

1138 Anacletus II, born Pietro Pierleoni, an antipope (1130-38), died; he was acknowledged only in Rome and Sicily; elected in opposition to Innocent II (1130-43); excommunicated (1134) by the Council of Pisa.

1366 Heinrich Suso, German mystic, died at about 66; an itinerant preacher, he was a renowned pupil of Meister Eckhardt; his book, "The Little Book of Eternal Wisdom," was a classic of German mysticism; beatified 1831.

1509 Giovanni Morone, Italian cardinal and papal diplomat, was born in Milan; papal nuncio to Germany, Bishop of Novara (west of Milan) (1553-60), of Ostia (port of Rome) (1570-80); presided at Council of Trent; nominated for pope by Cardinal Charles Borromeo but election was blocked (died 1580).

1540 St. Edmund Campion, English Jesuit martyr, was born in London; originally an Anglican, became a Catholic (1578) and left England; sent back (1580) to coerce temporizing Catholics; attacked Anglican Church at the 1581 Oxford commencement, arrested and offered his life if he returned to the Anglican Church; refused, charged with conspiracy against the Crown, executed (1581); beatified 1886, canonized 1970.

1554 Jesuit College of Sao Paulo, Brazil was founded.

1627 Robert Boyle, noted British physicist and chemist, was born in Munster, Ireland; endowed the Boyle lectures for the defense of Christianity against unbelievers (died 1691).

1688 Abbe de St. Vallier was consecrated as the second bishop of Quebec, succeeding Bishop Francois de Laval.

1783 William Colgate, industrialist and philanthropist, was born in Kent, England; founder, head of an American soap, toiletries company; founder of American Bible Society (died 1857).

1807 William Adams, Presbyterian clergyman and theologian, was born in Colchester, Conn.; a founder (1836), president, Union Theological Seminary (1873-80) (died 1880).

1863 Rufus M. Jones, a founder of American Friends Service Committee (1917), was born in South China, Me.; professor of philosophy, Haverford College (1904-34); shared 1947 Nobel Peace Prize (died 1948).

1874 Hewlett Johnson, known as the "Red Dean" for his friendliness to Communism, was born in Manchester, England; Dean of Manchester Cathedral (1924-31), of Canterbury Cathedral (1931-66) (died 1966).

1875 John F. Noll, Catholic Bishop of Ft. Wayne, Ind. (1925-56) and noted writer and editor, was born in Ft. Wayne; wrote "Kind Words From Your Pastor," which was used by other clergy and went through 24 printings; founded *Parish Monthly*, which became *Family Digest*, and *Our Sunday Visitor* and *The Priest*, a monthly (died 1956).

1885 (John) William Wand, Bishop of London (1945-55), was born in Grantham, England; Archbishop of Brisbane, Australia (1934-43), Bishop of Bath and Wells (1943-45) (died 1977).

1900 House of Representatives refused (268 to 50) to seat Rep. Brigham H. Roberts of Utah because of his plural marriages.

1905 Maurice Roy, Catholic Archbishop of Quebec (1947-81) and primate of Canada (1956-81), was born in Quebec; elevated to cardinal 1965 (died 1985).

1959 Pope John XXIII announced plans to call the first ecumenical conference since 1870 for the purpose of reuniting Christian communities separated from Rome.

1983 Pope John Paul II signed a new code of canon law, containing 1,752 canons, which were to become effective Nov 27, 1983; the revised code, ordered 24 years earlier, outlined the rights of clergy and lay people for the first time.

JANUARY 26

Feast day in the Catholic Church of St. Timothy, companion of St. Paul, who called him "My son in the Lord," and of St. Titus, a disciple of St. Paul.

Former feast day of St. Polycarp, Bishop of Smyrna, who was burned at the stake (about 168); called the "teacher of Asia;" his martyrdom led to the start of observance days.

404 St. Paula died; a Roman matron who settled in Bethlehem, where she founded two convents; also observed as her feast day.

1108 St. Alberic (or Aubrey), founder of the Cistercian monks, died; also observed as his feast day.

1188 St. Eystein of Norway, originally Eystein Erlandsson, died; chaplain to the Norwegian king, he became Archbishop of Nidaros; also observed as his feast day.

1657 William Wake, English prelate, was born near Dorchester; Archbishop of Canterbury (1716-37), he negotiated with French Jansenists on a proposed union with the Anglican Church (died 1737).

1790 William Capers, Methodist missionary to the Creek Indians, was born in St. Thomas Parish, S.C.; editor, *Wesleyan Journal* and *Southern Christian Advocate*; secretary, Southern missions; Methodist, South bishop (1846-55) (died 1855).

1799 Samuel Gobat, Anglican bishop, was born in Switzerland; served as the second Anglican-German Bishop of Jerusalem (1854-79) (died 1879).

1837 Daniel S. Tuttle, Episcopal prelate, was born in Windham, N.Y.; served as missionary bishop of Montana (1869-86), Bishop of Missouri and presiding Episcopal bishop (1903-23) (died 1923).

1838 Joseph Cook, originally Flavius Josephus, Congregational clergyman, was born in Ticonderoga, N.Y.; gained fame for his defense of Christianity against biblical critics, freethinkers, and evolutionists; author (Biology, Current Religious Perils) (died 1901).

1853 Arthur F. W. Ingram, Anglican prelate, was born near Worcester, England; Canon of St. Paul's Cathedral, Bishop of London (1901-39); leader in Oxford settlement; founder (1888), Oxford Home in London's East End (died 1946).

1902 Andrew B. Davidson, Scottish biblical scholar, died at 71; a member of the Old Testament revision committee (1870-84); spent life on language research, historical interpretation of the Old Testament; his commentary on the Book of Job (1862) was the first scientific treatment of the Old Testament in English.

1905 John C. Heenan, Archbishop of Westminster (1963-75), was born in Ilford, England; superior, Catholic Missionary Society (England Wales) (1947-51), Bishop of Leeds (1951-57), Archbishop of Liverpool (1957-63), elevated to cardinal 1965 (died 1975).

1912 The Cathedral of Khartoum, Sudan, was dedicated by the Bishop of London.

1961 Henry D. A. Major, a leader of the English modernist movement, died at 90; he was the last Church of England priest to be charged with heresy for trying to reconcile science and religion.

1972 The 16-volume Encyclopedia Judaica, published in Jerusalem, was released.

1985 Pope John Paul II began a 12-day visit to South America.

JANUARY 27

Former feast day of St. John Chrysostum, patriarch of Constantinople; now observed in the Catholic Church on September 13.

417 Pelagius, a British monk whose doctrine was considered heretical, was excommunicated by Pope Innocent I; doctrine denied original sin and held that man could be righteous by the exercise of free will.

672 St. Vitalien, pope from 657 to 672, died; also observed as his feast day.

847 Sergius II, pope from 844 to 847 died; during his reign Rome was sacked by the Saracens (846).

1800 James H. Otey, first Episcopal Bishop of Tennessee (1834-63), was born in Liberty, Va. (died 1863).

1806 Joseph Octave Plessis was named Bishop of Quebec and primate of Canadian Catholics, succeeding Bishop Pierre Dunand.

1808 David F. Strauss, German theologian and biographer, was born near Stuttgart; author of one of the most sensational religious books of the 19th Century, "Leben Jesu;" interpreted Gospel accounts of life of Jesus as a myth; professor at Zurich, but strong opposition forced him to leave (died 1874).

1812 Henry T. Anderson, theologian who translated the New Testament from the original Greek (1864), was born in Caroline County, Va. (died 1872).

1825 William H. Green, Presbyterian clergyman, was born in Groveville, N.J.; a noted Hebrew scholar and the American leader of the ultraconservative school of biblical criticism (died 1900).

1847 Henry S. Holland, Anglican clergyman and author, was born in Wimbledon, England; considered one of the most brilliant preachers and writers of his time; sought to relate Christian principles to the social and economic problems of human living; a founder of the Christian Social Union; wrote hymns (Judge eternal, throned in splendor) (died 1918).

1850 John F. Genung, Baptist biblical scholar, was born in Willseyville, N.Y.; served in Amherst College (1882-1919); author (The Epic of the Inner Life, Ecclesiastes, A Guidebook to the Biblical Literature) (died 1919).

1973 Pope Paul VI proclaimed sainthood of Teresa Jornet Ibars, a 19th Century Spanish nun who founded the Congregation of Little Sisters of Abandoned Old People.

1977 The Vatican, affirming the refusal of the Catholic Church to ordain women as priests, said they cannot qualify because Jesus was a man and His representative on earth must have a "natural resemblance" to him.

1979 Pope John Paul II opened the third Latin American Bishop's Conference in Mexico City.

JANUARY 28

Former feast day of St. Peter Nolasco, French-born cofounder of the Order of Our Lady of Mercy (de Mercede) (the Mercedarians or Nolascans); canonized 1628; observances dropped in 1969.

814 St. Charlemagne, founder of the Holy Roman Empire, died; also observed as his feast day, primarily among college students in France.

1119 Gelasius II, pope from 1118, died.

1549 Elias Levitas (Elijah ben Asher ha-Levi), German-born rabbi, died at 80; taught in various Italian colleges; a noted Hebrew grammarian whose work led Christendom to return to documentary sources for its doctrine.

1573 The Compact of Warsaw was signed, guaranteeing Polish religious freedom.

1600 Clement IX, pope from 1667 to 1669, was born as Giulio Rospigliosi in Pistoia, Italy.

1621 Paul V, pope from 1605 to 1621, died.

1768 Jean Louis L. de Cheverus, Catholic prelate, was born in Mayenne, France; became first Bishop of Boston (1808-23); returned to France, became Archbishop of Bordeaux (1823-36); elevated to cardinal 1836 (died 1836).

1769 Thomas F. Middleton, Anglican prelate, was born in Kedleston, England; first Anglican Bishop of Calcutta (1814-22), the see included all of India and Australia; founded Bishop's College, Calcutta (died 1822).

1799 Richard Rothe, German Protestant theologian, was born in Posen; author of a three-volume "Theologische Ethick" (a system of speculative theology) (died 1867).

1809 Richard V. Whelan, Catholic Bishop of Richmond, Va. (1841), was born in Baltimore; served an area of 60,000 sq. mi., developed area that later became West Virginia of which he became bishop (1850) (died 1874).

1834 Sabine Baring-Gould, Anglican rector and hymnist, was born in Exeter, England; edited 15-volume "Lives of the Saints" and various other theological works; hymns include "Now the day is over" and "Onward Christian soldiers" (died 1924).

1856 Reuben A. Torrey, evangelist, was born in Hoboken, N.J.; a successor of Dwight L. Moody, he was superintendent of the Moody Bible Institute (1889-1908); dean, Bible Institute, Los Angeles (1912-24); pastor, Church of the Open Door, Los Angeles (1915-24) (died 1928).

1864 Samuel McComb, clergyman and theologian, was born in Londonderry, Ireland; associated with the Emmanuel Movement ("moral treatment of nervous disorder") in Boston; canon, Cathedral of the Incarnation, Baltimore (died 1938).

1893 Abba Hillel Silver, American Reformed rabbi and Zionist leader, was born in Neinstadt, Lithuania; rabbi, Cleveland Temple (1917-63); chief spokesman for the Jewish Agency in the United Nations debate over the founding of Israel (died 1963).

1978 The first bishops were named in the provisional Anglican Church of North America, an outgrowth of the schism over the Episcopal Church decision to ordain women as priests.

JANUARY 29

Feast day of St. Francis de Sales, French bishop, author and Doctor* of the Church.

570 St. Gildas the Wise, monk and first British historian, died; wrote the only history of the Celts; also observed as his feast day.

904 Sergius III was consecrated as pope, served until 911; became pope after arranging the assassination of his predecessor (Leo V) and a rival claimant; rebuilt basilica of St. John Lateran, which had been destroyed by an earthquake.

1118 Paschal II, pope from 1099 to 1118, died.

1523 "Disputation" was ordered by the Swiss Government to test the truth of the teachings of Huldreich Zwingli; he prepared 67 proofs in setting up his church reforms; Johannes Faber, vicar-general of the Catholic Bishop of Constance, discussed only one of the proofs; Zurich Council held that Zwingli was not convicted of error; a second disputation led to virtual elimination of the Catholic Church in Zurich.

1656 Samuel Andrew, Congregational clergyman, was born in Cambridge, Mass.; helped found Yale U., acting rector (1707-19); pastor of Milford (Conn.) Congregational Church (1685-1713) (died 1738).

1688 Emanuel Swedenborg, theologian, was born in Stockholm; rejected the traditional doctrines of the Trinity, original sin, vicarious atonement, a chief devil, and eternal punishment as an expression of divine vengeance; taught that eternal life was an inner condition beginning with earthly life, that gradual redemption occurs through personal regulation of spiritual states; did not try to found a sect but groups sprang up after his death (1772); wrote numerous theological studies and "Heaven and Hell," an account of his spiritual experiences.

1876 Christophoros III, Greek Orthodox patriarch of Alexandria (1939-67), was born in Azyts, Greece (died 1967).

1972 The historic separation of white and black Methodist conferences in South Carolina ended when the two conferences met together for the first time, voted to accept a plan of union.

1978 The Reformed Protestant Dutch Church of New York City celebrated its 350th birthday.

1982 The World Council of Churches Committee on Faith and Order, meeting in Lima, Peru, took a major step toward resolving some theological disagreements that have divided Christian churches for centuries.

JANUARY 30

Feast day among many Episcopal parishes of St. Charles I, king of England (1625-49), who was beheaded (Jan 30, 1649) on orders of Oliver Cromwell and the Puritans.

Feast day in Orthodox Church of St. Hippolytus, who set himself up as the first anti-pope (217-235); known as "chief of the bishops of Rome;" a noted theologian, to whom is attributed the "Canons of Hippolytus" and various instructions.

680 St. Bathildis, French queen, died; wife of Clovis II and benefactor of many monasteries; founder of the Abbey of Corgie (near Amiens, France); also observed as her feast day.

1563 Franciscus Gomarus (Francis Gomar), Scholastic Calvinist theologian, was born in the Netherlands; led the attack on Jacobus Arminius, who objected to the shift in Calvinism to medieval Scholasticism,* with emphasis on predestination; instrumental in getting the Synod of Dort to condemn Arminianism* (died 1641).

1592 Clement VIII was elected pope, served until 1605; ordered revisions in the Vulgate*, breviary, and liturgical books; the revised Vulgate (known as the Clementine), was issued in 1592, served as the standard Bible text of the Catholic Church for more than 300 years.

1617 William Sancroft, English prelate, was born near London; Archbishop of Canterbury (1678-91); reign marked by an effort to renew the strength of the Anglican establishment; refused to read James II's Declaration of Indulgences (1688) which exempted Catholics and dissenters from penal statues; tried, acquitted of seditious libel; deprived of his see as a nonjuror* (1690) (died 1693).

1792 John H. Hopkins, Episcopal prelate, was born in Dublin, Ireland; first Episcopal Bishop of Vermont (1832-68) (died 1868).

1799 Thomas C. Upham, Congregational clergyman and theologian, was born in Deerfield, N.H.; taught mental and moral philosophy, Bowdoin College (1825-67); one of the early advocates of international peace by tribunals (died 1872).

1801 Pierre Jean deSmet, Jesuit missionary, was born in Termonde, Belgium; labored 30 years among the American Indians of the Midwest and Pacific Northwest (died 1870).

1839 John F. Bentley, church architect, was born in Doncaster, England; developed an English form of Gothic in building, decorating churches and convents; designed Westminster Cathedral (died 1902).

1840 Father Damien, Catholic missionary, was born in Tremeloe, Belgium as Joseph deVeuster; served leper colony on Molokai Island, Hawaii, where he died of leprosy in 1888.

1889 Jose Garibi y Rivera, the first Mexican cardinal, was born in Guadalajara, Mexico; elevated to cardinal 1958 (died 1972).

1889 Antonio Caggiano, Argentine Catholic prelate, was born; Bishop of Rosario (1935-59), Archbishop of Buenos Aires (1959-76); named cardinal 1946 (died 1976).

1948 Mahatma Gandhi, Hindu religious leader, was assassinated.

JANUARY 31

410 St. Marcella died; an ascetic whose Rome home became the center of Christian influence; also observed as her feast day.

1561 Menno Simons, Dutch religious reformer, died at about 65; originally a Catholic, he became an Anabaptist* and founded a moderate sect known as the Mennonites; his most important work was "The Foundations of Christian Doctrine."

1583 Peter Bulkeley, Puritan clergyman, was born in Bedfordshire, England; a "thundering preacher and a judicious divine;" founder of Concord, N.H. (died 1659).

1668 Herman Busenbaum, Jesuit theologian, died at 68; wrote "Medulla theologiae moralis," a celebrated book which went into more than 200 editions; used as a text in many seminaries.

1673 St. Louis Marie de Montfort, priest and theologian, was born in France; founder, Congregation of the Daughters of Wisdom and the Company of Mary (Montfort Fathers); canonized 1947 (died 1716).

1686 Hans Egede, Lutheran missionary, was born in Norway; first to preach the Gospel to Eskimos in Greenland; founded a seminary in Copenhagen to train missionaries to Greenland (died 1758).

1714 Howal Harris, Welsh revivalist, was born; a founder of Welsh Calvinistic Methodism and the first lay preacher in the movement (died 1773).

1737 Jacob Duche, Anglican clergyman, was born in Philadelphia; chaplain to the Continental Congress (1775-77); had change of heart, wrote to George Washington asking him to have Congress recall the Declaration of Independence; left with the Loyalists but returned in 1792 (died 1798).

1752 Ceremony for the Profession of Sister St. Martha Turpin was held at the Ursuline convent in New Orleans; she was the first American-born Catholic nun.

1854 Ludwig Pastor, theological historian, was born in Aachen, Germany; wrote a monumental 16-volume "History of the Popes" (died 1928).

1888 St. John Bosco, founder of the Salesian Society and co-founder of the Salesian Sisters, died at 73; also observed as his feast day.

1915 Thomas Merton, Trappist monk, was born in France; wrote the popular "Seven Storey Mountain" (died 1968).

FEBRUARY 1

Former feast day in the Catholic Church of St. Ignatius, Bishop of Antioch and a powerful theologian and church leader; martyred under Trajan (about 110); a Father* of the Church; now observed October 17.

523 St. Brigit of Ireland, abbess of Kildare and patron saint of Ireland, died at about 70; by her prayers and miracles she reputedly exercised great influence on the church in Ireland; also observed as her feast day.

772 Adrian I was named pope, served until 795; a firm, skilful, and tactful ruler; summoned Charlemagne to drive back the Lombards threatening Rome (773-774); founder of the Papal States, the temporal power of popes; presided over the Second Nicene Council (787); long pontificate was marked by attempts to gain as much territory and privileges from the strife between the Franks and Lombards.

1241 Boniface of Savoy was named Archbishop of Canterbury, served until 1270.

1691 Alexander VIII, pope from 1689 to 1691, died at 81.

1763 Thomas Campbell, a founder of the Disciples of Christ Church, was born in Scotland; with his son, Alexander, and Barton W. Stone, established the Baptist sect which later became the Churches of Christ (originally Disciples of Christ) (died 1854).

1787 Richard Whatley, English prelate, was born in London; Archbishop of Dublin (1831-63), supported Catholic emancipation, advocated state endowment of Catholic clergy; a founder of Broad Church policy; exerted self in favor of common unsectarian religious education for Protestant and Catholic schools (died 1863).

1820 George H. Houghton, Episcopal clergyman, was born in Deerfield, Mass.; founder, rector, Church of the Transfiguration (better known as the Little Church Around the Corner), New York City (1849-97) (died 1897).

1831 Henry M. Turner, Methodist bishop who advocated return of blacks to Africa, was born in Newberry Court House, S.C. (died 1915).

1877 A decree was issued granting equal rights to Chinese Christians.

1889 Crisanto Luque, Archbishop of Bogota (1950-59), was born in Tenja, Colombia; elevated to cardinal 1953 (died 1959).

1899 William O. Brady, Catholic Archbishop of St. Paul, was born in Fall River, Mass. (died 1961).

1963 The Lutheran Free Church merged into the American Lutheran Church.

1970 Pope Paul VI said that priestly celibacy was a fundamental principle of the Catholic church and could not be questioned.

1984 John J. O'Connor, Catholic prelate, was named Archbishop of New York; served as military chaplain for 27 years, retiring as a rear admiral; Bishop of Scranton, Pa. (1983).

FEBRUARY 2

Feast of the Candlemas, a feast of Mary marked by a procession with candles; better known as the feast day commemorating the pontification of the Blessed Virgin Mary.

962 Otto I, the Saxon king, was crowned by Pope John XII, establishing the Holy Roman Empire; ended in 1806 with the Napoleonic conquests.

1257 St. Bonaventure (Bonaventura) was named minister general of the Franciscan Order, served until 1273.

1594 Giovanni F. da Palestrina, a leader in the development of church music, died at 68; composed exclusively in medieval church modes; his work marks the apex of attainment in the field of older church music.

1640 St. Joan of Lestonnac died; founder of the Religious of Notre Dame of Bordeaux; canonized 1949; also observed as her feast day.

1649 Benedict XIII, pope from 1724 to 1730, was born as Pietro Francesco Orsini in Gravina, Italy.

1656 The partially-completed Cathedral of Mexico City was dedicated.

1745 Hannah More, English religious writer, was born near Bristol; a popular poet and dramatist, she renounced the social life, concentrated on religious efforts, setting up Sunday schools and writing (Sacred Dramas, Religion of the Fashionable World, Practical Piety, Shepherd of Salisbury Plain) (died 1833).

1769 Clement XIII, pope from 1758 to 1769, died at 76.

1831 Gregory XVI was named pope, serving until 1846; with the help of Austria, suppressed revolt in Papal States (1831-32); despite political difficulties, he did much for missions, created many new bishoprics and vicarates; opposed the separation of church and state.

1881 The first Young People's Society of Christian Endeavor was founded in the Williston Congregational Church, Portland, Me. by its pastor, Francis E. Clark; incorporated 1885.

1882 The Knights of Columbus was organized by Rev. Michael McGivney in New Haven, Conn.

1926 An apostolic letter of Pope Pius XI protested against the religious and educational provisions of the French constitution and directed bishops to refrain from political activities.

1956 The Netherlands Reformed Church agreed to permit the celebration of Holy Communion interchangeably with the Evangelical Lutheran Church (which approved in May).

1981 Pope John Paul II named Msgr. Jean-Marie Lustiger Archbishop of Paris; the Jewish-born prelate had been Bishop of Orleans.

1983 Archbishop Joseph L. Bernardin of Chicago was among the 18 new cardinals invested by Pope John Paul II.

1986 Dalai Lama, exiled spiritual leader of Tibetan Buddhists, met with Pope John Paul II in New Delhi on the second day of the papal visit to India.

FEBRUARY 3

Feast day in the Catholic Church of St. Blasius (or Blaise), martyred Bishop of Sebaste (modern Siras, Turkey); reputedly a doctor who saved a child from choking on a fish bone; his feast day also includes the blessing of throats.

619 St. Lawrence of Canterbury died; accompanied St. Augustine to England in 597, became Archbishop of Canterbury in 608; also observed as his feast day.

865 St. Anskar, the "apostle of the North," died at about 64; built first Christian church in Sweden, served as first Archbishop of Hamburg (831-865); in Germany, he is known as St. Scharies; also observed as his feast day.

1683 John Myles, pioneer Baptist clergyman, died at 62; in 1667, he and one of his parishioners were fined 5 pounds each by the General Court of Plymouth Colony "for their breach of order in setting up of a publicke meeting without the knowledge and approbation of the Court;" he was banished, founded the town of Swansea.

1786 Wilhelm Gesenius, Protestant theologian, was born in Nordhausen, Germany; a pioneer in Hebrew philology, prepared a Hebrew grammar (died 1842).

1811 George F. Pierce, Methodist, South bishop (1854-84), was born in Greene County, Ga.; president, Emory College (Ga.) (1848-54) (died 1884).

1842 Sidney Lanier, American poet, was born in Macon, Ga.; wrote several Presbyterian hymns (Into the woods, my Master went) (died 1881).

1864 The Christian Union, composed of Protestant congregations opposed to "political preaching" during the Civil War, was formed in Columbus, Ohio.

1888 Translation of the Bible into Japanese was completed.

1896 A meeting in New York City protested the recall of W. Ballington Booth, head of the Salvation Army in the United States.

1943 Four chaplains aboard the Dorchester - Alexander Goode, John P. Washington, George L. Fox, Clark V. Poling - gave up their lifejackets to others and went down with the ship.

1988 National Religious Broadcasters, representing most television and radio evangelists, voted 324 to 6 in Washington for self-regulation by requiring members soliciting tax-exempt donations to meet the standards of its Ethics and Financial Accountability Commission.

FEBRUARY 4

856 Rabanus Maurus, abbot of Fulda (northeast of Frankfurt, Germany) (822-847) and Archbishop of Mainz (847-856), died at about 72; one of the greatest theologians of his age; venerated as a saint but not formally canonized.

1189 St. Gilbert of Sempringham, founder of the Gilbertines, the only medieval religious order of English origin, died at about 93; canonized 1202; also observed as his feast day.

1505 St. Joan of France, deposed queen, died; she founded the Annonciades of Bourges; also observed as her feast day.

1529 Ludwig Haetzer (Hetzer), Swiss reformer and theologian, was beheaded for heresy; a leader of iconoclasts and Anabaptists*, co-translator of the Hebrew prophets into German.

1555 John Rogers, English reformer and theologian, was burned at the stake as a heretic; the first Protestant martyr of Mary I's reign, he edited and published a complete Bible (1537) under the pseudonym of Thomas Matthew; continued Tyndale's version of the Old Testament.

1575 Pierre de Berulle, cardinal and statesman, was born in Serilly, France; founder of the Oratory (congregation of priests); one of the most important figures in 17th century French spiritual life (died 1629).

1790 John Bachman, Lutheran theologian and naturalist, was born in Rhinebeck, N.Y.; founded Lutheran Synod of South Carolina and the South Carolina Theological Seminary; collaborated with Audubon on "The Viviparous Quadrupeds of North America" (died 1874).

1810 Finis Ewing and two others organized the first presbytery of the Cumberland Presbyterian Church.

1833 George H. Hepworth, Unitarian and Congregational clergyman, was born in Boston; Unitarian pastorates in Boston, New York (1858-72), Congregational pastorates in New York, Newark (1872-85); with New York newspapers, he published weekly sermons; author (Rocks and Shoals, Hiram Golf's Religion) (died 1902).

1850 David L. Anderson, Methodist missionary to China, was born in Summerhill, S.C.; founder, first president, Soochow U. (1901-11) (died 1911).

1856 Ernest D. Burton, educator and theologian, was born in Granville, Ohio; chairman, New Testament and Early Christian Literature Department, U. of Chicago (1892-1923); Chicago U. president (1923-25) (died 1925).

1873 George Bennard, Salvation Army officer and evangelist, was born in Youngstown, Ohio; remembered for his hymns, "The old rugged cross" and "Sweet songs of salvation" (died 1958).

1883 George K. A. Bell, Anglican Bishop of Chichester, was born on Hayling Island, England; very active in ecumenical movements, serving as first chairman of central committee (1948-54), then honorary president, World Council of Churches; condemned indiscriminate bombing of German citizens in World War II, which probably kept him from being named Archbishop of Canterbury (died 1958).

1906 Dietrich Bonhoeffer, Lutheran theologian, was born in Breslau, Germany; taught a theology of "the church of the world;" an anti-Nazi, he worked underground for the church; arrested by Gestapo (Apr 5, 1943), hanged April 9, 1945; author (The Cost of Discipleship, Ethik, Letters and Papers from Prison).

1924 Rev. Harry Emerson Fosdick was cleared of charges of heresy by a vote of 111 to 28 by the New York Presbytery.

1945 Aleksei was crowned patriarch of Moscow and Russia and the head of the Russian Orthodox Church; served until 1970.

FEBRUARY 5

Feast day of St. Agatha, Sicilian martyr and patron saint of Catania and Palermo; legend has it that her intervention stilled an eruption of Mt. Etna in Sicily.

518 St. Alcimus Eopicius Avitus, Bishop of Vienne (south of Lyon, France), died; a strong opponent of Arianism* and noted writer, especially his poetry (one epic dealing with the history of the world from the Fall of Man to the Flood and the Exodus contained 2,522 hexameter verses, each line containing six metrical feet).

1265 Clement IV, the French-born Guy le Gros Foulques, was named pope; served until 1268; had been papal legate to England when named pope.

1597 St. Peter Baptist and 25 Japanese companions were martyred by Emperor Tagosama, who sought to stamp out Christianity; also observed as the feast day for them.

1599 The Parliament of Paris forced Henry IV of France to register the nearly year old Edict of Nantes, which granted a large measure of religious liberty to French Protestants (Huguenots).

1631 Roger Williams landed at the Massachusetts Bay Colony from England; after many difficulties founded Rhode Island Colony and the first Baptist congregation in North America; pastor at Salem, Mass. (1631-35), banished by the Massachusetts General Court for his doctrines and outspoken criticism of its abuse of power; originally a Baptist, he withdrew (1639) from all church connections, accepting no creed but maintaining a fundamental belief in Christianity; obtained a charter for Providence Plantations in Narragansett Bay (1644); president of the colony (1654-57); famed as the apostle of religious toleration.

1703 Gilbert Tennent, Presbyterian clergyman and evangelist, was born in Armagh County, Ireland; a leader in the "Great Awakening;" in 1740, he preached a sermon, "The Dangers of Unconverted Ministry," attacking ministers who resisted the Awakening and helped bring on the Presbyterian division (died 1764).

1723 John Witherspoon, a Presbyterian leader, was born near Edinburgh, Scotland; organizer of the Presbyterian Church in the United States along national lines; moderator of the first general assembly (1789); president, College of New Jersey (later Princeton) (1768-94); member, Continental Congress (1776-79, 1780-81, 1782); signer of Declaration of Independence (died 1794).

1837 Dwight L. Moody, foremost evangelist of the latter 19th Century, was born in Northfield, Mass.; organized Illinois St. Church, Chicago, an independent and nondenominational church; became an evangelist, blending simple American optimism and evangelical Arianism*; founded Northfield Seminary for girls, Mt. Hermon School for boys, and the Chicago (later Moody) Bible Institute (died 1899).

1838 Abram J. Ryan, Catholic priest and poet known as the "poet of the Confederacy," was born in Hagerstown, Md.; served as a Confederate chaplain (1862-65) (died 1886).

1889 The College of Ottawa was made a Catholic university by the Pope.

FEBRUARY 6

Feast day in the Catholic Church of St. Titus, who worked with the Apostle Paul.

337 St. Julius I elected as pope, served until 352; reign was marked by building five new churches in Rome, including St. Maria in Trastevere and the Basilica Julia (now the Church of the Twelve Apostles).

891 St. Photius, patriarch of Constantinople (858-867), died; excommunicated by Pope Nicholas I (863); Photius issued an encyclical (867) against the Western Church - the immediate cause of the great schism; restored (877), but again excommunicated (882) and banished to an Armenian cloister (886); also observed as his feast day.

1140 Thurstan, Norman Archbishop of York (1121-1140), died; in constant controversy with leaders; founded many monasteries in northern England.

1608 Antonio Vieira, Jesuit missionary, was born in Lisbon, Portugal; considered one of the greatest preachers of the era; served as missionary and Jesuit provincial in Brazil; imprisoned (1665-67) on the urging of the Brazilian slaveowners because of his defense of the rights of the natives (died 1697).

1740 Clement XII, pope from 1730 to 1740, died at 70.

1754 Andrew Faller, Baptist clergyman and missionary, was born near Cambridge, England; first secretary (1792) of the Baptist Missionary Society (died 1815).

1778 William O'Bryan, founder of the Bible Christian Church, was born near Plymouth, England; church, also known as Bryanites, was an offshoot of Wesleyan Methodism and later joined the United Methodist Church (died 1868).

1814 Edward F. Sorin, educator and theologian, was born near Laval, France; founder, first president, Notre Dame U. (1844-65); superior general, Congregation of Holy Cross (1869-93) (died 1893).

1861 George Tyrell, Catholic reformer, was born in Dublin, Ireland; sought a dogma that would coexist with modern knowledge; dismissed from the Jesuits for his "Letter to a Professor of Anthropology;" responded to attacks on Modernism; author (The Faith of the Millions, Hard Sayings, Christianity at the Crossroads) (died 1909).

1875 Cyril F. Garbett, Anglican prelate, was born; Bishop of Winchester (1932-43), Archbishop of York (1942-55); served as sort of ambassador-at-large for the Church of England during World War II (died 1955).

1922 Pius XI was named pope, serving until 1939; reign was marked by the signing of the Lateran Treaty, recognizing Italy's rule of Rome and the sovereign independence of Vatican City; issued encyclicals condemning Naziism and atheistic Communism.

1974 The Vatican published a revised liturgy for the sacrament of penance that made possible a fundamental shift in setting of the historic ritual from simple encounter between priest and the penitent to a communal rite.

1977 Black Rhodesian guerilla killed seven white Catholic missionaries at St. Paul's Mission in Rhodesia.

FEBRUARY 7

Former feast day of St. Romauld, founder of the Camaldolese Benedictines (Hermits); now observed June 19.

590 Pelagius II, pope from 579 to 590, died.

1478 Sir Thomas More, English saint and author, was born in London; appeared as champion of king against Luther's reform measures (1523); succeeded Wolsey as lord chancellor (1529), the first layman to hold the office; sought more rational theology and radical reform of clergy, but supported the historic church; refused to accept Henry VIII's Act of Supremacy and to sanction his marriage to Anne Boleyn; when he was beheaded July 6,1535, he declared that he "died the King's good servant but God's first;" author of "Utopia," which described communal ownership, universal education, and religious toleration; canonized 1935.

1550 Julius III was elected pope, served until 1555; pontificate favored Jesuits and encouraged Francis Xavier to Christianize Japan, but was marred by nepotism; a high point was the return of England to the Roman obedience with the accession of Mary to the throne.

1779 William Boyce, English composer and organist, died at 69; his compilations of more than two centuries of English church music kept alive the sacred music from the Tudor period on.

1824 Robert S. Maclay, Methodist missionary, was born in Concord, Pa.; organized Anglo-Chinese College, Foochow, China (1881), Anglo-Japanese College, Tokyo (1883), the Philander Smith Biblical Institute, Tokyo (1884) (died 1907).

1844 Frederic X. Katzer, Catholic prelate, was born in Ebensee, Austria; consecrated Bishop of Green Bay, Wis. (1886), Archbishop of Milwaukee (1891-1903) (died 1907).

1872 Martin J. Spalding, Catholic Archbishop of Baltimore, died at 62.

1872 Henry W. Robinson, English Baptist theologian and Old Testament scholar, was born in Northampton; wrote valuable textbook (The Religious Ideas of the Old Testament); his most important work was in Hebrew psychology and Old Testament theology (died 1945).

1878 Pius IX, pope from 1846 to 1878, died.

1886 Yehezkel Abramsky, rabbinical scholar and writer, was born in Dashkovtsy, Lithuania; head of ecclesiastical court of British United Synagogue; author of 24-volume "Hazon Yehezkel," a commentary on Tosefta (supplementary digest of Jewish laws) (died 1976).

1895 Pierre Van Paasen, Unitarian Fellowship minister and author, was born in Garcum, Netherlands; author best known for best selling, "Days of Our Years" (died 1968).

1985 David J. duPlessis Center for Christian Spirituality was dedicated at the Fuller Theological Seminary, Pasadena, Cal.

FEBRUARY 8

Feast day of St. John of Matha, co-founder with St. Felix of Valois of the Trinitarian Order; served as first general superior.

1577 Robert Burton, English clergyman and author, was born near Birmingham; vicar, St. Thomas' at Oxford (1616-40), author of the classic, "The Anatomy of Melancholy," a collection of causes and cures of all types of melancholy, including religious (died 1832).

1718 Jean Joseph Amiot, Jesuit missionary to China for about 50 years, was born in Toulon, France; writings aided greatly in European knowledge of eastern Asia (died 1793).

1795 Pierre Jean Beckx, general of the Jesuit Order (1853-84), was born near Antwerp; served as procurator* of Jesuits in Austria (1847-48), provincial (1852-53); influential advisor to Pope Pius IX; author (Der Monat Maria) (died 1887).

1844 Samuel A. Barnett, clergyman and social reformer, was born in Bristol, England; made significant contribution to reform and improvement of education and cities; author (Practicable Socialism, Religion and Progress, Religion and Politics) (died 1913).

1847 Hugh P. Hughes, Methodist leader, was born in Gaermarthen, Wales; founder of the *Methodist Times*; first president, National Free Church Council; opened West London Mission (1886) (died 1902).

1849 Roman National Assembly divested the Pope of all temporal power, adopted a republican form of government.

1878 Martin Buber, Jewish religious philosopher, was born in Vienna; made important contributions to 20th Century thought; worked for development of Hasidism* and recognition of cultural significance of Judaism; professor at Hebrew University, Jerusalem (1938-65); his major work, "I and Thou" (died 1965).

1966 The Vatican revealed that the office charged with the censure of books had been abolished in a reorganization of the Sacred Congregation for the Doctrine of the Faith.

1972 The Joint Study Commission on Possible Catholic Membership in the National Council of Churches recommended that the American Catholic Church become a member; recommendation went to the National Council of Catholic Bishops.

FEBRUARY 9

Former feast day in the Catholic Church of St. Cyril (376-444), patriarch of Alexandria (412-444); now observed June 27.

1119 Calixtus II, born Guido of Vienna, was crowned pope, serving until 1124; a reforming pope, he condemned clerical marriages, simony*, violations of the Truce of God, and forgers of ecclesiastical documents; the Concordat of Worms and the First Lateran Council took place during his reign.

1414 Thomas Arundel, Archbishop of Canterbury (1396-97, 1399-1414), died at 61; chancellor of England (1386-89, 1391-96, 1399, 1407, 1412); took part in the overthrow of King Richard II.

1555 John Hooper, called the "first Puritan," was burned at the stake, the first prominent victim of Catholic Queen Mary's counter-reformation; he had been Bishop of Gloucester and Worcester.

1802 Horatio Potter, Episcopal prelate, was born in Beekman, N.Y., brother of Alonzo Potter; served as Episcopal Bishop of New York (1854-87) (died 1887).

1831 Elders of the Mormon Church, by a "revelation," were directed to go out and preach the gospel "two by two."

1837 Alfred Ainger, English clergyman, was born in London; master of Temple Church, one of the most popular clergymen in London; biographer, editor of Charles Lamb's works (died 1904).

1877 Trinity (Episcopal) Church in Copley Square, Boston, was dedicated; replaced the original church which burned in the great Boston fire of 1872.

1930 The Protestant Federation, Metropolitan Russian Church, and the Grand Ravvi of French Jews denounced the anti-religious policy of Russia.

1988 Immanuel Jakobovits, Great Britain's chief rabbi, was elected to the House of Lords, the first rabbi to serve there.

FEBRUARY 10

Feast day of St. Scholasticus (about 453), twin sister of St. Benedict and the founder of a convent.

1791 Henry E. Milman, historian and divine, was born in London; wrote various religious histories, hymns (When our heads are bowed with woe; Ride on: ride on in majesty); dean of St. Paul's (1849-68) (died 1868).

1824 Thomas K. Beecher, Congregational clergyman, was born in Litchfield, Conn., the sixth son of Lyman Beecher; a pioneer in the "institutional church" movement; pastor of the Independent Congregational Church, Elmira, N.Y. (1854-1900) (died 1900).

1829 Leo XII, pope from 1823 to 1829, died at 68.

1829 Richard S. Willis, music editor and composer, was born in Boston; editor, *The Musical World*, numerous hymn collections; remembered for music for "It came upon a midnight clear" (died 1900).

1846 Mormons began heading westward out of Illinois.

1867 Sir Robert A. Falconer, Canadian theologian and educator, was born on Prince Edward Island; with Pine Hill College (theological), Halifax - professor (1892-1907), president (1904-07); president, U. of Toronto (1907-32) (died 1943).

1910 Dominique G. Pire, priest and social worker, was born in Dinant, Belgium; founded various charitable organizations, including Aid to Displaced Persons; awarded 1958 Nobel Peace Prize (died 1969).

1928 The Polish Government signed a concordat with the Vatican.

1939 Pius XI, pope from 1922 to 1939, died.

1969 The Greek Orthodox Church adopted a new constitution, under which the Holy Synod, composed of 67 bishops and presided over by the Archbishop of Athens, is the ruling body; a General Ecclesiastical Assembly meets annually.

FEBRUARY 11

Feast day in the Orthodox Church of St. Blasius (Blaise), martyred Bishop of Sebaste (modern Siras, Turkey).

Feast day of Our Lady of Lourdes, commemorating the first of several appearances by the Blessed Virgin Mary to Bernadette Soubirous.

Feast day of Caedmon (died about 680), the earliest English Christian poet; a laborer at Whitby Monastery, Caedmon allegedly received in a vision the gift of composing verses to God; became a monk.

731 St. Gregory II, pope from 715 to 731, died.

821 St. Benedict of Aniane, French monastic reformer who wrote guides for monastic life, died at about 70; founded monastery of Aniane (near Montpelier), which became the center of reform for all French monastic houses; also observed as his feast day.

824 Paschal I, pope from 817 to 824, died; also observed as his feast day.

1535 Gregory XIV, pope from 1590 to 1591, was born in Somma, Italy as Niccolo Sfondrati.

1600 Jose de Acosta, Spanish Jesuit missionary, died at 61; missionary to New World, second provincial of Peru; author of a valuable history of the West Indies.

1649 William Carstares (or Carstairs), Presbyterian clergyman, was born near Aberdeen, Scotland; leader of the Scottish Church at the time of the Revolution settlement; chaplain to William of Orange, whom he accompanied to England (1688), the King's chief advisor on Scottish affairs (1693-1702), principal of Edinburgh U. (1703-15) (died 1715).

1729 Solomon Stoddard, Congregational clergyman, died at 84; first librarian at Harvard U. (1667-74), pastor at Northampton, Mass. for more than 50 years and the religious and political leader of Western Massachusetts; advocated a synod-governed national church.

1836 Washington Gladden, Congregational clergyman and leader, was born in Pottsgrove, Pa.; pastor, First Congregational Church, Columbus, Ohio (1882-1918); moderator, National Council of Congregational Churches (1904-07); called the "father of American social gospel;" author (Plain Thoughts on the Art of Living, Being a Christian); wrote hymn, "O Master, let me walk with Thee" (died 1918).

1858 Visions of Bernadette Soubirous began in Lourdes, continuing through July 16, during which the Virgin Mary is believed to have revealed herself 18 times.

1884 Pope Leo XIII issued an encyclical letter to French bishops calling on them to redouble their efforts to discover heresy and infidelity.

1923 St. Thérèse of Lisieux was beatified.

1926 The Mexican Government ordered the nationalization of all church property.

1929 Three documents were signed by Mussolini and Cardinal Pietro Gasparri re-creating the Papal State under the name of "State of Vatican City;" the documents (1) recognized the Holy See and the Kingdom of Italy as separate and independent sovereignties, (2) agreed on the religious activities of the Catholic Church in Italy, and (3) the Pope was granted an indemnity of 750 million lire and 1 billion lire in state bonds.

1975 St. Patrick's Cathedral and Temple Emanu-El in New York City planned a year of dialogue on problems that have strained relations between members of their faiths.

1982 Pope John Paul II began a seven-day, four-nation journey to West Africa.

FEBRUARY 12

Feast day of St. Meletius, Archbishop of Antioch (360-381); died while presiding over the Council of Constantinople.

Feast of the Seven Holy Founders (six Florentine merchants and St. Bonfilius), who founded the Order of Servites (Servants of Mary) in 1233.

1049 St. Leo IX was consecrated as pope, served until 1054; his reign was marked by reform, including elimination of simony* and clerical marriage; he was the first pope to impress his authority on the church in general by extensive tours and synods; also began appointing non-Romans to papal administrative posts.

1608 Daniello Bartoli, Jesuit historian, was born in Ferrara, Italy; wrote "Storia della Campagnia di Gesu" and several biographies (died 1685).

1663 Cotton Mather, most famous Puritan cleric, was born in Boston, son of Increase Mather; assistant, then pastor, of Boston's Second (Congregational) Church (1684-1728); a leader in the prosecution of the Salem "witches" but later thought the trials unfair; wrote more than 450 books, most celebrated of which was "Magnalia Christi Americana," an ecclesiastical history of New England (died 1728).

1679 Joseph Greaton, Jesuit missionary, was born in London; leader in the building of St. Joseph's Church in Philadelphia, the first completely public Catholic church in the English colonies (died 1753).

1812 William H. Burleigh, Unitarian editor and hymn writer, was born in Woodstock, Conn.; editor, *Christian Freeman*; among his hymns was "Lead us, O Father, in the paths of peace" (died 1871).

1836 Charles E. Cheney, Episcopal reformer, was born in Canandaigua, N.Y.; rector of Christ Church, Chicago (1860-1916); tried for heresy (1869), convicted and deposed, but proceedings were declared legally null and void (1874); a founder, Bishop of Chicago, of the Reformed Episcopal Church (1878-1916) (died 1916).

1903 Randall T. Davidson was named Archbishop of Canterbury.

1929 Pope Pius XI appeared on the balcony of St. Peter's and gave the Papal blessing to some 100,000 persons gathered in the square, a day after the Papal State was re-created.

1984 Rev. Roland H. Bainton, a leading scholar on the history of the Reformation, died at 89; taught ecclesiastical history at Yale (1920-62); author of 32 books, including a best-selling Luther biography and Sunday School texts.

FEBRUARY 13

Feast day in the Catholic Church of St. Agabus, Christian prophet in Jerusalem in the First Century; regarded as an apostle and one of the 70 disciples of Jesus; mentioned in Acts as foretelling the famine under Claudius and St. Paul's imprisonment.

Feast day of St. Catherine de Ricci, prioress of the Dominican convent at Prato (10 miles northwest of Florence) (1552-90).

Feast day of St. Gregory II, pope from 715 to 731.

1130 Innocent II, born Gregorio Papareschi, was named pope; served until 1143; elected by small committee of cardinals, others named Anacletus II; Innocent was supported by the French and Bernard of Clairvaux; Anacletus controlled Rome, but when he died in 1138, the schism ended and Innocent returned to Rome.

1130 Honorius II, pope from 1124 to 1130, died.

1480 Girolamo Aleandro, Italian prelate and diplomat, was born near Venice; as papal nuncio to Germany, and later France, he had a major role in condemning Martin Luther at the Diet of Worms (1521); thereafter he concentrated on repressing Lutheranism and fostering church reform; compiled a Greek-Latin lexicon (1512), elevated to cardinal 1538 (died 1542).

1582 Gregory XIII issued a bull announcing that his calendar reform commission had completed its work.

1602 Alexander Newell, English clergyman, died at about 95; dean of St. Paul's Cathedral, London (1560-1602), who incurred royal disfavor by his tactless preaching; wrote the small catechism in the Prayer Book, which is still the official catechism of the Church of England.

1674 Jean de Labadie, French religious reformer, died at 64; a Jesuit converted to Calvinism, he was deposed (1668) and formed his own separatist church, the Labadists.

1728 Cotton Mather, Puritan religious leader, died at 65.

1766 Louis G. V. Dubourg, Catholic prelate and educator, was born in Cap Francis, Santo Domingo; president, Georgetown College (1796-98); founder, president, St. Mary's College (1803-12); Bishop of New Orleans (1815-20) (died 1833).

1798 Christian F. Schwartz, who was known as "the apostle of India" for his 50 years as a missionary there, died at 71.

1880 John LaFarge, Jesuit priest who fought racism, was born in Newport, R.I.; his efforts helped found first national Catholic project on behalf of black education (Cardinal Gibbons Institute, Ridge, Md.), a precursor of the Catholic interracial movement; an editor of *America*, Jesuit weekly newspaper (died 1963).

1909 Mario Casaregio, Archbishop of Guatemala and the first Central American to be named a cardinal, was born in Figueros de Castropal (died 1984).

1926 The Mexican Government ordered the deportation of foreign monks and nuns; closing of convents begun where schools giving religious instruction existed.

FEBRUARY 14

Former feast day of St. Valentine, apparently intended to commemorate the martyrdom of two saints of the same name - a Roman priest martyred under Emperor Claudius II and a bishop of Terni; observance dropped in 1969.

869 St. Cyril, an "apostle to the Slavs," with his brother, St. Methodius, died; the Greek brothers devised a Slavic alphabet (known as the Glagolithic) giving Slavs their first written language; Pope John Paul II in 1980 proclaimed both patron saints of Europe; also observed as their feast day.

1130 Anacletus II was elected anti-pope by a majority of the cardinals, recognized only in Rome and Sicily; reigned until 1138.

1599 Alexander VII, pope from 1655 to 1667, was born in Siena as Fabio Chigi; an ineffectual pontiff, he enriched Rome with art masterpieces (the Bernini colonnade at St. Peter's) and extensive additions to the Vatican Library; issued a bull against the Jansenists.

1760 Richard Allen, first Black Methodist clergyman, was born in Philadelphia; a founder, bishop, African Methodist Episcopal Church (1816-31) (died 1831).

1792 William Goodell, Congregational missionary to the Near East for 42 years, was born in Templeton, Mass.; translated Bible into Armeno-Turkish (died 1867).

1816 James Morison, theologian and reformer, was born near Edinburgh, Scotland; with the United Secession Church and co-founder, with his father, Robert, of the Evangelical Union (Morisonians), which merged with the Congregationalists after his death in 1893; had been ousted from the United Church for preaching universal atonement.

1830 Richard A. Lipsius, Protestant theologian, was born in Jena, Germany; helped found the Evangelical Protestant Missionary Union and the Evangelical Alliance; did much to unravel problem of early Christian apocryphal literature (died 1892).

1833 Archbishop Panet of Quebec died and was succeeded by Joseph Signay.

1847 Anna Howard Shaw, clergywoman and physician, was born in Newcastle-on-Tyne, England; denied ordination by the American Methodist Church, she was ordained by the Protestant Methodist Church (1880); resigned to spearhead women's suffrage movement; president, American Woman Suffrage Assn. (1904-15) (died 1919).

1910 Catholic Bishop Neil MacNeil was named Archbishop of Vancouver.

1913 James A. Pike, Episcopal clergyman who renounced his church and formed the Foundation for Religious Transition, was born in Oklahoma City (died 1969).

FEBRUARY 15

1145 Lucius II, pope from 1144, was killed while leading a papal army in battle to restore order in Rome.

1145 Eugenius III, born Bernardo Pignatelle, was elected pope; served until 1153; a pupil of St. Bernard of Clairvaux, he became the first Cistercian pope; an ardent reformer of the morals of the clergy and of monastic observance; refused to renounce temporal power and was expelled from Rome by a mob (1145); made preparations for Second Crusade from France.

1288 Nicholas IV, born Girolano Masci, was elected pope; served until 1292; first Franciscan pope, his acts were circumscribed by the powerful Colonna family; had been general of the Franciscan Order (1274-88).

1662 James Renwick, Scottish Covenanter*, was born in Moniaive, Scotland; a field preacher for the Cameronians, who had declared Charles II a tyrant and usurper; captured and executed (1688), the last of the martyrs of the Covenant.

1730 Thomas Bray, English clergyman, died at 74; founder of the Society for the Promoting of Christian Knowledge (1698) and the Society for the Propagating of the Gospel (1701); established about 80 parochial libraries in the American colonies; created "Associates of Dr. Bray" to assure permanence of the libraries (1723), which is still active.

1772 Robert Finley, Presbyterian clergyman and educator, was born in Princeton, N.J.; organized (1816) American Colonization Society to plan a colony in Africa for American blacks as a solution for the slavery problem; president, U. of Georgia (1817) (died 1817).

1775 Pius VI was named pope by a conclave which met for four months; served until 1799; reign marked by rising tide of atheism and secularism; established see of Baltimore (1789), the first in America; released American clergy (1781) from jurisdiction of vicar apostolic in England; constant struggle with French and the king of Naples; taken prisoner by French and imprisoned (1798) in Valence.

1782 William Miller, whose predictions led to formation of Adventist Church, was born in Pittsfield, Mass.; predicted Second Coming in 1843 and 1844; his movement failed after that but led to formation of the Adventist Church (died 1849).

1822 Henry B. Whipple, Episcopal prelate, was born in Adams, N.Y.; first Bishop of Minnesota (1859-1901); successfully campaigned against injustice and cruelty of government handling of Indians (died 1901).

1843 Russell H. Conwell, Baptist clergyman and lecturer, was born in Worthington, Mass.; most noted lecturer on the Chautauqua circuit, delivering his famous "Acres of Diamonds" speech more than 6000 times; founder, first president, Temple U. (1888-1925); founder, Samaritan Hospital (1891) (died 1925).

1881 William W. Sweet, church historian, was born in Baldwin, Kans.; professor of theological subjects at DePauw (1913-27), U. of Chicago (1927-46) (died 1959).

1925 30,000 Catholics paraded in Rennes to protest the anti-religious policy of the French government.

1966 Anthony Bashir, Metropolitan Archbishop of Syrian Antiochan Church of North America (1936-66) died in Boston at 68.

FEBRUARY 16

Feast day in Orthodox Church of St. Flavian, patriarch of Constantinople (446-449).

309 St. Pamphilus, a priest and teacher of Caesarea (ancient seaport of Roman Palestine) and a devout Christian teacher in Alexandria, died at about 69; imprisoned (307-309) during persecution under Emperor Maximius and martyred; also observed as his feast day in the Orthodox Church.

1075 Orderic Vitalis, Anglo-Norman chronicler, was born near Shrewsbury, England; spent life in Norman abbey at St. Evroult; wrote history of Normandy and England (died 1142).

1497 Philipp Melancthon, Reformation leader, was born in Bretten, Germany; an associate of Martin Luther and during Luther's absence, leader of the Reformation cause; served as scribe of the Reformation; his attitude to Christianity was far more humanistic than that of most reformers; he cared for learning and his commentaries on the Scriptures broke new ground; originated the first systematic theology of the Protestant Reformation, the Protestant public school system, and the basic Protestant creed (died 1560).

1516 Gaspard de Coligny, Huguenot leader, was born in Chatillon-sur-Loing, France, the son of the marshal of France; became an admiral, was converted to Protestantism while a prisoner in Spain (1557-59), became co-leader of the Huguenots; killed in St. Bartholomew Day massacre (1572).

1560 Jean DuBellay, French prelate, died at 68; Bishop of Paris and Archbishop of Bordeaux (1544-53), elevated to cardinal 1535.

1692 Giovanni D. Mansi, Italian prelate and historian, born; Archbishop of Lucca (13 miles northeast of Pisa) (1765-69); known especially for history of church councils to 1509 (died 1769).

1852 Charles Taze Russell, a founder of Jehovah's Witnesses, was born in Pittsburgh; known as "Pastor Russell;" founded International Bible Students Assn., which became Jehovah's Witnesses; founder of the *Watchtower* (1879) (died 1916).

1892 Anselmo M. Albareda, prefect of the Vatican Library (1936-62), was born in Barcelona, Spain (died 1966).

1892 An encyclical of Pope Leo XIII to the French bishops urged submission to the government of the Republic.

1930 Episcopal Bishop William T. Manning of New York endorsed the action of the Vatican and the Archbishop of Canterbury in denouncing the anti-religious policy of the Soviet Union; invited all faiths to attend a special service at the Cathedral of St. John the Divine.

1966 The Central Committee of the World Council of Churches called for a Vietnam cease fire "of sufficient duration" to serve as a cooling-off period and as an opportunity to explore possibilities of negotiation.

FEBRUARY 17

443 St. Mesrob, patriarch of Armenia, died; honored as creator of the Armenian and Georgian alphabets.

661 St. Finan, Bishop of Lindisfarne (an offshore Island in the North Sea), died; sought to retain Celtic customs against the Romanized English customs; also observed as his feast day.

1613 St. Noël Chabanel, Jesuit missionary, was born in France; missionary to North American

Indians, killed by a Huron Indian (Dec 8, 1649); canonized (1930) along with six other North American martyrs.

1708 William Rittenhouse, Mennonite clergyman and industrialist, died at 64; first pastor of Germantown (Pa.) church, first American Mennonite bishop (1703); built first American paper mill (1690).

1785 Nachman Krochmal, Jewish scholar, was born in Brody, Russia (formerly Austria); made important contributions to the study of Jewish religion and history; author (Guide to the Perplexed of Our Time) (died 1840).

1826 Oblates of Mary Immaculate, one of the largest Catholic missionary congregations, was approved by Pope Leo XII.

1865 Ernst P. W. Troeltsch, liberal Protestant theologian, was born near Augsburg, Germany; leading theologian of religio-historical school; his writings prepared revolution in Protestant thought (died 1923).

1891 Omaha (Neb.) Theological Seminary was founded by the Presbyterian churches of the Midwest.

1966 The apostolic constitution, "Paenitemini," was issued by Pope Paul VI, revising the rules of penitential observance in the Catholic Church.

1968 Isaac Rivkind, emeritus chief of Hebraica at the Jewish Theological Seminary of America, died in New York City at 73.

1982 The Chicago Circuit Court ruled that $4.6 million belonging to Elijah Muhammad was an asset of his estate and should not be transferred to the Muslim sect he founded.

FEBRUARY 18

Feast day in the Catholic Church of St. Flavian, patriarch of Constantinople (446-449); deposed and excommunicated by the Council of Ephesus (449); said to have died from severe injuries inflicted on him by theological opponents; canonized as a martyr by the Council of Chalcedon (451).

Feast day in the Orthodox Church of St. Leo I the Great, pope from 440 to 461.

676 St. Colman, third Irish Bishop of Lindisfarne (offshore island in the North Sea), died; opposed anti-Celtic decisions of Synod of Whitby and, with others, moved to Iona.

999 Gregory V, pope from 996 to 999, died.

1546 Martin Luther died in Eisleben, the town where he was born; his body was interred in the Church of All Saints, Wittenberg, on the door of which he is said to have posted his 95 Theses.

1688 The earliest known protest was issued against slavery by the Germantown (Pa.) Mennonites in their monthly meeting held at Richard Worrell's.

1781 Henry Martyn, English missionary to India, was born in Truro; translated New Testament into Urdu and Persian (died 1812).

1856 Charles S. Nash, Congregational clergyman and theologian, was born in Granby, Mass.; with Pacific Theological Seminary (1891-1920), dean (1906-11), president (1911-20) (died 1926).

1869 "Chicago Protest" of the Episcopal Church was launched by Charles E. Cheney, who helped organize and headed the Reformed Episcopal Church; brought to trial for heresy and deposed; refused to leave Christ Church, Chicago, where he served (1860-1916); court held that church property belonged to the parish, not the diocese; Cheney served as Bishop of Chicago (1878-1916).

1880 Pope Leo XIII issued an encyclical on marriage as a sacrament, condemned divorce.

1889 Aloysius J. Muench, Archbishop of Fargo, N.D. (1950-59), was born in Milwaukee; elevated to cardinal 1959; papal nuncio to Germany (1959-62) (died 1962).

1915 Matthias Defregger, auxiliary Catholic bishop of Munich, Germany, was born in Munich; became center of controversy over his Army service when Italian villagers were killed on Nazi orders; Defregger refused to carry out the order.

1946 Three American Catholic archbishops were elevated to cardinal - John J. Glennon of St. Louis, Francis J. Spellman of New York, and Samuel A. Stritch of Chicago.

1973 The 40th Eucharistic Congress opened in Melbourne, Australia.

FEBRUARY 19

Feast day of St. Mesrob, developer of the Armenian alphabet, and translator of the Scriptures from Syriac to Armenian.

607 Boniface III became pope, served only until Nov. 12th; before his death, he secured an edict from Emperor Phocas confirming the primacy of the pope.

973 Benedict VI was consecrated as pope (had been elected Sep. 6, 972); served until 974; a faction of Roman nobles imprisoned and murdered him in August 974.

1552 Melchor Klesl (or Khlesl), cardinal and statesman, was born in Vienna; tried to promote a tolerant religious policy during the Counter Reformation; chancellor to Archduke (later Emperor) Matthias, virtual head of imperial politics (1612-18); imprisoned (1618-23) for advising against war with revolting Bavarians, acquitted (died 1630).

1621 Gregory XV was named pope, served until 1623; established the Congregation for the Propagation of Faith and the secret election of popes by two-thirds of the cardinals.

1672 Charles Chauncy, nonconformist Puritan clergyman, died at 80; fled England, served pastorates in Plymouth and Scituate; beliefs led to dispute and schism; second president, Harvard (1654-72).

1793 Sidney Rigdon, Mormon leader, was born in Piney Fork, Pa.; a Baptist clergyman, he became associated with Joseph Smith in formative years of the church; differed with Smith on polygamy; hoped to assume leadership on Smith's death (1844), but was excommunicated; formed short-lived secession movement (died 1876).

1802 Leonard Bacon, Congregational clergyman, was born in Detroit; sometimes called the "Congregational Pope;" pastor, First Congregational Church, New Haven, Conn. (1825-81); a founder, editor, *New York Independent* (1847-63); a leader in antislavery movement; wrote hymn, "O God, beneath Thy guiding hand" (died 1881).

1978 The Congregation of the Laity conference in Los Angeles was attended by lay church members from many denominations.

1988 Pope John Paul II in an encyclical letter condemned the rivalry between superpowers which subjected poor nations to imperialistic "structures of sin" that deny freedom and development.

FEBRUARY 20

Feast day in the Orthodox Church of St. Agatho, pope from 678 to 687.

1431 Martin V, pope from 1417 to 1431, died.

1469 Cajetan, Italian cardinal and theologian, was born Tommaso de Vic; general of the Dominican Order (1508-18), Bishop of Gaeta (about 50 miles north of Naples) (1519-34); Pope Leo X sent him to Germany to unite the princes against the Turks; while there he sought unsuccessfully to get Martin Luther to recant and win him back to the church; was one of 19 cardinals who met with Pope Clement VII and rejected request of Henry VIII for divorce from Catherine of Aragon (died 1534).

1513 Pope Julius II, who served from 1503, died.

1719 Joseph Bellamy, Puritan clergyman, was born in Cheshire, Conn.; pastor, Bethlehem, Conn. (1748-90); created a divinity school in home, where many prominent New England clergy were trained; author (True Religion Delineated); an architect of the "new divinity" in New England (died 1790).

1778 Robert Bruce, Presbyterian clergyman, was born in Scone, Scotland; minister of the Associate (now First) United Presbyterian Church, Pittsburgh (1808-46); instrumental in establishing Duquesne College (died 1846).

1791 The first Methodist class in Canada was held in Hay Bay, near Napanee in Upper Canada.

1803 John W. Nevin, theologian and educator, was born near Strasbourg, Pa.; his teachings were basic to the Mercersburg theology; professor, Mercersburg (Pa.) Seminary (1840-53); acting president, Marshall College (1841-53); president, Franklin & Marshall College (1866-76); editor, *Mercersburg Review*, an influential theological journal (died 1886).

1822 Henry F. Durant, lawyer and clergyman, was born in Hanover, N.H.; a successful Massachusetts lawyer, he became a lay preacher on the death of his son, conducting revival meetings; founder, treasurer, Wellesley College (1870-81) (died 1881).

1831 Patrick J. Ryan, Catholic prelate, was born in Thurles, Ireland; bishop coadjutor of St. Louis (1872-84), Archbishop of Philadelphia (1884-1911) (died 1911).

1849 Joseph M. Levering, Moravian prelate, was born in Hardin County, Tenn.; a bishop (1888-1908) and president of church's governing body (1903-08) (died 1908).

1878 Leo XIII was elected pope, served until 1903; his reign saw the growth of Catholic school systems, marked the beginning of an end of the era when the Catholic Church was essentially European; wrote many important encyclicals on marriage, Freemasonry, the Bible, education; opened the Vatican archives to scholars.

1888 Georges Bernanos, Catholic novelist, was born in Paris; his most memorable work was "The Diary of a Country Priest" (died 1948).

1901 Robert W. Stopford, Anglican Bishop of London (1961-73), was born in Liverpool; vicar general in Jerusalem and the Middle East (died 1976).

1907 The U.S. Senate confirmed (42 to 28) the election of Reed Smoot of Utah, defeating a proposal to unseat him because of his membership in the Mormon Church.

FEBRUARY 21

Feast day in the Orthodox Church of St. Eustathius of Antioch, Bishop of Antioch (324-330), who was exiled for his opposition to Arianism*.

1431 The interrogation of Joan of Arc began before Pierre Cauchon, Bishop of Beauvais.

1595 St. Robert Southwell, English poet and Jesuit, was tortured and executed; worked under cover until exposed; author (Mary Magdalen's Funeral Tears, An Epistle of Comfort); poet (St. Peter's Complaint); canonized along with 40 other martyrs of England and Wales in 1970; also observed as his feast day.

1801 John Henry Newman, Anglican leader of the Oxford Movement, was born in London; movement sought to return the Church of England to the high ideals of the latter 17th Century; became a Catholic (1845), a priest (1847), cardinal (1879), broke down some of the prejudices of the English against Catholic priests; vicar of the Oxford University Church (1828-43), urging Anglican reaffirmation of the doctrine of apostolic succession; replied to Charles Kingsley's charge of Catholic indifference to truthfulness in his "Apologia pro Vita Sua" (1864), a literary masterpiece of his spiritual history; his main contributions lay more in the field of psychological analysis and acute moral perception than in strictly theological matters; ranks among leading modern Christian thinkers and one of the very great masters of English prose; wrote hymn, "Lead, kindly light" (died 1890).

1824 Mother Mary Angela, nun and educator, was born near Brownsville, Pa.; superior of the Sisters of the Holy Cross in the United States and head of St. Mary's Academy, near Notre Dame U. (died 1887).

1881 Jonah B. Wise, American rabbi, was born in Cincinnati; rabbi, Portland, Ore. (1906-25) and Central Synagogue, New York City (1925-59); a founder and head of United Jewish Appeal (1930-58) (died 1959).

1881 Marc Boegner, a leading figure in French Protestantism, was born in Epinal, France; president, Protestant Federation of France (1929-61), president, National Council of the Reformed Church of France (1938-50), president, World Council of Churches (1948-50) (died 1970).

1899 Bernard W. Griffin, British Catholic prelate, was born in Birmingham; Archbishop of Westminster (1943-56), elevated to cardinal 1946 (died 1956).

1968 Sayid Ali al-Mirghani, head of the Khatmia religious sect in Sudan, died in Khartoum at 89.

1988 Rev. Jimmy Swaggart, a television evangelist, confessed to sins before 8000 members of his congregation in Baton Rouge, La. and said he would absent himself from his pulpit for "an indeterminate time."

FEBRUARY 22

Feast day in the Catholic Church of St. Joseph of Arimathea, who provided the tomb in which Jesus' body was laid after the Crucifixion; legend has it that he took the Holy Grail, the cup that had been used in the Last Supper, to England.

Feast day in the Orthodox Church of St. Telesphorus, martyred pope from about 125 to 136.

606 Sabinian, pope from 604 to 606, died.

1072 Stigaud, Archbishop of Canterbury (1052-72), died; unrecognized by the pope; deposed (1070) and imprisoned until his death; charged with usurpation and plurality*.

1281 Martin IV, born Simon de Brie, was elected pope; served until 1285; excommunicated Greek Emperor Michael Paleologus (1281), thus destroying the union between Eastern and Western churches achieved at the Council of Lyons (1274).

1455 Johann(es) Reuchlin, humanist and educator, was born near Stuttgart, Germany; the grand uncle of Philipp Melancthon, he enhanced the success of the Reformation by preventing the destruction of Jewish books and awakening the forces of liberalism; while helping Protestantism, he did not support Luther; promoter of Greek and Hebrew studies in Germany (died 1522).

1471 Jan Rokycana, one of the chief religious leaders of the Hussites, died; served as archbishop of the Hussite church.

1592 Nicholas Ferrar, English deacon, was born in London; set up Little Gidding, a religious community which represented a return to the ascetic tradition; used by T.S. Eliot as a theme in and the title for one of his "Four Quartets;" introduced bookbinding as an industry of the community, which was broken up by Parliament (died 1637).

1793 Isaak M. Jost, Jewish historian, was born in Germany; wrote various histories of the Jewish people, translated the Mishnah* into German with a commentary (died 1860).

1805 Sarah F. Adams, English poet, was born in Harlow; wrote words for many hymns, including "Nearer, My God, to Thee" for which her sister, Eliza Flower, wrote the music (died 1848).

1810 The American Catholic parochial school system was begun by Mother Elizabeth Ann Seton in Emmittsburg, Md.

1819 James Russell Lowell, author and editor, was born in Cambridge, Mass.; editor, *Atlantic Monthly* (1857-62), *North American Review* (1863-72); wrote the hymn "Once to every man and nation" (died 1891).

1820 Randolph S. Foster, Methodist prelate and educator, was born in Williamsburg, Ohio; served as a bishop (1872-1902); president, Northwestern U. (1857-60); president, Drew Theological Seminary (1870-72) (died 1903).

1849 Charles R. Brown, theologian, was born in East Kingston, N.H.; Baptist clergyman; professor of Old Testament, Newton Theological Institute for 30 years (died 1914).

1855 Henry G. Ganss, Catholic priest and composer, was born in Darmstadt, Germany; served parishes in central Pennsylvania; among his hymns was the papal hymn, "Long live the pope," which was translated into 25 languages (died 1912).

1896 The Christian Catholic Apostolic Church was formed in Chicago by John A. Dowie, a former Congregational clergyman; became a fanatical megalomaniac, identified self as messenger of the Covenant (1899), proclaimed himself Elijah the Restorer (1901); built Zion City, 42 miles from Chicago, which was occupied by his followers but wholly owned by him; in 1906, followers rebelled and deposed him.

1961 The National Council of Churches endorsed birth control as a means of family limitation.

1976 The New York State Board of Regents denied the application of the Unification Theological Seminary to become a degree-granting institution chartered by the State.

1981 The Southern Baptist Foreign Mission Board said that it will not pay ransom or yield to demands of anyone who takes one of its missionaries hostage.

FEBRUARY 23

155 St. Polycarp, Second century Bishop of Smyrna, died; according to legend, he was to be burned at the stake but the flames would not touch him, and when pierced with a sword, his blood quenched the flames; also observed as his feast day.

1072 St. Peter Damian, Italian hermit monk, died at 65; an original leader of the 11th Century reform movement and famous as an uncompromising preacher against worldliness and simonical practices of the clergy; trusted advisor to several popes; Bishop of Ostia (port of Rome) (1057-69), papal legate to Germany (1069), a Doctor* of the Church; also observed as his feast day.

1417 Paul II, pope from 1464 to 1471, was born Pietro Barbo in Venice; he was a nephew of Pope Eugenius IV.

1447 Eugenius IV, pope from 1431 to 1447, died at 64.

1730 Benedict XIII, pope from 1724 to 1730, died at 81.

1798 Thomas Evans, Quaker clergyman, was born in Philadelphia; made extensive compilations of Quaker history, doctrine (died 1868).

1832 John H. Vincent, Sunday School teacher and Methodist prelate, was born in Tuscaloosa, Ala.; general agent of the Methodist Sunday School Union (1866-86}; helped organize training school for Sunday School teachers; a co-founder of the Chautauqua Movement, an outgrowth of the Sunday School teachers assembly; bishop (1888-1904) (died 1920).

1833 Mormon Church decided to establish a permanent city at Kirtland, Ohio.

1902 Ellen Stone, American missionary captured by Turkish brigands in September 1901, was released on payment of ransom of $72,500 raised by public subscription.

1945 Rev. Allan (A.) Boesak, one of the most influential spokesmen of non-white South Africa, was born in Kakamas, South Africa; president, World Alliance of Reformed Churches (1982-).

1982 The U.S. Supreme Court ruled that members of Old Order Amish Church who operate businesses must pay Social Security and unemployment taxes despite their religious belief that paying taxes is sin.

FEBRUARY 24

Feast day in the Anglican Church of St. Matthias, disciple chosen to fill the place vacated by Judas Iscariot.

1528 Domingo Banez (sometimes Vanez or Baines), theologian, was born in Spain; a leading exponent of the traditional scholastic theology; taught in several Spanish universities (died 1604).

1536 Clement VIII, pope from 1592 to 1605, was born as Ippolito Adobrandini in Fano, Italy.

1816 Charles Inglis, first Anglican bishop in North America, died at 82; served in the mid-Atlantic colonies, later as Bishop of Nova Scotia.

1883 Amleto Cicognani, apostolic delegate to the United States, was born in Brisighella, Italy; elevated to cardinal 1958 (died 1963).

1902 Gladys M. Aylward, missionary to China, was born in Edmonton, England; her fictionalized biographies (The Small Woman) became a popular movie (died 1970)

1988 The U.S. Supreme Court ruled unanimously that public figures who are victims of a satirical attack — even one that is pornographic and "outrageous" — may not sue for damages; the decision rejected a $200,000 judgment won by Rev. Jerry Falwell against *Hustler Magazine*.

FEBRUARY 25

Feast day of St. Ethelbert, king of Kent (560-616); married daughter of Frankish king, who brought Christianity to England; she converted him (597) and he became the first Christian English king; promulgated first written code of British laws.

Feast day of St. Tarasius (died 806), patriarch of Constantinople (784-806).

779 St. Walburga, English missionary to Germany, died at about 69; sister of Sts. Willibald and Winnibald; said to have aided St. Boniface in converting Germans; also observed as her feast day.

1296 Pope Boniface VIII issued the bull, "Clericis laicos," to protect the clergy of England and France from paying ecclesiastical revenues to laymen without the approval of Rome.

1536 Jacob (Leonhard) Hutter, Austrian Anabaptist* leader, was burned at the stake in Innsbruck; organized the Hutterites in a communal form of life; about 18,000 Anabaptists now live in the western United States and Canada.

1570 Pope Pius V issued a bull of excommunication, "Regnans in excelsis," against Queen Elizabeth I.

1801 John M. Odin, Catholic prelate, was born in Ambierle, France; the first Bishop of Texas (1848-57), Archbishop of New Orleans (1857-70) (died 1870}.

1927 Bruce Ritter, Franciscan priest who founded Covenant House (1972), an international child care agency that operates short-term crisis centers, was born in Trenton, N.J.

1968 Archbishop Makarios was elected to a second five-year term as president of Cyprus.

FEBRUARY 26

1273 Robert Kilwardby was consecrated as Archbishop of Canterbury; served until 1278; became cardinal Bishop of Porto and Santo Rufino (1278); on going to Rome, he took with him the registers and judicial records of Canterbury which have never been recovered.

1732 St. Joseph's Church in Philadelphia was completed and the first mass was celebrated by the Rev. Joseph Greaton; this was the first completely public Catholic church in the American colonies.

1846 George C. Stebbins, hymn composer, was born in East Carleton, N.Y.; worked with Dwight L. Moody and wrote many popular hymns (Take time to be holy; Jesus is tenderly calling; I've found a friend) (died 1945).

1857 Charles M. Sheldon, Congregational clergyman, was born in Wellsville, N. Y.; his religious novel, "In His Steps," was an outstanding best seller (23 million copies in 23 languages) (died 1946).

1865 Mexican decree promulgated provisions for liberty of worship and sales of church property.

1884 Francesco Bergongoni-Duca, Italian cardinal, was born; wrote the Lateran Treaty, which gave Vatican City its independence from Italy (died 1954).

1928 Pope Pius XI in his lenten address scored the immodesty of the dress of women.

1981 The Theology Commission of the Lutheran Church, Missouri Synod, recommended that the Synod break relations with the American Lutheran Church, which it considered too liberal in its interpretation of the Bible.

FEBRUARY 27

1659 Henry Dunster, English-born Baptist clergyman and educator, died at about 50; served as the first president of Harvard (1640-54); forced to resign because of his views on infant baptism; became pastor in Scituate, Mass. (1655-58).

1717 Johann D. Michaelis, German biblical scholar, was born in Halle; pioneered in the use of historico-critical study in biblical interpretation; did important work in Hebrew and Arabic studies and on early versions of the Bible (died 1791).

1720 Samuel Parris, English-born clergyman, died at 67; started the Salem witchcraft trials when he supported accusations against his West Indian slave; appeared for the prosecution in many cases but later admitted his error in accepting "spectral evidence;" resigned his pastorate 1696.

1746 Samuel Spring, Congregational clergyman, was born in Northbridge, Mass.; served church in Newburyport, Mass. (1777-1819); extreme Calvinist in theology; instrumental in founding American Board of Commissioners for Foreign Missions and the Andover Seminary (died 1819).

1767 A royal decree expelled the Jesuits from New Spain (the Western Hemisphere).

1773 Christ Church in Alexandria, Va. was completed after six years of construction at a total cost of about $4070; George Washington purchased a pew for himself and his family for $100.

1813 The Maine Literary and Theological Institute was chartered; became Colby University in 1867.

1826 Howard Crosby, Presbyterian clergyman, was born in New York City; served Fourth Ave. Presbyterian Church, New York City (1863-91); founder, Society for the Prevention of Crime (1877) (died 1891).

1799 Johann J. Dollinger, church historian, was born in Bamberg, Germany; professor of church history, Munich (1826-73); a leading German Catholic who refused to accept the decree of papal infallibility; excommunicated (1871) (died 1890).

1823 Ernest Renan, French author, was born near Brest; wrote the "History of the Origin of Christianity," which included the popular "Life of Jesus" (died 1892).

1857 Alfred F. Loisy, Catholic theologian, was born in Ambrieres, France; founder of modernism in France; taught at College de France (1911-27); works condemned by the church, excommunicated (1908) (died 1940).

FEBRUARY 28

Feast day of St. Oswald, Archbishop of Worcester (961-992) and York (972-992).

468 St. Hilary, pope from 461 to 468, died.

1551 Martin Bucer (also Butzer), German divine, died in England at 60, where he had been promoting the Reformation; sought to mediate between Zwingli and Luther; after Zwingli's death, he became leader of Reformed churches in Switzerland and southern Germany; helped draw up the Tetrapolitan confession* for the Diet of Augsburg (1530); tried to unite Protestants and Catholics at the Diet of Ratisbon.

1574 The first great auto-da-fé of the Mexican inquisition took place in Mexico City; 63 persons were punished, five were publicly burned.

1638 The National Covenant was signed, giving rise to the formation of Covenanters, Scottish Presbyterians who fought to maintain their chosen form of church government and worship.

1799 Samuel S. Schmucker, theologian and educator, was born in Hagerstown, Md.; founder, professor at Gettysburg (now Lutheran) Theological Seminary (1826-64); a founder, first president, Gettysburg College (1832-34); leader of the low-church Lutheran party in America (died 1873).

FEBRUARY 29

Feast day of St. John Cassian in the Orthodox Church, where he is regarded as a saint.

992 St. Oswald, English prelate, died; as Archbishop of York (972-992), he helped promote monastic reforms; also served as Archbishop of Worcester (961-992); his feast day is observed February 28.

1468 Paul III, pope from 1534 to 1549, was born as Alessandro Farnese in Canino, Italy.

1528 Patrick Hamilton, first Scottish Presbyterian martyr, was burned at the stake; after meeting Martin Luther, he became a Protestant reformer and returned to Scotland; he was soon found guilty of heresy.

1604 John Whitgift, Archbishop of Canterbury (1583-1604), died at about 74; a stern disciplinarian, he strove to establish rigid religious uniformity; a vigorous opponent of Puritanism.

1692 John Byrom, English poet and hymnologist, was born near Manchester; among his hymns is "Christians, awake, salute the happy morn;" author of the phrase "tweedledum and tweedledee" (died 1763).

1736 Ann Lee, founder of the American Shakers, was born in Manchester, England; established first American Shaker colony at what is now Watervliet, N.Y. (1776) (died 1784).

1834 James Bassett, Presbyterian missionary, was born near Hamilton, Canada; organized the Tehran (Iran) Presbyterian Church (1876) (died 1906).

1888 Domenico Tardini, Italian prelate, was born in Rome; served as secretary of state for Pope John XXIII (1958-61); elevated to cardinal 1958 (died 1961).

MARCH 1

Feast day (primarily in Wales) of St. David, patron saint of Wales.

492 St. Felix III, pope from 483 to 492, died; also observed as his feast day.

492 St. Gelasius I became pope, served until 496; considered one of the great architects of the papacy, declaring that the world is ruled by the Holy Roman Empire and the priests, but the latter are pre-eminent, with the Church of Rome above all; tried to heal schism between East and West; a notable writer of the period, primarily of letters, but also part of the liturgy known as the Gelasian Sacramentary.

705 John VII, a native of Greece, was elected pope; served until 707; renowned for his eloquence, education, and taste for art.

1389 St. Antcninus (Antonino) was born; established convent of San Marco at Florence; Archbishop of Florence (1446-59); counsellor of popes and statesmen because of his integrity and wisdom; endeared himself to the people by caring for the sick and needy in times of plague and famine; canonized 1523 (died 1459).

1546 George Wishart, an early Scottish martyr of the Reformation, was burned at the stake as a heretic for advocating the Reformation.

1625 John Robinson, English Separatist clergyman, died at about 50; pastor to the Pilgrims while they were in Holland; did not accompany them to America because only a minority of his congregation chose to go and he stayed with the majority.

1670 Carolina Colony established the Church of England as the official church of the colony.

1807 Wilford Woodruff, a Mormon leader, was born in Avon, Conn.; a member of the advance party to Utah; president of the Mormon Church (1889-98); declared end of plural marriages (1890) (died 1898).

1812 Augustus W. N. Pugin, English ecclesiastical architect, was born in London; a leader in reviving Gothic architecture in England (died 1852)

1816 John B. Kerfoot, Episcopal clergyman, was born in Dublin; first Bishop of Pittsburgh (1866-81) (died 1881).

1821 Joseph H. Reinkens, Old Catholic Church leader, was born in Aachen, Germany; associated with movement which opposed doctrine of papal infallibility (1870), named as its first bishop (1873) (died 1896).

1921 Terence J. Cooke, Catholic prelate, was born in New York City; Archbishop of New York (1968-83), elevated to cardinal 1969 (died 1983)

1925 Dr. Harry Emerson Fosdick left the First Presbyterian Church, New York City, refusing to accept the requirements of the General Assembly.

1930 The legal union of the Church of England in India with the Church of England was terminated.

1958 Pope Pius XII named Samuel Stritch, Archbishop of Chicago, to the newly-created post of proprefect of the Sacred Congregation for the Propagation of the Faith.

1959 Archbishop Makarios III returned to Cyprus after a three-year exile.

MARCH 2

Feast day of Heinrich Suso, German mystic; beatified 1831.

672 St. Chad (or Ceadda), English prelate, died; bishop of East Saxons (664), Litchfield, York, and Mercians; one of the most popular English saints; also observed as his feast day.

1459 Adrian VI, only Dutch pope (1522-23), was born as Adrian Dedel in Utrecht; tutor to Archduke Charles (later Charles V of Spain); grand inquisitor (1516) and regent (1520) of Spain; as pope, failed in efforts to reform church and to oppose advances of the Turks.

1791 John Wesley, co-founder of Methodism, died in London at 87.

1803 Mary Francis Clarke, founder of the Sisters of the Blessed Virgin Mary (1833), was born; (died 1887).

1810 Leo XIII, pope from 1878 to 1903, was born as Giocchino Vincenzo Pecchi near Rome.

1816 Tuve N. Hasselquist, Lutheran leader, was born in Hassläröd, Sweden; president, Augustana (Ill.) synod (1860-70); president, Augustana College and Theological Seminary (1863-91) (died 1891).

1876 Pius XII, pope from 1939 to 1958, was born in Rome as Eugenio Pacilli.

1877 Luigi Maglione, Italian cardinal and diplomat, was born; nuncio to Switzerland (1920-26), to France (1926-35); elevated to cardinal 1935; prefect of the Congregation of the Council (1935-39), secretary of state to Pope Pius XII (1939-44) (died 1944).

1930 The Catholic Hour, one of the oldest religious radio programs, was inaugurated.

1939 Pius XII was named pope, served until 1958; tried to prevent world war, relaxed rules for fasting before communion, allowed masses in the evening and use of the vernacular.

1979 More than 1,100 evangelical Christian groups, with $1 billion in combined income for 1978, announced the formation of an umbrella agency, the Evangelical Council for Financial Accountability.

1980 Swiss voters in a national referendum rejected a proposal to ban all ties between church and state.

1981 The Vatican reaffirmed its century-old prohibition against Catholics becoming Masons.

MARCH 3

468 St. Simplicius was elected pope, served until 483; during his reign, Western Europe fell before the barbarians.

1193 Saladin, one of the greatest and most religious Muslim leaders, died; sultan of Egypt and Syria, he campaigned successfully to drive the Christians from Palestine, fighting an army of Crusaders under Richard I of England and Philip II of France; lost Caesarea and Jaffa and was ordered to accept a three-year truce (1192).

1263 Hugh of St. Cher, French cardinal, died at 64; Dominican scholar, reputedly the first compiler of a concordance* of the Bible, the first to divide the Old and New Testaments into chapters; best known for correcting, indexing Latin version of the Bible.

1431 Eugenius IV, born Gabriello Condulmieri, a nephew of Pope Gregory XII, was elected pope; served to 1447; engaged in long struggle with the Council of Basel, which refused his order to disband; convened Council of Ferrara (1439); was deposed by the Council of Basel (1439), which elected antipope, Felix V; schism lasted throughout his reign; a patron of art and literature.

1500 Reginald Pole, English prelate, was born near Birmingham; Archbishop of Canterbury (1556-58); left England (1529) to avoid taking sides on Henry VIII's desire to divorce Catherine of Aragon; while traveling, he criticized Henry on the matter, as a result of which his mother and brother in England were executed; Pole served as presiding legate at the Council of Trent, which embodied Pole's views on original sin and his doctrine of justification by faith; just missed election as pope in 1549; returned to England (1554) (died 1558).

1520 Matthias Flacius Illyricus, Lutheran reformer, was born near Trieste; a pioneer in church history studies, notably his 13 volume Magdeburg Centuries; a pupil of Luther; first representative of verbal inspiration among Lutheran theologians, championed orthodoxy in various religious controversies (died 1575).

1604 Faustus Socinus, Italian theologian, died at 65; developed an anti-Trinitarian doctrine (Socinianism*), which adhered to the authority of the Scriptures; denounced by the Inquisition and forced to live in Switzerland and Poland.

1791 French Revolutionaries, who earlier had taken over the property of the clergy (Nov 2,1789), transferred silver plate used in the churches to the mint, where it was coined.

1801 Blessed Teresa Verzeri, congregation founder, was born in Italy; founded (1847) the Daughters of the Sacred Heart; beatified 1946 (died 1852).

1819 Alexander Crummell, Black Episcopal clergyman, was born in New York City; was refused admission to the General Theological Seminary so he read for orders and was ordained in 1844; president of Liberia College 20 years, then rector, St. Luke's Church, Washington, D.C. (1872-94) (died 1898).

1832 William C. Doane, Episcopal prelate, was born in Boston, the son of Bishop George W. Doane; first Episcopal Bishop of Albany, N.Y. (1869-1913); author of the hymn, "Ancient of days" (died 1913).

1891 Damaskinos, political and church leader, was born in Dhoroitsa, Greece; Archbishop of Athens (1941-49) and regent of Greece during the 1944-46 civil war (died 1949).

1919 Two American Catholic bishops were elevated to archbishop - Patrick J. Hayes of New York and Albert A. Daeger of Santa Fe, N.M.

1974 A joint committee of American Catholic and Lutheran theologians issued a study declaring that papal primacy need no longer be a "barrier" to reconciliation of the churches.

MARCH 4

254 St. Lucius, pope from 253 to 254, died; also observed as his feast day.

561 Pelagius I, pope from 556 to 561, died.

1583 Bernard Gilpin, English clergyman, died at 66; his annual journeys through neglected sections of Northumberland and Yorkshire, where he preached and ministered to the poor, gave him the title of "Apostle of the North."

1756 The first American professor of divinity, Naphtali Daggett, was installed at Yale College.

1784 Johann W. Ebel, Lutheran clergyman and teacher, was born in East Prussia; pastor in Königsberg; founder of the mystic and theosophic Mucker Society, dissolved (1839) on charges of immorality and sectarianism, which were found untrue after a six year trial (died 1861).

1838 The first American Jewish Sunday School was established in Philadelphia.

1861 Arthur C. McGiffert, theologian, was born in Sauquoit, N.Y.; teacher, professor, Lane Theological Seminary; with Union Theological Seminary, professor of church history (1893-1927), president (1917-26); author of "A History of Christianity," criticism of which led him to leave the Presbyterian Church (died 1933).

1878 The Roman Catholic hierarchy in Scotland was revived by Pope Leo XIII.

1881 The Toronto Baptist College was incorporated.

1987 A federal judge banned 31 textbooks from Alabama public schools saying they illegally promoted "the religion of secular humanism;" the ruling was overturned Aug. 27 by the U. S. Circuit Court of Appeals.

MARCH 5

475 St. Gerasimus, a hermit, died; legend has it that he drew a thorn from the paw of a lion; also observed as his feast day.

1179 The Third Lateran Council opened to discuss schisms, ended March 19; promulgated 27 canons, including the papal election by the College of Cardinals.

1409 The Council of Pisa opened, deposed Gregory XII and Benedict XIII , and elected Alexander V as pope in their place; council ended August 7.

1605 Clement VIII, pope from 1592 to 1605, died at 69.

1820 Alvah Hovey, Baptist educator, was born in Greene, N.Y.; theology professor, Newton Theological Institution (1849-1903), president (1868-1903) (died 1903).

1830 Theodore T. Munger, Congregational clergyman and theologian, was born in Bainbridge, N.Y.; pastor, North Church, New Haven; helped explain public extremism about Civil War in theological terms (died 1910).

1869 Michael von Faulhaber, Catholic prelate, was born in Heidenfeld, Germany; Archbishop of Munich (1917-52); elevated to cardinal 1921; author of concordat between Bavaria and the Pope; a vigorous opponent of Naziism (died 1952).

1895 Moses Feinstein, religious leader, was born in Uzda, Russia; influential, widely-respected Jewish Orthodox rabbi who helped make New York's Mesivta Tiferet Jerusalem one of the leading American yeshivas; solved contemporary religious problems for Orthodox Jews throughout the world (died 1986).

1939 Moses Gaster, Rumanian-born Jewish scholar and rabbi, died at 73; chief rabbi of the Sephardic (Jews of Spanish or Portuguese origin) communities in England (1887-1919).

1981 Teaching evolution in public schools did not violate the rights of religious fundamentalists, a California Superior Court judge ruled.

1984 The U. S. Supreme Court ruled 5-4 that public financing of a Nativity scene did not of itself violate the doctrine of separation of church and state.

MARCH 6

Feast day of St. Colette (1381-1447), Flemish reformer of the Poor Clares and founder of the Colettine Poor Clares; established 17 convents in her lifetime; canonized 1807.

766 St. Chrodegang died; Bishop of Metz (742-766) and one of the chief ecclesiastical reformers of his time; also observed as his feast day.

1447 Nicholas V, born Tommasso Parentucelli, was elected pope; served until 1455; probably the best of the Renaissance popes, a patron of the arts and literature; restored many ruined churches and founded the Vatican Library; led a blameless personal life, free from nepotism, and anxious to reconcile religion with the new learning; brought about the submission of the last antipope (Felix V) and the dissolution of the moribund council of Basel (1449).

1611 Pierre Joseph Marie Chaumonot, Jesuit missionary, was born in Burgundy, France; served with the Indians in New York and Canada (1639-93); wrote a Huron grammar and a dictionary of dialects (died 1693).

1642 A papal bull issued by Urban VIII forbade the reading of Jansen's "Augustinus."

1662 Francis Atterbury, English prelate, was born in Milton; Bishop of Rochester and Dean of Westminster (1713-22); a zealous participant in many literary, political, and ecclesiastical controversies of his time; banished for complicity in Jacobite plot (1723); regarded as the best preacher of his day (died 1732).

1741 Henri Marie Dubreuil de Pontbriand was appointed Catholic Bishop of Quebec; was consecrated April 9.

1811 Edward H. Browne, Anglican prelate, was born near London; Bishop of Winchester (1873-90); his "Exposition of the 39 Articles" was long a standard authority (died 1891).

1874 Nikolai A. Berdysev, Russian religious philosopher, was born in Kiev; influential in Russian religious revival (1904-14), expelled (1922) by Bolsheviks because of his basic concept that the highest value was a person as a spiritual entity; founded a religious philosophical academy in Paris; author (Freedom of the Spirit, Destiny of Man) (died 1948).

1984 The U.S. Senate (81 to 13) confirmed William A. Wilson as the American ambassador to the Vatican, thus reopening diplomatic relations with the Holy See after more than a century.

MARCH 7

1274 St. Thomas Aquinas, Christian philosopher and theologian, died at about 50; often called the Angelic Doctor; systematized Latin theology and wrote some of the most beautiful eucharistic hymns in the church's liturgy; his teaching drew a sharp distinction between reason and faith; his own influence was great in his own time, waned between the 16th and 19th centuries, but since mid-19th Century has undergone a revival; canonized 1323, named a Doctor* of the Church (1567), made patron of all Catholic universities (1880); also observed as his feast day.

1608 Nakae Toju, Japanese Confucianist scholar, was born; called the sage of Omi; founder in Japan of the Wang Yang-ming School of Neo-Confucianism (died 1648).

1638 Anne Hutchinson settled in exile on the island of Aquidneck, R.I., where 19 settlers formed a town which later became Portsmouth; she had been banished from Massachusetts for her religious opinions.

1644 Samuel Gorton (about 1592-1677), English-born founder of a religious sect, was banished from Massachusetts; settled in Rhode Island; his sect, the Gortonians, rejected outward religious ceremonies, held that Christ was both human and divine, that heaven and hell exist only in the mind.

1693 Clement XIII, pope from 1758 to 1769, was born in Venice as Carlo della Torre Rezzonico.

1724 Innocent XIII, pope from 1721 to 1724, died at 69.

1832 Galusha Anderson, Baptist clergyman and educator, was born in Clarendon, N.Y.; president of the old U. of Chicago (1878-85) (died 1918).

1836 James M. Thoburn, Methodist missionary, was born in St. Clairville, Ohio; missionary to India (1859-1908), missionary bishop (1888-1908) (died 1922).

1855 Marie Joseph Lagrange, French theologian, was born in Bourg-en-Bresse, France; one of the leading Catholic biblical scholars; his monumental commentaries on the four Gospels became a standard work (died 1938).

1893 Thomas D. Roberts, Catholic Archbishop of Bombay (1937-50), born; successfully argued with the Vatican that his successor should be an Indian (died 1976).

1921 Archbishop Dennis J. Dougherty of Philadelphia was elevated to cardinal.

1964 Pope Paul VI celebrated mass in a Rome parish church in Italian rather than Latin and facing the congregation, thus implementing decisions of the Ecumenical Council.

1971 Patriarch Kiril of the Bulgarian Orthodox Church died/

1979 The Consultation on Church Union, meeting in Cincinnati, enthusiastically greeted a proposal that might soon pave the way for common ordained clergy among the nation's 10 largest Protestant denominations.

MARCH 8

Feast day in the Orthodox Church of St. Agabus, Christian prophet of the First Century; regarded as an apostle and one of the 70 disciples of Christ.

Feast day of St. Felix of Dunwich, first Bishop of East Anglia (about 631-648); helped introduce monastic life to Britain.

1118 Gregory VIII, born Mauritius Burdinus, was set up by Henry V of Germany as anti-pope; served until 1121; never able to assert himself in Rome and spent much time in prison.

1144 Celestine II, pope from 1143 to 1144, died.

1495 St. John of God, congregation founder, was born in Portugal as Juan Ciudad; founded the Hospitaller Order of St. John of God; canonized 1650 and declared the patron of hospitals and sick persons; also observed as his feast day (died 1550).

1607 Johann von Rist, German poet and Lutheran hymnist, was born near Hamburg; a most prolific hymnist with more than 650 hymns (Lord Jesus Christ, the living bread; Praise and thanks to Thee be sung; O Jesu! welcome, gracious name) (died 1667).

1715 Louis XIV of France announced he had put an end to all exercise of the Protestant religion.

1856 W. Bramwell Booth, Salvation Army leader, was born in Halifax, England; headed the Army (1912-29}; while serving under his father, William, founder of the Army, he was the chief organizer and chief of staff (1880-1912) (died 1929).

1884 George S. Duncan, internationally-renowned New Testament scholar, was born in Forfar, Scotland; professor, St. Andrew's; author (Jesus Son of Man) (died 1965).

1948 The U. S. Supreme Court ruled that religious education in public schools is a violation of the First Amendment.

1962 The General Council of the United Presbyterian Church in the U.S. issued a "Letter on Freedom of Pulpit and Pew," which attacked right wing extremists who would "substitute militant anti-communism for the Gospel of Jesus Christ."

1964 Pope Paul VI called for a dialogue between Catholics and Protestants with the aim of finding common ground.

1976 The U.S. Supreme Court refused to review a decision by the Tennessee Supreme Court that snake handling and drinking of poison can be enjoined as public nuisances even when they are part of a religious ritual.

MARCH 9

Feast day of St. Frances of Rome, a founder of the Benedictine Oblates (1425), superior (1426-40).

Feast day in the Catholic Church of St. Gregory, Bishop of Nyassa (371-395); one of the most acute intellects of the Fourth Century; influenced mystical tradition of the Eastern Church.

1463 St. Catherine of Bologna, a founder and abbess of the convent of Poor Clares (1456-63), died; also observed as her feast day.

1568 St. Aloysius Gonzaga, Jesuit and the patron saint of youth, was born in Italy; died in 1591 while ministering to those stricken by famine and pestilence in Rome; canonized 1726.

1903 Albert G. Meyer, Catholic prelate, was born in Milwaukee; Archbishop of Milwaukee (1953-58), of Chicago (1958-65); elevated to cardinal 1959 (died 1965).

1907 John A. Dowie, founder of the Christian Catholic Apostolic Church, died in Zion City, which he also founded, at the age of 60.

1907 Mircea Eliade, teacher of religious history (U. of Chicago), was born in Bucharest; he was noted for research in symbolic language used in religions; author (The Myth of the Eternal Return, The Sacred and the Profane) (died 1986).

1956 The British deported Archbishop Makarios III of Cyprus to the Seychelles Islands.

1971 Kyrillos VI, 116th patriarch of the Coptic Orthodox Church (1959-71), died in Cairo at 69.

1982 The Vatican refused to give liberal theologian Dr. Hans Kung an audience with the pope until he changed his views, especially on papal infallibility.

MARCH 10

483 St. Simplicius, pope from 468 to 483, died; advanced the jurisdiction of Rome considerably during his reign; also observed as his feast day.

1045 Sylvester III, pope since January 20, resigned to return to his bishopric in Sabina (a suburb of Rome, also called Mallianum).

1528 Balthasar Hübmaier; German Anabaptist leader, was burned at the stake in Vienna; involved in Peasants' War, he supported the Anabaptist* cause with his writing.

1810 John McCloskey, Catholic prelate, was born in Brooklyn, N.Y.; first president, Fordham U. (1841-42), first Bishop of Albany, N.Y. (1847-64); Archbishop of New York (1864-85); first American cardinal (1875) (died 1885).

1823 John B. Dykes, clergyman and hymn composer, was born in Hull, England; wrote music for many well-known hymns (Lead, kindly light; Nearer, my God, to Thee; Jesus, lover of my soul; Holy, Holy, Holy) (died 1876).

1880 Commissioner George S. Railton and seven women arrived in New York City from London on the steamer Australia and set up the Salvation Army in the United States; the first service was held in Castle Garden.

1897 Carl H. Kraeling, theologian and archaeologist, was born in Brooklyn, N.Y.; author (John the Baptist, The Synagogue) (died 1966).

MARCH 11

Feast day of St. Oengus (8th-9th Century), an Irish monk associated with the movement to reform Irish monasticism, the reformed monks calling themselves "Fellows of God."

604 St. Gregory I (the Great), pope from 590 to 604, died.

859 St. Eulogius of Cordoba was beheaded; his violent opposition to Mohammedanism led to his imprisonment, martyrdom; also observed as his feast day.

1513 Leo X was elected pope, served to 1521; reign marked by religious controversy with Martin Luther and the latter's excommunication, and with Johann Reuchlin; terminated the Fifth Lateran Council (1517) to prevent a schism.

1521 Andrew Forman, Scottish prelate, died at about 56; served as Archbishop of Bourges (1513-14) and Archbishop of St. Andrews and primate of Scotland (1514-21).

1547 Council of Trent was moved to Bologna because of an outbreak of the plague; the last two sessions held there.

1742 Samuel Provoost, first Episcopal Bishop of New York (1786-1801), was born in New York City; chaplain of U.S. Senate (1789-1801) (died 1815).

1794 Giovanni Perrone, Jesuit theologian, was born near Turin, Italy; active in condemnation of Hermesian* heresy and in formulation of the doctrine of the Immaculate Conception (died 1876).

1796 Francis Wayland, Baptist clergyman and educator, was born in New York City; a leading American preacher, served First Baptist Church, Boston (1821-27); president, Brown U. (1827-55) (died 1865).

1827 Daniel Dorchester, Methodist clergyman, was born in Duxbury, Mass.; served as superintendent of American Indian schools (1889-1907) (died 1907).

1965 Rev. James Reeb, Unitarian clergyman from Boston, died in Selma, Ala. from a beating he received two days earlier while working on a civil rights drive.

1966 Morris Adler, American rabbi and educator, died in Detroit at 60; author (Great Passages from the Torah, World of the Talmud).

1985 Father Leonardo Boff, 47-year old Brazilian Franciscan, was "silenced" by the Vatican, forbidden to write or lecture because "some of Boff's opinions were such as to endanger the sound doctrine of the faith."

1986 The controversy over his teaching of the Catholic doctrine ended when Rev. Charles E. Curran of Catholic U., Washington, D.C. was ordered by the Vatican to retract his views on birth control and other sexual issues or lose his right to teach Catholic doctrine.

MARCH 12

Feast day of St. Theophanes (about 758-818), Byzantine monk and historian who founded a monastery at Sigriano; opposed the iconoclastic policy of Emperor Leo V and died in exile.

417 St. Innocent I, pope from 401 to 417, died.

1022 San Simeon the New Theologian died; Byzantine mystic and spiritual writer, abbot of the monastery at St. Mamas (Constantinople) (981-1005); also observed as his feast day.

1088 Urban II, born Odo (or Udo) was elected pope, served until 1099; convoked councils (1095) at Piacenza and Clermont, initiated great crusading movement with the First Crusade (1095), giving papacy a great source of strength and prestige; also observed as his feast day.

1144 Lucius II, born Gerard, was named pope, served until 1145.

1364 Ralph (Ranulf) Higden, English Benedictine monk, died; author of "Polychronicon," a universal history.

1607 Paul Gerhardt, greatest German Protestant hymn writer, was born near Wittenberg; made German translation from Latin of "O sacred head now wounded;" among his hymns are "Jesus, Thy boundless love to me;" "All my heart this night rejoices," and "Give to the winds thy fears" (died 1676).

1663 August H. Francke, German pietistic clergyman and philanthropist, was born in Halle; helped found the "Colegium philobiblicum" for a closer study of the Scriptures; founded a charity school at Halle (1695), to which were added other schools, an orphanage, all later combined into the Francke Institutions (died 1727).

1685 George Berkeley, Irish philosopher and prelate, was born near Dublin; served as Bishop of Cloyne (near Cork) (1734-53); wrote on religious and economic problems (Principles of Human Knowledge); celebrated for his metaphysical doctrine, a form of subjective idealism (died 1753).

1712 Thomas A. Arne, English composer, was born in London; best known for his "Rule Brittania;" also wrote music for Anglican hymns (Am I a soldier of the cross; Let Zion's watchmen all awake) (died 1778).

1758 James Lee, Methodist clergyman, was born in Prince Georges County, Md.; assistant to Bishop Francis Asbury (1797-1800); presiding elder, South District of Virginia (1801-15); author of first history of American Methodism (died 1816).

1786 First Presbyterian church service was held in Montreal by Rev. John Bethune.

1805 Justin Perkins, missionary in Persia (Iran), was born in West Springfield, Mass.; known as the "apostle of Persia," serving Nestorian Christians (1833-69); opened schools, reduced modern Syriac* to writing (died 1869).

1811 John S. B. Monsell, Irish Anglican clergyman, was born in Londonderry; rector of St. Nicholas at Guildford, wrote several hymns (Fight the good fight with all thy might; Worship the Lord in the beauty of holiness) (died 1875).

1826 Robert Lowry, Baptist clergyman, was born in Philadelphia; composer of hymns (Savior, Thy dying love; I need Thee every hour; Low in the grave He lay) (died 1899).

1853 A Roman Catholic hierarchy was re-established in the Netherlands.

1896 Commander Frederick S. Tucker, son-in-law of William Booth, was named head of the Salvation Army in the United States; arrived April 2.

1910 Laszlo Lekai, Catholic primate of Hungary (1975-86), was born in Zalalovo, Hungary; elevated to cardinal 1976 (died 1986).

1979 Pope John Paul II met with leaders of world Jewish organizations and called for "fraternal dialogue and fruitful cooperation."

MARCH 13

Feast day in the Catholic Church of St. Nicephorus, patriarch of Constantinople (806-815); refused to obey Emperor Leo's edict against worship of images, deposed.

Feast day of Boniface of Savoy, Archbishop of Canterbury (1241-70); died enroute to a Crusade.

483 St. Felix III was named pope, served until 492; began schism between Orthodox and Catholic churches, which lasted 34 years.

1622 An auto-da-fe at Cartagena, Colombia burned an English Protestant; inquisition decreed in 1610.

1733 Joseph Priestley, renowned English scientist and theologian, was born near York; best known for his work in chemistry and electricity; held various Presbyterian pastorates in England; then to the United States, where he was an early advocate of Unitarianism; wrote 4-volume history of the Christian Church and a 4-volume work on the Scriptures (died 1804).

1800 Pius VII was unanimously elected pope, served until 1823; reign marked a transition between the troubles of the French Revolution and the quiet pontificates that followed; crowned Napoleon (1804) but later opposed his aggressions; held prisoner by Napoleon at Savona and Fontainebleau (1809-14), returned to Rome; restored Jesuit order (1814); suppressed carbonari (a secret group originally formed to promote the Italian republic) and restored order in Rome (1815-23).

1815 James C. Hepburn, Presbyterian medical missionary to Japan, was born in Milton, Pa.; compiled first Japanese-English dictionary, supervised first complete translation of the Bible into Japanese (1888) (died 1911).

1832 John T. Gulick, Congregational missionary to the Far East, was born in Hawaii; missionary to China (1865-75) and Japan (1875-99); evolutionist, author (Evolution, Racial and Habitudinal) (died 1923).

1833 William F. Warren, Methodist theologian, was born in Williamsburg, Mass.; president, Boston Theological School (1867-73); a founder, first president, Boston U. (1873-1903); theological school became part of university (died 1929).

1857 Brigham H. Roberts, Mormon leader and publicist, was born in Warrington, England; a missionary leader, orator, editor of the Salt Lake Tribune (1890-96); wrote much about the Mormon Church, including six-volume centennial history; elected to House of Representatives (1898) but refused seat because of his plural marriages (died 1933).

1908 Andover Theological Seminary was moved from Andover, Mass. to Cambridge, where it became affiliated with Harvard U.

1911 Lafayette R. Hubbard, sect founder, was born in Tilden, Neb.; originated Scientology, a movement based on dianetics, a method of achieving mental and physical health (died 1986).

1965 Rt. Rev. Fan Stylian Noli, founder and bishop of the Albanian Orthodox Church in America (1930-65), died in Ft. Lauderdale, Fla. at 83.

1970 The Consultation on Church Union submitted preliminary plans to unite nine Protestant denominations into a single church.

1988 Conservative Judaism in America issued its first statement of principles, rejecting fundamentalism in all religions.

MARCH 14

Feast day in the Orthodox Church of St. Benedict, the father of Western monasticism.

1009 St. Bruno of Querfort, German missionary bishop; he and 18 companions were murdered by heathens; with St. Adalbert, he is a patron of Prussia.

1638 Johann G. Gichtel, Protestant mystic and ascetic, was born in Regensburg, Germany; spent most of his life in Amsterdam; founder of a small sect which condemned marriage and church services (died 1710).

1698 Lodowick Muggleton, English sectarian, died at 89; he and his cousin, John Reeve, presented themselves as the two witnesses of Revelation xi, messengers of a new dispensation (1652); denied the Trinity, held that the devil became incarnate in Eve; made converts who called themselves Muggletonians.

1774 John Vine Hall, English writer, was born in Diss, Norfolk; a reformed drinker, he wrote "The Sinner's Friend" (1821), which went through about 300 editions, was translated into 30 languages (died 1860).

1835 William F. Moulton, Wesleyan Methodist clergyman, was born near Birmingham, England; translated Winer's "Grammar of New Testament Greek;" a reviser of the New Testament (1870-81); author of "History of the English Bible" (died 1898).

1835 Henry B. Swete, biblical and patristic* scholar, was born in Bristol, England; did important work on biblical texts; divinity professor, Cambridge (1890-1915) (died 1917).

1897 The Polish National Catholic Church of America was organized in Scranton, Pa.

1925 Archbishop Ruch of Strasbourg called a three-day strike of French Catholic school children as a protest against setting up some nondenominational schools.

1979 The Christian Church (Disciples of Christ) and the United Church of Christ took the first step toward some form of union.

MARCH 15

Feast day in the Catholic Church of St. Longinus, the "soldier with the spear" at the Crucifixion.

Feast day of St. Louise de Marillac, co-founder with St. Vincent de Paul, of the Sisters of Charity.

1672 Charles II issued the first declaration of indulgence in which he asserted his right to suspend all penal legislation enacted by Parliament against both Catholic and Protestant dissenters; he was forced by Parliament to cancel the declaration and to pass the Test Act (1673), driving Catholics from office.

1708 John Hulse, clergyman and philanthropist, was born in Middlewich, England; bequeathed most of his inherited property to Cambridge U.

for the advancement of religious learning (scholarships, lectures) (died 1790).

1711 Eusebio F. Kino (or Climi), Italian Jesuit missionary to Mexico and the American Southwest, died at about 66; discovered, described the Casa Grande ruins in the Gila Valley of Arizona.

1729 The first Catholic nun to be professed in the United States was Sister St. Stanislaus Hachard at the Ursuline convent in New Orleans.

1816 Richard H. Wilmer, Episcopal Bishop of Alabama (1862-1900), was born in Alexandria, Va. (died 1900).

1820 St. Clement Hofbauer, the "apostle of Vienna," died; early leader of the Redemptorists; canonized 1909; also observed as his feast day.

1875 Archbishop John McCloskey of New York became the first American cardinal; consecrated April 27.

1875 Israel Rosenberg, American rabbi, was born in Lomza, Poland; president, Union of Orthodox Rabbis (1940-56) (died 1956).

1988 Catholic Bishop Eugene A. Marino was elevated to Archbishop of Atlanta by Pope John Paul II, the first black Catholic archbishop in the United States; since 1985, he had been secretary of the National Conference of Catholic Bishops.

1641 The General Court declared Rhode Island a democracy, adopted a new constitution granting freedom of religion for all citizens.

1649 St. Jean de Brebeuf, French Jesuit missionary to North American Indians, was captured and burned at the stake at St. Ignace on the Sturgeon River near Lake Huron; canonized 1930 along with six other North American martyrs.

1750 Samuel Stanhope Smith, Presbyterian clergyman and educator, was born in Pequa, Pa.; professor of moral philosophy, Princeton U. (1779-1812), president (1795-1812) (died 1819).

1823 William H. Monk, English musician and composer, was born in London; served as organist at various churches, edited hymn collections for the Church of Scotland; wrote numerous hymns (Abide with me; Let us with gladsome mind) (died 1889).

1875 Clerical control over parish funds was taken away by the German government.

1878 Clemens A. Galen, Catholic bishop, was born in Dinklage, Germany; Bishop of Münster (1933-46) and an effective opponent of Naziism; elevated to cardinal 1946 (died 1946).

1970 The new English Bible was published; translated directly from ancient texts, it was the work of British scholars of the major Protestant churches who were assisted by literary experts; its language departed radically from the King James Version.

MARCH 16

1072 Adalbert, Archbishop of Bremen-Hamburg (1045-72), died at about 72; papal legate, then vicar, in northern Europe; gained influence as counselor and companion of Henry III and as tutor of Henry IV, Holy Roman Emperor, and for a time was virtual ruler of the Empire.

1445 Johann Geiler von Kaiserberg, theologian, was born in Switzerland; regarded as forerunner of the Reformation; preacher at the Cathedral of Strasbourg (1478-1510), where his sermons excoriated vices and social evils of the day (died 1510).

MARCH 17

Feast day of St. Patrick, patron saint of Ireland; named bishop (432) and assigned by Pope Celestine I to convert the Irish; founded churches and converted many throughout Ireland; founded church and monastery at Armagh.

659 St. Gertrude of Nivelles, abbess of a Belgian convent (Nivelles), died at 34; widely invoked as patroness of travelers; also observed as her feast day.

1677 Thomas Boston, Scottish Calvinist, was born in Dunse, Scotland; one of the 12 "Marrow Men" (defenders of "The Marrow of Modern

Divinity"), defending Calvinism against the charge that it was too free in offers of salvation; author (The Fourfold State) (died 1732).

1696 Antoine Court, Protestant clergyman, was born in Villeneuve-de-Berg, France; founder, head of seminary at Lausanne (1729-60); a leader in restoring the Reformed Church in France (died 1760).

1780 Thomas Chalmers, Scottish religious leader, was born in Anstruther, Scotland; a founder and first moderator of the Free Church of Scotland; gained wide reputation as a preacher, administrator of poor relief; professor of moral philosophy and theology (1923-43); leader of evangelical section of Church of Scotland, led withdrawal of 470 ministers (1843) from general assembly to form the Free Church (died 1847).

1781 Ebenezer Elliott, English poet, was born in New Foundry, Yorkshire; known as the corn-law rhymer, he is also remembered for the hymn, "When wilt Thou save the people?" (died 1849).

1809 Ambrose L. M. Phillips de Lisle, Catholic leader, was born in England; a leading figure in the 19th Century Catholic revival and founder of Mt. St. Bernard, the first post-Reformation English Trappist monastery (died 1878).

1823 Charles P. Krauth, Lutheran theologian and educator, was born in Martinsburg, W. Va.; professor of systematic theology, Lutheran Theological Seminary, Philadelphia; editor, *The Lutheran;* member of American Revision Committee of English Version of the Bible (died 1883).

1832 Moncure D. Conway, Unitarian clergyman and active abolitionist, was born in Stafford County, Va.; pastor of a Washington, D.C. church from which he was dismissed for his opposition to slavery; pastor in London, England (1864-84); editor, *The Dial* (1860-61), *Commonwealth* (1862); author (Demonology and Devil Lore, Life of Thomas Paine) (died 1907).

1874 Stephen S. Wise, Zionist leader and rabbi, was born in Budapest; rabbi and founder, Free Synagogue, New York City (1907-49); president, American Jewish Congress; founder, president, Jewish Institute of Religion; founder, Zionist Organization of America (died 1949).

1887 Wilfrid Parsons, Catholic clergyman and editor, was born in Philadelphia; editor-in-chief, *America*, Catholic weekly (1925-36); with Georgetown and Catholic universities (died 1958).

1918 Oliver Plunkett, Archbishop of Armagh, Ireland, who was executed at Tyburn in 1861, was beatified.

1929 Peter L. Ludwig, a lay Lutheran theologian who developed a sociological theory of religion (The Sacred Canopy), was born in Vienna.

1963 Mother Elizabeth Ann Seton, American-born founder of the Sisters of Charity of St. Joseph, was beatified in Rome by Pope John XXIII.

MARCH 18

Feast day in the Catholic Church of St. Alexander, Bishop of Cappadocia (now central Turkey) and first bishop coadjutor of Jerusalem; built theological library in Jerusalem (died 251).

Feast day of St. Cyril, Bishop of Jerusalem (315-387), a Doctor* of the Church; opposed Aryan heresy, deposed from bishopric (357), continued to defend orthodoxy, restored to his see (about 379); best known for a series of discourses given during Lent for those to be baptized on Easter.

417 St. Zosimus became pope, served until 418.

731 Gregory III was consecrated as pope, served until 741; Syrian-born pontiff who condemned iconoclasm, convoked a council in Rome (731).

1086 St. Anselm of Lucca, Italian Benedictine prelate, died; noted for his crusade against lay investiture; patron of Mantua, Bishop of Lucca (1071-86); also observed as his feast day.

1123 First Lateran Council was held but did little more than reiterate decrees of earlier councils; lasted until April 5; rights of investiture were settled by treaty between Pope Calixtus II and Emperor Henry V.

1227 Honorius III, pope from 1216 to 1227, died.

1789 Charlotte Elliott, Anglican hymn writer, was born in England; wrote about 150 hymns (Just as I am, without one plea; My God, my Father, while I stray; O Holy Saviour, friend unseen) (died 1871).

1795 Demetrius A. Gallitzin (1770-1840), first Catholic priest to receive full theological training in the United States, was ordained by Bishop John Carroll in Baltimore.

1804 Johannes A.A. Grabau, Lutheran leader, was born in Obenstedt, Germany; led about 1000 persons from Prussia, where the Lutheran and Reformed churches had combined; helped organize, headed Buffalo Synod of the Lutheran Church (died 1879).

1828 Charles Voysey, English theist, was born in London; founded Theistic Church (1871) in London after being ousted from Anglican Church for heterodoxy (disagreement with accepted church doctrine) (died 1912).

1847 Robert A. Hume, American Congregational missionary to India, was born in Bombay, India; founder, president, United Divinity College at Ahmednagar (1878-1926) (died 1929).

1857 Henry Berkowitz, rabbi, was born in Pittsburgh; one of the first rabbis ordained in the United States (1883); served Rodolph Sholem Congregation, Philadelphia, for 30 years (died 1924).

1870 Bishop John J. Lynch was named the first Catholic Archbishop of Toronto.

1881 Julian Morgenstern, rabbi and educator, was born in St. Francisville, Ill.; with Hebrew Union College - professor of Bible and Semitic languages (1907-47); president (1921-47) (died 1976).

1889 Francis J. Haas, Catholic prelate and labor expert, was born in Racine, Wis.; director, National Catholic School of Social Service, Washington (1931-37); dean of Social Service School, Catholic U. (1937-43); first chairman, U.S. Committee on Fair Employment Practices (1943); Bishop of Grand Rapids, Mich. (1943-53) (died 1953).

1898 Lawrence J. Shehan, Catholic prelate, was born in Baltimore; Archbishop of Baltimore (1961-74), elevated to cardinal 1965 (died 1974).

1956 Nicholai Velimirovich, Serbian Orthodox Church bishop, died in South Canaan, Pa. at about 74.

1960 Catholic Bishop James Walsh was sentenced to 20 years for espionage and counter-revolutionary activities by a Communist court in Shanghai.

MARCH 19

Feast day of St. Joseph, husband of Mary; declared a patron of the Universal Church by pope Pius IX in 1870.

416 Pope St. Innocent I wrote a letter to Decentius, Bishop of Eugubium (southeast of Florence), which was important for the history of the canon of the Mass; also spoke of confirmation as reserved for bishops and mentioned rites of unction and penance.

1227 Gregory IX, born Urgolino, the Count of Segni, was elected pope, served until 1241; pontificate featured a long struggle with Emperor Frederick II, whom he twice excommunicated; helped develop the Holy Office of the Inquisition.

1534 Jose de Anchieta, Portuguese Jesuit missionary, was born in the Canary Islands; known as the "apostle of Brazil;" author of an Indian grammar and works on Brazil; virtues declared heroic by Pope Clement XII (1736) (died 1597).

1657 Jean Le Clerc, French theologian, was born in Geneva, Switzerland; editor of three influential encyclopedias; a biblical scholar, a champion of free thought and an enemy of all dogmatism, defended the unlimited rights of reason in the domain of faith (died 1736).

1684 Jean Astruc, French physician and theologian, was born; began scholarly investigation of the sources of the Pentateuch* because of his interest in the Pentateuchal laws of cleanliness (died 1766).

1711 Thomas Kenn (also Ken), English prelate and hymnologist, died at 74; Bishop of Bath and Wells (1684-91); attended Charles II's deathbed; one of seven who petitioned against James II's Declaration of Indulgence (1688), acquitted of a charge of seditious libel; refused to take oath of allegiance to William and Mary; wrote several hymns (Awake, my soul; Glory to Thee, my God, this night; Praise God, from whom all blessings flow).

1721 Clement XI, pope from 1700 to 1721, died at 72.

1748 Elias Hicks, liberal Quaker missionary and active abolitionist, was born in Hempstead, N.Y.; opposed set creed and was blamed for the Quaker schism (1827-28), dividing liberal elements from conservatives in many congregations, with liberals known as "Hicksites" (died 1830).

1770 John M. Mason, Presbyterian clergyman and educator, was born in New York City; began theological seminary (1804), which later became the Union Theological Seminary (died 1829).

1786 Edward Bickersteth, English clergyman and hymnist, was born near Liverpool; secretary, Church of England Missionary Society (1816-30); compiled a popular 700-page hymnbook (Christian Psalmody); edited 50-volume Christian's Family Library; wrote hymns (O God, rock of ages; Peace, perfect peace) (died 1850).

1804 James B. Taylor, secretary of Foreign Missions Board, Southern Baptist Convention (1846-71), was born in Barton-on-Humber, England (died 1871).

1811 Andrew P. Peabody, Unitarian clergyman and editor, was born in Beverly, Mass.; pastor, South Parish Church, Portsmouth, N.H. (1833-60); owner, editor, *North American Review* (1853-63); professor, Harvard (1860-81) (died 1893).

1813 David Livingstone, Scottish explorer and missionary, was born near Glasgow; "found" by Henry Stanley in Africa, where he had been a missionary (1841-55) and explorer (died 1873).

1879 Thomas Plassman, president, St. Bonaventure (N.Y.) College and Seminary (1920-49), was born in Avenwedde, Germany (died 1959).

1896 Edwin E. Aubrey, theologian, was born in Glasgow, Scotland; chairman, U. of Chicago theology department (1933-44); president, Crozier Theological Seminary (1944- 49) (died 1956).

1937 Pope Pius XI issued the encyclical, "Divini redemptoris," condemning Bolshevik Communism.

1977 Rt. Rev. Silvano Wani was elected archbishop of the Anglican Church in Uganda.

1987 Jim Bakker, founder of the PTL (Praise the Lord) ministry, turned control of the ministry and its Heritage USA theme park in South Carolina over to Jerry Falwell, head of the Moral Majority, after admitting to a sexual scandal seven years earlier.

MARCH 20

Feast day of Blessed John of Parma, Franciscan minister general (1247-57).

Former feast day of St. Joachim, father of the Blessed Virgin Mary; now observed July 25.

687 St. Cuthbert, English monk, died at about 52; headed monastery of Melrose (661-676), then Bishop of Hexham, Lindisfarne; also observed as his feast day.

1292 John Peckham, English Catholic prelate, died at about 53; Archbishop of Canterbury (1279-92); insisted on discipline and sought to increase ecclesiastical power; voluminous writer on science and theology.

1383 St. John of Nepomuk, patron saint of Bohemia, died; confessor to queen of Wenceslaus IV, by whom he was tortured and drowned in the Moldau River (1383) for refusing to reveal contents of queen's confession; canonized 1729.

1544 St. Cuthbert Mayne, English martyr, was born; first seminary priest to die (1577) for Catholicism in England under Elizabeth I; canonized 1970.

1808 Daniel D. Whedon, Methodist theologian, was born in Onandaga, N.Y.; editor, *Methodist Quarterly Review* (1856-84); widely known for his 14 volumes of Bible commentaries (died 1885).

1840 James R. Miller, Presbyterian clergyman and author, was born in Harshaville, Pa.; editorial superintendent, Presbyterian Board of Publications (1887-1912); author of eight-volume "Devotional Hours with the Bible," of which more than 2 million copies were sold (died 1912).

1854 Frank Samuel Child, Congregational clergyman and author, was born in Exeter, N.Y.; pastor, First Church, Fairfield, Conn. (1879-1922); author (Old New England Town, A Colonial Witch) (died 1922).

1889 The Baptist Convention of Ontario and Quebec was established.

1931 The practice of birth control was defended by the Federal Council of Churches of Christ in America.

1972 The United Church of Christ, one of the most active Protestant denominations on social issues, announced it is disbanding its Christian Social Action Council; will emphasize aid to local churches rather than large scale national programs.

1984 A constitutional school prayer amendment permitting organized spoken prayer in public schools was rejected by the U. S. Senate.

1987 The American Lutheran Church voted in favor of merging with the Lutheran Church in America and the Association of Evangelical Lutheran Churches to form the Evangelical Lutheran Church in America; the merger of the churches into the new 5.3 million member church will become effective Jan. 1,1988.

MARCH 21

Feast day of St. Nicholas of Flüe (1417-87), Swiss ascetic who lived in the Ranft Valley for 19 years with no food save the Eucharist; his sanctity attracted many for advice; patron saint of Switzerland; canonized 1947.

Feast day of St. Serapion (or Sarapion), Egyptian bishop and author of an anti-Manichean* thesis; reputed author of a sacramentary discovered in 1874, valued as one of the earliest large liturgical compilations.

547 St. Benedict, father of Western monasticism, died at about 67 at Monte Cassino, where he had founded a monastery that became the foundation of the Benedictine Order; declared patron saint of Europe by Pope Paul VI (1964).

1474 St. Angela Merici, founder of the Ursuline nuns, was born near Verona (died 1540).

1556 Thomas Cranmer, Archbishop of Canterbury (1533-55), was burned at the stake for treason during the reign of Queen Mary I.

1734 Robert Wodrow, Scottish churchman, died at 55; served as historian of the Church of Scotland.

1778 Charles Wesley, co-founder of Methodism, died at 81.

1809 Alessandro Gavazzi, a founder of the Free Church of Italy, was born in Bologna; organized Italian Protestants in London (1850-60), helped set up the Free Church (1870), established theological school in Rome (1875) (died 1883).

1811 Nathaniel Woodard, Anglican clergyman, was born in Basildon, Scotland; founder of the Woodard schools, which combined Anglican and public school education at a moderate cost (died 1891).

1812 William G. Ward, English theologian, was born in London; a leader of the Oxford Movement; he left the Anglican Church for the Catholic Church; known as "Ideal" Ward for his treatise, "The Ideal of a Christian Church," in praise of Catholicism (died 1882).

1813 James J. Strang, Mormon leader, was born in Scipio, N.Y.; formed his own sect, the "Strangites" (died 1856).

1829 Eugene A. Hoffman, Episcopal educator, was born in New York City; dean, General Theological Seminary, New York City (1879-1902) (died 1902).

1843 Date set by William Miller for the second coming of Christ, which became his "first disappointment;" the second occurred in October 1844; his movement gave rise to the formation of the Adventist Church (1845).

1896 Ballington Booth, former head of the American Salvation Army, named officers of the new Volunteers in America, an organization he formed after his resignation from the Army.

1937 Pope Pius XI issued the German encyclical, "Mit brennender sorge" (With burning anxiety), expressing his belief that Naziism is fundamentally unchristian, attacked the idea of a German national church.

1956 Spyridon, Archbishop of Athens and primate of Greece, died in Athens at 82.

1965 Rev. Martin Luther King Jr. led a 54-mile civil rights march from Selma to Montgomery, Ala.

1974 Pope Paul VI, in an "apostolic exhortation" called Marian Devotion, called for increasing devotion to the Virgin Mary, calling such action fully in keeping with modern women's rights movements and the search for Christian unity.

MARCH 22

Feast day in the Catholic Church of St. Zacharias (or Zachary), pope from 741 to 752; had great influence over the kings of the Lombards; encouraged missionary work of St. Boniface.

1454 John Kempe, English cardinal and Archbishop of Canterbury (1452-54), died at about 74; far more a politician than a churchman, taking little interest in his dioceses (Rochester, Chichester, London, York).

1556 Reginald Pole was consecrated as Archbishop of Canterbury, served until 1558.

1687 The first Anglican service was held in South Meeting House in Boston on Good Friday; on Easter Sunday, the Anglican service was from 11 AM to 2 PM; the Congregationalists had to wait for their service until the Anglicans finished.

1745 Joseph Proud, Swedenborgian (New Church) clergyman and hymn writer, was born in Beaconsfield, England; originally a Baptist clergyman, he attracted large congregations in Birmingham, Manchester, and London; wrote many hymns still used in New Church services (died 1826).

1812 Stephen P. Andrews, founder of Universology, was born in Templeton, Mass. (died 1886).

1819 William H. Elder, Catholic prelate, was born in Baltimore; Bishop of Natchez, Miss. (1857-83); Archbishop of Cincinnati (1883-1904) (died 1904).

1882 A new anti-polygamy act was passed by the Congress, imposing penalties on the practice; forbidding polygamists from voting, holding public office, or serving on juries; and placed elections in Utah under the supervision of a five-man presidential board.

1930 Pat (Marion G.) Robertson, televangelist, was born in Lexington, Va.; set up nation's first Christian television station which grew into CBN (Christian Broadcasting Network), one of four largest cable networks.

1982 Pericle Felici, Catholic prelate, died at 70; the leading Catholic conservative and Vatican expert on canon law, a noted classical scholar; twice considered in 1978 for the papal vacancy.

1982 The final report of the Anglican-Roman Catholic International Commission was issued, reaching a great measure of agreement on the Eucharist, ministry and authority of the church, including papal authority.

1984 Bernard F. Law, 52-year old Missouri Catholic bishop, began his duties as the Archbishop of Boston.

MARCH 23

1555 Julius III, pope from 1550 to 1555, died.

1806 Robert S. Candlish, early leader of the Free Church of Scotland, was born in Edinburgh; minister of St. George's, Edinburgh (1834-73); took a leading part in forming independent Free Church; principal of New College, Edinburgh (1862-73) (died 1873).

1815 Ezekiel Robinson, Baptist clergyman and educator, was born in South Attleboro, Mass.; president, Rochester Theological Seminary (1860-72), Brown U. (1872-89) (died 1894).

1836 Crawford H. Toy, theologian and educator, was born in Norfolk, Va.; professor, of Hebrew, Harvard U. (1880-1909); author (History of the Religion of Israel, Judaism and Christianity, Introduction to the History of Religion) (died 1919).

1861 Uchimura Kanzo, Japanese Christian essayist and theologian, was born in Tokyo; a government school teacher, he refused as a Christian to bow before the signature of the emperor on the Imperial Rescript on Education; founder-editor of an influential magazine (*Biblical Studies*) and taught the Bible in his home; wrote a widely circulated autobiography, "How I Became a Christian" (died 1930).

1861 Francis Bourne, English cardinal, was born in London; successfully defended the Catholic voluntary school system against government restriction (1906); named Archbishop of Westminster (1903), elevated to cardinal 1911; instrumental in organizing the International Eucharistic Congress in London 1908 (died 1935).

1878 John S. Stamm, Evangelical bishop (1926-56), was born in Alida, Kan.; senior bishop, president of board of bishops (1936-46) (died 1956).

1905 (Lewis) John Collins, British founder and chairman of the interdenominational Christian Action movement (1946-73), was born (died 1982).

1966 Archbishop of Canterbury Arthur M. Ramsey exchanged public greetings with Pope Paul VI in the first official visit to a Catholic pontiff by the head of the Anglican Church.

MARCH 24

Former feast day of the Archangel Gabriel, messenger of God; now observed Sep 29.

1381 St. Catherine of Sweden, superior of the Brigittines (1373-81), died at 50; succeeded her mother, St. Bridget, as superior; never formally canonized but commemorated as a saint by the Brigittines.

1396 Walter Hilton, English devotional writer, died at about 56; known for "The Scale of Perfection."

1455 Nicholas V, pope from 1447 to 1455, died at 68.

1650 Sir Jonathan Trelawny, English prelate, was born in Pelynt, Cornwall; Bishop of Bristol (1685-1707), of Winchester (1707-21); one of seven bishops who opposed James II's Declaration of Indulgence (1688), spent a month in the Tower of London (died 1721).

1707 Countess of Huntingdon (Selina Hastings), English religious leader, was born in Staunton Harold, England; founder of the Calvinistic Methodist sect known as "Countess of Huntingdon's Connexion;" worked with the Wesleys, sought to reconcile differences between the Wesleys and George Whitefield; built 64 chapels and a seminary in Wales (died 1791).

1795 Beriah Green, clergyman and abolitionist who helped organize the American Anti-Slavery Society, was born in Preston, Conn. (died 1874).

1797 Antonio Rosmini-Serbati, Italian priest and philosopher, was born in Rovereto, Italy; founder of the Fathers of Charity (1828), modeled on the Jesuit order; served as advisor to Pope Pius IX; worked in interest of Italian confederation and fell from favor, his works were condemned (died 1855).

1820 Fanny (Frances J.) Crosby, one of the greatest Protestant hymn writers, was born in Southeast, N.Y.; although blind, she produced more than 5000 poems, hymns, and secular songs (Safe in the arms of Jesus, Rescue of the perishing, Blessed assurance, Jesus is tenderly calling; Pass me not, O Gentle Savior; I am Thine, O Lord; Sweet hour of prayer; Savior, more than life to me) (died 1915).

1890 Harold H. Rowley, internationally-famed Old Testament scholar, was born in Leicester, England (died 1969).

1924 Two American Catholic archbishops were elevated to cardinal - Patrick J. Hayes of New York and George W. Mundelein of Chicago.

1945 Pope Pius XII authorized the use of a new version of the Psalms from the Hebrew, prepared by the Pontifical Biblical Institute.

1972 Thirty-three leading Catholic theologians in Europe and North America appealed to priests and laymen to counteract what they termed a crisis in leadership.

1980 Catholic Archbishop Oscar Arnulfo Romero y Galdanez was shot and killed while saying mass in San Salvador.

1985 Pope John Paul II named 28 new cardinals, increasing the number to 152, but only 120 under the age of 80 will be eligible to vote for a new pope.

MARCH 25

Feast of the Annunciation, celebrating the bringing of the news to the Virgin Mary of the incarnation of Christ; observed in the Anglican, Catholic and Orthodox churches.

Feast day of St. Dismas, traditional name of the penitent thief who died on the cross beside Jesus.

708 Constantine, a Syrian, was consecrated as pope, served until 715.

1558 Marcos de Niza, Italian Franciscan friar, died at about 63; reached the "seven cities" of the Zuni Indians in New Mexico (1539); provincial of the Franciscan Order in Mexico (1541-58).

1570 Johann Walther, German Lutheran composer and hymnist, died at 74; a friend of Martin Luther, whom he assisted in developing the German mass; composed religious and church music.

1594 St. Jean de Brebeuf, French Jesuit missionary, was born in Conde-sur-Vire, France; served among the Indians in Canada (1625-49); executed by the Indians; patron saint of Canada; canonized along with six other North American martyrs (1930) (died 1649).

1634 George Bull, British prelate, was born in St. Cuthbert, England; Archbishop of Llandaff (1686-1705), Bishop of St. Davids in Wales (1705-10); fame rests on "Defensio Fidei Nicenal," which shows that the doctrine of the Trinity was held by anti-Nicene fathers (died 1710).

1687 The Church of England replaced the Congregational Church in Old South Meeting House in Boston on orders of Gov. Edmund Andros.

1740 Construction of the Bethesda orphanage began under auspices of the English evangelist, George Whitefield; main building burned in 1773, was never rebuilt.

1790 President Washington attended the consecration of the new Trinity Church in New York City, sitting in a canopied pew set apart for the president; the original building, constructed in 1696, was destroyed by fire Sep 21,1776.

1797 John Winebrenner, American religious leader, was born in Walkerville, Md.; a German Reformed clergyman with an outspoken attitude against slavery and drink; formed (1830) the Church of God, which regarded the Bible as the only rule of faith and practice (died 1860).

1803 Richard H. Froude, Anglican clergyman, was born in Dartington, England; a close friend of John Henry Newman and a leader in the Oxford Movement; wrote three of the "Tracts of the Times" (died 1836).

1812 Michael Baumgarten, German theologian was born near Hamburg; active promoter of free church life and an opponent of the Lutheran hierarchy; stood for complete separation of church and state (died 1889).

1822 Albrecht Ritschl, German theologian, was born in Berlin; influenced a generation of Protestant historians; founded a school of theology, still important, which sought to eliminate all metaphysical elements from religion, that Christian theology should rest on appreciation of the inner life (died 1889).

1823 Godfrey Thring, Anglican hymn writer, was born in Alford, England; his hymns included "From the Eastern mountains" and "Saviour, blessed Saviour" (died 1903).

1865 Arthur Hinsley, Catholic leader, was born in Carlton, England; rector of the English College in Rome (1917-28); Archbishop of Westminster (1935-43); elevated to cardinal 1937 (died 1943).

1884 Peter Guilday, Catholic editor and historian, was born in Chester, Pa.; founder, editor, *Catholic Historical Review* (1915-47); founder, secretary, American Catholic Historical Assn (1919-41) (died 1947).

1968 Pope Paul VI approved a three year experiment of Sodalities of Our Lady; changed to Christian Life Communities.

1980 The Most Rev. Robert Runcie was enthroned as the 102nd Archbishop of Canterbury.

1981 Moral Majority Inc. began a newspaper advertising campaign denying it is anti-Semitic or opposed to women's rights.

1983 Pope John Paul II declared a "Holy Year" to end Easter Sunday 1984.

1988 American Catholic bishops refused to set aside their controversial policy statement on AIDS;

they voted to hold a broad discussion of the subject in June.

MARCH 26

655 Deusdedit was consecrated as the first Archbishop of Canterbury of English origin, served until 664.

668 St. Theodore of Tarsus was consecrated as the seventh Archbishop of Canterbury, first to rule the entire English church; served until 690.

752 Stephen II was elected pope, served until 757; allied papacy with the Frankish dynasty, which determined the relations between the papacy and the Empire for centuries.

1663 Bishop Francoise Xavier de Laval obtained a royal grant to establish a theological seminary in Quebec, which later became Laval U.; the Petite Seminaire opened Oct 9,1668.

1780 Moses Stuart, American Hebraist, was born in Wilton, Conn.; professor of sacred literature, Andover Theological Seminary; translated many German works, including a Hebrew and Greek grammar of the New Testament; sought to show the importance of German scholarship in biblical criticism (died 1852).

1886 John Baillie, Scottish churchman, was born in Gairloch, Scotland; a founder and president (1954-60) of the World Council of Churches (died 1960).

1900 Giovanni Urbani, Archbishop of Venice (1958-69), was born in Venice; president of the Italian Bishops Conference, elevated to cardinal 1958 (died 1969).

MARCH 27

Former feast day in the Catholic Church of St. John of Damascus, eminent theologian and a Doctor* of the Eastern Church; author of the standard textbook of dogmatic theology in the Orthodox Church (Fount of Knowledge); canonized by both Eastern and Catholic churches; gave impetus to Greek hymnody and music, wrote hymns (The day of resurrection: come ye faithful).

1191 Clement III, pope from 1187 to 1191, died.

1378 Gregory XI, pope from 1370 to 1378, died at 47.

1416 St. Francis of Paola, Franciscan leader, was born in Paola, Italy; founder of the Minim Friars (1436), patron of Italian seamen; canonized 1519 (died 1507).

1716 George Keith, Scottish-born founder of Christian Quakers, died at 88; a friend of William Penn; later formed own sect (1692), then ordained in the Anglican Church, becoming a missionary (1700) in Pennsylvania, converting many Quakers.

1753 Andrew Bell, educator and clergyman, was born in St. Andrews, Scotland; developed system of teaching, using older students as monitors; Church of England asked him to set up such schools (1807); became superintendent (1811) of National Society for Promoting the Education of the Poor in the Practices of the Established Church (died 1832).

1765 Franz Xaver von Baader, German Catholic theologian and social philosopher, was born in Munich; attempted unsuccessfully to create a theosophy founded on metaphysical principles and the divine truths of the Old and New Testaments; visualized society as united by the universal application of the principle of love (died 1841).

1802 Taylor Lewis, classical scholar and Orientalist, was born in Northumberland, New York; specialist in study of religion; author (The Six Days of Creation, The Bible and Science, The Divine Human in the Scriptures) (died 1877)

1842 George Matheson, Scottish Free Church clergyman, was born in Glasgow; devoted much of his life to writing, remembered for the hymn, "O love that wilt not let me go" (died 1906).

1882 Archbishop McCabe of Ireland was elevated to cardinal.

1905 Robert S. Marsden, a founder of the Orthodox Presbyterian Church (1936), was born in Philadelphia (died 1960).

1962 Segregation in all Catholic schools in the New Orleans diocese was ordered ended by Archbishop Joseph F. Rummel.

1972 The Institute for Jewish Policy Planning and Research, sponsored by the Synagogue Council of America, was formed to draft long-range goals for Jewish organizations and to undertake research in problems affecting American Jews.

1979 Commander Ernest Holtz was installed as national commander of the Salvation Army in Centennial Memorial Temple, New York City.

MARCH 28

Feast day of St. John of Capistrano, Italian theologian and the most famous Franciscan preacher of the 15th Century; canonized 1724.

1134 St. Stephen Harding, English-born abbot, died at about 86; a co-founder of the Abbey of Citeaux (south of Dijon, France), which was the first abbey of the Cistercians; became abbot 1109; wrote the rules of the Cistercian Order.

1285 Martin IV, pope from 1261 to 1285, died.

1515 St. Theresa de Avila, Spanish mystic, was born; originated the Carmelite Reform (restoration of the original observance of austerity); foundress of the Discalced Carmelites; canonized 1622, made Doctor* of the Church (1970)(died 1582).

1592 John (Johannes, Jan) A. Comenius, Czech theologian, was born in Nivnice, Czechoslovakia; sometimes called the "grandfather of modern education" because he wrote the first textbook with pictures; a leader of a persecuted Moravian brotherhood sect; hoped for a utopian church which would unite all religions in Christian love, felt education was the surest way to attain that goal (died 1670).

1599 Catholic Archbishop Lobo Guerrero arrived in Colombia.

1703 Construction of the first Episcopal church in New Jersey began in Burlington; the first service was held Aug 22.

1787 Theodore Frelinghuysen, Dutch Reformed layman and public official, was born in Millstone, N.J.; called a "Christian statesman" because of his involvement in religious, charitable enterprises - president, American Bible Society (1846-62); president, American Tract Society (1842-48); president for 16 years, American Board of Commissioners for Foreign missions; U.S. senator (1829-35); chancellor, New York U. (1839-50); president, Rutgers U. (1850-62) (died 1862).

1811 John A. Neumann, Catholic prelate, was born in Prahatice, Czechoslovakia; Bishop of Philadelphia (1852-60); founded schools and seminary; co-founder, Sisters of Notre Dame (1877) and Sisters of the Third Order of St. Francis (1855); beatified 1963 as the first American prelate proposed for canonization; canonized 1977 (died 1860).

1859 George W. Clinton, African Methodist Episcopal bishop (1896-1921) and educator, was born in Lancaster County, S.C.; founder, editor, *AME Zion Quarterly Review*; editor, *Star of Zion* (died 1921).

1886 Richard C. Trench, Anglican prelate and author, died at 79; Archbishop of Dublin (1864-84); wrote and edited sacred poems and other theological works (Notes on the Parables, Notes on the Miracles).

1895 Spencer W. Kimball, head of the Mormon Church (1973-85), was born in Salt Lake City (died 1985).

1967 Pope Paul VI issued an encyclical, "Populorum Progressis" (On the Development of People), urging an end to suffering throughout the world.

1982 Two fires damaged the altar of Salisbury Cathedral, where the original copy of the Magna Carta is housed; document was not damaged.

MARCH 29

537 Vigilius was consecrated as pope, served until 555; condemned by the Council of Constantinople for seeking to annul decrees of the Council of Chalcedon; kept out of Rome for seven years, then died on his return.

828 Gregory IV was named pope, served until 844: started renovation and embellishment of churches in Rome.

1058 Stephen IX, pope from 1057 to 1058, died.

1602 John Lightfoot, English biblical critic and Hebraist, was born near Birmingham; first Christian scholar to call attention to importance of the Torah* and assisted Brian Walton with the Polyglot Bible (died 1675).

1819 Isaac M.Wise, founder of American Reformed Judaism, was born in Steingrub, Czechoslovakia; rabbi in Cincinnati (1855-1900); a founder, president, Hebrew Union College, Cincinnati (1875-1900); founder, *American Israelite* and *Die Deborah*, weekly newspapers; author (The Cosmic God) (died 1900).

1883 Edward W. Benson was consecrated as Archbishop of Canterbury; served until 1896.

1892 Joseph Mindszenty, Hungarian Catholic primate, was born in Szombathely, Hungary; opposed Nazis and Communists; imprisoned November 1944 on charge of treason, released (1945) and rearrested Dec 26, 1948 by Communists; imprisoned for life; released Oct 30, 1956 and took refuge in the American legation in Budapest; permitted to leave Hungary Sep 29,1971 and went to Vienna; elevated to cardinal 1946 (died 1975).

MARCH 30

Feast day of St. John (St. John Climacus), abbot of Mt. Sinai and author of "Klimax" (Ladder of Divine Ascent), which sums up the teaching of the desert fathers.

1135 Moses Maimonides, master of rabbinic literature, was born in Cordoba, Spain; after Moslem capture of Cordoba (1148), he went to Egypt, became physician to Sultan Saladin and rabbi of Cairo; tried to reconcile rabbinic Judaism with Aristotelian philosophy as modified by Arabic interpretation; believed in freedom of the will, condemned asceticism; author of "Guide to the Perplexed", which had a profound influence on Christian thought in the Middle Ages (died 1204).

1191 Celestine III, born Giacinto Bobo, was elected pope at the age of 85; crowned Henry VI of Germany as emperor; confirmed statutes of the Teutonic Order of Knights and approved the orders of Knights Templar and Hospitallers.

1486 Thomas Bourchier, Archbishop of Canterbury (1454-86), died at about 76; named lord chancellor (1455), cardinal (1467); he was much involved in the political issues of the times, maintaining a balance between the conflicting interests of Lancaster and York.

1533 Thomas Cranmer was consecrated as Archbishop of Canterbury; served until 1556.

1555 Robart Ferrar, English Protestant martyr, was burned at the stake; Bishop of St. David's (1548-54), condemned for denial of Catholic doctrine of the Eucharist.

1765 Juan Antonio Llorente, priest and historian, was born in Spain; general secretary, Inquisition (1789-1801); wrote history of the Spanish Inquisition (died 1823).

1820 James A. Corcoran, Catholic editor, was born; co-editor, *United States Catholic Miscellany* (1846-61); editor, *American Catholic Quarterly Review* (1876-89) (died 1889).

1871 The Boston University School of Theology was formed by the merger of the Boston Theological Seminary and Boston University.

1901 The court decision in the Delpit case held that marriages of Roman Catholics by Protestant clergymen were valid.

1982 High ranking Anglican and Catholic churchmen found after a 12-year study that the Pope would be the "universal primate" if the two churches united.

1984 Karl Rahner, a leading Catholic theologian, died at 80; played key role in introducing vernacular in the Mass, in opening dialogues with other denominations.

MARCH 31

1492 The Spanish rulers, Ferdinand and Isabella, expelled all Jews from Spain; 160,000 left the country.

1499 Pius IV, pope from 1559 to 1565, was born Giovanni Angelo Medici in Milan, Italy.

1631 John Donne, renowned English metaphysical poet, died at 58; dean of St. Paul's (1621-24) and preached sermons unexcelled in the 17th Century.

1675 Benedict XIV, pope from 1740 to 1758, was born in Bologna as Prospero Lorenzo Lambertini.

1816 Francis Asbury, bishop and first American Methodist superintendent, died at 71.

1820 American missionaries from New England arrived in Hawaii; included Hiram Bingham, Asa Thurston, Dr. Thomas Holman, Samuel Whitney, and Samuel Ruggles.

1825 John Marriott, Anglican rector, died at 45; remembered for the hymn "Those whose almighty word."

1829 Pius VIII was named pope, served until 1830.

1835 John LaFarge, outstanding church muralist, was born in New York City; his finest work is in the Church of the Ascension, New York City; developed opalescent glass for churches (died 1910).

1923 Msgr. Butchkaivitch, Vicar General of the Catholic Church, was convicted of opposition to the Soviet Government and executed.

APRIL 1

1132 St. Hugh of Grenoble died at 80; Bishop of Grenoble, France (1080-1132); canonized 1134; also observed as his feast day.

1605 Leo XI was named pope, served only about four weeks before his death April 27.

1764 Henry Ware, theologian, was born in Sherborn, Mass.; Hollis professor of divinity, Harvard U. (1805-40), whose courses led to the formation (1816) of the Harvard Divinity School; considered one of the founders of American Unitarianism (died 1845).

1792 The first New Church (Swedenborgian) sermon in the United States was delivered by Rev. James Wilmer in Baltimore, Md.

1811 James McCosh, Scottish theologian and educator, was born near Glasgow; professor of logic and metaphysics, Queens College, Belfast (1852-68); president, Princeton U. (1868-88), one of its most influential presidents; author (The Method of Divine Government, Christianity and Positivism) (died 1894).

1844 George Harris, Congregational clergyman and educator, was born in East Machias, Me., nephew of Samuel Harris (6/14/1814); professor, Andover Theological Seminary (1883-99), president of faculty; co-editor, *Andover Review* (1884-93); tried for heresy for certain articles, acquitted; president, Amherst College (1899-1912) (died 1922).

1849 Blessed Ludovic Pavonia, founder of the Congregation of Sons of Mary Immaculate (Claretian Missionaries) (1847), died at 65.

1858 Columba Marmion, Benedictine monk and theologian, was born in Ireland; noted theologian of Christian asceticism*; abbot of Maredsous (Namur, Belgium) (died 1923).

1871 Robert S. Franks, theologian best known for "A History of the Doctrine of the Work of Christ," was born in Ridcar, England (died 1964).

1874 Ernest W. Barnes, Anglican prelate and author, was born in England; Bishop of Birmingham (1924-53), a leader in the Church of England modernist movement; author of the controversial "The Rise of Christianity" (died 1953).

1925 Hebrew University in Jerusalem opened and was dedicated.

1959 Archbishop Iakovos was enthroned as head of the Greek Archdiocese of North and South America at the Cathedral of the Holy Trinity in New York City.

APRIL 2

Former feast day of St. Margaret Clitherow, English "martyr of York;" put to death for harboring priests (1586); canonized 1970.

999 Sylvester II, born as Gerbert, was consecrated as the first French pope, served until 1003; Archbishop of Reims (991-998), Ravenna (998-999); sought to eliminate simony* and nepotism.

1013 John XVI, pope from 997 to 998, died in prison; a Greek native, he assumed the papacy after the expulsion of Gregory V; when Gregory was restored, John was captured (March 998) and imprisoned until his death.

1234 St. Edmund of Abingdon was consecrated as Archbishop of Canterbury, served until 1240.

1285 Honorius IV, born Giacomo Savelli, was elected pope; served until 1287; a great nephew of Honorius III; effected a temporary halt to the feud between the Empire and the papacy; policies resulted in a further decline of the power and prestige of the papacy.

1507 St. Francis of Paola, founder of the Minim Friars (1436), died at 31; also observed as his feast day.

1806 Giacomo Antonelli, papal secretary, was born in Sonnino, Italy; secretary of state to Pope Pius IX (1848-76); headed the first constitutional ministry of the Papal States, re-established the absolute power of papal administration; elevated to cardinal 1846 (died 1876).

1846 William H. Cobb, Congregational clergyman, was born in Rochester, Mass.; librarian of Congregational Library, Boston (1887-1923) (died 1923).

1858 George B. Foster, Baptist theologian, was born in Alderson, W. Va.; professor, U. of Chicago

(1895-1918); debated publicly with Clarence Darrow on "Is life worth living?" (died 1918).

1866 Francis Hodur, religious leader, was born in Zorki, Poland; founder (1897) of the Polish National Catholic Church of America; prime bishop (1907-53) (died 1953)

1914 A ten-day constitutional convention opened in Hot Springs, Ark. to form the Assemblies of God, one of the largest of the charismatic groups known as Pentecostal, with more than 1 million members.

1978 Canon Mary Simpson became the first woman priest of the Anglican Church to preach in Westminster Abbey.

APRIL 3

Feast day of St. Joseph the Hymnographer (about 810-886), the most prolific Greek hymn writer.

1058 Benedict X, born Johannes Mincius, was named pope by the nobles who dominated the papacy; served until 1059; lived 20 years longer as a prisoner in the monastery of St. Agnes, where he died

1287 Honorius IV, pope from 1285 to 1287, died.

1593 George Herbert, English devotional poet, was born in Montgomery Castle; his best known prose work is "A Priest at the Temple;" he wrote several Anglican hymns (Let all the world in every corner sing; Teach me, my God and King) (died 1633).

1771 Hans N. Hauge, Norwegian lay preacher, was born; founder of Norwegian Pietism*; jailed (1804-11) (died 1824).

1822 Edward Everett Hale, Unitarian clergyman and author, was born in Boston; nephew of Edward Everett; pastor, South Congregational Church, Boston (1856-1901); chaplain, U.S. Senate (1903-09); author (The Man Without a Country) (died 1909).

1814 Lorenzo Snow, Mormon leader, was born in Mantua, Ohio; president, Mormon Church (1898-1901); when anti-polygamy law went into effect, he was convicted and jailed (1886); decision overturned by the Supreme Court (1887); as president, he was the first to enunciate the doctrine of eternal progression in the aphorism, "As man now is, God Once was; as God now is, man may be" (died 1901).

1822 Henry M. Field, Presbyterian and Congregational clergyman and editor, was born in Stockbridge, Mass.; editor, *The Evangelist* (1854-90) (died 1907).

1851 John J. Hughes, Catholic Bishop of New York, became its first archbishop.

1986 Sayyed Mohammad Kazem Sharat-Madari, one of the first Shi-ah grand ayatollahs, died in Tabriz, Iran.

APRIL 4

397 St. Ambrose, one of the great Fathers* of the Catholic Church, died at about 57; pioneered in adapting pagan funeral oration to Christian Latin use; father of hymnology in the Western Church, writing such hymns as "Deus creator omnium," "Veni redemptor gentium;" a famed preacher, partly responsible for the conversion of St. Augustine; maintained the independence of the church against civil power; served as Bishop of Milan (374-397).

636 St. Isidore of Seville, Spanish encyclopedist and theologian, died at about 76; Archbishop of Seville (about 600-636); known particularly for his vast medieval encyclopedia; canonized 1598, declared a Doctor* of the Church (1722); also observed as his feast day.

896 Formosus, pope from 891 to 896, died at about 80; there is much dispute over his legitimacy as a pope; he had been excommunicated by Pope John VIII but restored by Marinus.

1139 Second Lateran Council was called by Pope Innocent II primarily to condemn the followers of Arnold of Brescia and to end the schism caused by the election of the anti-pope, Anacletus II.

1292 Nicholas IV, pope from 1288 to 1292, died.

1589 St. Benedict the Black died at 63; patron of Blacks in North America; canonized 1807; also observed as his feast day.

1660 Declaration of Breda (Holland) was issued by Charles II, indicating his readiness to grant his subjects a "liberty of tender consciences" in religion.

1742 Charles Wesley preached before the University of Oxford on the text, "Awake, thou that sleepest," a sermon which became the most popular Methodist tract.

1748 William White, pioneer Episcopal leader, was born in Philadelphia; he "Americanized" the Anglican Church, led move to create the Protestant Episcopal Church of America; presiding bishop (1795-1836); rector, Christ Church, Philadelphia (1776-1836); introduced principle that laity should share with clergy in church government; drafted original constitution of church and collaborated with William Smith in preparing American revision of The Book of Common Prayer (died 1846).

1805 Prosper-Louis P. Guerenger, French Benedictine monk, was born in Sable-sur-Sarthe, France; restored Benedictines in France, serving as first abbot and head of Benedictine congregation of France (died 1875).

1810 James F. Clarke, Unitarian clergyman and author, was born in Hanover, N.H.; founder, minister, Church of the Disciples, Boston (1841-50, 1854-88); author (Ten Great Religions, Common Sense in Religion) (died 1888).

1813 Jorgen E. Moe, Norwegian prelate, was born; Bishop of Kristiansand (1875-81); best known for his collection of folklore, a poet and author of children's stories (died 1882).

1825 Charles W. Shields, Episcopal theologian and educator, was born in New Albany, Ind.; professor of the harmony of science and religion, Princeton U. (1865-1903) (died 1904).

1835 Pallotine Fathers was founded by St. Vincent Pallotti.

1862 Ernest W. Shurtleff, Congregational clergyman, was born in Boston; organized American church in Frankfurt, Germany (1905-06); wrote the hymn, "Lead on, O King Eternal" (died 1917).

1870 George A. Smith, Mormon leader, was born in Salt Lake City; president, Mormon Church (1945-51) (died 1951).

1968 Terence J. Cooke was installed as the seventh Catholic Archbishop of New York.

1968 The Rev. Martin Luther King Jr., clergyman and civil rights leader, was assassinated in Memphis, Tenn.

1980 French Archbishop Marcel Lefebvre, suspended from all priestly duties in 1976, celebrated the forbidden 16th century Latin mass on Italian soil for the first time at the unconsecrated San Simeon Piccolo Church in Venice.

APRIL 5

582 Eutychius, patriarch of Constantinople, died at about 70; served as patriarch from 552 to 565 and 577 to 582; presided at Fifth Ecumenical Council (553), conducted consecration ceremonies for St. Sophia (562).

1419 St. Vincent Ferrer, Spanish Dominican friar, died at 69; reputed to be the greatest preacher of his time, took active part in movement to end papal schism; canonized 1445; also observed as his feast day.

1808 Mark A. D. Howe, Episcopal prelate, was born in Bristol, R.I.; the first Bishop of Central Pennsylvania (1871-95) (died 1895).

1809 George A. Selwyn, Anglican prelate, was born in London; first Bishop of New Zealand (1841-68) (died 1878).

1865 The first American Unitarian Assn. convention was held in New York City.

1882 William L. Sperry, Congregational theologian, was born in Peabody, Mass.; professor of practical theology, Andover Theological Seminary (1917-25); also with Harvard Divinity School (1908-53), dean (1922-53) (died 1954).

APRIL 6

Feast day of St. Sixtus I, pope from about 116 to 125; may have been a presbyter whose name went on the papal list because he was a martyr.

Former feast day in Ireland of St. Celestine I, pope from 422 to 432, who sent the first bishop to Ireland; observance moved to July 27 in 1922, later dropped.

1249 St. Louis IX, king of France, was taken prisoner by Moslems during a Crusade.

1252 St. Peter Martyr (Peter of Verona), Dominican priest, died at 46 when he was assassinated by members of Catharist* sect; general inquisitor in Northern Italy and preached against Catharist heresy; canonized 1253.

1593 John Greenwood and Henry Barrow, early English martyrs, were hanged; Greenwood, leader of the London Separatists, denied the scriptural authority of the English church and repudiated royal supremacy; Barrow defended separatism and congregational independence; both were considered forerunners of Congregationalism.

1785 Rev. John Pierpont, Unitarian clergyman, was born in Litchfield, Conn.; served pastorates in Boston (1819-45), Troy, N.Y. (1845-49), and West Medford, Mass. (1849-58); best remembered as composer of "Jingle bells" (died 1866).

1810 Edmund H. Sears, American Unitarian clergyman, was born in Sandisfield, Mass.; wrote a number of hymns (It came upon a midnight clear, Calm on the listening ear of night) (died 1876).

1830 The Church of Jesus Christ of Latter Day Saints (Mormons) was organized by Joseph Smith and Oliver Cowdery at Fayette, N.Y.; original church began with six persons.

1839 Joseph Smith and several Mormon colleagues were arrested, charged with murder, treason, and other crimes; escaped while being taken to Columbia, Mo.

1858 President Buchanan issued a proclamation declaring the Mormon government of Utah in rebellion; Col. Thomas L. Kane was sent to mediate the differences; met with Brigham Young, who had been removed as governor and newly-appointed Gov. Alfred Cumming; rebellion ended in June, Cumming took over June 30.

1869 William B. Hale, Episcopal clergyman and editor, was born in Richmond, Ind.; served as a clergyman (1893-1900); editor, various magazines and newspapers (1900-13); served as President Wilson's confidential agent in Mexico (1913); disgraced by revelation that he was a paid agent of Germany in the United States (1917) (died 1924).

1893 The Mormon Tabernacle in Salt Lake City was dedicated; had been under construction for 40 years.

1973 Talks on a merger of nine Protestant denominations with 25 million members were postponed indefinitely by the Consultation on Church Union, which voted to support cooperation on the local level.

1981 The U. S. Supreme Court ruled 8-1 that a Jehovah's Witness who quit his Indiana factory job rather than make parts for military equipment may not be denied unemployment insurance benefits.

APRIL 7

Feast day of St. Hegesippus, Second Century Christian writer; author of a Christian church history of his time, of which only a fragment exists.

858 Benedict III, pope from 855 to 858, died; restored Rome, which had been devastated by the Saracens in 846.

1024 Benedict VIII, pope from 1012 to 1024, died.

1449 Felix V, who served as the last anti-pope, voluntarily resigned the pontificate and urged his followers to acknowledge Nicholas II as pope.

1506 St. Francis Xavier, a founder of the Society of Jesus (Jesuits), was born in Navarre, Spain; known as the "apostle of the Indies" because of his missionary work in the Far East; considered one of the greatest Christian missionaries, who reputedly made more than 700,000 conversions; canonized 1622, named patron of all missions 1927 (died 1552).

1571 John Hamilton, Archbishop of St. Andrews (1547-71), was hanged for alleged complicity in the murders of Lord Darnley and the regent, Moray; unable to avert the Scottish Reformation in 1560; imprisoned (1563) and on his release became an active partisan of Mary Stuart.

1640 (Jean) Louis Hennepin, Flemish Nicollet friar and explorer, was born in Ath, Belgium; arrived in Canada (1675), accompanied LaSalle through the Great Lakes (1679) and the upper Mississippi River (1680) (died 1705).

1652 Clement XII, pope from 1730 to 1740, was born as Lorenzo Corsini in Florence, Italy.

1719 St. Jean Baptist de la Salle died; founder of the Institute of the Brothers of Christian Schools; also observed as his feast day.

1780 William Ellery Channing, champion of the liberal wing of the Congregational Church, was born in Newport, R.I.; wing later became the Unitarian Church (1825); pastor, Federal St. Church, Boston (1803-42); an organizer of the American Unitarian Assn. (1852); exercised wide influence on social and philanthropic issues (died 1842).

1807 Charles Pettigrew, an organizer and bishop of the Episcopal Church in North Carolina, died at 59; helped establish the U. of North Carolina.

1848 Randall T. Davidson, Archbishop of Canterbury (1903-28), was born in Edinburgh; furthered Church of England's participation in ecumenical movements; guided the church through theological controversy over modernism, disestablishment of the church in Wales, and the dispute over Prayer Book revisions; resigned (1928) because of poor health (died 1930).

1851 Anna G. Spencer, liberal clergywoman and reformer who was a leader in various women's causes, was born in Attleboro, Mass. (died 1935).

1884 Charles H. Dodd, Divinity professor at Cambridge and a biblical scholar, was born in Wrexham, Wales; author of 20 books (The Founder of Christianity) (died 1973).

1890 Hugh Martin, active in student Christian movements, was born in Glasgow, Scotland; treasurer, World Student Christian Federation (1928-35); helped found SCM Press, Religious Book Club (died 1964).

1907 Joshua L. Liebman, rabbi and educator, was born in Hamilton, Ohio; best known for his popular book, "Peace of Mind" (died 1948).

1965 The Dilowa Hutukhtu, the "living Buddha" of the Yellow Sect of Mahayana Buddhism, died in New York City at 82; at one time he was spiritual and temporal leader of 900 lamas and three lamaseries.

APRIL 8

1378 Urban VI, born Bartolomeo Prignani, was elected pope, served until 1389; violent and overbearing manner led French members of Sacred College to declare his election void (1378), elected Clement VII as anti-pope; Urban served in Rome, Clement in Avignon, thus starting the great schism.

1455 Calixtus III was elected pope, served until 1458; sought unsuccessfully to launch crusade against Ottoman Turks, who had taken Constantinople (1453); revised trial verdict of Joan of Arc by annulment of her sentence and declaring her innocence.

1730 The first Jewish synagogue (Shearith Israel) in New York City and the nation was consecrated.

1808 The Catholic Diocese in Baltimore — the first in the United States - was raised to an archdiocese.

1857 A small group of Dutch immigrants, meeting in Zeeland, Mich., organized the Christian Reformed Church.

1876 Augusto Alvaro da Silva, Archbishop of Bahai and Brazil's first cardinal, was born in Recife, Brazil; elevated to cardinal 1953 (died 1968).

1925 Tikhon, first patriarch of Moscow (1917-25) after the restoration of the Russian Orthodox Church, died.

1965 The Vatican announced the creation by Pope Paul VI of a secretariat for relations with non-believers.

1988 The Executive Presbytery of the Assemblies of God in Springfield, Mo. defrocked television evangelist Rev. Jimmy Swaggart after he refused to stop preaching for a year for publicly-admitted sins; Swaggart resigned from the Assemblies, saying a year's absence would destroy his ministry.

APRIL 9

715 Constantine, pope from 708 to 715, died.

1555 Marcellus II was elected pope, served only one month.

1597 John Davenport, English-born Puritan founder of the New Haven (Conn). Colony (1638), was baptized; with Theophilus Eaton, he helped draw up a code of laws; pastor of First Church, New Haven (1638-68), First Church, Boston (1668-70) (died 1670).

1598 Johann Crüger, composer and organist, was born near Guben, Germany; wrote music for many hymns (Come, heavenly spirit, heavenly dove; Now thank we all our God; Talk with us, Lord; Ah, Holy Jesus) (died 1662).

1761 William Law, English controversial and devotional writer, died at about 75; spiritual director for John and Charles Wesley, John Byrom; wrote "Serious Call to a Devout and Holy Life," which deeply influenced the evangelical revival.

1816 The African Methodist Episcopal Church was established in Philadelphia by Bishop Richard Allen.

1830 Joseph Parker, English Congregational clergyman, was born near Newcastle; a fervid pulpit orator; edited "The People's Bible;" author (Ecce Deus, A Preacher's Life) (died 1902).

1862 Charles H. Brent, Episcopal clergyman, was born in Newcastle, Canada; missionary bishop to the Philippines (1901-18); chief of chaplains with American forces in World War I; Bishop of Western New York (1918-26); bishop in charge of Episcopal churches in Europe (1926-28); principal force in ecumenical movement to have Episcopal Church sponsor Faith and Order World Conference in Lausanne (1927), served as conference president (died 1929).

1893 Michael J. Ready, Catholic prelate, was born in New Haven, Conn.; general secretary, National Catholic Welfare Council (1936-44), Bishop of Columbus (1944-57) (died 1957).

1945 Dietrich Bonhoeffer, Lutheran theologian and active anti-Nazi, was hanged by the Gestapo.

APRIL 10

847 St. Leo IV was consecrated as pope, served until 855; defended Rome against the Saracens.

1028 St. Fulbert, Italian-born Bishop of Chartres (1006-28), died at 68; campaigned vigorously against simony,* clerical marriages, and control of the church by the nobility; also observed as his feast day.

1554 Thomas Goodrich, Bishop of Ely (1534-54), died; assisted in compiling the first Book of Common Prayer.

1585 Gregory XIII, pope from 1572 to 1585, died at 83.

1644 William Brewster, Pilgrim leader, died at 84; served as elder and preached regularly for the Puritan congregation in Plymouth, from its founding until 1629, when the first ordained minister arrived.

1794 Edward Robinson, biblical scholar, was born in Southington, Conn.; professor, Union Theological Seminary (1837-63); considered the father of biblical geography; founder, editor, *American Biblical Repository* (1831-35); founder (1843) of "Bibliotheca Sacra" (died 1863).

1806 Leonidas Polk, Episcopal missionary bishop to the Southwest, was born in Raleigh, N.C.; Bishop of Louisiana (1841-61); a founder, University of the South (1860); major general in the Confederate Army, he was killed at Pine Mountain (June 14, 1864).

1827 William A. P. Martin, Presbyterian missionary to China, was born in Livonia, Ind.; founded mission in Peking (1863); professor, president, T'ungwen Kuan, a Chinese college in Peking (1869-94) (died 1916).

1829 William Booth, Salvation Army founder, was born in Nottingham, England; a preacher of the Methodist New Connection, he broke with the church over his fervent preaching; became an independent itinerant revivalist, founding East London Revival Society, which became the Christian Mission in Whitechapel, then the Salvation Army (died 1912).

1878 Maximos Saigh, Melchite patriarch of Antioch and all the Orient (1947-67), was born in Aleppo, Syria; elevated to cardinal 1965 (died 1967).

1888 Nathaniel Micklem, theology professor in various British schools, was born in Brondesbury, England; author (A Book of Personal Religion) (died 1976).

1921 Gregory V (about 1746-1821), ecumenical patriarch of Constantinople, was declared a saint and martyr of the Greek Orthodox Church.

1970 Patriarch Aleksei of Moscow and 14 other bishops signed a "tomos" granting total ecclesiastical independence to the Orthodox Church in America.

APRIL 11

Former feast day in the Catholic Church of St. Leo I the Great, pope from 440 to 461; now observed December 10.

672 Adeodatus became pope, served until 676.

678 Donus (or Domnus), pope from 676 to 678, died.

1079 St. Stanislaus (or Stanislaw), martyred Polish bishop and patron saint of Poland, died; also observed as his feast day.

1506 Construction began on a new Vatican basilica; completed 1626.

1698 Charles Morton, Puritan clergyman, died at 71; Harvard fellow (1692), first vice president (1697); urged prosecutions for witchcraft at Salem; author of textbooks on science and logic used at Harvard.

1721 David Zeisberger, American-Moravian missionary among the Indians, was born in Zauchenthal, Czechoslovakia; helped set up settlements in Ohio, which were destroyed during the Revolution; then built towns in Ohio, Michigan, and Canada after the war (died 1808).

1794 Edward Everett, Unitarian clergyman, was born in Dorchester, Mass.; congressman, Massachusetts governor (1836-40), minister to Great Britain (1841-45); president, Harvard (1846-49); gave dedication oration at Gettysburg (which lasted two hours), when Lincoln made his classical brief address (died 1865).

1836 William P. DuBose, Episcopal theologian, was born in Winnsborough, S.C.; founder, dean, theology department, U. of the South, Sewanee, Tenn. (1871-1908); one of greatest theological minds in Episcopal Church (died 1918).

1853 Samuel D. Chown, Canadian Methodist clergyman, was born near Kingston; a leading advocate of church union; as general superintendent, Methodist Church, he influenced union of Presbyterian, Methodist, and Congregational churches in Canada (1925) (died 1933).

1903 Brigham Young, head of the Mormon Church, died in Salt Lake City at 76.

1963 Pope John XXIII issued the encyclical, "Pacem in terris," dealing with relations among men, their rights and duties as citizens; conduct of affairs among nations.

1980 Efforts to allow ordination of women as Mormon ministers were overwhelmingly rejected by delegates to the church's biennial world convention in Independence, Mo.

1980 Rev. Hans Kung accepted a compromise settlement with Tübingen University in Bonn, West Germany that would allow him to continue on the faculty without examining candidates for the priesthood.

1988 A preliminary 164-page pastoral letter was distributed to American Catholic bishops discussing sexism in the church; the letter is the third of three letters, one on peace was issued in 1983 and the economy in 1986.

APRIL 12

352 St. Julius I, pope from 337 to 352, died; also observed as his feast day.

806 St. Nicephorus was selected to be patriarch of Constantinople, served until 815.

1204 Troops of the Fourth Crusade captured and pillaged Constantinople, virtually destroying the Byzantine Empire and any hope of Christian unity.

1443 Henry Chichele, Archbishop of Canterbury (1414-43), died at about 81; diplomat, serving as envoy to many countries; erroneously blamed in Shakespeare's "Henry V" for urging the conquest of France to divert Parliament from disendowment of the Church; founder (1437) of two colleges at Oxford - St. Bernard's and All Souls.

1500 Joachim Camerarius, classical scholar and Lutheran theologian, was born in Germany; mediated between Protestants and Catholics during the Reformation; helped Philip Melancthon formulate the Augsburg Confession (1530) (died 1574).

1562 Huguenot leaders at Orleans signed a manifesto, stating that as loyal Frenchmen they were driven to take up arms for liberty of conscience, leading to more than three decades of violence.

1778 John Strachan, first Anglican Bishop of Toronto (1839), was born in Aberdeen, Scotland; established King's College (1843), Trinity U. (1852); popular resentment over exclusive endowment of Episcopal education led to making King's College into the U. of Toronto (died 1867).

1811 Daniel R. Goodwin, theologian and educator, was born in North Berwick, Me.; president, Trinity College, Hartford (1853-60); provost, U. of Pennsylvania (1860-68); professor, Philadelphia Divinity School (1865-90), dean (1868-83) (died 1890).

1818 Michael Heiss, Catholic educator and prelate, was born in Pfahldorf, Germany; first rector, St. Francis (Wis.) Seminary (1856-68); first Bishop of LaCrosse, Wis. (1868-90); one of the planners of curriculum for Catholic seminaries (died 1890).

1830 Charles C. Grafton, Episcopal prelate, was born in Boston; helped organize (1865) Society of St. John the Evangelist (Cowley Fathers); Bishop of Fond du Lac, Wis. (1889-1912) (died 1912).

1898 Louis Nazaire Begin was named Archbishop of Quebec on the death of Cardinal Tascherau.

APRIL 13

Feast day in the Catholic Church of St. Martin I, pope from 649 to 655.

1055 Victor II, born Gebhard, was consecrated as pope, served until 1057; reformed clergy during his reign; a strong supporter of Emperor Henry III, to whom he was related and to whom he owed his election.

1059 Pope Nicholas II, following the Lateran Council of 1059, issued the bull setting up the electoral procedure by which a pope would be named by the cardinals.

1506 Blessed Pierre Favre, French co-founder of the Jesuits, was born near Geneva, Switzerland; met Ignatius of Loyola as a student at U. of Paris and helped him found the Society of Jesus; founded Jesuit colleges in Cologne (1544) and Spain; beatified 1872 (died 1546).

1598 Edict of Nantes was promulgated by Henry IV granting a broad measure of religious liberty, civil rights, and security to French Protestants, the Huguenots.

1768 Franciscan fathers sent to replace the Jesuits arrived in California.

1789 The first general conference of the New Jerusalem Church (New Church) was held in London.

1791 Pope Pius VI issued the brief, "Caritas," denouncing the French Constitution which separated the French church from the papacy; called it heretical, sacrilegious and schismatic.

1823 Sabato Morais, Jewish theologian, was born in Leghorn, Italy; a founder, president, Jewish Theological Seminary, New York City (1886-97); rabbi in Philadelphia (1851-97) (died 1897).

1824 William Alexander, Anglican archbishop, was born in Ireland; Archbishop of Armagh and primate of Ireland (1896-1911) (died 1911).

1828 Joseph B. Lightfoot, Anglican Bishop of Durham (1879-89) and biblical critic, was born in Liverpool; noted for work on New Testament and Apostolic Fathers; served on New Testament revision committee (died 1889).

1829 The Catholic Emancipation Act, passed by Parliament, received royal assent; within three weeks, the first Catholic was elected to Parliament (Earl of Surrey).

1835 Louis A. Lambert, Catholic priest and editor, was born in Charleroi, Pa.; wrote popular conservative answer to agnosticism (Notes on Ingersoll) (died 1910).

1846 The Norwegian Evangelical Lutheran Church of North America was organized by Elling Eielson at Fox River, Ill.

1851 William Q. Judge, theosophist, was born in Dublin, Ireland; charter member of the Theosophical Society, organizer of branches; after schism, headed American section of the Society; founder, editor, *The Path* (1886-96) (died 1896).

1874 Anson P. Stokes, Episcopal clergyman who was secretary of Yale U. (1899-1921), was born in New York City; canon residentiary, National Cathedral, Washington, D.C. (1924-39); author (Church and State in the United States) (died 1956).

1908 The Methodist Conference of New England lifted the ban on dancing, card playing, and theater-going.

1919 Madalyn O'Hair, atheist, was born in Pittsburgh; successfully campaigned against prayer in the public schools with victory in the U.S. Supreme Court case.

1933 Paul Tillich, theologian, was suspended from the U. of Frankfurt because of his book, "The Socialist Decision."

1986 Pope John Paul II made an unprecedented visit to the central synagogue of Rome, saying his visit was designed to contribute to good relations.

APRIL 14

Feast day of St. Benezet (about 1165-1184), French saint, who reputedly directed the building of the famous Pont d'Avignon across the Rhone, the remains of which are now a pilgrimage site.

Feast day of St. Elmo, popular name of St. Peter Gonzales, Dominican patron of seamen.

Former feast day of St. Justin Martyr (about 100-165), greatest of early Christian apologists; a Father* of the Church; opened first Christian school in Rome; said to have been scourged and martyred in Rome; now observed June 1.

911 Sergius III, pope from 904 to 911, died.

1682 Avvakum (1620-82), Russian founder of the Old Believer movement in the Russian Orthodox Church, was burned at the stake; exiled to Siberia (1653), returned (1662), tried and imprisoned (1666).

1802 Horace Bushnell, Congregational clergyman, was born in Bantam, Conn.; called the "father of American religious liberalism;" considered one of the most creative, liberal minds in 19th Century American theology; pastor of North Church, Hartford (1833-59); author (Christian Nurture, God in Christ) (died 1876).

1832 Brigham Young was converted to and baptized in the Mormon faith.

1847 Brigham Young and a party of Mormons left Council Bluffs for the West.

1883 First edition of the *Journal of Christian Science* was issued, consisting of eight pages of three columns each, with the stated purpose of being "an independent Family paper to promote Health and Morals;" designed to be bimonthly, with a subscription price of $1 a year and 17 cents per copy.

1957 Pope Pius XII reiterated his conviction that nuclear weapons should not be used and expressed the hope that all nations would master the use of nuclear energy to serve man.

1982 Churches of Christ in Poland were officially recognized after 20 years.

APRIL 15

1816 Johann B. Franzelin, Catholic cardinal and theologian, was born in Austria; prepared the "schema" (outline) discussed at the First Vatican Council; prefect of the Sacred Congregation of Rites (1876-86) (died 1886).

1832 Herbert Vaughan, English Catholic prelate, was born in Gloucester; Archbishop of Westminster (1892-1903), elevated to cardinal 1903; largely responsible for passage of the Education Act (1902) whereby British denominational schools became state supported; built Westminster Cathedral (died 1903).

1859 Thomas Louis Connally was appointed Catholic Archbishop of Halifax.

1886 Jesse M. Bader, president and general secretary of the World Convention of Churches of Christ (Disciples) (1930-63), was born in Bader, Ill. (died 1963).

1901 Anglican Archbishop William Bennett Bond was elected Metropolitan of Canada.

APRIL 16

556 Pelagius I was consecrated as pope, originally named in 555; served until 561; rebuilt Rome after war with Goths; many Western bishops were opposed to him.

1521 Martin Luther arrived at Worms to appear before the Diet, composed of notables of church and state.

1612 Abraham Calovius (Calov), Lutheran theologian, was born in Prussia; professor of theology at Wittenberg (1650-86); champion of Lutheran orthodoxy, was a true exemplar of Lutheran scholasticism (died 1686).

1783 St. Benedict Joseph Labre died at 35; patron of displaced persons; canonized 1881; also observed as his feast day.

1879 St. Bernadette of Lourdes died; also observed as her feast day, except in France where it is observed Feb. 18.

1887 Stephen E. Keeler, Episcopal Bishop of Minnesota (1944-56) was born in New Canaan, Conn. (died 1956).

1927 Cardinal Joseph A. Ratzinger, prefect of the Sacred Congregation for the Doctrine of the Faith (1981-), was born in Marktylam Inn, Germany; Archbishop of Munich (1977-81), elevated to cardinal 1977.

1962 Catholic Archbishop Joseph F. Rummel of New Orleans excommunicated three persons for attempting to provoke opposition to his orders desegregating church schools.

1967 *National Catholic Reporter*, an independent American Catholic periodical, made public the formerly secret reports of the Papal Commission on Birth Control, revealing that a majority of the commission favored liberalization of the church's stand.

APRIL 17

Feast day of St. Anicetus, pope from 155 to 156; died a martyr.

Feast day of St. Stephen Harding, abbot of Citeaux (mother house of Cistercians, 16 miles south of Dijon, France), which he helped found (1109-34); co-founder of the Cistercian Order; canonized 1623.

326 St. Alexander, patriarch of Alexandria, died; primarily concerned with putting down the Melitian* and Arian* schisms; also observed as his feast day.

1111 St. Robert de Molesmes, French churchman, died; a co-founder of the monastery at Citeaux (see above) and one in the forest of Molesmes (1075).

1635 Edward Stillingfleet, Anglican prelate, was born near Southampton; sought compromise between Presbyterian and Episcopal creeds and defended the Church of England against charge of schism; archdeacon of London (1677), dean of St. Paul's (1678-89), Bishop of Worcester (1689-99) (died 1699).

1640 Reorus Torkillus, the first American Lutheran clergyman, arrived in Wilmington, Del.

1680 Kateri Tekakwitha, first North American Indian ever presented for sainthood, died at 24; her practice of heroic virtue was recognized in 1943; known as the "Lily of the Mohawks."

1708 Ambrose, Archbishop of Moscow (1768-71) was born; martyred (1771) by a mob during the plague when he removed an icon to prevent the spread of infection; translated Hebrew psalter and many Greek and Latin Fathers.

1772 Archibald Alexander, theologian and educator, was born in Lexington, Va.; a founder, first professor, Princeton Theological Seminary (1812-51); president, Hampden Sydney College (1796-1801, 1802-07); pastor, Pine St. Church, Philadelphia (1807-12) (died 1851).

1808 Charles F. Barnard, Unitarian clergyman, was born in Boston; founder, pastor (1836-66), Boston's Warren St. Chapel, "the children's church" (died 1884).

1842 Charles H. Parkhurst, Presbyterian clergyman and reformer, was born in Framingham, Mass.; pastor, Madison Square Church (1880-1918); a sermon in February 1892, attacking political corruption and organized vice led to the Lexow investigation, the defeat of Tammany Hall, and the election of a reform administration in New York City; president, Society for the Prevention of Crime (died 1933).

1970 Sergei V. S. Aleksei, head of the Russian Orthodox Church (1944-70), died in Moscow at 92.

APRIL 18

Feast day of Mme. Acarie, born Barbara Avrillot (1566-1618), "Marie of the Incarnation," founder of the Carmelites of the Reform in France (1603); beatified 1791.

309 St. Eusebius was named pope, served until August 17, when he was banished by Emperor Maxentius; died in exile in Sicily.

1161 Theobald, Archbishop of Canterbury (1138-61), died; resisted efforts of monasteries to throw off episcopal control; introduced the study of civil law and established canonical jurisprudence in England.

1521 Martin Luther appeared before Emperor Charles V and other nobles at the Diet of Worms; was asked about his writings and whether he would recant; Luther said he would recant if convinced of any error of Scripture or by evident reason; otherwise he would abide by his conscience, which was bound by the word of God; he reputedly said, "Here I stand, I can do no more."

1587 John Foxe, English Protestant clergyman and author, died at 71; wrote "The Book of Martyrs" (1563), a Latin history of Christian martyrdom.

1743 James Blair, Scottish-born Episcopal clergyman and educator, died at 88; founder, first president (1693-1743), College of William & Mary, Williamsburg, Va.; pastor, Bruton Parish Church, Williamsburg (1710-43).

1835 Henry A. Buttz, theologian, was born in Middle Smithfield, Pa.; with Drew Theological Seminary, Madison, N.J., as professor (1868-80), president (1880-1912), president emeritus (1912-20) (died 1920).

1902 Menachem M. Schneerson, rebbe (spiritual leader) of Lubanitch Hasidim (1951-), was born in Nikolayev, Russia; one of the most important figures in Jewry.

1906 The trial on heresy charges of Rev. Algernon S. Crapsey, rector of St. Andrew's Episcopal Church, Rochester, began before an ecclesiastical court in Batavia, N.Y.; known for social work, but it was charged he had made heretical remarks about the divinity of Christ; convicted Dec 5, expelled from ministry.

1909 Beatification ceremony for Joan of Arc held in St. Peter's, Rome.

APRIL 19

Feast day of St. Alphege, Archbishop of Canterbury (1005-1011) and martyr; stoned to death by the Danes during a drunken feast because he would not ransom himself at the expense of his poor tenants.

1054 St. Leo IX, pope from 1049 to 1054, died; also observed as his feast day.

1127 St. Felix of Valois was born in France; one of the founders of the Order of the Most Holy Trinity (Trinitarians) (died 1212).

1836 Adoniram J. Gordon, Baptist clergyman and hymn writer, was born in New Hampton, N. H.: served Boston churches and was active in missionary work, founding the Boston Missionary Training School (now Gordon College, Gordon Divinity School); wrote many hymns (My Jesus, I love Thee; I shall see the King in His beauty) (died 1895).

1870 Jay T. Stocking, Congregational clergyman, was born in Lisbon, N.Y.; wrote the hymn, "O master, workman of the race" (died 1936).

1886 The Bishop of Madrid was assassinated.

1887 Catholic University of America was incorporated; chartered by Pope Leo XIII on March 7, 1889.

1911 The completed portion of the Cathedral of St. John the Divine in New York City was consecrated.

1959 The Coptic Church chose as its 116th patriarch Archpriest Mina el Baramoussy el Metawahad, who was enthroned as Kyrillos VI.

1978 The U. S. Supreme Court struck down as unconstitutional the last state (Tennessee) ban on the eligibility of priests and ministers to run for public office.

1980 The United Methodist Church rejected by a vote of 728 to 225 efforts to ease its stand against homosexual practices at its general conference in Indianapolis.

APRIL 20

Feast day of St. Agnes of Montepulciano, prioress of a Dominican convent; several remarkable prophecies and cures are attributed to her; canonized 1726.

1012 Benedict VIII was consecrated as pope; served until 1024; an effective ruler, a progressive and strong pontiff; supported monastic reform, suppressed clerical immorality and added the Nicene creed* to the Roman rite; defeated the Saracens by taking Sardinia from them; brother of John XIX, who succeeded him.

1139 The Second Lateran Council, with Pope Innocent II presiding, opened with 1000 church leaders attending; the principal topic of discussion was the preservation of the temporal possessions of the clergy.

1164 Victor IV, antipope from 1159 to 1164, died.

1314 Clement V, the first Avignon pope, who served from 1305 to 1314, died.

1494 Johannes Agricola, religious reformer, was born in Eisleben, Germany, as Johannes Sneider; a disciple of Luther; proponent of Antinomianism,* thus opposing Luther and Melancthon; general superintendent and court preacher for the Elector of Brandenburg (1540-66); made a popular collection of German proverbs (died 1566).

1586 St. Rose of Lima, patron saint of South America, was born in Lima, Peru; she was the first person born in the New World to be canonized by the Catholic Church (1671) (died 1617).

1594 Matthäus A. von Löwenstein, German hymn writer, was born in Silesia; his best known hymn was "Lord of our life and God of our salvation" (died 1648).

1745 Nathanael Emmons, Congregational clergyman and teacher, was born in East Haddam, Conn.; pastor, Franklin (Mass.) Church (1773-1825); also trained theological students for the Congregational ministry (died 1840).

1785 The first state Methodist conference was held in Louisburg, N.C. with Superintendents Francis Asbury and Thomas Coke present.

1802 William H. Furness, Unitarian clergyman and abolitionist, was born in Boston; served the First Unitarian Congregational Church, Philadelphia (1825-75); pioneer in pointing out distinction between Jesus of history and Christ of theology; hymn writer (died 1896).

1821 Cornelis W. Opzoomer, Dutch theologian, was born in Rotterdam; leader of the empirical-positivistic school of philosophy and champion of modern theology; dreamed of a church of the future based on piety alone, embracing all Christians (died 1892).

1839 Last of the Mormons left Missouri, ending a long civil war.

1842 John M. Farley, Catholic prelate, was born in Armagh County, Ireland; the fourth Archbishop of New York (1902-18), elevated to cardinal 1911 (died 1918).

1855 The first Bohemian church in the United States (St. John Nepomunk) opened in St. Louis.

1884 Pope Leo XIII issued the encyclical, "Humanum genus," condemning the Masonic order; clarified 10 years later to include other secret societies, forbidding membership in them under pain of mortal sin.

1911 The Portuguese Government issued a decree calling for separation of church and state, the Catholic religion no longer being the national church.

APRIL 21

Feast day in the Orthodox Church of St. Januarius, Bishop of Veneveto and patron saint of Naples.

1073 Alexander II, born Anselmo da Baggio, pope from 1061 to 1073, died; under the electoral law of 1059, he was the first pope chosen by a synod to examine the claims of Honorius II; made papal control over the church outside Rome more effective; renewed the decrees against simony* and enforced clerical celibacy.

1109 St. Anselm, Italian-born Archbishop of Canterbury (1093-1109), died at about 76; first of the Scholastic philosophers and one of the most important thinkers between St. Augustine and Thomas Aquinas; founder of Scholasticism;* originator of the ontological argument for the existence of God (based on the idea of a perfect being) and the satisfaction theory of atonement; became the major figure in the investiture controversy by refusing to pay money to William II Rufus, lest it be construed as payment for the archbishopric; controversy continued until the Concordat of Worms; his most important work was "Cur deus homo" (Why God became man); canonized 1494; also observed as his feast day.

1142 Pierre Abelard, French philosopher and theologian, died; as theologian, he is noteworthy for his doctrine of revelation and his conception of the relation between faith and knowledge; best remembered for the legendary romance with Heloise; wrote hymns (O what their joy and their glory must be).

1393 John Capgrave, Augustinian theologian, was born in Lynn, England; provincial of Augustinian hermits in England; author of a catalogue of English saints, the life of St. Katherine (died 1464).

1534 Elizabeth Barton, "the nun (or maid) of Kent," was executed; an English ecstatic* whose prophecies about Henry VIII's marital policies created public disquiet; an ecclesiastical commission said her prophesies were sincere; became a Benedictine nun (1527); confession extorted from her that trances were feigned (1533).

1649 The Province of Maryland enacted the Toleration Act, designed to remove the charge that the colony was intolerant of Protestants; it said in part: "...noe person or persons whatsoever... professing to believe in Jesus Christ, shall from henceforth bee any waies troubled, Molested or discountenanced for or in respect of his or her religion nor in the free exercise thereof...nor any way compelled to the beleefe or exercise of any other religion against his or her consent."

1778 Thomas McAuley, Presbyterian clergyman, was born in Colerain, Ireland; founder, first president, Union Theological Seminary (1835-40) (died 1862).

1783 Reginald Heber, Anglican prelate and hymn writer, was born in Malpas, England; Bishop of Calcutta (1823-26); wrote many hymns (Holy, holy, holy; The Son of God goes forth to war, From Greenland's icy mountains, God that madest earth and heaven) (died 1826).

1795 St. Vincent Pallotti, Catholic priest and order founder, was born in Rome; founder, Pallotine Fathers, designed to maintain, extend and promote Christian piety and belief (died 1850).

1805 James Martineau, English clergyman and theologian, was born in Norwich; helped found Irish Unitarian Christian Society (1830), became a leader in the Unitarian movement and an outstanding theologian of his time; author (Types of Ethical Theory, A Study of Religion) (died 1900).

1808 Johann B. Wichern, German theologian, was born in Hamburg; founder of home missions in Germany (died 1881).

1856 Johnson Oatman, gospel hymn writer, was born near Medford, N.J.; wrote many hymns (No, not one; Count your blessings; Higher ground, sweeter than all) (died 1926).

1864 The first of seven weekly pamphlets was issued by (Cardinal) John Henry Newman; they were collected as "Apologia Pro Vita Sua," a defense of his life and religious opinions.

1870 Edward S. Ames, philosophy and theology professor, U. of Chicago (1900-58), was born in Eau Clair, Wis.; a leading advocate of modernism in the Disciples of Christ Church; author (Psychology of Religious Experience, Religion) (died 1958).

1885 Irish Catholic bishops were summoned to Rome and rebuked by Pope Leo XIII for disloyalty.

1927 Archbishop Mora y del Rio was charged with complicity in the Limon massacre; he denied the charge but said that Mexican Catholics had the right to fight for their rights.

1968 The Uniting General Conference of the Methodist and Evangelical United Brethren churches opened in Dallas; resulted in the United Methodist Church with 11 million members.

1972 The United Methodist Church General Conference adopted what were described as landmark doctrinal guidelines designed to help people understand their religion in contemporary society.

1981 The American Civil Liberties Union charged the Pittsburgh cable television contract with Warner Cable Corp. violated church-state separation by providing Christian Associates of Southwest Pennsylvania with a channel and equipment for religious-oriented programming.

APRIL 22

Feast day of St. Soter, pope from 166 to 174 or 175; venerated as a martyr but nothing is known of his martyrdom.

296 St. Gaius (or Caius), pope from 283 to 296, died; also observed as his feast day.

536 St. Agapetus I, pope from 535 to 536, died; a strong defender of orthodoxy; also observed as his feast day.

835 Kobo Daishi, Japanese Buddhist monk, died at 61; founder of a Buddhist sect, Shingon (True World), and established a monastery on Mt. Koya; also an accomplished calligrapher, artist, and poet.

1164 Paschal III, born Guido of Crema, was elected as anti-pope; recognized only in few parts of the Catholic world; served until 1168.

1669 Richard Mather, English-born colonial religious leader, died at 63; pastor in Dorchester, Mass. (1636-69); one of the authors of the Bay Psalm Book and the Cambridge Platform, the standard statement for many years of Congregational doctrine in New England.

1688 Jonathan Dickinson, Presbyterian clergyman and educator, was born in Hatfield, Mass.; a leading defender of Presbyterianism; obtained charter for the College of New Jersey (which later became Princeton), first president (1746-47) (died 1747).

1711 Eleazar Wheelock, Congregational clergyman, was born in Windham, Conn.; planned widespread educational system for Indians, but plan failed because of governmental disapproval and unsatisfactory results among the Indian graduates; opened school in Lebanon, Conn. (1754), asked by New Hampshire to move school to Dresden (now Hanover), opened to all and eventually became Dartmouth U. (1769) (died 1799).

1759 James Freeman, pioneer American Unitarian, was born in Charlestown, Mass.; a lay leader in King's Chapel, New York City, he was refused ordination in the Episcopal Church because of his substantial revisions to the Book of Common Prayer; ordained as a Unitarian instead (1787) and King's Chapel became the first Unitarian church in the United States; served there until 1826 (died 1835).

1766 Alexander V. Griswold, colonial Episcopal prelate, was born in Simsbury, Conn.; Bishop of the Eastern Diocese (1810-43), which was most of New England; at his death, area had grown to five dioceses (died 1843).

1775 Georg Hermes, Catholic theologian, was born in Dreierwalde, Germany; tried to demonstrate the rational necessity of Christianity for personal self-realization and human dignity, trying to adjust Catholicism to Immanuel Kant's philosophy; writings were condemned by Pope Gregory XVI (1835) (died 1831).

1801 Elijah C. Bridgman, Congregational missionary and Orientalist, was born in Belchertown, Mass.; first American missionary to China; wrote Chinese language manuals and helped translate Bible into Chinese; helped organize Society for the Diffusion of Useful Knowledge and the Medical Missionary Society (died 1862).

1842 Alexander Kohut, leader of Conservative Judaism, was born in Feligyhaza, Hungary; a founder of the Jewish Theological Seminary of America (1887); author of modern version of Aruch Hashalem (died 1894).

1889 Henry D. Moyle, first counselor to the president of the Mormon Church, was born in Salt Lake City (died 1963).

1927 The Archbishop of Mexico and five other Catholic dignitaries were deported after the Limon massacre.

1960 The American Lutheran Church was founded in Minneapolis by the merger of the Evangelical Lutheran, American Lutheran, and United Evangelical Lutheran churches.

1967 William A. Irwin, American Bible scholar, died in Wheaton, Md. at 82; author (The Old Testament, Keystone of Human Culture).

APRIL 23

Feast day of St. George, patron saint of England; reclassified (1969) as an optional memorial in the Catholic Church; according to legend, George conquered the dragon (the Devil) and rescued the King's daughter, Sabra (representing the Church).

997 St. Adalbert, Bishop of Prague (983-988) and Benedictine missionary to Prussia, died; he was murdered by Germans who thought he was a Polish spy; tradition attributes oldest Polish religious song (Bogurodzica - "Mother of God") to him; also observed as his feast day.

1073 St. Gregory VII, born Hildebrand, was elected pope; served until 1085; ranks as one of the most important popes; decreed (1075) against lay investiture of bishops and abbots, which led to a long struggle with Emperor Henry IV of Germany; while his actions led to divisions in the Church, he did much to regenerate the Church and to centralize it in Rome; he was the first pope to excommunicate a ruler (Henry IV); Gregory was driven from Rome (1084) and died in Salerno (1085); canonized 1584.

1500 Johannes Stumpf, Swiss theologian, was born; one of the most important personalities of the Swiss reformation; his chronicle was a standard work until the 18th Century; a friend of Zwingli (died 1578).

1522 St. Catherine of Ricci, Dominican mystic and nun, was born in Italy; prioress of Dominican convent at Prato (10 miles northwest of Florence) (1552-90); chiefly remarkable for an ecstasy into which she was rapt for 28 hours a week for years; canonized 1746 (died 1590).

1538 John Calvin and Guillaume Farel, whom Calvin was helping, were ordered by the Geneva General Assembly to leave and cease their planned reforms.

1586 Martin Rinkart, German hymn writer, was born in Eilenberg; hymns included "Now then we all our God" and "Let all men praise the Lord" (died 1649).

1720 Elijah ben Solomon, Talmudic scholar, was born in Lithuania; foremost Talmudic scholar of his day, exerted great influence on Jewish education, contending that study of astronomy and mathematics are essential (died 1797).

1803 Adin Ballou, Universalist clergyman, was born in Cumberland, R.I.; founded Hopedale Community at Milford, Mass. (1841), the first utopian enterprise, and promised "to promote the holiness and happiness of all mankind;" community ended 1868 (died 1890).

1813 Antoine F. Ozanam, French historian and Catholic leader, was born in Milan, Italy; a founder of the Society of St. Vincent de Paul (died 1853).

1828 Fenton J. A. Hort, biblical scholar, was born in Dublin; professor of divinity, Cambridge U. (1878-91); with B. F. Westcott, edited a critical edition of the Greek New Testament (died 1892).

1905 Nathan H. Knorr, president of the Watch Tower Bible and Tract Society (1942-77), was born in Bethlehem, Pa. (died 1977).

1964 The Presbyterian Church in the United States opened its general assembly in Montreat, N.C.; enacted a change in the Book of Church Order permitting the ordination of women as deacons, elders, and ministers.

1982 William C. Townsend, biblical scholar, died at 85; founded (1935) the Wycliffe Bible Translators Organization, which translated the New Testament into more than 130 languages.

APRIL 24

624 St. Mellitus, third Archbishop of Canterbury (619-624), died; also observed as his feast day.

858 St. Nicholas I (the Great) was elected pope, served until 867; conducted a vigorous administration, protected minor clergy, and established a wholly new concept of the power and dignity of the papacy; deposed the archbishops of Cologne and Trier for sanctioning the adulterous marriage of an emperor.

1342 Benedict XII, pope from 1334 to 1342, died at 57.

1581 St. Vincent de Paul, founder of Catholic orders, was born near Toulouse, France; founder of the Congregation of the Priests of the Mission (Lazarists or Vincentians) and of the Sisters of Charity; canonized 1787; declared universal patron of works of charity 1885 (died 1660).

1585 Sixtus V was elected pope; served until 1590; regarded as one of the greatest popes because of achievements in reforming the central administration of the church; revised rules for the College of Cardinals, limiting the number to 70; built the Vatican Library and the Lateran Palace, completed the dome of St. Peter's Basilica; authorized a new edition of the Septuagint (1587), published a new edition of the Vulgate Bible.

1809 Joseph A. Alexander, Presbyterian theologian and educator, was born in Philadelphia, the son of Archibald Alexander (4/17/1772); taught at Princeton U. and Seminary; remarkable linguist who helped prepare the first American edition of Donnegan's Greek lexicon; did much to introduce German theological writing in the United States (died 1860).

1868 St. Mary Euphrasia Pelletier died at 72; founder, Institute of Our Lady of Charity of the Good Shepherd; also observed as her feast day.

1964 The Standing Conference of Orthodox Bishops deplored all vestiges of segregation and reiterated its support for prayer and Bible reading in the public schools.

1985 Pope John Paul II named two new American cardinals - Archbishop John J. O'Connor of New York and Archbishop Bernard F. Law of Boston.

APRIL 25

Feast day of St. Mark, an apostle and the traditional author of the second Gospel.

1214 Louis IX (St. Louis), king of France (1226-70), was born; renowned for his sanctity, led two Crusades, dying of the plague on the Second; canonized 1297 (died 1270).

1518 The chapter of German Augustinians met in Heidelberg and relieved Martin Luther of his duties as district vicar in the wake of his campaign against indulgences.

1599 Oliver Cromwell, English lord protector, was born near Cambridge; sought to strengthen tolerance, leaving all forms of worship to the free choice of the worshipers (died 1658).

1778 James Relly, English reformer, died at 56; a coworker of George Whitefield, he broke away because of his belief in salvation for all; preached Universalism in London; his convert, John Murray, formed the American Universalist Church.

1787 Justin Edwards, Congregational clergyman and theologian, was born in Westhampton, Mass.; president, Andover Theological Seminary (1836-42); a founder of the American Temperance Society (died 1853).

1792 John Keble, Anglican clergyman, was born in Fairford, England; had a leading role in founding the Oxford Movement with his sermon in 1833 on national apostasy*, wrote religious verse (The Christian Year), many hymns (Blest are the pure in heart; Sun of my soul, Thou saviour dear; New every morning is the love (died 1866).

1815 Richard W. Church, dean of St. Paul's Cathedral (1871-90), was born in Lisbon, Portugal; one of the most distinguished Anglican preachers and writers of the 19th Century; author (The Gifts of Civilization, The Oxford Movement) (died 1890).

1819 Charles J. Ellicott, Anglican prelate, was born near Stamford, England; Bishop of Gloucester and Bristol (1863-97), until it was divided, then Bishop of Gloucester (1897-1905); chairman of New Testament revision committee for 11 years (died 1905).

1839 Samuel J. Stone, Anglican clergyman, was born in Whitmore, England; best known for the hymn, "The church's one foundation" (died 1900).

1887 Charles E. Fuller, radio evangelist who conducted "The Old Fashioned Revival Hour," was born in Los Angeles (died 1968).

1926 Dr. Henry Sloan Coffin was elected president of the Union Theological Seminary, New York City.

1956 The Methodist General Conference opened in Minneapolis, during which it granted full clergy rights to women.

1967 Janie McGaughey of the Presbyterian Church in the United States became the first in her denomination to become moderator of a presbytery (Atlanta).

1981 Archbishop of Canterbury Robert Runcie spoke at the 350th anniversary of Christ Episcopal Church in Stevensville, Md.

APRIL 26

Feast day of St. Marcellinus, pope from 296 to 304.

Feast day of St. Paschasius Radbertus, abbot of Corbie (near Amiens, France) and author of the first monograph on the Eucharist.

Former feast day of St. Anacletus, the third pope (76-88); observance ended 1969.

757 Stephen II, pope from 752 to 757, died.

1806 Alexander Duff, Presbyterian missionary, was born in Moulon, Scotland; first missionary to India from the Church of Scotland, helped found schools and the University of Calcutta; founder, *Calcutta Review* (died 1878).

1814 Mary Duncan, Scottish Presbyterian hymn writer, was born in Kelso; wrote many hymns for her children (Jesus, tender shepherd, hear me) (died 1840).

1832 Conference in Independence, Mo. recognized Joseph Smith as president of the high priesthood of the Mormon Church.

1847 The Missouri synod of the Lutheran Church met for the first time in Chicago.

1904 Paul Emile Leger, Catholic prelate, was born in Valleyfield, Quebec: Archbishop of Montreal (1950-53), emeritus (1953-), elevated to cardinal 1953.

1958 Samuel Stritch of Chicago was given the highest Vatican post ever given an American - proprefect of the Vatican's Sacred Congregation for the Propagation of Faith.

APRIL 27

Feast day of St. Peter Canisius, Jesuit scholar and a Doctor* of the Church.

1803 Paul Cullen, Catholic prelate, was born near Ballitore, Ireland; first Irish cardinal (1866) and Archbishop of Dublin (1852-78) (died 1878).

1843 Ira Barnes Dutton, Catholic missionary, was born in Stowe, Vt.; assisted and succeeded Father Damien in serving the lepers on Molokai Island (died 1931).

1875 Archbishop John McCloskey of New York was invested as the first American cardinal in St. Patrick's Cathedral.

1960 The National Council of the Protestant Episcopal Church again endorsed sit-ins by blacks in the South.

1976 The Vatican announced the appointment of 19 new cardinals, including one American - Archbishop William W. Baum of Washington, D.C.

1981 Anglican prelates from 36 nations began a six day meeting in Washington; 27 bishops issued a joint statement May 1 condemning the world's arms race, rejected the notion of a "just" war.

APRIL 28

Feast day of St. Louis Marie de Montfort, founder of the Montfort Fathers (Company of Mary) and the Congregation of the Daughters of Wisdom.

Former feast day of St. Paul of the Cross, founder of the Passionists; now observed Oct. 19.

1522 The See of Santiago de Cuba was created, with Fra Juan Umite as the first bishop.

1819 Ezra Abbot, biblical scholar, was born in Jackson, Me.; professor of New Testament, Harvard Divinity School (1872-84); one of the original members of the American New Testament Revision Committee (died 1884).

1829 The Duke of Norfolk took his seat in the House of Lords, the first Catholic peer seated under the Emancipation Act.

1841 St. Peter Chanel; missionary to the South Seas, was martyred; canonized 1954; also observed as his feast day.

1960 The 100th general assembly of the Southern Presbyterian Church declared that marital sexual relations without procreative intentions were not sinful.

APRIL 29

Feast day of St. Giuseppe Cottolengo, founder of a charitable institution and 14 religious congregations.

Feast day of St. Robert de Molesmes, French abbot and founder of a monastery in the forest of Molesmes (1075-1111).

1109 St. Hugh of Cluny died at 85; abbot of the monastery at Cluny (near Macon, France) (1049-1109); took leading part in organizing the First Crusade; canonized 1120; also observed as his feast day.

1380 St. Catherine of Siena, greatest of the 14th Century Italian mystics, died at 33; her visions were responsible for Pope Gregory XI's decision to return to Rome from Avignon (1377) and for recognition of Pope Urban VI (1380); canonized 1460, declared a patron saint of Italy (1939); also observed as her feast day.

1670 Clement X was elected pope as the compromise candidate after a long conclave; served until 1676; opposed Louis XIV policy of extending the rights of royalty and promoted peace among the European states.

1749 John Philip Boehm, a founder of the German Reformed Church in Pennsylvania, died at 66.

1795 Lorrin Andrews, Congregational missionary to Hawaii (1828-41), was born in East Windsor, Conn.; published a Hawaiian dictionary and grammar, translated the Bible into Hawaiian; published first newspaper in Hawaii (1834); became first associate justice of the Hawaiian Supreme Court (1852-55) (died 1868).

1834 Joseph H. Gilmore, Baptist clergyman, was born in Boston; wrote lyrics for the hymn, "He leadeth me" (died 1918).

1836 Marist Fathers (Society of Mary), a religious congregation founded by Jean Claude Colin, was approved by the pope.

1856 Ira M. Price, Oriental scholar, was born near Newark, Ohio; professor, Semitic languages and literature, U. of Chicago (1900-25); wrote treatises on Old Testament history (died 1939).

1891 Phillips Brooks, minister of Trinity Church, Boston, was elected Episcopal Bishop of Massachusetts; served until 1893.

1980 Washington for Jesus rally in Washington, D.C. attracted 200,000 evangelical Christians to the city; a speaker declared the world to be "aflame in sin."

1986 The Council of Bishops of the United Methodist Church unanimously voted for "clear and unconditional" opposition to the use of nuclear weapons.

APRIL 30

Feast day of St. Pius V, pope from 1566 to 1572.

Feast day in the Orthodox Church of St. James (the Great), an apostle and patron saint of Spain.

Former feast day of St. Catherine of Sienna (1347-80), greatest 14th Century Italian mystic; now observed April 29.

1240 Jacques (Jacob) de Vitry, French prelate and historian, died at about 60; Bishop of Acre (northwest Israel seaport) and prominent in Fifth Crusade; cardinal Bishop of Tusculum (ancient city, south of Rome) (1227-40); Latin patriarch of Jerusalem (1239); wrote "Historia Orientalis," a valuable source book of 13th Century history and customs.

1623 Francoise de Laval, first Catholic Bishop of Canada (1674-88), was born in Montigny-sur-Avre, France; founded Quebec Seminary, which became the first Canadian Catholic university (died 1708).

1651 St. Jean Baptiste de La Salle, founder of the Brothers of the Christian Schools, was born in Reims, France; canonized 1900 (died 1719).

1771 Hosea Ballou, Universalist theologian, was born in Richmond, N.H.; most influential American Universalist leader for more than 50 years; wrote many Universalist hymns (When God descends with man to dwell); author (Treatise on the Atonement)(died 1852).

1785 Spencer H. Cone, Baptist clergyman, was born in Princeton, N.J.; a founder, president, American and Foreign Bible Society (1837-50); president, American Bible Union (1850) (died 1855).

1798 Thomas Binney, English nonconformist, was born in Newcastle-on-Tyne; Congregationalist who felt sermons occupied too much of the service, favored more responsive reading; wrote hymn, "Eternal light, eternal light" (died 1874).

1816 George Bowen, American missionary, was born in Middlebury, Vt.; known as the "white saint of India," where he served the Methodist Church (1848-88) (died 1888).

1822 Hannibal W. Goodwin, Episcopal clergyman, was born in Taughannock, N.Y.; inventor of photographic film (1887) (died 1895).

1905 A decree was issued in Russia improving the liberty of worship for all.

1986 Paramilitary police in India's state of Punjab seized control of the Golden Temple in Amritsar, the holiest shrine of Sikhdom.

MAY 1

Feast day of Sts. Philip and James, the apostles.

1045 Gregory VI, born Johannes Gratianus, assumed the role of pope; served until Dec. 20, 1046, when he was deposed and banished to Germany; accused of buying pontificate from Benedict IX.

1551 Second session of the Council of Trent opened, continued to April 28, 1552 without any accomplishments.

1555 Pope Marcellus II, who served only a month, died.

1572 St. Pius V, pope from 1566 to 1572, died at 68; canonized 1712.

1672 Joseph Addison, essayist and editor, was born in Amesbury, England; best known for his essays in *The Tatler* and *The Spectator*; Anglican hymn writer (The spacious firmament on high; When all Thy mercies, O my God; How are Thy servants blest, O Lord) (died 1719).

1759 Jacob Albright, a founder of the Evangelical Church, was born near Pottstown, Pa.; served as bishop of a Methodist sect (The Newly Formed Methodist Conference); after failing to get approval of the Methodist leaders, the sect became the Evangelical Church, then merged with the United Brethren Church; Albright College at Reading, Pa. was named for him (died 1808).

1827 John Bascom, educator and theologian, was born in Genoa, N.Y.; president, U. of Wisconsin (1874-87); author of "The Natural Theology of Social Science," which was critical of Protestant conservatism, and "Sociology," which paved the way for social gospel (died 1911).

1839 Mormons began buying land in Commerce, Ill. on the east bank of the Mississippi and renamed it Nauvoo.

1843 Thomas O'Gorman, Catholic prelate and author, was born in Boston; served as Bishop of Sioux Falls, S.D.; accompanied William Howard Taft to help adjudicate the friar land claims in the Philippines; author of a nine-volume history of the Catholic Church in the United States (died 1921).

1845 Fourteen Southern conferences of the Methodist Church met in Louisville, Ky. and organized the Methodist Episcopal Church, South as a result of differences of opinion over the slavery question.

1848 The main body of Mormons, led by Brigham Young, left Missouri for Utah.

1881 Pierre Teilhard de Chardin, French Jesuit priest and paleontologist, was born in Sarcenat, France; participated in the discovery of the "Peking man" in China; sought to create a synthesis between science and religion; author (The Phenomenon of Man) (died 1955).

1888 John F. O'Hara, Archbishop of Philadelphia (1951-60), was born in Ann Arbor, Mich.; president, Notre Dame U. (1934-39), elevated to cardinal 1958 (died 1960).

1895 Leo Sowerby, composer and organist, was born in Grand Rapids, Mich.; organist at Cathedral of St. James, Chicago (1927-62); composed the oratorio, "Christ Reborn" (died 1968).

1931 The first American Bahai house of worship was opened in Wilmette, Ill.

1965 Pope Paul VI issued the encyclical, "Mense maio," an appeal for world peace.

1966 A legal measure took effect whereby the Church of England was allowed to modify its form of public worship if approved by the convocations of Canterbury and York and the Church Assembly, without first getting permission from Parliament.

1972 Rt. Rev. Paul Moore Jr., 52-year old civil rights activist and a vigorous opponent of the Vietnam War, became the 13th Episcopal Bishop of New York; enthroned Sep 23.

MAY 2

Feast day of St. Eugenius I, pope from 654 to 657.

373 St. Athanasius the Great, patriarch of Alexandria (328-373), died; a Doctor* of the Church, he spent his life "planting trees under which men of later ages might sit;" known as the "father of Orthodoxy;" exiled five times for his opposition to Arianism;* also observed as his feast day.

1507 Martin Luther celebrated his first mass.

1576 Bartolomé de Carranza, Spanish Dominican Archbishop of Toledo, died at 73; confidant of Charles V and Philip II, confessor to Mary Tudor; imprisoned for eight years by the Inquisition on a charge of heretical writings.

1602 Athanasius Kircher, Jesuit educator, was born in Germany; taught mathematics and Hebrew in the College of Rome; credited with the invention of the magic lantern (died 1680).

1796 John G. Palfrey, Unitarian clergyman and editor, was born in Boston; editor, owner of the *North American Review* (1835-45); congressman, Boston postmaster; author of a history of New England and volumes of sermons (died 1881).

1821 William Taylor, Methodist missionary, was born in Rockbridge County, Va.; served as missionary to the Gold Rush in California (1849-56); became missionary in various parts of the world, then missionary Bishop of Africa (1884-96) (died 1902).

1832 The Seamen's Bethel in New Bedford, Mass. was dedicated.

1837 Selah Merrill, Congregational clergyman and archaeologist, was born in Canton Centre, Conn.; headed Eastern Palestine archaeological expeditions (1876-77), American consul in Jerusalem (1882-85, 1891-93, 1898-1907) (died 1909).

1844 Aaron Wise, rabbi and theologian was born in Erlau, Hungary; a rabbi in New York City (1875-96); a founder, Jewish Theological Seminary, New York City (1886) (died 1896).

1851 Graham Taylor, Congregational clergyman and educator, was born in Schenectady, N.Y.; founder, resident warden, Chicago Commons Social Settlement (1894), which became one of the most widely-known American social settlements (died 1938).

1860 Theodore Herzl, founder of Zionism, was born in Budapest; wrote "Der Judenstaat," advocating a Jewish state in Palestine (died 1904).

1871 Francis P. Duffy (Father Duffy), Catholic priest, was born in Coburg, Canada; organizer, priest, Church of Our Saviour, South Fordham, N.Y.; chaplain of the 69th Regiment, New York National Guard (later the 165th Infantry), which he accompanied to Mexico and Europe (died 1932).

1927 Emilio Castro, general secretary, World Council of Churches (1985-), was born in Montevideo, Uruguay.

1956 Racial segregation in Methodist churches was ordered abolished by the General Conference meeting in Minneapolis.

1986 Eva Burrows, a native of Newcastle, Australia, was named general and world leader of the Salvation Army.

1988 The General Conference of the United Methodist Church in St. Louis refused by a vote of 676 to 293 to allow the ordination of practicing homosexuals.

MAY 3

Feast of the Invention (finding) of the Cross, commemorating the discovery by St. Helena (326) of the cross on which Jesus was crucified; Helena was the mother of Roman emperor Constantine.

Feast day of St. Alexander I, pope from 105 to 115; tradition asserts he added words commemorating the institution of the Eucharist to the canon of the mass.

996 Gregory V, born Bruno of Carinthia, was named pope; served until 999; the first German pope, he was expelled during 997-998 by forces of the anti-pope, but restored by his uncle, Emperor Otto III.

1410 Alexander V, born Pietro Philargi, pope in 1409-10, died; only recognized in small part of Christendom; more concerned with recovery of Papal States than reform of the church.

1512 The Fifth Lateran Council opened; made final attempt at papal reform before the Lutheran revolt, to avoid a split with the French; ended March 6, 1517.

1675 Thomas Chalkley, Quaker missionary, was born in Southwark, England; pioneer missionary in the American colonies (died 1741).

1675 Massachusetts enacted a law requiring the locking of church doors during the service because too many people were leaving before the sermons were completed.

1758 Benedict XIV, pope from 1740 to 1758, died at 83.

1786 St. Giuseppe Cottolengo, founder of a charitable institution and 14 religious congregations, was born; canonized 1934 (died 1842).

1794 James O. Andrew, Methodist prelate, was born in Wilkes County, Ga.; through marriage he became a slave owner; the 1844 General Conference directed him to desist from his clerical duties until he got rid of the slaves; this led to the division of the Methodist Church (1845); he served as a Methodist South bishop (1846-66) (died 1871).

1812 The theological seminary of the Presbyterian Church was located at Princeton U.

1819 Samuel D. Alexander, Presbyterian clergyman who was minister of the 15th St. (later Phillips) Church, New York City (1856-89), was born in Princeton, N. J. (died 1894).

1833 The Mormons adopted the name of Latter Day Saints.

1863 Loyal L. Wirt, superintendent of the Alaska mission (1898-1900), was born in Lamont, Mich.; built Alaska's first hospital in Nome (1899) (died 1961).

1870 Sir Frank Fletcher, English educator, was born in Atherton, England; head master, Charterhouse (1911-35); known for Anglican hymn, "O Son of man, our hero strong and tender" (died 1954).

1873 Arthur W. Moulton, Episcopal Bishop of Utah (1920-46), was born in Worcester, Mass. (died 1962).

1880 Charles Bradlaugh, a member of Parliament from Northampton and an atheist, refused to take the oath of allegiance and was excluded by the Commons; eventually (June 1884) the courts upheld his exclusion and in January 1886 he took the oath.

1923 The All Russian Church Conclave unfrocked Patriarch Tiakhon, expelled him from the church as a traitor.

1959 Blessed Mother Margaret d'Youville, founder of the Grey Nuns, was beatified in ceremonies in Rome.

1959 The Unitarian and Universalist churches voted to merge the American Unitarian Assn. and the Universalist Church of America.

1971 The Vatican announced that Polish and Vatican officials had met to discuss church-state relations for the first time since World War II.

1972 The Church of England, for the second time in three years, rejected reunification with the Methodist Church.

1983 The National Conference of Catholic Bishops after more than a year's study issued a pastoral letter urging the cessation of development, production and deployment of nuclear weapons.

1988 The General Conference of the United Methodist Church in St. Louis approved a new hymnal which retains most of the old favorite hymns.

MAY 4

1038 St. Gothard (Gotthard), Bishop of Hildesheim (in lower Saxony) (1022-38), died; reformed many monasteries in Upper Germany; also observed as his feast day.

1493 Pope Alexander VI issued the bull, "Inter caetera," which set the boundary between Portuguese and Spanish lands in the New World following its discovery by Christopher Columbus.

1613 James Sharp, Scottish ecclesiastic, was born near Aberdeen; chosen to plead the cause of the moderate party before Cromwell, he betrayed the party and served the interests of the English bishops in re-establishing the episcopacy in Scotland; named Archbishop of St. Andrew and primate of Scotland (1661-79); murdered by a group of fife lairds and farmers May 3,1679.

1800 John McL. Campbell, Scottish theologian, was born in Kilninver; ousted from Church of Scotland ministry because of his views on personal assurance of salvation and on the universality of the atonement; his followers were Campbellites or Disciples of Christ (died 1872).

1829 The first English Catholic member, the Earl of Surrey, was elected to Parliament.

1841 Alexander V. G. Allen, theology professor, Cambridge (1869-1908), was born in Otis, Mass.; author (Continuity of Christian Thinking) (died 1908).

1886 Michael A. Corrigan, Catholic Bishop of Newark, was installed as the third Archbishop of New York; served until 1902.

1889 Francis J. Spellman, Archbishop of New York (1939-67), was born in Whitman, Mass.; auxiliary bishop of Boston (1932-39), elevated to cardinal 1946 (died 1967).

1892 Angus Dun, Episcopal Bishop of Washington (1944-62), was born in New York City; dean, Episcopal Theological School, Cambridge, Mass. (1940-44) (died 1971).

1895 Gerald P. O'Hara, Catholic archbishop who was apostolic delegate to Great Britain (1954-63), was born in Green Ridge, Pa. (died 1963).

1969 Black leader James Foreman disrupted services at New York City's Riverside Church to press demands that American churches and synagogues pay $500 million as reparations to blacks.

1988 Catholic Bishop Eugene A. Marino was installed as Archbishop of Atlanta, the first black American archbishop.

1988 Rev. Robert Schuller announced sharp cutbacks in his highly-rated "Hour of Power" broadcast ministry because of the problems facing television evangelism in the wake of recent scandals involving Jimmy Swaggart and Jim Bakker.

MAY 5

Former feast day of St. Pius V, pope from 1566 to 1572; now observed April 30.

449 St. Hilary, Bishop of Arles (France) (429-449), died at about 48; sought to establish primacy over church in South Gaul; deprived of his rights by Pope Leo I; also observed as his feast day.

553 Second Council of Constantinople opened; strengthened doctrinal decisions of the Council of Chalcedon (451) and virtually destroyed Nestorianism*; council ended June 2.

1504 Stanislaus Hosius, Polish Catholic prelate, was born in Cracow; Bishop of Kulm (Chelmno) and Ermeland (1549-79); elevated to cardinal 1561; active opponent of Protestant Reformation (died 1579).

1813 Sören Kierkegaard, philosopher and theologian, was born in Copenhagen; among the first rank of modern philosophical writers, he became a force in existentialism, personalist theologies, and studies of mass society in the 20th Century; one of the most personal thinkers, he exerted considerable influence on contemporary thought; held that an individual freely chooses his own truth on the subjective basis of faith, that religion is an individual matter, and that the relation of the individual to God involves suffering (died 1855).

1851 A Catholic university was founded in Ireland.

1852 Pietro Gasparri, canonist and Catholic cardinal, was born in Capovalazza de Ussita, Italy; as secretary of the Congregation for Extraordinary Ecclesiastical Affairs, he led in revising the Code of Canon Law; served as secretary of state to Popes Benedict XV and Pius XI (1914-38); negotiated the Lateran Concordat (1929) setting up Vatican City (died 1934).

1852 Friedrich von Hügel, British Catholic religious philosopher, was born in Florence, Italy; founder of London Society for the Study of Religion, which became the center for modernist groups; also an Old Testament scholar; author (The Mystical Element of Religion) (died 1925).

1887 Geoffrey F. Fisher, Archbishop of Canterbury (1945-61), was born in Nuneaton, England; initiated revision of English canons, last codified in 1603; president, World Council of Churches (1946-54); first Archbishop of Canterbury to visit the Vatican since 1397 (died 1972).

1979 Pope John Paul II warned professors teaching faith and morals in Catholic universities to follow church doctrine or face dismissal.

1980 Rev. Robert Drinan, the only Catholic priest in Congress, was barred from seeking re-election to his Massachusetts seat in the House of Representatives by the superior general of the Society of Jesus (Jesuits), of which Drinan was a member.

1980 A group of conservatives who believe every word of the Bible is literally true began a movement to gain control of the Southern Baptist Convention.

MAY 6

1210 The Cathedral in Reims, France was destroyed by fire; a new cathedral was begun the following year.

1501 Marcellus II, pope in 1555, was born as Marcellus Cervini in Montepulciano, Italy; presided at the Council of Trent (1545), served as Vatican librarian; elected pope in April 1555, died May 1.

1574 Innocent X, pope from 1644 to 1655, was born Giovanni Battista Pamfili in Rome.

1606 John Norton, Puritan clergyman, was born in Hertfordshire, England; pastor of First Church, Boston, after John Cotton (1652-63); helped obtain confirmation of Massachusetts charter; active in prosecution of Quakers in Massachusetts Colony; author of first Latin book (on New England government) produced in the colonies (died 1663).

1638 Cornelis Otto Jansen, Catholic reformer, died at 53 of the plague; his writings brought about a reappraisal of the church's piety and role in national and international politics; the work on which he labored for 22 years, "Augustinus," devoted to St. Augustine's doctrines, was published after his death; the Church declared it heretical for its acceptance of predestination and its teaching that grace is reserved only for the elect.

1702 Friedrich C. Oetinger, Protestant theologian and theosophist, was born in Germany; leader of Pietists* and a disciple of Jakob Böhme and Swedenborg (died 1782)

1746 William Tennent, Presbyterian clergyman, died at 72; best known for his "Log College" in Pennsylvania, where he taught about 21 of the most gifted Presbyterian clergymen.

1776 Luigi Lambruschini, Catholic statesman and cardinal, was born in Genoa; papal secretary of state (1836), Archbishop of Genoa (1819) (died 1854).

1778 Henry Philpotts, Anglican Bishop of Exeter (1831-69), was born near Bristol; successfully agitated for the revival of convocation, religious orders (died 1869).

1796 Johann A. Möhler, Catholic church historian, was born in Igersheim, Germany; renowned as the "theologian of church unity" (died 1838).

1829 Phoebe A. C. Hanaford, first woman regularly ordained in New England, was born on Nantucket Island; became pastor of the Universalist Church in Hingham, Mass. (1868) (died 1921).

1858 Samuel B. McCormick, Presbyterian clergyman and educator, was born in Westmoreland County, Pa.; president, Coe College, Cedar Rapids, Iowa (1897-1904); chancellor, Western U. of Pennsylvania, which he moved to Pittsburgh, renamed it the U. of Pittsburgh, developed it into a modern institution (1904-20) (died 1928).

1865 Edward C. Chorley, Episcopal historiographer, was born in Manchester, England; historiographer of Episcopal Church (1919-49); founder, editor, Episcopal Church history magazine (1923-49) (died 1949).

1887 Michael Browne, master general of the Dominican Order (1955-63), was born in County Tipperary, Ireland; elevated to cardinal 1962 (died 1971).

1956 The Swiss Guards, who help guard the Vatican, celebrated their 450th anniversary.

1986 The first American Indian to become a Catholic bishop, Rev. Donald E. Pellotte, 41, was ordained in Gallop, N.M.

MAY 7

Feast day of St. Stanislaus (Stanislaw), patron saint of Poland.

721 St. John of Beverly, to whose miraculous intercession Henry V gave credit for his victory at Agincourt (Oct 25, 1415), died; Bishop of York (705-721), founder of abbey at Beverly; also observed as his feast day.

1274 The second Council of Lyon began on the call of Pope Gregory X to end the Greek schism, rescue the Holy Land, and effect moral reform; council adopted a creed for reunion of the churches but this was later rejected by the Byzantines; council ended June 17.

1342 Clement VI, born Pierre Roger, was elected pope; served until 1352; established himself at Avignon; although guilty of nepotism and prodigality, he was a benefactor of the poor and a good theologian; the most controversial aspect of his reign was his decree that the papacy alone had final rights on granting ecclesiastical benefices.

1508 Nil Sorski, Russian mystic and saint, died at 75; he was the first to write about the contemplative life and asceticism; also observed as his feast day in Russia.

1605 Nikon, Russian prelate, was born in Valdemanovo; patriarch of Moscow and head of the Russian Church (1652-66); revised sacred books and church services, which was unpopular and caused a schism in the church; deposed (1680) and sentenced to banishment; recalled to Moscow but died on the return trip in 1681.

1728 Blessed Rose Venerini, religious teacher and founder of the Venerini Sisters, died at 62; beatified 1952.

1738 George Whitefield, Methodist evangelist, arrived in Savannah, Ga.

1797 Edward Bass, rector of St. Paul's Church in Newburyport, Mass. (1752-89), was consecrated as the first Episcopal Bishop of Massachusetts, which then included Rhode Island and New Hampshire.

1806 William B. Ullathorne, Catholic Bishop of Birmingham (1851-89), was born in Pocklington, England; organized Catholic Church in Australia.

1823 Harriet S. Cannon, Episcopal order founder, was born in Charleston, S. C.; founder, mother superior, Sisters of St. Mary (1865-96) (died 1896).

1851 Adolf von Harnack, German theologian and church historian, was born in Dorpat, Estonia (Russia); had a major influence on historical theology; probably the most outstanding patristic* scholar of his generation; his major work, "History of Dogma," is still one of the principal tools of historical theologians (died 1930).

1894 Francis Brennan, Catholic prelate, was born in Shenandoah, Pa.; named to Sacred Rota in Rome (the Catholic Church's highest court of appeals); became the first American dean of the Rota (1959-67); elevated to cardinal 1967 (died 1968).

1978 Pope Paul VI conducted beatification rites for Sister Maria Enrichetta Cominici in St. Peter's Basilica.

MAY 8

615 St. Boniface IV, pope from 608 to 615, died.

685 St. Benedict II, pope from 684 to 685, died; also observed as his feast day.

1521 St. Peter Canisius, Jesuit theologian, was born in Nijmegen, Netherlands; re-established the Catholic Church in parts of Germany and Poland, serving as the first Jesuit provincial in Germany (1556); a strong opponent of Protestantism; wrote many catechisms, the chief of which, "Catechismus Major," has been issued in 130 editions; canonized 1925 as the "second apostle of Germany;" named a Doctor* of the Church (died 1597).

1559 The Act of Supremacy was enacted in England, making the Anglican Church the state religion with the ruler as head of the church.

1721 Innocent XIII became pope, serving until 1724.

1786 St. Jean Baptiste Vianney, Catholic priest, was born in Dardilly, France; noted for supernatural powers ascribed to him; known as the Cure d'Arts, patron of parish priests, thousands of whom came each year to seek his counsel; canonized 1925 (died 1859).

1792 A Moravian mission was established by David Zeisberger at Oxford in Upper Canada.

1842 Michael Power was consecrated as the first Catholic Bishop of Toronto.

1845 The Virginia Baptist Foreign Missionary Society called for a consultative convention in Augusta, Ga. and 293 delegates from nine states organized the Southern Baptist Convention, with Dr. W. B. Johnson of South Carolina president.

1894 (Alfred) Edwin Morris, fifth Archbishop of Wales (1957-71), was born in Lye, England; Bishop of Llandaff (1931-34), of Monmouth (1945-57) (died 1971).

1895 Fulton J. Sheen, Catholic prelate, was born in El Paso, Ill.; auxiliary bishop of New York (1951-66); a celebrated radio, television personality (The Catholic Hour 1930-52); national director, Society for the Propagation of Faith (1950-67); Bishop of Rochester, N.Y. (1966-69) (died 1979).

1898 Alojzije Stepinac, Yugoslav Catholic prelate, was born in Croatia; Archbishop of Zagreb (1937-45); a symbol of the fight for religious freedom against the Nazis, jailed from 1945 to 1951; elevated to cardinal 1952 (died 1960).

1959 Archbishop Egidio Vagnozzi, the seventh apostolic delegate to the United States, arrived.

1970 The first woman in the history of the Canadian Unitarian Council, Mrs. Mary Lu MacDonald, was elected president at the annual meeting in Toronto.

1982 Rev. Billy Graham, against the urging of the Reagan Administration, spent five days preaching in Moscow.

1984 Benjamin Weir, American Presbyterian clergyman, was kidnapped in Beirut, Lebanon; released Sept. 9, 1985.

MAY 9

Feast day in the Catholic Church of St. Gregory of Nazianzus (in Cappadocia, eastern Asia Minor) (about 330-390), one of the great Doctors* of the Church and one of the Cappadocian Fathers; one of the greatest champions of orthodoxy against Arianism*; author (Theological Orations, On His Life).

Feast day in the Orthodox Church of St. Christopher, patron of wayfarers.

1707 Dietrich Buxtenhude, Danish organist and composer of church music, died at about 70; exerted great influence on church organ music and church cantatas.

1797 Walter Colton, Congregational clergyman and founder of *The Californian,* the first California newspaper, was born in Rutland, Vt.; served as a Navy chaplain (1831-51) (died 1851).

1852 The first American Catholic plenary council was convened in Baltimore with representatives from six metropolitan and 27 suffragan sees, an abbot and superiors of many religious orders; represented a membership of an estimated 1.6 million.

1869 Alexander III, Greek Orthodox patriarch of Antioch and All the East (1930-58), was born in Damascus (died 1958).

1882 Edward F. Mooney, Catholic prelate, was born in Mt. Savage, Md.; named archbishop and apostolic delegate to India (1926-31), to Japan (1931-33); Archbishop of Rochester (1933-37), first Archbishop of Detroit (1937-46), elevated to cardinal 1946 (died 1958).

1902 William Howard Taft was sent to Rome to negotiate with the pope for the sale of friars lands in the Philippines and withdrawal of the friars; pope declared it was impossible to withdraw the 40 orders of friars.

1906 Episcopal Rev. Algernon S. Crapsey was found guilty of heresy; suspended from office May 15, formally dismissed from the ministry Dec 5.

1939 Kateri Tekakwitha, the "lily of the Mohawks," was beatified in Rome.

1969 The Catholic Church issued a revised liturgical calendar that eliminated more than 200 saints.

1971 The new patriarch of the Church of Ethiopia, Abuna Theophilos, was enthroned.

1988 Pope John Paul II warned bishops in Bolivia to protect Catholics from evangelical preachers on his arrival for a five-day visit.

MAY 10

Feast day of St. Antoninus (Antonio), Archbishop of Florence (1446-59); a founder of modern moral theology and Christian social ethics.

Feast day in the Orthodox Church of St. Simon, one of the apostles.

946 Agapetus II was named pope; served until 955; hampered in his reign by the power of Alberic, the secular master of Rome.

1569 St. Juan de Avila, Spanish missionary and ascetic writer, died at 69; known as the "apostle of Andalusia;" canonized 1970; also observed as his feast day.

1793 Robert E. B. Baylor, Baptist clergyman who helped found the Baptist Education Society and Baylor U., was born in Lincoln County, Ky.; served as a U.S. district judge (1845-61) (died 1873).

1818 Arthur Cleveland Coxe, Episcopal prelate and author, was born in Mendham, N.J.; Bishop of Western New York (1865-96); wrote numerous hymns (How beauteous were the marks; O where are kings and empires now?); author (Christian Ballads) (died 1896).

1843 Kaufman Kohler, rabbi and educator, was born in Furth, Germany; president, Hebrew Union College, Cincinnati (1903-21); served Sinai Temple, Chicago (1872-79), Temple Beth-el, New York City (1879-1903); a leader of American Reformed Judaism (died 1926).

1886 Karl Barth, Protestant theologian, was born in Basel, Switzerland; professor at Bonn (1900-34), left after refusing to take oath of allegiance to Hitler; acknowledged leader of the "theology of crisis;" distinguished for the revolution he wrought in 20th Century Protestant theology, trying to lead theology away from what he believed to be the fundamentally erroneous outlook of modern religious philosophy and bring it back to the principles of the Reformation; one of the most influential forces in modern religious thought; author (The Word of God and Theology, Christian Doctrine, I Believe) (died 1968).

1895 Sir Israel Brodie, chief rabbi, United Hebrew Congregations of the British Empire (1948-65), was born in Newcastle-on-Tyne, England (died 1979).

1939 The Methodist Episcopal Church, the Methodist Episcopal Church South, and the Methodist Protestant Church issued a declaration of union in Kansas City, Mo. to form the Methodist Church with more than 8 million members.

1963 The Balzan Peace Prize was awarded to Pope John XXIII.

MAY 11

Feast day in the Orthodox Church of Sts. Cyril and Methodius, Greek brothers and missionaries to the Slavs; reputed to have invented the Cyrillic alphabet and translated the Gospels and liturgical books into Old Slavonic.

603 St. Comgall, founder and first abbot of Bangor and founder of Irish monasticism, died; also observed as his feast day.

1313 Robert Winchelsey (or Winchelsea), Archbishop of Canterbury (1293-1313), died at about 68; strenuously upheld privileges of the clergy and papal authority.

1682 General Court of Massachusetts repealed laws which (1) banned observing Christmas and (2) provided capital punishment for returning Quakers.

1788 Henry Cooke, Irish Presbyterian leader, was born in County Down, Ireland; successfully led orthodox drive to exclude Arianism* from Irish Presbyterian churches and colleges (died 1868).

1816 The American Bible Society was formed in New York City by delegates from 35 Bible societies.

1825 The American Tract Society was organized in New York City.

1961 The American Unitarian Assn and the Universalist Church of America officially became the Unitarian Universalist Association.

MAY 12

Feast day of St. Epiphanius (about 315-402), Bishop of Constantia (367-402); founded and headed a monastery in Palestine; champion of traditionalistic orthodoxy; author of a treatise on heresies (Panarion).

Feast day of St. Germanus, patriarch of Constantinople (715-730), who led resistance against iconoclasm*.

254 St. Stephen I was elected pope, served to 257; defended the validity of heretic baptism.

1003 Sylvester II, pope from 999 to 1003, died.

1012 Sergius IV, pope from 1009 to 1012, died.

1328 Nicholas V, born Pietro Rainalducci, was named antipope by Louis of Bavaria; imprisoned (1330) until his death (1333).

1671 Erdmann Neumeister, Lutheran theologian and hymnist, was born near Leipzig; a vehement antagonist of Pietism*; remembered for several hymns (Jesus, great and wondrous star; Sinners Jesus will receive) (died 1756).

1753 Georg Gleig, Episcopal prelate, was born in Boghall, Scotland; Bishop of Brechin (1808-40), primus (presiding bishop) of Scotland Episcopal Church (1816-37) (died 1840).

1802 Henri Lacordaire, Dominican leader, was born in Receu-sur-Ource, France; re-established Dominican Order in France, becoming its provincial; renowned for his sermons at Notre Dame (died 1861).

1816 George L. Prentiss, Presbyterian clergyman and educator, was born in Gorham, Me.; organizer and pastor, Church of the Covenant, New York City (1862-73); professor, Union Theological Seminary (1873-91), of which he wrote a history (died 1903).

1827 Gustav Gottheil, Reformed rabbi, was born in Pinne, Poland; rabbi, Temple Emanu-el, New York City (1875-1901); a founder, Jewish Theological Seminary, New York City; active in founding Federation of American Zionists (1898) (died 1903).

1848 Peter T. Forsyth, theologian and educator, was born in Aberdeen, Scotland; outstanding Scottish Congregationalist theologian, educator; served as chairman of the Congregational Union of England and Wales (died 1921).

1865 Bernard Levinthal, rabbi, was born in Vilna, Russia; served Philadelphia congregation (from 1891); founder, president of Orthodox Rabbinical Association of America (died 1952).

1866 William T. Manning, Episcopal prelate, was born in Northampton, England; rector of Trinity Church, New York City (1908-21), Bishop of New York (1921-46) (died 1949).

1880 John Henry Newman, a leader of the Oxford Movement, was elevated to a Catholic cardinal.

1887 Society of Jesus (Jesuits) was reconstituted and rechartered in Quebec Province.

1950 Rose Philippine Duchesne, founder of the first convent of the Sacred Heart in the New World, was beatified in St. Charles, Mo.

1972 Pope Paul VI gave national and regional hierarchies a stronger role in the selection of bishops, although the final decision remained with the Pope and the Roman Curia.

1982 Portuguese police seized a man dressed in clerical garb and carrying a knife as he moved toward Pope John Paul II, who was visiting the Shrine of Fatima.

1985 The first woman Conservative rabbi, Amy Eilberg, 30, was ordained during graduation ceremonies at the Jewish Theological Seminary in New York City.

MAY 13

Former feast day of St. Robert Bellarmine, Italian cardinal and noted theologian; now observed May 17.

609 All Saints Day festival was instituted by Pope Boniface IV; date later changed to Nov. 1 when Pope Gregory III dedicated a chapel in St. Peters to all saints; made a universal observance in 835 by Pope Gregory IV.

649 Theodore I, pope from 642 to 649, died.

1615 Innocent XII, pope from 1691 to 1700, was born as Antonio Pignatelli in Spinazzola, Italy.

1638 Richard Simon, French biblical critic, was born in Dieppe; pioneered modern biblical study; his critical history of the New Testament brought angry responses from both Catholics and Protestants (died 1712).

1655 Innocent XIII, pope from 1721 to 1724, was born as Michelangelo Conti in Poli, Italy.

1742 Manasseh Cutler, Congregational clergyman, was born in Killingly, Conn.; served congregation at Ipswich Hamlet (now Hamilton), Mass. (1771-1823); prepared account of New England flora; an organizer of Ohio Co. to colonize the Ohio River Valley and helped draft Ordinance of 1787 for governing the Northwest Territory (died 1823).

1779 Jacob Bunting, English Wesleyan clergyman, was born in Manchester; fought to retain ministerial supervision of the church; his main work was to transform the Methodist Society into a church with a sound and consolidated organization, independent of the Church of England; president of the first Wesleyan Theological College (Hoxton 1835-58) (died 1858).

1792 Pius IX, pope from 1846 to 1879, was born as Giovanni Maria Mastai-Ferretti near Ravenna, Italy.

1834 St. Andrew Hubert Fournet died; co-founder of the Daughters of the Cross; canonized 1933; also observed as his feast day.

1836 Bishop Jean Jacques Lartigne was named the first Catholic Bishop of Montreal.

1842 Sir Arthur S. Sullivan, noted English composer, was born in London; best known for his operettas (Gilbert and Sullivan) and "The Lost Chord;" wrote numerous hymns (Onward, Christian soldiers; Angel voices, ever singing; Draw Thou my soul, O Christ; Come ye faithful, raise the strain) (died 1900).

1860 Percy S. Grant, ultra-liberal Episcopal clergyman, was born in Boston; served Church of the Ascension, New York City (1893-1924), which became a forum for the expression of views on social conditions; became radical leader among the clergy; engaged in doctrinal dispute with Bishop William T. Manning (1923), resigned (1924) (died 1927).

1873 Mexico decreed that no religious rite may take place outside church buildings.

1889 Teodosio Clemente DeGouveia, Archbishop of Mozambique (1941-62), was born in Sao Jorge, Madeira; elevated to cardinal 1946 (died 1962).

1925 A bill requiring daily Bible readings in all public schools was passed by the Florida legislature.

1931 Jim (James W.) Jones, Peoples Temple cult leader, was born in Lynn, Ind.; Temple with 900 members ended in mass suicide and murder in Guyana after Congressman Ryan and three others were killed after visiting the Temple.

1967 Archimandrite Ieronymos Kotsonis, professor of canon law and chaplain to King Constantine, was chosen Archbishop of Athens and primate of Greece.

1981 Pope John Paul II, while riding in an open car in St. Peters Square in Rome, was wounded by a gun-wielding assailant.

MAY 14

Feast day of St. Michael Garicoïts, founder of the Priests of the Sacred Heart of Bétharram (1838).

Feast day of St. Matthias, the apostle chosen to replace Judas Iscariot.

Feast day in the Catholic Church of St. Pachomius (about 290-346), founder (about 318) of the coenobitic* Christian monastic community on an island in the Nile, whose members agreed to abide by the rules of conduct established by him.

Feast day of Blessed Magdalen di Canossa, founder of the Canossan Daughters of Charity (1808); beatified 1941.

964 John XII, pope from 955 to 964, died.

1572 Gregory XIII was named pope, served until 1585; reign marked by reform of the Julian calendar (1582) and the Gregorian calendar is still in use; established permanent papal nuncios in principal countries; vigorous opponent of Protestantism; strengthened the Jesuits; revised canon law.

1752 Timothy Dwight, Congregational clergyman, was born in Northampton, Mass., the grandson of Jonathan Edwards; served Greenfield (Conn.) Church (1783-95); eighth president of

Yale U. (1795-1817); author (Theology, Explained and Defended); wrote the hymn "I love Thy Kingdom, Lord" (died 1817).

1754 John Leland, pioneer Baptist clergyman, was born in Grafton, Mass.; led assault on privileges of Anglican clergy in Virginia; author, "Short Essays on Government," which advocated separation of church and state (died 1841).

1835 James Drummond, Unitarian theologian, was born in Dublin; advocated doctrinal freedom, rejected the Resurrection and nature miracles; taught at Manchester College (died 1918).

1864 Adam C. Welch, one of the greatest Scottish biblical scholars, was born in Jamaica, the son of a Presbyterian missionary; professor of Hebrew and Old Testament interpretation at New College, Edinburgh; developed new theory of the growth of Israel's religion (died 1943).

1872 Elia Dalla Costa, Archbishop of Florence (1931-61), was born in Vicenza, Italy; elevated to cardinal 1933; credited with having saved art treasures and city of Florence from World War II damage (died 1961).

1881 St. Mary Mazzarello died at 44; co-founder of Daughters of Our Lady Help of Christians (1872); canonized 1951; also observed as her feast day.

1899 Dr. Charles A. Briggs, suspended from the Presbyterian Church (1893) on charges of heresy, was ordained as an Episcopal clergyman.

1902 (Helen) Flanders Dunbar, leader in American psychosomatic and clinical pastoral education movement, was born in Chicago; director, Joint Commission on Religion and Medicine of the Federal Council of Churches and the New York Academy of Medicine (died 1959).

1905 Joseph T. O'Callahan, Catholic chaplain aboard the aircraft carrier Franklin (1945) when it was bombed by the Japanese, was born in Roxbury, Mass.; his valor earned him the Congressional Medal of Honor (died 1964).

1956 Pope Pius XII approved the transplanting of corneas from the eyes of dead persons to restore the sight of the blind.

1961 Pope John XXIII urged a well-planned and boldly-executed worldwide attack on hunger and poverty.

1965 Metropolitan Leonty, American primate of the Russian Orthodox Greek Catholic Church of America, died at 88.

1978 Leaders of the Greek Orthodox Church considered suspending their membership in the World Council of Churches because of it being run "by a Protestant elite."

MAY 15

Feast day in the Orthodox Church of St. Pachomius, founder of coenobitic* Christian monasticism.

Former feast day of St. Jean Baptiste de LaSalle, French founder of the Brothers of the Christian Schools; now observed April 7.

884 Marinus I (also known as Martin II), pope from 882 to 884, died.

1796 The day predicted for the Second Coming by Congregational clergyman David Austin; he waited all day with his congregation in Elizabeth, N.J. and then preached on the text, "My Lord delayeth His coming."

1816 Sylvanus D. Phelps, Baptist clergyman and hymn writer, was born in Suffield, Conn.; pastor, First Baptist Church, New Haven; among his hymns is "Savior, Thy dying love" (died 1895).

1817 The first general convention of the New Jerusalem Church in America was held in Philadelphia.

1817 Debendranath Tagore, Indian philosopher, was born in Calcutta; known as the "Maharshi," great sage or seer; leader of the movement to reform Hinduism (died 1905).

1823 Thomas L. Harris, Universalist clergyman and mystic, was born in Fenny Stratford, England; after attempts at two cooperative communities, he founded the Independent Christian Congregation, New York City (1848) (died 1924).

1846 Philo M. Buck, pioneer Methodist missionary to India (1870-1914), was born in Corning, N.Y.; superintendent, Meernt District (1893-1914) (died 1924).

1866 Karl Holl, German theologian, was born in Tübingen; his erudite study of Luther's doctrine gave a new direction to Luther interpretation and remains a classic work on the subject (died 1926).

1876 The New York Society of Ethical Culture was founded by Felix Adler; the first society of the Ethical Culture movement, it emphasized "deed rather than creed" and applied itself to education and social reform.

1880 (F. K.) Otto Dibelius, Evangelical (Lutheran) Bishop of Berlin and staunch anti-Nazi and anti-Communist worker (1945-66), was born in Berlin; a founder, first chairman (1949-61) of the German Evangelical Church Council (died 1967).

1888 Catholic Bishop John Ireland of St. Paul, Minn., was elevated to archbishop.

1891 Pope Leo XIII issued the encyclical, "Revum novarum," rejected both the Marxist theory of class conflict and the laissez-faire capitalism of the 19th Century European liberalism.

1926 The Mexican Government ordered the deportation of the papal envoy, Msgr. George Caruana, who had entered the country without disclosing his identity.

1931 Pope Pius XI issued the encyclical, "Quadragesimo anno," reaffirming and elaborating the theses of Leo XIII on social and economic matters.

1972 The U.S. Supreme Court ruled 7-0 that the Amish religious sect is exempt from state compulsory education laws requiring children to attend school beyond the eighth grade; such compulsion was said to violate the constitutional rights to freedom of religion.

1978 The U.S. Supreme Court let stand a decision denying a Quaker conscientious objector the right, on the basis of religious convictions, to refuse to pay part of his income taxes that went to finance the Vietnam War.

MAY 16

Feast day of St. Brendan, Irish saint and hero of legendary voyages in the Atlantic during the Fifth and Sixth centuries; founder and head of a monastery in Cloufert, County Galway (557-577).

Feast day of St. John of Nepomuk (about 1340-1393), patron saint of Bohemia.

1265 St. Simon Stock, general of the Carmelite Order (about 1247-65), died; also observed as his feast day.

1605 Paul V became pope, served until 1621; promoted church reforms set up by the Council of Trent, completed St. Peter's Basilica, enlarged the Quirinal Palace and Vatican Library; weakened papal authority by his struggle with Venice.

1611 Blessed Innocent XI, pope from 1676 to 1689, was born as Benedetto Odescalchi in Como, Italy.

1843 Robert Morison, Scottish theologian, helped his son, James, organize a new denomination, the Evangelical Union, in Kilmarnock, Scotland; the new group was called Morisonians, who broke from Calvinism.

1862 Elwood Worcester, Episcopal clergyman, was born in Massillon, Ohio; while rector of Emmanuel Church, Boston (1904-29), he developed the theory that a combination of religion and medicine could help cure nervous disorders (known as the Emmanuel Movement) (died 1940).

1885 David D. Pool, rabbi of Shearith Israel, New York City synagogue for Spanish and Portuguese (1907-55), was born in London (died 1970).

1920 The canonization of Joan of Arc was celebrated in Rome.

MAY 17

Feast day of St. Robert Bellarmine, Italian cardinal and theologian.

352 Liberius became pope, served until 366.

884 St. Adrian III, born Agapetus, was elected pope, served until 885; dealt severely with factious Roman nobility; died enroute to Worms to help settle the question of succession.

1410 John XXIII was elected pope, served until 1415; deposed by the Council of Constance.

1630 John Howe, Puritan clergyman, was born in Loughborough, England; domestic chaplain to Oliver Cromwell and his son, Richard; noted for his ecumenical efforts; author (The Living Temple of God) (died 1705).

1791 Richard P. Miles, Catholic Bishop of Nashville (1837-60), was born in Prince Georges County, Md.; built numerous schools, hospitals and churches (died 1860).

1794 Frederic Monod, French Protestant leader, was born in Switzerland; founder (1849) of the Free Church of France (died 1863).

1831 Robert Machray, Anglican bishop, was born in Aberdeen, Scotland; first primate of the Church of England in Canada (died 1904).

1838 William H. Hare, Episcopal prelate, was born in Princeton, N.J.; missionary Bishop of Niobrara (Nebraska, Dakotas) for 37 years; known as the "apostle of the Sioux" (died 1909).

1844 Julius Wellhausen, Old Testament scholar, was born near Hanover, Germany; his theory produced a revolution in Old Testament criticism (died 1918).

1881 New Church Theological School was incorporated by the New Jerusalem Church; originally in Waltham, Mass., it was later moved to Boston, then Cambridge.

1881 Gavrilo, Serbian Orthodox leader, was born; patriarch of Yugoslavia (1938-50) (died 1950).

1882 Sisters of Charity of the North West Territories was incorporated.

1925 St. Therese of Lisieux, French nun, was canonized.

1936 Nahum Sokolow, Jewish author and Zionist leader, died at 75; president, World Zionist Organization (1931-35); led Zionist delegation to Paris conference (1919), instrumental in obtaining minority rights for Jews in Europe.

1947 The Conservative Baptist Association of America was formed in Atlantic City, N.J.

1964 Pope Paul VI announced the formation of a special Vatican secretariat to maintain relations with the world's non-Christian religions.

MAY 18

Feast day of St. Eric, patron of Sweden.

526 St. John I, pope from 523 to 526, died.

1631 The General Court of Massachusetts decreed that "no man shall be admitted to the body politic but such as are members of some of the churches within the limits" of the colony.

1692 Joseph Butler, Anglican prelate, was born near Oxford, England; served as Bishop of Bristol, Durham, and dean of St. Paul's (1740-50); ranks among the greatest exponents of natural theology and ethics in England since the Reformation; influential author (Analogy of Religion, Sermons on Human Nature) (died 1752).

1766 The Church of the United Brethren in Christ was formed in Lancaster, Pa.

1769 Clement XIV was elected pope, served until 1774; issued apostolic brief (1773) suppressing the Jesuits; founded the Clementine Museum at the Vatican.

1834 Sheldon Jackson, Presbyterian missionary, was born in Minaville, N.Y.; served as missionary, superintendent of missions in the Great Plains and mountain states; after 1877, his main interest was Alaska, where he helped secure legislation for a territorial government (died 1909).

1843 The Free Church of Scotland came into existence when 203 members of the General Assembly of the Church of Scotland marched out of St. Andrew's Church and into Tanfield Hall, a half mile away, and constituted themselves into the Free Church; Thomas Chalmers was named moderator by acclamation.

1868 Edward L. Parsons, Episcopal Bishop of California (1924- 41), was born in New York City (died 1960).

1894 The General Assembly of the Presbyterian Church, meeting in Washington, reconsidered heresy charges against Dr. Charles A. Briggs; reversed the acquittal by the New York Presbytery and formally suspended him (June 1) from the ministry.

1920 John Paul II, elected pope in 1978, was born in Wodowice, Poland as Karol Wojtyla.

1926 Aimee Semple McPherson, founder of the International Church of the Foursquare Gospel in Los Angeles, disappeared at the beach; it seemed she had drowned but a month later she turned up in Mexico, claiming she had been kidnapped; it developed that she had run off with a former operator of her radio station.

1967 The new Methodist Church of the Caribbean and the Americas was inaugurated in Antigua.

1982 Rev. Billy Graham was awarded the Templeton Prize for Progress in Religion at a ceremony in Buckingham Palace.

MAY 19

715 Gregory II was elected pope, served until 731; sent St. Boniface to preach in Germany, renovated churches, and encouraged monastic life.

804 Alcuin, English educator and theologian, died at about 69; preceptor (teacher) of the palace school of Charlemagne (782-796), which kept learning alive during the Dark Ages; his edition of Gregorian Sacramentary was a basis for the Roman Missal, helping attain some uniformity in Western Christendom liturgy.

988 St. Dunstan, Archbishop of Canterbury (959-988), died at about 79; treasurer and chief advisor to King Eldred, thus virtually ruler of the kingdom; driven out by Edwy (955-57); recalled and made Bishop of London, then Archbishop of Canterbury; rebuilt the abbey of Dunstan, reformed monastic life; also observed as his feast day.

1296 Pope Celestine V, who only served five months in 1294 and resigned, died; canonized 1313; also observed as his feast day.

1303 St. Yves of Brittany, French lawyer and cleric, died at 50; patron saint of lawyers; also observed as his feast day.

1805 Joshua V. Himes, Christian clergyman and a leader in the Second Advent movement, was born; pastor of several Christian churches in Boston (1830-42); became chief assistant and publicist to William Miller, who predicted the Second Coming in 1843 and 1844 (died 1895).

1819 The Jesuits were reinstated in Mexico under a royal decree of Sep. 17, 1815.

1880 The U. S. Supreme Court upheld the right of the government to dissolve the Mormon Church Corporation.

1923 Cardinal Robert Bellarmine was beatified.

1925 Malcolm X, Muslim leader, was born in Omaha as Malcolm Little; leader of the Black Muslims (1963-64); founder, Organization of Afro-American Unity (1964); assassinated Feb. 21, 1965.

1930 Bishop James Cannon Jr. was exonerated by the Methodist Episcopal Church of stock market manipulation charges.

1956 Pope Pius XII condemned artificial insemination as immoral and absolutely illicit.

1968 Nicholas enthroned as the new Orthodox patriarch of Alexandria in the Cairo Cathedral.

1972 The United Presbyterian Church in the U.S.A. voted 411 to 310 to withdraw from the Consultation on Church Union, formed more than a decade earlier to seek a merger of the major Protestant denominations.

1976 Thelma D. Adair was elected moderator of the United Presbyterian Church in the U.S.A., the first black woman to hold that office.

MAY 20

Feast day of St. Yves (or Ivo) of Chartres, most learned canonist of his day; Bishop of Chartres (1090-1116); upheld rights of the church against royal encroachment; compiled a collection of canon law.

Feast day of St. Ethelbert, king of East Anglia (in England), murdered (about 974) by King Offa of Mercia, whose daughter he sought to marry; venerated at Hereford as patron of its cathedral.

325 First Council of Nicaea opened to deal with the Arian* controversy; ended July 25.

1277 Pope John XXI died of injuries sustained when the ceiling in his castle collapsed on him; had served since 1276.

1444 St. Bernardino of Siena, Italian Franciscan theologian, died; a leading promoter of the Franciscan Order of the Observant, serving as vicar general (1437-44); canonized 1450; also observed as his feast day.

1470 Pietro Bembo, cardinal and author on linguistics, was born in Venice; elevated to cardinal 1539; served as Bishop of Gubbio (also called Eugubium, southeast of Florence) (1541-44) and Bergamo (1544-47); author of "Discussions of the Italian Language," which restored the classic tradition in Italian language and literature (died 1547).

1690 John Eliot, English missionary to the American Indians for 30 years, died; published an Indian language catechism (1653) and the Bible (1661-63), which was the first Bible published in America.

1806 Edward R. Ames, Methodist prelate, was born in Amesville, Ohio; served as bishop (1852-79); founder of seminary at Lebanon, Ill., which became McKendree College (died 1879).

1825 Antoinette L. B. Blackwell, social reformer and pastor, was born in Henrietta, N.Y.; reportedly the first woman to serve as a regularly-appointed pastor (Congregational Church, South Butler, N.Y.) (died 1921).

1851 Mother Alphonsa, originally Rose Hawthorne, the youngest daughter of author Nathaniel Hawthorne, was born in Lenox, Mass.; founder of Servants of Relief for Incurable Cancer and a home in Hawthorne, N.Y., where she served from 1901 to her death in 1926.

1903 The French Chamber of Deputies rejected a motion (278- 247) for the separation of church and state.

1960 The Southern Baptist Convention criticized the election of Catholics to public office, stating: "When a public official is inescapably bound by the dogma and demands of his church, he cannot consistently separate himself from these."

1973 The Cathedral Church of St. John the Divine in New York City celebrated its 100th anniversary and installed the Very Rev. J. P. Morton as its new dean.

1978 The Museum of the Jewish Diaspora, tracing the history and life of the Jews over the centuries, opened at Tel Aviv University.

1979 The Mormon Church announced it would build a religious complex at its founding site near Waterloo, N.Y. to commemorate the 150th anniversary of the church.

MAY 21

Feast day in the Orthodox Church of St. Helena (died about 330), reputed discoverer of Christ's cross, and of her son, Constantine I the Great; the cross was said to have been discovered when Constantine was building his church on Golgotha.

1541 Johannes Faber of Leutkirch, Catholic prelate, died at 63; a friend of Erasmus and a onetime sympathizer with Zwingli and Melancthon; later became a vigorous opponent of Lutherans; served as Bishop of Vienna, envoy to Spain and England.

1738 Charles Wesley, co-founder of Methodism, said he found himself "at peace with God" and two days later wrote his "conversion hymn" — "Where shall my wond'ring Soul begin? How shall I all to Heaven aspire?"

1780 Elizabeth Fry, English Quaker philanthropist, was born in Norfolk; a Quaker minister, she was active in prison reform; founded an order of nursing sisters (died 1845).

1841 Joseph Parry, Welsh hymn composer, was born in Merthyr, Wales; among his hymns are "Jesus, lover of my soul" and "Watchman, tell us of the night" (died 1903).

1846 The new Trinity Church in New York City was dedicated.

1908 Stephen F. Bayne, Episcopal prelate, was born in New York City; Bishop of Olympia (Wash.) (1947-59); executive officer of the Anglican Communion (1960), director of the Anglican overseas department (died 1974).

1964 Eller G. Hawkins, a black minister from New York, was elected moderator of the General Assembly of the United Presbyterian Church of the U.S.A.

1964 The Baptists met in Atlantic City to celebrate the 150th anniversary of the organization of the denomination's missionary work in North America.

1965 Very Rev. Pedro Arrupe was elected father general of the Society of Jesus (Jesuits) by the 30th general congregation meeting in Rome.

1965 Metropolitan Anastassy, primate of Russian Orthodox Church in America (1936-64), died in New York City at 91.

1967 General Assembly of the Presbyterian Church in the U.S.A. adopted the Confession of 1967, the first major new confession to be adopted by Presbyterians since the Westminster Confession of 1647.

1978 The General Assembly of the United Presbyterian Church in the U.S.A. overwhelmingly disapproved the ordination of avowed practicing homosexuals.

1980 The Egyptian Government held a nationwide referendum on amendments to the constitution that among other changes would make the Islamic religious code the principal source of legislation.

1988 Rev. Jimmy Swaggart preached for the first time since he lost his credentials as an Assemblies of God minister.

MAY 22

Feast day of Blessed Joachim de Mas y de Vedruna, Spanish-born founder of the Carmelites of Charity (1820); beatified 1940.

896 Stephen VI was elected pope, served until 897; imprisoned and then strangled (August 897) by revolting populace, which was shocked by his judgment of Formosa, his predecessor.

1667 Alexander VII, pope from 1655 to 1667, died at 68.

1715 Francois Joachim de Pierre de Bernis, French prelate and poet, was born; elevated to cardinal 1758; was Archbishop of Albi (47 miles northeast of Toulouse), ambassador to Rome, where he forced Pope Clement XIV to suppress the Jesuits (1773) (died 1794).

1772 Ram Mohun Roy, Indian religious reformer, was born in West Bengal; principal leader of the 19th Century renascence of Hinduism, founder of a reformed Hindu sect, the Brahmo Samaj; successfully led movement to ban the rite of suttee (death for the widow at her husband's funeral) (died 1833).

1786 Arthur Tappan, silk merchant and philanthropist, was born in Northampton, Mass.; a founder of American Missionary Assn. and the American Anti-Slavery Society; a donor of Lane Theological Seminary and Oberlin College (died 1865).

1789 The Presbyterian General Assembly held its first meeting in Philadelphia's Second Church.

1851 Emil G. Hirsch, liberal rabbi and educator, was born in Luxembourg; rabbi, Sinai Congregation, Chicago (1880-1923); first to have only a Sunday service in the synagogue; editor, *Reform Advocate* (1891-1923); professor of rabbinic philosophy, U. of Chicago (1892-1923) (died 1923).

1908 Leslie E. Cooke, associate general secretary, World Council of Churches (1955-67), was born in Brighton, England (died 1967).

MAY 23

230 St. Urban I, pope from 222 to 230, died.

1423 Benedict XIII, antipope from 1394 to 1423, died; pledged to end schism but resisted every effort to end the split in the papacy.

1498 Girolamo Savonarola was burned at the stake.

1555 Paul IV became pope, served until 1559; cofounder, first superior of the Order of Theatines (1524); continued reforms of Paul III, reorganized the Inquisition, of which he had charge as a cardinal; unpopular because of nepotism.

1810 Martin J. Spalding, Catholic prelate, was born near Lebanon, Ky.; Bishop of Louisville (1848-64), Archbishop of Baltimore (1864-72) (died 1872).

1844 Bab (Mirza Ali Muhammed) revealed his mission and formulated principles of Baha-i faith; held doctrine of spiritual unity of all peoples allowed for no racial or religious prejudice; a strong crusader for international peace.

1844 Abdul-Baha, foremost opponent of Bahai faith, was born, the son of Bahaullah, a founder of the faith; imprisoned in Turkish penal colony at Acre (1868-1908); succeeded father as Bahai leader (1892-1921); freed from prison by Young Turks, journeyed through the United States, Europe (1911-13) preaching the Bahai faith; lived in Palestine (1914-21) (died 1921).

1852 Cleland K. Nelson, Episcopal prelate, was born in Cobham, Va.; Bishop of Georgia (1892-1907), first Bishop of Atlanta (1907-17) (died 1917).

1862 Hermann Gunkel, Old Testament scholar, was born in Springe, Germany; one of the first to develop the method of form criticism (died 1932).

1960 The American Unitarian Association and the Universalist Church of America, in their national conventions in Boston, voted to approve merger of the churches.

1979 Members of the United Presbyterian Church in the U.S.A. and the Presbyterian Church in the United States took communion in a joint worship service, marking the first time the two churches came together to hold annual conventions since the church split over the Civil War issue of slavery.

MAY 24

Feast day of St. Vincent of Lérins (died about 450), noted for his memoranda responding to heresies, arguing that the final Christian truth is the Holy Scripture.

1089 Blessed Lanfranc, Italian-born Archbishop of Canterbury, died at about 84; served from 1070 to 1089; rebuilt the cathedral which had been destroyed by fire in 1067; established a library, compiled a book of constitutions for the monastic community; also observed as his feast day.

1430 Joan of Arc was captured and later tried before Pierre Cauchon, Bishop of Beauvais, who used inquisitorial procedures; condemned and was burned at the stake; condemnation was annulled July 7, 1456 and she was canonized 1920.

1689 The British Parliament passed the Act of Toleration, designed to relieve the legal disabilities of Protestant dissenters.

1738 John Wesley, co-founder of Methodism, underwent a personal experience while attending a meeting in Aldergate St., London; during the reading of Luther's Preface to the Epistle to the Romans, "I felt my heart strangely warmed. I felt I did trust in Christ...for salvation;...and an assurance was given me that He had taken away *my* sins...and saved *me* from the law of sin and death."

1768 Thomas Bacon, Anglican clergyman, died at about 68; served in Maryland and Delaware (1744-68); compiled the laws of Maryland (1765).

1807 Pope Pius VII canonized St. Angela Merici, founder of the Ursulines.

1810 Abraham Geiger, rabbi and theologian, was born in Frankfurt, Germany; led the Jewish reform movement in Germany, a pioneer in Reform Judaism (died 1874).

1876 Maurilio Fossati, Archbishop of Turin (1930-65), was born in Arona, Italy; elevated to cardinal 1933 (died 1965).

1877 Bishop George Conroy, apostolic delegate to Canada, arrived in Quebec.

1878 Harry Emerson Fosdick, spokesman for modern liberal Christianity, was born in Buffalo, N.Y.; pastor, First Baptist Church, Montclair, N.J. (1904-15); Riverside Church, New York City (1926-46); professor of practical theology, Union Theological Seminary (1908-46); author (The Manhood of the Master, The Meaning of Prayer, Successful Christian Living); wrote the hymn "God of grace, God of glory" (died 1969).

1882 Carlyle B. Haynes, Seventh Day Adventist clergyman, was born in Bristol, Conn.; president of various conferences, including Michigan, South America (died 1958).

1891 William F. Albright, biblical archaeologist and Near East scholar, was born in Coquimbo, Chile; noted for excavations at Gibesh and Sault, Tell-Beit Mirsim and others (died 1971).

1892 Cuthbert A. Simpson, theology professor and Anglican dean, was born in Charlottetown, Prince Edward Island; taught at General Theological Seminary, New York City, and Oxford; first American citizen to be made dean of an Anglican cathedral (Christ Church, Oxford) (died 1969).

1894 The trial of Professor Henry Preserved Smith (1847-1927) on heresy charges began before the Presbyterian General Assembly; convicted 306 to 101; professor of biblical literature, Amherst College (1898-1906), of religious history, Meadville Theological School (1907-13); librarian, Union Theological Seminary (1913-25); pioneer in modern biblical criticism in the United States.

1929 The general assemblies of the Church of Scotland and of the United Free Church of Edinburgh voted to unite as a national body, the Church of Scotland.

1956 Ceremonies throughout India celebrated the 2500th anniversary of Buddhism.

1962 The newly-formed Canadian Unitarian Council was approved as an official agency of the Unitarian Universalist Association.

1980 The Vatican issued an order seeking to suppress what it termed abuses in Catholic worship, such as the "manipulation of liturgical texts for social and political ends."

MAY 25

Feast day of St. Madelaine Sophie Barat, founder of the Society of the Sacred Heart.

Feast day of St. Boniface IV, pope from 608 to 615.

709 St. Aldhelm (Ealdhelm), English prelate, scholar and poet, died at about 69; founded monastic communities and several churches; wrote Latin verse, a treatise on Latin prosody, including his famous 101 riddles and English songs; his chief contribution was the extension of faith into southern England and his literary influence on the continent; canonized 1080; also observed as his feast day.

735 Bede (the Venerable), Anglo-Saxon theologian and the first great English scholar, died at about 63; spent most of his life (628-735) at the monastery at Jarrow; author (Ecclesiastical History of the English People); his works spread throughout Europe and won him the name of "the teacher of the Middle Ages."

1085 St. Gregory VII, pope from 1073 to 1085, died in exile in Salerno; his dying words: "I have loved justice and hated iniquity; therefore, I die in exile;" also observed as his feast day.

1085 Blessed Victor III, born Desidarius, was named pope by his predecessor, Gregory VII, who died this day; had been abbot of Monte Cassino (1057-68), during which 70 books were copied; consecrated pope May 9,1087 and reigned only until Sep.16,1087; convened synod at Capua.

1261 Alexander IV, pope from 1254 to 1261, died; ineffectual in dealing with serious political problems and during his reign Rome was lost to papal control; established the Inquisition in France; founded order of Augustinian hermits.

1510 Georges d'Amboise, French cardinal, died at 50; served as chief minister to King Louis XII and papal legate in France; ambitious to become pope but was passed over twice.

1528 Jakob Andrea, Lutheran theologian and writer, was born near Stuttgart; active promoter of Lutheran Church in Germany and in producing the "Formula of Concord," designed to end Lutheran discord (died 1590).

1550 Camillus de Lellis, founder of Ministers of the Sick (Camillians or Agonizants), was born in Buchianico, Italy; served as general of the order (1596-1604); canonized 1746 (died 1614).

1793 Stephen T. Badin became the first Catholic priest to be ordained in the United States; served as vicar general of Kentucky.

1803 Ralph Waldo Emerson, renowned American essayist, was born in Boston; served as a Unitarian clergyman (Second Church, Boston 1829-32); resigned over doctrinal differences; he was a connecting link between America's early theological and its later secular culture (died 1882).

1805 William Paley, English theologian and philosopher, died at 62; published lectures (Principles of Moral and Political Philosophy) which became the ethical textbook at Cambridge; also wrote arguments favoring existence of God, refutation of deists.

1810 William Henry Channing, Unitarian clergyman, was born in Boston, nephew of William Ellery Channing; served in camps, hospitals during the Civil War; editor, *The Present*, a Socialist periodical (1843-44); chaplain, House of Representatives (1863-64) (died 1884).

1824 Daniel K. Flickinger, missionary leader, was born in Sevenmile, Ohio; secretary, United Brethren Missionary Society (1857-85); missionary bishop (1885-89) (died 1911).

1825 The American Unitarian Association was organized in Federal St. Church, Boston.

1835 Henry C. Potter, Episcopal prelate, was born in Schenectady, N.Y., the son of Alonzo Potter; Bishop of New York (1887-1908), launched the building of the Cathedral of St. John the Divine (died 1908).

1847 John A. Dowie, Scottish faith healer and church founder, was born in Edinburgh; founder of the Christian Catholic Apostolic Church and Zion City, north of Chicago; proclaimed himself Elijah the Restorer; eventually deposed by a revolt of his followers (died 1907).

1865 John R. Mott, YMCA and missionary leader, was born in Livingston Manor, N.Y.; general secretary, YMCA (1915-31), head of American YMCA Council, world alliance (1926-37); founder, Foreign Missions Conference (1893); general secretary, World's Student Christian Federation (1892-1920), chairman (1920-28); chairman, International Missionary Council (1921-42); played important role in founding the World Council of Churches, honorary president at its first meeting (1948); shared 1946 Nobel Peace Prize (died 1955).

1879 Cyril C. Martindale, most famous English Jesuit of the 20th Century, was born in Kensington, England; involved in Catholic international university movement and planning eucharistic congresses (died 1963).

1879 St. Patrick's Cathedral in New York City was dedicated.

1892 The General Assembly of the Presbyterian Church considered heresy charge against Dr. Charles A. Briggs; remanded matter to New York Presbytery.

1914 Archbishop Louis N. Bégin of Quebec was elevated to cardinal.

1926 Our Lady of Victory Shrine and church in Lackawanna, N.Y. was consecrated as a basilica.

1930 Randall Thomas Davidson, former Archbishop of Canterbury, died at 82.

1950 The North American Baptist Association was organized in Little Rock, Ark. to encourage and foster missionary cooperation.

1975 Pope Paul VI proclaimed the sainthood of St. John Baptist de la Concepcion, Spanish preacher of the counter-reformation movement, and St. Vincenta Maria Lopez Vicuna, 19th Century Spanish nun who founded the Daughters of St. Mary Immaculate.

MAY 26

Feast day in England and Wales of St. Augustine, first Archbishop of Canterbury (about 601 to between 604 and 609); known as the "apostle of the English;" sent to England by Pope Gregory I with 40 monks.

Feast day of St. Eleutherius, pope from 175 to 189.

Feast day of St. Quadratus, the earliest (Second Century) Christian apologist.

1478 Clement VII, pope from 1523 to 1534, was born in Florence, Italy as Giulio de Medici, a cousin of Pope Leo X; his reign was marked by shifty diplomacy and intrigue; a procrastinator, he delayed so long on the request of Henry VIII to annul his marriage to Catherine of Aragon that Henry broke with the church; a similar delay in reforms encouraged the spread of Protestantism.

1595 St. Philip Neri, a leader in the counter-Reformation and founder of the Institute of Oratory (Oratorians), died at 80; also observed as his feast day.

1647 Catholic priests were forbidden to enter the territory under Puritan jurisdiction under a Massachusetts law; the first offense would result in banishment, the second death.

1700 Count Nikolaus Zinzendorf, German religious and social reformer, was born in Dresden;

reorganized the Unitas Fratrum* into the Moravian Brethren (Renewed Church of the United Brethren); established Moravian congregations in Pennsylvania; wrote several hymns (O Thou to whose all-searching light; Jesus still leads us) (died 1760).

1745 Jonathan Edwards Jr., son of the noted colonial preacher, was born in Northampton, Mass.; pastor, White Haven Church, New Haven (1769-95); president, Union College, Schenectady, N.Y. (1799-1801); chiefly remembered for "New England Theory of Atonement" (died 1801).

1845 Samuel J. Barrows, Unitarian editor (*Christian Register* 1880-96), was born in New York City; helped in passage of New York's first probation law, a federal parole law (died 1909).

1863 Shailer Mathews, theologian, was born in Portland, Me.; a leader in Social Gospel movement; dean, U. of Chicago Divinity School (1908-33); author (Patriotism and Religion) (died 1941).

1927 The founder of the Christian Endeavor Society, Rev. Francis E. Clark, died at 75 in Newton, Mass.

MAY 27

Feast day of St. Bede the Venerable (673-735), Anglo-Saxon theologian who epitomized the early brilliant flowering of Christianity and culture; named a Doctor* of the Church 1899.

Feast day of St. John I, pope from 523 to 526.

535 John II, pope from 533 to 535, died.

1329 Pope John XXII issued the bull, "In agro dominico," condemning various propositions of Meister Eckhart (about 1260-1327), who founded German mysticism; as Dominican vicar general, provincial, he championed a type of pantheistic philosophy.

1464 Isidore of Kiev, metropolitan of Russian Orthodox Church (1435-39), died at about 79; an architect of the reunion of the Catholic and Russian Orthodox churches (1439); elevated to cardinal; papal legate to Greece (1444-48) and Constantinople (1453-59); titular patriarch of Constantinople (1459-64).

1564 John Calvin died at 55.

1663 Thomas Emlyn, dissenting English clergyman, was born in Stamford, England; the first English minister of religion to publicly adopt the name Unitarian and the last dissenter to be imprisoned (died 1741).

1668 Three Baptists - Thomas Gold, William Turner, and John Farnum-were banished by the General Court of Massachusetts.

1705 Michael Wigglesworth, English-born Puritan clergyman and author, died at 74; later Congregational pastor in Malden (1656-1705); author of theological verse (The Day of Doom).

1796 Henry B. Bascom, Methodist prelate and teacher, was born in Hancock, N.Y.; president, Madison College, Uniontown, Pa. (1827-29), Transylvania U., Lexington, Ky. (1842-49); chaplain to U.S. Congress (1824-26); an organizer of the Methodist Episcopal Church, South, and Bishop of Kentucky (1850) (died 1850).

1799 George W. Doane, Episcopal prelate, was born; Bishop of New Jersey (1832-59), a leader of the High Church party; author of many hymns (Softly now, the light of day; Thou art the way; Father of mercies, hear) (died 1859).

1819 Julia Ward Howe, author and lecturer, was born in New York City; best known for "The Battle Hymn of the Republic" (died 1910).

1821 Sir Henry W. Baker, English clergyman and hymn writer, was born in London; editor of "Hymns Ancient and Modern," the most representative collection of hymns in use in the Church of England, to which he contributed 25 originals and translated hymns (Thy king of love my shepherd is; O God of love, O king of peace; Art thou weary, art thou languid) (died 1877).

1857 Belleville Seminary of the Methodist Episcopal Church was chartered.

1892 Archbishop Michael (Thucydides Constantinides) of the Greek Orthodox Church of North and South America was born in Maroneia, Greece; named spiritual leader of about 1 million Americans of Greek descent in 1949, serving until his death in 1958.

1901 Josef Wendel, Archbishop of Munich (1952-60), was born in Bliekastel, Germany; known as the "cardinal of peace" for his efforts to secure world understanding of Germany's post-World War II problems (died 1960).

1902 Peter Marshall, Presbyterian clergyman (New York Ave. Presbyterian Church, Washington, D.C. 1937-49), was born in Coalbridge, Scotland; immortalized in book, "A Man Called Peter" (died 1949).

1917 A new "Codex Juris Canonici" was promulgated by a papal bull; effective May 19,1918.

1924 The Methodist General Conference, meeting in Springfield, Mass., lifted the ban on dancing and theater attendance.

1982 Rev. Sun Myung Moon, Unification Church leader, testified under oath about his religious beliefs and said he met and had conversations with Buddha.

MAY 28

Feast day in the Catholic Church of St. Augustine, founder of the Christian church in southern England and the first Archbishop of Canterbury (597-607).

576 St. Germain (Germanus), French abbot and Bishop of Paris (555-576), died at about 80; president of the councils of Paris (557, 573); gained fame as a miracle worker, strove to bring peace and stability to decaying Merovingian reign; also observed as his feast day.

640 Severinus was enthroned as pope; had been named in 638, served until Aug 2, 640.

1779 Thomas Moore, Irish poet, was born in Dublin; wrote the hymn, "Come, ye disconsolate" (died 1852).

1789 Bernard S. Ingemann, Danish educator and writer, was born in Torkilstrup, Denmark; poet and novelist, professor of Danish language and literature; wrote well-known hymn, "Through the night of doubt and sorrow" (died 1862).

1819 Frederic D. Huntington, Episcopal prelate, was born in Hadley, Mass.; originally a Unitarian; named first Episcopal Bishop of Central New York (1869-1904) (died 1904).

1835 Mrs. Annie S. Hawks, Baptist hymn writer, was born in Hoosick, N.Y.; best remembered for "I need Thee every hour" and "Thine, most gracious Lord" (died 1918).

1881 Augustin Bea, main architect of Catholic ecumenical policy, was born in Riedböhringen, Germany; president of the Vatican Secretariat for Christian Unity; elevated to cardinal 1959 (died 1968).

1919 Royal decree in Rumania emancipated Jews, who were given all rights of citizenship.

1958 The United Presbyterian Church was formed in Pittsburgh by the merger of the Presbyterian Church in the U.S.A. and the United Presbyterian Church of North America.

1968 The Unitarian Universalist Association decided to entrust the church's race program to a newly-formed Black Affairs Council.

1982 Pope John Paul II began a six-day visit to Great Britain; had audience with Queen Elizabeth.

MAY 29

1138 Victor IV, born Gregory Conti and antipope for two months, resigned his claims, submitting to Innocent II.

1415 John XXIII, born Baldassare Cossa and pope from 1410 to 1415, was deposed by the Council of Constance; lived as a prisoner in Germany (1416-19), died shortly thereafter.

1546 David Beaton (1494-1546), primate of Scotland and Archbishop of St. Andrews (1539-46), was murdered in St. Andrews in revenge for his ordering the execution as a heretic of George Wishart, a Reformation preacher; elevated to cardinal 1538.

1583 John Penry, Welsh Puritan, was executed; with Puritan colleagues, he published the "Martin Marprelate" tracts (1588), satirizing the bishops and defending the Presbyterian discipline; hanged on charge of inciting rebellion.

1647 Freemen from four Rhode Island towns (Providence, Portsmouth, Newport, Warwick) met in Portsmouth and drafted a constitution, establishing freedom of conscience, separating church and state, providing rights to towns, and created the Providence Plantations.

1698 Trinity Church in Wilmington, Del. was begun; completed at cost of 800 pounds, then a considerable sum; completed church was 60 feet long, 30 feet wide, 20 feet tall.

1724 Benedict XIII was named pope, served until 1730; had been Archbishop of Benevente since 1686; unsuccessful in attempts to reform clergy and left secular matters to Cardinal Coscia.

1786 Charles J. Blomfield, English prelate, was born in Bury St. Edmunds, England; Bishop of London (1828-56); noted Greek scholar and edited plays of Aeschylus and Greek lyric poets (died 1857).

1819 William J. Mann, Lutheran clergyman and educator, was born in Stuttgart, Germany; professor, Lutheran Seminary, Philadelphia (1864-92); author (Lutheranism in America) (died 1892).

1849 James W. Bashford, Methodist prelate and educator, was born in Fayette, Wis.; president, Ohio Wesleyan U. (1889-1904); Methodist Bishop of China (1904-15); revealed Japanese demands of China Government to President Wilson (died 1919).

1873 The Mexican congress adopted constitutional amendments which declared for religious tolerance, separation of church and state, describing marriage as a civil contract, and prohibited monastic orders.

1874 Gilbert K. Chesterton, noted English writer, was born in London; author (Orthodoxy; Why I am a Catholic); hymn writer (O God of earth and altar) (died 1935).

1924 The French Government accepted a $1 million gift from John D. Rockefeller for the reconstruction of Reims Cathedral and Fontainebleau Palace.

1960 The Inter-Church Center on Riverside Drive, New York City, was completed; housed headquarters of several denominations and the National Council of Churches.

1961 The U.S. Supreme Court by an 8-1 vote upheld the constitutionality of state blue laws prohibiting commercial activity on Sunday.

1982 Pope John Paul II and Archbishop of Canterbury Robert Runcie prayed together in Canterbury Cathedral marking the resumption of relations between the Anglican and Catholic churches.

1986 Nell Alexander, the first woman president of the Baptist Union of Great Britain and Ireland, died at 71.

1988 Pope John Paul II named 25 new cardinals, including Archbishop James A. Hickey of Washington and Edmund C. Szoka of Detroit.

MAY 30

Feast day of St. Felix I, pope from 269 to 274.

727 St. Hubert, Belgian Bishop of Maastricht and Liege, died at about 72; patron saint of hunters; according to legend, he was converted while hunting after seeing a stag with a cross between its antlers.

1252 St. Ferdinand of Castile (Ferdinand III), king of Castile and Leon, died at 53; founder, U. of Salamanca; canonized 1671; also observed as his feast day.

1416 Jerome of Prague, a disciple of John Hus who was condemned as a heretic by the Council of Constance, was burned at the stake.

1431 Joan of Arc was burned at the stake; canonized 1920; also observed as her feast day (except in New Orleans, where the observance is May 9).

1525 Thomas Münzer, German religious reformer, was executed; disagreed with Luther, became increasingly radical in his socio-political ideas; a leader in the Peasants War and inaugurated war against the nobility and clergy.

1596 John Leslie, Catholic prelate and historian, died at 69; championed Catholicism during the Reformation; one of the commissioners sent to bring Mary, Queen of Scots, to Scotland; one of her staunchest supporters and advisor on ecclesiastical matters; banished (1573), became suffragan, vicar general of the archbishropic of Rouen.

1639 Metrophanes Kritopoulos, Greek Orthodox patriarch of Alexandria (1636-39), died at 50; important for his exposition of the Orthodox faith.

1672 George Fox (1624-91), Quaker founder, arrived in Newport for a visit and was entertained cordially by Rhode Island Governor Nicholas Eaton. "Most of the pupils had never heard of Friends before; but they were mightily affected with the meeting, and there is a great desire amongst them after the Truth," Fox was quoted as saying; he developed his preaching as a protest against the Presbyterian system; frequently imprisoned but continued preaching until his death in 1691.

1746 John H. Livingston, Dutch Reformed clergyman and educator, was born in Poughkeepsie, N.Y.; last American to go to Holland for theological training and ordination; helped reunite Dutch Reformed Church in the United States; president, theology professor, Queens (later Rutgers) College (1810-25) (died 1825).

1812 The Reformed Mennonite Church was formed.

1839 Hermann Adler, British rabbi, was born in Hanover, Germany; served as Britain's chief rabbi (1891-1911), succeeding his father, Nathan; a strong proponent of Zionism (died 1911).

1850 William Lawrence, Episcopal prelate, was born in Boston; Bishop of Massachusetts (1893-1926); dean, Episcopal Theological School, Cambridge (1888-93); author (The American Cathedral, Life of Phillips Brooks) (died 1941).

1867 The Free Religious Association was formed in New York City by Octavius B. Frothingham, former Unitarian clergyman, and others; Frothingham served as president (1867-78).

1903 Thomas Corbishley, Jesuit priest who was active in the ecumenical movement in Europe, was born in Preston, England (died 1976).

1971 The Provincial Council of the Russian Orthodox Church, meeting in Zagorsk, elected Metropolitan Pimen to become Patriarch of Moscow and All Russia.

MAY 31

1064 A council in Mantua withdrew recognition of Honorius II, who had been anti-pope since 1061.

1567 Guy de Bray (Guido de Brés), Belgian reformer, was executed as a heretic; born a Catholic, he was converted to Calvinism; author of the Belgic Confession*.

1653 Pope Innocent X issued the bull, "Cum occasione," condemning five propositions of Jansenism.

1680 Joachim Neander, German hymn writer, died at 30; first important hymn writer of the German Reformed Church (Praise to the Lord, the Almighty King, the King of Creation).

1684 Timothy Cutler, Anglican leader and educator, was born in Charlestown, Mass.; rector of Yale College (1720-22), resigned to become Anglican rector of Christ Church, Boston (1723-65); dominant Anglican spokesman of his time and a leader of anti-revival forces (died 1765).

1691 John Tillotson (1630-94) was consecrated as Archbishop of Canterbury, serving until 1694; dean of Canterbury (1670-75), of St. Paul's in London (1689-91); reluctantly assumed archbishop role on deposition of nonjuror* Sancroft.

1701 Alexander Cruden, Scottish author of a biblical concordance*, was born in Aberdeen; his complete concordance of the Scripture is still the standard for the King James Version (died 1770).

1761 Samuel Finley, Irish-born Presbyterian evangelist, was named president of the College of New Jersey (later Princeton), serving until his death in 1766 at 51; expelled from Connecticut as a "vagrant" when he preached without permission of the parish pastor.

1810 Alexander V. Griswold was named Episcopal bishop of the "Eastern" diocese — most of New England; served until 1843.

1821 The first American Catholic cathedral, Cathedral of the Assumption of the Blessed Virgin Mary in Baltimore, Md., was dedicated by Archbishop Marechal.

1857 Pius XI, pope from 1922 to 1939, was born as Achille Ambrogio Damiani Ratti in Desio, Italy.

1898 Norman Vincent Peale, noted clergyman and author, was born in Bowersville, Ohio; pastor, Marble Collegiate Reformed Church, New York City (1932-); co-founder (1937) of American Foundation for Religion and Psychiatry; author (The Power of Positive Thinking, A Guide to Confident Living).

1939 Terence Waite, personal assistant to Archbishop of Canterbury Robert Runcie, was born in Styal, England; active in negotiating for the release of hostages in Lebanon; taken hostage in Lebanon in 1987.

1956 Synod of Evangelical Lutheran Church accepted an agreement with the Netherlands Reformed Church, which it had approved earlier, for the celebration of Holy Communion by ministers of either church in the other.

1980 Pope John Paul II arrived in France for a three-day visit, the first by a pope since 1814.

JUNE 1

Feast day of St. Angela Merici, founder of the Ursulines.

Feast day of St. Justin Martyr (about 100-165), greatest of the early Christian apologists; a Father* of the Church; opened the first Christian school in Rome.

1637 Jacques Marquette, French explorer and Jesuit missionary, was born in Leon; first white man to explore the Upper Mississippi Valley (died 1675.)

1660 Mary Dyer, Quaker missionary, was hanged in Boston for sedition; had been banished (1657) but returned from Rhode Island twice to visit imprisoned Quakers; reprieved after second visit but she refused to stay away, seeking repeal of the "unrighteous law of banishment."

1762 Edmund I. Rice, congregational founder, was born in Callan, Ireland; founder, superior, Irish Christian Brothers (1822-38) (died 1844).

1783 The Order of St. Patrick was established in Ireland.

1793 Henry F. Lyte, Anglican clergyman and hymn writer, was born in Ednam, Scotland; best known for "Abide with me," "Pleasant are thy courts," "Jesus I my cross have taken" (died 1847).

1801 Brigham Young, Mormon leader, was born in Whitingham, Vt.; became a Mormon (1832), a member of the quorum of 12 apostles (1835); directed Mormon settlement in Nauvoo, Ill. (1838), succeeded Joseph Smith as head of the Mormon Church (1847) and directed mass migration to and settlement in Utah; first governor of Utah Territory (1849-57) (died 1877).

1803 William Ellery Channing, the "apostle of Unitarianism," was ordained and installed as pastor of the Federal St. Church, Boston; served there until his death in 1842.

1823 John Tulloch, Church of Scotland clergyman and educator, was born near Perth; principal, theology professor, St. Mary's College, St. Andrews; founder of liberal church party; active in reorganizing education in Scottish schools and universities (died 1886).

1827 Charles E. Freppel, French Catholic prelate and public official, was born in Alsace; Bishop of Angers (165 miles southwest of Paris) (1870-91); founder of Catholic university there; served as leader of the Clerical Party in the Chamber of Deputies (1881-91) (died 1891).

1830 The first conference of the Mormon Church was held in Fayette, N.Y.

1846 Gregory XVI, pope from 1831 to 1846, died at 81.

1918 An executive order was issued exempting conscientious objectors from military service, assigning them to farm work or positions with the Quakers.

1980 The United Presbyterian Church general assembly in Detroit amended the church constitution to state that local church property will be held in trust for the entire denomination, making it more difficult for local churches to leave the fold.

JUNE 2

657 St. Eugenius I, pope from 654 to 657, died.

829 St. Nicephorus, patriarch of Constantinople (806-815), died at about 71; also observed as his feast day in the Orthodox Church.

1535 Leo XI, pope from April 1 to April 27, 1605, was born as Alessandro Ottaviano de Medici in Florence, Italy.

1751 John Bampton, English canon of Salisbury, died at about 61; endowed one of Protestant Christendom's most distinguished lectureships.

1812 Archibald Alexander, noted Presbyterian clergyman, became the first professor at Princeton Theological Seminary, which he helped found.

1835 St. Pius X, pope from 1903 to 1914, was born as Giuseppe Melchiore Sarto near Venice.

1979 Pope John Paul II arrived in Poland for a nine-day visit, the first by a pope to a Communist country.

JUNE 3

Feast day of St. Kevin, founder of the monastery at Glendalough, County Wicklow in Ireland in the Seventh Century.

253 St. Lucius I was elected pope, served until 254.

545 St. Clotilda, Frankish queen, died; retired to abbey of St. Martin at Tours after her husband's death; also observed as her feast day.

574 Benedict I was consecrated as pope, served until 579.

1162 Thomas à Becket was consecrated as Archbishop of Canterbury, served until 1170.

1620 The Recollet Fathers laid the cornerstone of their church, Notre Dame des Anges, in Quebec; opened as parish church May 25, 1621.

1647 British Parliament, under Puritan control, ordained that Christmas and other holidays should no longer be observed.

1726 Philip William Otterbein, a founder of the United Brethren Church, was born in Dillenburg, Germany; served German Reformed pastorates in Pennsylvania and Maryland; with Martin Boehm and six lay evangelists formed the United Brethren Church (1789), with the first annual conference held in 1800 (died 1813).

1811 Henry James Sr., philosopher who was influenced by Swedenborgianism and Fourierism, was born in Albany, N.Y.; author (Christianity the Logic of Creation, Relation to Life) (died 1882).

1812 Norman Macleod, a leading Presbyterian clergyman of the 19th Century, was born in Campbelltown, Scotland; served the Barony Church, Glasgow (1851-72); chaplain to Queen Victoria; editor, *Edinburgh Christian Magazine* (1849-60), *Good Words* (1860-72) (died 1872).

1822 Thomas Gallaudet, Episcopal clergyman and teacher of deaf, was born in Philadelphia, the son of Thomas Gallaudet (1787-1851); founded, St. Ann's Church for Deaf Mutes, New York City (1859) and Gallaudet Home for Aged and Infirm Deaf Mutes, near Poughkepsie (1885) (died 1902).

1963 Pope John XXIII, pope from 1958 to 1963, died at 82.

1972 The first woman rabbi in the United States, Sally J. Priesand, was ordained in Cincinnati's I.M.Wise Temple.

1979 The Episcopal Church Standing Commission on Human Affairs and Health recommended that homosexuals be allowed to be ordained as priests if able and willing to conform their behavior to that which church affirms to be wholesome.

1980 Catholic and Eastern Orthodox representatives, meeting for the first time since 1054, agreed they would try to get their churches to meet again.

1985 The Vatican and the Italian Government ratified a concordat replacing the Lateran Treaty of 1929; the new treaty no longer recognized Catholicism as the Italian state religion but affirmed the independence of Vatican City.

JUNE 4

Feast day in the Orthodox Church of St. Martha, sister of Mary andLazarus; the patron saint of housewives.

Feast day of St. Optatus (about 370), Bishop of Milevis in North Africa; his arguments formed starting point for St. Augustine's refutation of Donatism*

Feast day of St. Vincentia Gerosa, co-founder of the Sisters of Charity for Lovers; canonized 1950.

1608 St. Francis Caraccioli, founder of Clerici Regulares Minores (1588), died at 45; canonized 1807; also observed as his feast day.

1663 William Juxon, Archbishop of Canterbury (1660-63), died at 81; Bishop of London (1633-49); attended Charles I at his trial and on the scaffold.

1820 The Mariners' Church was opened in New York City by the New York Port Society.

1836 Chauncey Goodrich, Congregational missionary to China (1865-1925), was born in Hinsdale, Mass.; translator, dean of Gordon Memorial Theological Seminary, Peking U. (died 1925).

1857 Benjamin F. Mills, evangelist, was born in Rahway, N.J.; provided a link between America's revival tradition and social gospel; made innovations in revival techniques, organizing the "District Combination Plan of Evangelism" (died 1916).

1869 Charles Stelzle, Presbyterian clergyman, was born in New York City; a leader in efforts to adjust church to meet modern economic conditions; author (The Workingman and Social Problems, Gospel of Labor) (died 1941).

1878 Frank N. D. Buchman, founder of Moral Rearmament, was born in Pennsburg, Pa.; originally a Lutheran clergyman (1909-15) working among students at Penn State U.; launched Moral Rearmament movement in Washington (1938), spread worldwide; evolved a religion called "A First Century Christian Fellowship" then served as a YMCA missionary in Japan, Korea, and India (died 1961).

1900 Nelson Glueck, archaeologist and rabbi, was born in Cincinnati; discovered many important historical sites in Israel and Jordan; president, Hebrew Union College (1947-71) and the Jewish Institute of Religion (1949), which were later merged (died 1971).

1902 Otto Weber, German theologian who was an interpreter of Karl Barth, was born in Cologne; author (Karl Barth's Church Dogmatics, Ground Plan of the Bible) (died 1966).

1923 Archbishop Soldevila was murdered in Saragossa, Spain.

1979 The U. S. Supreme Court refused to hear the appeal of an Orthodox Jewish prisoner in Alabama who argued that prison authorities violated his freedom of religion by forcing him to shave and cut his hair.

1985 The U. S. Supreme Court struck down an Alabama law permitting one minute of prayer or meditation in the public schools.

JUNE 5

708 Jacob of Edessa, most important Syriac* writer, died at about 75; best known for his Syriac version of the Old Testament.

754 St. Boniface, English-born Benedictine missionary and "apostle of Germany," died when he and his companions were massacred during a mission to the Frisians; his devotion to the papacy and successful missionary work helped spread papal influence north of the Alps; also observed as his feast day.

1305 Clement V, born in France as Bertrand de Got, was elected pope, served until 1314; became first Avignon pope when he moved the papal residence from Rome (1309) at the request of his friend, King Philip the Fair of France; suppressed the Templars (1312), issued the decree, "Pastoralis cura," which proclaimed the absolute right of the pope over empire, and "Multorum querala," which attempted to control the Inquisition, to which he was opposed; did much to further scholarship, founded universities at Orleans (1306) and Perugia (1308).

1414 Jan Hus appeared before the three-day hearing of the Council of Constance but was not allowed to state his own beliefs, only to answer what are considered trumped-up charges; condemned to death.

1493 Justus Jonas, Protestant reformer, was born in Germany; professor of theology, Wittenberg (1521-41); a co-worker of Martin Luther, he translated his writings into German; preached the funeral oration for Luther (died 1555).

1590 Meletion Pegas was consecrated as patriarch of Alexandria; served until 1601.

1748 Charles H. Wharton, Episcopal clergyman who helped prepare constitution for the American Episcopal Church and Americanizing the prayer book, was born in St. Mary's County, Md. (died 1833).

1771 Sydney Smith, clergyman and essayist, was born near London; a founder, Edinburgh Review (1802), spent 20 years as a village parson and doctor in Yorkshire (1809-28), canon of St. Paul's, London (1831-45); wrote "Peter Plymley Letters" in defense of Catholic emancipation (died 1845).

1829 Marcus Jastrow, rabbi and lexicographer, was born in Rogasen, Poland; jailed in Poland as a patriot; rabbi, Rodelph Shalom Congregation, Philadelphia (1866-92); helped form Young Men's Hebrew Association (1875); compiler, "Dictionary of the Targumin, the Talmud Babli and Terushalmi and the Midrashic Literature" (died 1903).

1836 Johann Friedrich, theologian and historian, was born in Germany; professor of church history, Munich (1865-1905); excommunicated with Johann Döllinger, his teacher, for opposing the dogma of papal infallibility (1871); became a leader in the Old Catholic movement, helped establish the Old Catholic theological faculty at the University of Bern (1874) (died 1917).

1856 The Jesuits were again suppressed in Mexico by government decree.

1897 Charles Hartshorne, theologian who was an exponent of "process theology," was born in Kittaning, Pa.

1900 William E. R. Sangster, president, Methodist Conference of England (1950-58), was born in London (died 1960).

1930 Religious instruction in Italian secondary schools was made compulsory.

1970 President Nixon named Henry Cabot Lodge as his personal representative to the Vatican, the second president to do so (see Dec. 23, 1939).

1979 Pope John Paul II called on Poland's Communist Government to recognize the "cause of fundamental human rights, including the right to religious liberty."

JUNE 6

Feast day of St. Norbert, Archbishop of Magdeburg (1126-34), founder of the Canons Regular of Premontre (Premonstratenians, Norbertines, or White Canons), devoted to penitence and preaching; canonized 1582.

824 Eugenius II was consecrated as pope, served until 827; pontificate marked an important advance in the emancipation of the Papacy from the Frankish Empire.

1576 Giovanni Diodati, Calvinist, was born in Geneva, Switzerland; translated the Bible into Italian (1607) (died 1649).

1622 Claude Jean Allouez, Jesuit missionary, was born in St. Didier, France; began missionary work along the St. Lawrence River and the Great Lakes in 1658; said to have baptized more than 10,000 Indians; called the "founder of Catholicity in the West" (died 1689).

1684 Nathaniel Lardner, English biblical and patristic* scholar, was born near London; founder of modern school of critical research in early Christian literature; author of 17-volume, "The Credibility of the Gospel History" (died 1768).

1844 George Williams (1821-1905), English drygoods merchant, founded the Young Men's Christian Association (YMCA) in London.

1858 Claude J. G. Montefiore, English Jewish religious leader and scholar, was born in London; the first Jew whose writings on the New Testament had an influence on Christian scholars; promoted liberal reform in English Judaism; president, Anglo-Jewish Association (1896-1921), of a Liberal Jewish synagogue and University College, Southampton (1915-31); author (Elements of Liberal Judaism)(died 1938).

1860 William R. Inge, clergyman and philosopher, was born in Crayke, England; dean, St. Paul's Cathedral, London (1911-34); one of the best known churchmen of his generation, known as the "gloomy dean;" author (Christian Mysticism) (died 1954).

1874 Nicola Canali, Catholic prelate, was born in Rieti, Italy; a leader in Vatican City affairs, he announced the election of Pope John XXIII; elevated to cardinal 1935 (died 1961).

1966 Members from Christian Science churches in 50 countries came to Boston to observe the centennial of the discovery of Christian Science; work began on the expanded 15-acres headquarters complex.

1972 "Messengers" of the Southern Baptist Convention held their annual assembly, reaffirmed the Baptist commitment to religious freedom.

JUNE 7

Feast day of St. Colman of Dromore, first Bishop of Dromore in County Down, Ireland; founded a monastery there.

Feast day of St. Antony Gianelli, Bishop of Bobbio (40 miles northeast of Genoa) and founder of the Missioners of St. Alphonsus and the Sisters of St. Mary dell'Orto; canonized 1951.

431 Council of Ephesus opened to resolve differences between Alexandria and Constantinople; the principal decision was to condemn Nestorius, patriarch of Constantinople (433); however, decrees of the Council were not considered decisive dogmatic authority.

555 Vigilius, pope from 537 to 555, died.

1099 Crusaders besieged Jerusalem and the city fell July 15.

1804 Thomas S. Savage, first American Episcopal missionary to Africa, was born in Cromwell, Conn.; established a mission station in Liberia (1836-46); wrote a paper on the gorilla, previously unknown to scientists (died 1880).

1844 The first and only issue of the Nauvoo (Ill.) *Expositor* appeared, attacking Joseph Smith and Mormon polygamy; newspaper office was wrecked and burned on orders of Smith (June 10).

1845 John F. Goucher, Methodist clergyman and educator, was born in Waynesboro, Pa.; a benefactor, president, Baltimore Women's College (1890-1908), later renamed Goucher College (1922) (died 1922).

1857 Samuel M. Crothers, Unitarian clergyman and essayist, was born in Oswego, Ill.; pastor, The First Parish, Cambridge, Mass. (1894-1927); author of numerous essay collections (died 1927).

1870 The first General Assembly of the Presbyterian Church in Canada opened.

1886 Archbishop Elzear A. Taschereau (1820-98) of Quebec was named the first Canadian cardinal.

JUNE 8

410 St. Melania the Elder (about 342-210) died; founded a double monastery with Rufinus of Aquilea on the Mount of Olives; also observed as his feast day.

536 St. Silverius was consecrated as pope, served until 537; he was the son born to Pope Hormisdas before he entered the priesthood; twice exiled during his reign.

632 Mohammed died at 62.

1536 English clergy in convocation prepared articles on religion, issued in 1539 by Henry VIII; the articles acknowledged transubstantiation, communion in one kind, vows of chastity, private masses, celibacy of the clergy, and auricular confession; the articles were modified several times.

1647 The Cambridge Synod reconvened, attended by representatives of 29 Massachusetts churches; resulted in action announced in August 1648 of "A platform of church discipline gathered out of the word of God and agreed upon by the elders and messengers of the churches assembled in the synod of Cambridge in New England...;" eventually adopted (1651) by the congregations.

1757 Ercole Consalvi, cardinal and statesman, was born in Rome; instrumental in securing the election of Pope Pius VII (1800), who made him secretary of state; negotiated concordat with Napoleon (1801) (died 1824).

1809 Thomas Paine, political philosopher and author, died at about 73; best known for his writing on behalf of the colonial cause in American Revolution; also wrote "The Age of Reason," an uncompromising attack on the Bible.

1865 Henry Edward Manning, an archdeacon in the Anglican Church, was consecrated as Catholic archbishop of Westminster.

1886 Bishop Fabre was elevated to Archbishop of Montreal.

1887 Donald McMillan, American national commander of the Salvation Army (1953-57), was born in Middlesborough, England (died 1969).

JUNE 9

Feast day in the Orthodox Church of St. Cyril, patriarch of the Rumanian Orthodox Church (1925-39).

Feast day in the Orthodox Church of St. Cyril of Alexandria (about 376-444), early Christian theologian, Father* and Doctor* of the Church and patriarch of Alexandria (412- 444).

597 St. Columba, Irish missionary and one of Ireland's patron saints, died at about 76; as abbot, he founded monastery on the island of Iona (563), where he remained the rest of his life; also observed as his feast day.

1597 Jose de Anchieta, Portuguese Jesuit missionary, died at 64; a founder of the Jesuit mission in Brazil and known as the "apostle of Brazil."

1828 Thomas J. Potter, Catholic author and educator, was born in Scarborough, England; professor of sacred eloquence, All Hallow's College, Dublin; wrote the hymn, "Brightly gleams our banner" (died 1873).

1881 Luis M. Martinez, Catholic archbishop and the first Catholic primate of Mexico (1937-56), was born in Molino de Caballeros (died 1956).

1968 Archbishop Chrysostomos, Greek Orthodox Archbishop of Athens and primate of Greece (1962-67), died in Athens at 88.

1973 The $75 million Christian Science Church Center was formally opened in Boston.

1978 Mormon Church President Spencer W. Kimball said all worthy members of the church may be ordained to the priesthood without regard for race or color.

1981 Rev. Bailey Smith, a fundamentalist, was reelected president of the Southern Baptist Convention in Los Angeles.

1981 Representatives of 56 nations attended the Christian Science Church convention in Boston; Berthe S. Giradin of France was elected president.

1886 The Canadian Congregational Woman's Board of Missions was organized in Ottawa.

1906 The Christian Science Cathedral in Boston was dedicated.

1925 The United Church of Canada was formed by the organic union of the Congregational, Methodist, and Presbyterian churches of Canada.

1959 The new $2 million headquarters of the United Church of Canada in Toronto was dedicated.

1962 Archbishop Paul J. Hallinan of Atlanta announced that students would be admitted on a nonracial basis in Catholic schools of the Atlanta area beginning in the Fall.

1967 Joseph E. Ritter, Catholic prelate, died at 76; Archbishop of Indianapolis (1944-46), of St. Louis (1946-61); elevated to cardinal 1961.

1969 Pope Paul VI addressed the World Council of Churches in Geneva.

1978 The General Assembly of the Presbyterian Church in the United States elected Sara Bernice Moseley as its first woman moderator.

1980 Rev. Bailey E. Smith was elected president of the Southern Baptist Convention in St. Louis; delegates voted to "exhort" trustees of their seminaries not to employ liberal faculty members.

1983 The Presbyterian Church (USA) was formed by the merger in Atlanta of the United Presbyterian Church in the U.S.A. and the Presbyterian Church in the U.S., after a split of 122 years over the question of slavery and the Civil War.

1986 Rev. Adrian Rodgers of Memphis, a fundamentalist, was elected president of the Southern Baptist Convention.

JUNE 10

Feast day of St. Margaret of Scotland (about 1045-1093), queen consort of Malcolm III; began transition in Scotland from Celtic culture and Columban religious rites to feudal system and Roman ritual; canonized 1249.

JUNE 11

Feast day in the Orthodox Church of St. Bartholomew, one of the 12 apostles, who according to legend was flayed to death in Armenia.

Feast day of St. Barnabas, who accompanied St. Paul on his first missionary trip but later separated from him and went to Cyprus, where he founded the Cypriot Church; according to legend he was martyred in Salamis in AD 61.

1294 Roger Bacon, English Franciscan theologian, died at 80; noted physical scientist and philosopher who approached modern methods and was critical of the scholastic method of instruction.

1782 William Black, the first Canadian Methodist clergyman, preached his first sermon in Halifax, Nova Scotia.

1814 Henry W. Bellows, Unitarian clergyman, editor and humanitarian, was born in Boston; pastor, First Unitarian (later All Souls) Church, New York City (1839-92); founder, editor, *Christian Inquirer* (1847), *Christian Examiner* (1866-77); founder, president, U.S. Sanitary Commission, which cared for sick, wounded in Civil War; president, National Unitarian Conference (1865-79) (died 1882).

1881 Mordecai M. Kaplan, Jewish theologian, was born in Svencionys, Russia (Lithuania); founder of the Reconstructionist movement in Judaism; founder, Jewish Center, New York City; professor, Jewish Theological Seminary; author (Judaism as Civilization) (died 1983)

1882 Blessed Paula Frassinetti, founder of Sisters of St. Dorothy, died at 79; also observed as her feast day.

1910 Pope Benedict XV instructed Prussian bishops to abstain from publishing an encyclical that had angered German Protestants; Pope declared he had no intention of slighting non-Catholics.

1910 A royal order was published in Spain granting dissident religious establishments the right to show external signs of their beliefs on the walls of their churches and in their notices.

1936 The Presbyterian Church of America was formed in Philadelphia.

1944 The Church of St. Sava in New York City was elevated to cathedral status by the Serbian Orthodox Church.

1978 Bishop Harold L. Wright, the first black bishop in the New York Episcopal Diocese (1974-78), died at 46.

1983 Rev. John Randolph Taylor, 54-year-old pastor from Charlotte, N.C., was named the first moderator of the newly-merged Presbyterian Church (USA).

JUNE 12

816 St. Leo III, pope from 795 to 816, died; also observed as his feast day.

1774 Alexander McLeod, Presbyterian clergyman, was born on Mull Island off Scotland; pastor, First Reformed Presbyterian Church, New York City (1800-33); a vigorous opponent of slavery (died 1833).

1776 The Virginia Convention adopted the Bill of Rights, which exerted great influence on other colonies and in France; Patrick Henry drafted the section on religious freedom - "That religion, or the duty which we owe to our Creator, and the manner of discharging it, can be directed only by reason and conviction, not by force or violence; and therefore all men are equally entitled to the free exercise of religion according to the dictates of conscience; and that it is the mutual duty of all to practice Christian forbearance, love, and charity towards each other."

1819 Charles Kingsley, English clergyman and author, was born in Holne Vicarage, Devon, England; bast known for novels (Westward Ho, Water Babies, Hypatia); rector, Everly Established Church (1844-75) and a leading spirit in the Christian Socialist movement; jibe at Cardinal John Henry Newman ("Truth for its own sake has never been a virtue of the Roman clergy. Father Newman informs us that it need not and on the whole ought not to be.") led to the publication of "Apologia pro vita sua" in 1864 by Newman (died 1875).

1972 Expo '72, a fundamentalist conference organized by the Campus Crusade for Christ International, opened in the Dallas Cotton Bowl; about 80,000 delegates attended the five-day meeting.

1974 Delegates to the 117th annual meeting of the Southern Baptist Convention rejected a resolution that would give 10% representation to blacks and ethnic minorities and 20% to women on denominational boards and committees.

1974 Rt. Rev. John M. Allin was installed as the 23rd presiding bishop of the Episcopalian Church in ceremonies in the National Cathedral, Washington.

1979 The Southern Baptist Convention in a sharp move toward extreme conservative position elected Rev. Adrian P. Rogers president on the first ballot at its conference in Houston.

1980 A National Council of Churches panel proposed a major effort to introduce "non-sexist" language in local churches.

1984 Dr. Charles F. Stanley of Atlanta was elected president of the Southern Baptist Convention, the nation's largest Protestant denomination; Dr. Stanley, a former vice president of Moral Majority, gave control of the church to the "Bible inerrancy" wing, which had sought control for a decade.

1987 The scandal-wracked PTL (Praise the Lord) ministry filed for reorganization under the bankruptcy code blaming the "chaotic mismanagement" of founder Jim Bakker for piling up $70 million in debts.

JUNE 13

1003 John XVII, born in Rome as Sicco, was named pope, served only five months.

1231 St. Anthony of Padua, famous and lovable saint who performed many miracles, died at about 36; most celebrated follower of St. Francis of Assisi and a renowned preacher; also observed as his feast day.

1780 George Bourne, Presbyterian clergyman and antislavery writer, was born in Westbury, England; served pastorates in New York, Pennsylvania, and Virginia; moved to the Dutch Reformed Church in New York City; editor, *The Protestant*; wrote widely against slavery (died 1845).

1817 Emanuel V. Gerhart, German Reformed clergyman, was born in Freeburg, Pa.; president, Franklin & Marshall College (1854-65), Mercersburg Theological Seminary (1868-1904) (died 1904).

1979 Delegates to the Reformed Church of America's 173rd synod voted to amend the Book of Church Order to allow women to be ordained as ministers.

1982 The Reformed Presbyterian Church, Evangelical Synod, voted to merge with the Southern-rooted Presbyterian Church.

JUNE 14

Former feast day in the Catholic Church of St. Basil the Great, a Cappodocian Father*, famous for his organization of Greek monasticism; now observed Jan. 2.

1381 Simon of Sudbury, Archbishop of Canterbury (1375-81), was beheaded on London Bridge, the most distinguished victim of the Peasants' Revolt; he as chancellor and Sir Robert Hales, lord treasurer, were held responsible for the poll tax.

1662 Sir Henry (commonly Harry) Vane Jr., English Puritan statesman, was beheaded for treason; governor of Massachusetts (1636), lost re-election bid (1637) because he sided with Anne Hutchinson in a theological dispute; returned to England, knighted and became a member of Parliament; attacked Cromwell's Protectorate.

1748 Henry Alline, revivalist, was born in Newport, R.I.; called "the Whitefield of Nova Scotia," he produced an awakening in the area (died 1784).

1801 Heber C. Kimball, Mormon leader, was born in Sheldon, Vt.; one of the 12 Mormon apostles (1835), adviser to Brigham Young; chief justice of the State of Deseret (later Utah), lieutenant governor (1849-68) (died 1868).

1811 Harriet Beecher Stowe, author of "Uncle Tom's Cabin," was born in Litchfield, Conn.; wrote the hymn, "Still, still, with Thee, when purple morning breaketh" (died 1896).

1814 Samuel Harris, Congregational educator, was born in East Machias, Me.; professor of theology, Bangor (Me.) Seminary (1855-67); president, Bowdoin College (1867-71); theology professor, Yale Divinity School (1871-95) (died 1899).

1837 William Chatterton Dix, Anglican hymn writer, was born in Bristol; among his hymns were "As with gladness, men of old" and "Come unto me, ye weary" (died 1898).

1857 Walter W. Moore, first president, Union Theological Seminary (Virginia) (1904), was born in Charlotte, N.C. (died 1926).

1862 John J. Glennon, Catholic prelate, was born in Meath County, Ireland; Archbishop of St. Louis (1903-46), built a cathedral, seminaries, and high schools; elevated to cardinal 1946 (died 1946).

1895 Louis Finkelstein, Jewish theologian and rabbi, was born in Cincinnati; rabbi, Congregation Kehilath Israel, New York City (1919-31); president, Jewish Theological Seminary (1940-51), chancellor (1951 on).

1922 The Episcopal Synod of the Polish Orthodox Church proclaimed its independence from the Russian Orthodox Church.

1943 The U. S. Supreme Court ruled that under the Bill of Rights, school children could not be compelled to salute the flag if the ceremony conflicted with their religion; the case was brought by Jehovah's Witnesses.

1984 The Southern Baptist Convention passed a resolution opposing the ordination of women; the resolution was non-binding on local congregations and did not apply to women already ordained for the Baptist ministry.

1988 The Southern Baptist Convention elected Rev. Jerry Vines of Jacksonville, Fla. president, as the conservative fundamentalists narrowly retained their ten-year hold on the denomination.

1988 Rev. James E. Andrews was elected to a second four-year term as stated clerk of the General Assembly of the Presbyterian Church (U.S.A.).

JUNE 15

Feast day of St. Vitus, whose name is associated with a disease bearing his name; was a Christian child martyr of the late Third Century.

Feast day of St. Bernard of Menthon (932-1008), French Catholic priest who established the Alpine hospices that bear his name; patron saint of Alpinists; canonized 1681.

1215 The Magna Carta was signed by King John at Runnymede, near Windsor, at the insistence of the Archbishop of Canterbury and the lords; provided among other things for the freedom of worship with its opening words: "The Church of England shall be free."

1520 The papal bull, "Exsurge domine," issued by Pope Leo X against 41 articles of Martin Luther's teachings; this was followed by the burning of Luther's works in Rome.

1640 Fire destroyed the Chapel of Notre Dame de la Recouverance and the parish registers of Quebec.

1649 The first trial was held for witchcraft in Charlestown, Mass.; Margaret Jones was found guilty and executed.

1668 Padre Diego Luis de Sanvitores, Jesuit from Mexico, founded the first mission on the island of Guam.

1789 Josiah Henson, Methodist clergyman, was born a slave in Charles County, Md.; fled to Canada (1830), where he helped develop the British-American Institute, a school for Canadian blacks; mistakenly identified as the prototype for Harriet Beecher Stowe's "Uncle Tom" (died 1881).

1805 John M. Henni, Catholic prelate and editor, was born in Massanenga, Switzerland; founder, editor, *Wahrheitsfreund*, first German Catholic newspaper in the United States; first Bishop of Milwaukee (1844-81) (died 1881).

1807 William Nast, founder of the German Methodist Episcopal Church, was born in Stuttgart; an effective missionary among German settlers in the Midwest; editor, *Christiche Apologete* (1838-91) (died 1899).

1807 John B. McFerrin, Methodist clergyman and editor, was born in Rutherford County, Tenn.; editor, *Christian Advocate* (1840-58); book agent, Methodist Church, South (1858-66, 1878-87); secretary, Board of Missions (1866-78) (died 1887).

1875 Various Presbyterian churches united as the Presbyterian Church of Canada.

1888 Martin C. D'Arcy, Jesuit provincial of England (1945-76), was born near Bath, England; author (The Nature of Belief) (died 1976).

1982 Rev. Dr. James T. Draper, theological conservative, was elected president of the Southern Baptist Convention.

1982 The Presbyterian Church in the United States voted to rejoin the United Presbyterian Church in the U.S.A. after a 122-year schism that began as a result of the Civil War.

JUNE 16

676 Adeodatus, pope from 672 to 676, died.

1106 St. Benne, Bishop of Meissen (1066-85), died; his canonization in 1523 led Martin Luther to publish a violent brochure titled, "Against the New Idol and the Old Devil About to be Set up in Meissen;" patron saint of Bavaria and Munich; also observed as his feast day.

1846 Pius IX was named pope, served until 1878; reign marked by wide reforms in spiritual and ecclesiastical matters; forced to flee Vatican (1848) by insurrection, restored by French (1850); proclaimed dogma of the Immaculate Conception (1859-60); convened first Vatican Council (1869-70), which promulgated doctrine of papal infallibility; lost temporal power to King Victor Emmanuel (1870) and became the first "prisoner" of the Vatican; pontificate longest in history of the church.

1871 Sergey N. Bulgakov, theologian who developed "sophiology," was born in Livny, Russia; developed theological system which seeks to solve the problems of the relation between God and the world by the concept of the Divine Wisdom of "sophia;" expelled from Russia, became dean of the Orthodox Theological Seminary in Paris (1923-44) (died 1944).

1974 Rev. Dr. Lawrence W. Bottoms was elected moderator of the Presbyterian Church in the U.S., the first black leader in the 113-year history of the Southern denomination.

JUNE 17

Feast day in the Anglican Church of St. Alban, England's first Christian martyr; beheaded about 304 for helping a fugitive priest, who converted him, to escape.

Feast day of St. Botolph (Botulf), founder and first abbot of a monastery at Icanhoe in England (654); about 70 English churches are dedicated to him.

900 Fulk (or Foulques), Archbishop of Reims (883-900), was assassinated; served as chancellor for Charles the Simple (898-900), promoted political ambitions of the Carolingian* dynasty.

1207 Stephen Langton was consecrated as Archbishop of Canterbury; excommunicated by King John (1209), who favored John de Gray; returned 1213-15 and again 1217-28; sided with the lords and was the first subscribing witness to the Magna Carta; said to have led the transition from the feudal church of Lanfranc to a national church; promulgated (1222) set of constitutions still recognized as binding in English ecclesiastical courts.

1644 John of St. Thomas, Portuguese theologian and philosopher, died; a devout follower of St. Thomas Aquinas; author of two great works, "Cursus philosophics" and "Cursus theologius."

1669 Charles II authorized preparation of a bill to permit Lutherans in London to hold public services and to build a church.

1693 Johann G. Walch, German editor and theologian, was born in Jena; editor of Luther's works (24 volumes) and author of works on religious controversies (died 1775).

1700 Massachusetts enacted a law requiring Catholic priests to leave the colony within three months; if any priest remained he was to be considered an "incendiary and disturber of the public peace and safety and an enemy to the true Christian religion;" if found guilty, he could be imprisoned for life or executed.

1797 Alexander R. Vinet, Swiss Protestant theologian, was born near Lausanne; staunch advocate of religious liberalism and separation of church and state; had great influence on Protestantism (died 1847).

1859 John Wilbur Chapman, Presbyterian evangelist, was born in Richmond, Ind.; suceeded William Vaughan Moody, trained Billy Sunday (died 1918).

1864 William Cureton, English Semitic scholar, died at 56; discovered epistles of St. Ignatius and the "Curetonian Gospels," a fragmentary Syriac* version of the original of Matthew.

1884 Constantine Bohachevsky, American leader of Ukrainian Catholics, was born in Maniw, Ukraine; created system of parochial schools, was apostolic exarch of the American branch (1924-58), then metropolitan (died 1961).

1958 Pilgrim Holiness Church, meeting in Winona Lake, Ind., voted to approve a proposed merger with the Weslyan Methodist Church of America.

1962 Somdej Phra Wanarat, supreme patriarch of Thailand's Buddhists, died in Bangkok at 73.

1963 The U. S. Supreme Court ruled 8 to 1 that laws requiring recitation of the Lord's Prayer or Bible verses in public schools is unconstitutional.

1966 Pope Paul VI by a "motuproprio" transferred to the diocesan bishops powers formerly reserved to Rome to grant dispensations.

1985 Masaharu Taniguchi, founder of Seicho-no Ie ("House of Growth"), died at 92; organization espoused the principles of Buddhism, Christianity, and Shintoism.

JUNE 18

373 St. Ephraem, a Doctor* of the Church, died at about 67; a Syrian, deacon of the Church of Edessa (in western Macedonia) and a prolific writer of scriptural commentaries, homilies, and hymns; also observed as his feast day.

1802 Henry Durant, Congregational clergyman, was born in Acton, Mass.; went west with the gold rush, received charter for College (later University) of California (1855); first president, U. of California (1870-72) (died 1875).

1804 Peter Parker, first Protestant medical missionary to China, was born in Framingham, Mass.; served in China from 1834 to 1857 (died 1888).

1819 Samuel Longfellow, Unitarian clergyman and poet, was born in Portland, Me.; brother of Henry Wadsworth Longfellow, he wrote poetry (Thalatta) and numerous hymns (Holy Spirit, truth divine; I look to Thee in every need; O God, Thou giver of all good) (died 1892).

1825 Charles James Stewart was named Anglican Bishop of Quebec, succeeding Jacob Mountain.

1830 Elizabeth C.D. Clephane, Scottish hymn writer, was born in Edinburgh; best known for "Beneath the cross of Jesus" (died 1869).

1963 The American Baptist Association, meeting in Oklahoma City, questioned the decision of the Supreme Court regarding Bible reading and prayer in the public schools.

1982 Southern Baptist Convention delegates criticized professional football's Sunday television schedule because it interfered with religious services telecasts.

JUNE 19

Feast day of St. Bruno of Querfort, German missionary archbishop to the Slavs; martyred in Prussia.

Feast day in the Orthodox Church of St. Jude Thaddeus, one of the 12 apostles and the patron saint of lost causes or impossible things.

1027 St. Romauld, founder of the Camaldolese Order (1012), died at about 77; also observed as his feast day.

1341 St. Juliana Falconieri died at 71; founder of the Servite Nuns (about 1304), canonized 1737; also observed as her feast day.

1542 Leo Jud (Meister Leu), Swiss Protestant clergyman, died at 60; colleague of Zwingli at Zurich; aided in translating the Zurich Bible, made a Latin translation of the Old Testament.

1623 Blaise Pascal, French philosopher and mathematician, was born in Clermont Ferrand; noted for his mathematical accomplishments; became a Jansenist, wrote much in defense of Jansenism against Jesuit attacks (died 1662).

1770 Disciples of Emanuel Swedenborg, Swedish mystic, organized the Church of New Jerusalem, now called The New Church.

1782 Felicite R. de Lamennais, French priest and writer, was born in St. Malo; one of the most influential, controversial figures in the French church; advocated freedom in religious matters, was censured and condemned by the Pope and clergy; his great philosophical work was "Essai sur l'Indifference in Metiér de Religion" (died 1854).

1829 Charles C. Everett, Unitarian clergyman and theologian, was born in Brunswick, Me.; dean, Harvard Divinity School (1878-1900); a founder, editor, *New World*, a quarterly on religion and theology (died 1900).

1834 Charles H. Spurgeon, English Baptist clergyman, was born near London; the Metropolitan Tabernacle in London, accommodating 6000, was built for him and he preached there from 1861 to 1892, his weekly sermons were collected in 50 volumes; author (John Ploughman's Talks, John Ploughman's Pictures) (died 1892).

1851 Samuel M. Jackson, Presbyterian clergyman and editor, was born in New York City; Social Christian activist; editor-in-chief of 12 volume Schaff-Herzog Encyclopedia of Religious Knowledge (died 1912).

1872 The German Parliament voted 131-93 to expel the Jesuits.

1910 The first observance of Father's Day occurred in Spokane, Wash., under auspices of the Ministerial Association and the YMCA.

1977 Catholic Bishop John A. Neumann of Philadelphia, known for his development of parochial schools, was canonized, the first American male to achieve sainthood.

1987 The U.S. Supreme Court voted 7-2 to overturn a 1981 Louisiana law that required any public school teaching the theory of evolution to give equal time to the view of divine creation as a science.

JUNE 20

Feast day of St. Silverius, pope from 536 to 537.

930 Hucbald, Flemish monk and musical theorist, died at about 90; credited with laying the groundwork in church music of polyphony (simultaneous combinations of two or more independent melodic parts).

981 St. Adalbert, first Archbishop of Magdeburg, died; had general jurisdiction over the Slavs; also observed as his feast day.

1629 Three clergymen - Francis Higginson, Samuel Skelton, and Francis Bright - were invested with the authority of the Massachusetts Bay Colony and the church in Salem, which soon after was constituted by a covenant.

1658 Thomas Brattle, merchant and church leader, was born in Boston; chief organizer, Brattle St. Church; waged controversy with the Mathers, opposed the Salem witchcraft trials (died 1713).

1667 Clement IX was named pope, served until 1669; ended the Jansenist controversy which had been going on for 30 years; suppressed the Jesuits (1668).

1808 Samson R. Hirsch, Jewish religious leader, was born in Hamburg, Germany; founder of "Trennungs-Orthodoxie" (separatist Orthodoxy), a modernized Orthodox Jewish congregation and school system which sought to combine the Torah* and worldly wisdom (died 1888).

1868 Miron Cristea, Orthodox leader, was born in Toplita, Rumania; first patriarch of the Rumanian church (1925- 39) (died 1939).

1888 Pope Leo XIII issued the encyclical, "Libertas," seeking to affirm what is good about political liberalism, democracy, and freedom of conscience.

1926 The 28th International Eucharistic Congress of the Catholic Church began in a Chicago suburb, the first such meeting in the United States; attracted one million pilgrims; Cardinal John Bonzano, papal legate, presided.

1972 Judith Hird was ordained as pastor of the Holy Cross Lutheran Church in Tom's River, N.J., the first woman Lutheran pastor.

JUNE 21

Feast day in the Catholic Church of St. Eusebius of Samosata, martyr and Bishop of Samosata (present-day Samosat, Turkey) (361-380).

1002 St. Leo IX, pope from 1048 to 1054, was born as Bruno of Egisheim in Egisheim, France.

1591 St. Aloysius Gonzaga, patron saint of Catholic youth, died at 23; also observed as his feast day.

1639 Increase Mather, noted colonial clergyman, was born in Dorchester, Mass., son of Richard Mather; served as pastor of Boston's Second Congregational Church (1664-1723); president, Harvard (1685-1701); author of "Cases of Conscience Concerning Evil Spirits," which is credited with ending witchcraft executions (died 1723).

1792 Ferdinand C. Baur, Protestant theologian, was born in Schmiden, Germany; founder of the "Tübingen School," and the movement to apply the critical historical method to theology; a father of the modern history of dogma (died 1860).

1811 Matthew Simpson, Methodist leader and educator, was born in Cadiz, Ohio; served as bishop (1852-84), delivered the eulogy at funeral of President Lincoln; president, Garrett Biblical Institute, Evanston, Ill. (1859-84) (died 1884).

1825 William Stubbs, English prelate, was born near Leeds; canon of St. Paul's (1879-84), Bishop of Chester (1884-89), Oxford (1889-1901); important historical researcher; principal work, "The Constitutional History of England" (died 1901).

1870 The French consul and 22 Catholic priests and Sisters of Mercy, and many native converts, were massacred by a mob in Tientsin, China.

1892 Reinhold Niebuhr, influential American theologian, was born in Wright City, Mo.; with Union Theological Seminary (1930-60); pioneer in neo-orthodoxy, which sought to relate religious teachings to contemporary life and history; one of the most influential American theologians of the 20th century; author (Does Civilization Need Religion?, Moral Man and Immoral Society, The Nature and Destiny of Man) (died 1971).

1929 Agreement reached by the Mexican Government and the Catholic Church; the main point was the resumption of church services which had been suspended July 31, 1926.

1957 George S. Russell, British-Canadian clergyman, died in Toronto at 74; pastor, Deer Park United Church, Toronto (1929-57); president, Congregational Ministers' Crusade Against War (1925-29).

1963 Paul VI was consecrated as pope, served until 1978; he was the first pope to visit the Holy Land and the United States; the first pope to meet with the Orthodox patriarch in 500 years, when they revised the rules of penitential observance and modernized the church structure; reaffirmed the church's traditional view on clerical celibacy, artificial birth control.

JUNE 22

Feast day in the Catholic Church of St. Alban, England's first Christian martyr; beheaded about 304 for helping a fugitive priest, who converted him, to escape.

Feast day of St. Niceta, Bishop of Remesiana (Yugoslavia) (370-414); authorship attributed to him of celebrated hymn, "Te deum laudamus."

380 St. Eusebius of Samosata, martyr and Bishop of Samosata (Turkey) (361-380), died; reputedly killed by a thrown stone, thus becoming a martyr; also observed as his feast day in the Orthodox Church.

816 Stephen IV was elected pope, served until 817.

1276 Blessed Innocent V, pope from January 21 to June 22,1276, died at about 51; also observed as his feast day.

1535 St. John Fisher, English Catholic martyr, was beheaded for denying that Henry VIII was supreme head on earth of the Church of England and for opposing his divorce from Catherine of Aragon; Bishop of Rochester (1502-34); one of the greatest scholars of his day and his theological writings proved important during the Council of Trent; elevated to cardinal 1535; canonized 1935.

1552 The first Catholic Bishop of Brazil, Pedro Fernandes Sardinha, arrived in Bahia.

1622 Gregory XV issued a bull, "Inscrutabili divinae," which created the Congregation for the Propagation of Faith to supervise foreign mission activities.

1680 Ebenezer Erskine, founder of the Scottish Secession Church, was born near Edinburgh; censured prevalent doctrinal errors, advocated the right of the people to choose their pastors; was deposed; then with three fellow Church of Scotland clergymen formed the Secession Church (died 1754).

1750 Congregation in Northampton, Mass. dismissed Jonathan Edwards, famous colonial clergyman, after a long argument over the terms of church admission; Edwards had served the church since 1729; gave last sermon July 1.

1774 British Parliament passed the Quebec Act, designed to provide for the westward expansion of the territory of Quebec and the religious toleration of Catholics - "It is hereby declared that His Majesty's Subjects professing the Religion of the Church of Rome...may have, hold, and enjoy the free Exercise of the Religion of the Church of Rome...and that the Clergy of the said Church may hold, receive, and enjoy their accustomed Dues and Rights..."

1792 Domenico Barberi, called Dominic of the Mother of God, was born in Viterbo, Italy; a Passionist and mystic who served as a missionary in England (1841-49); beatified in 1963 (died 1849).

1929 Bishop Pascual Diaz was named Archbishop of Mexico City and the Catholic primate of Mexico.

1980 Lutherans and Catholics sang, prayed and affirmed their faith together in St. Patrick's Cathedral, New York City, in ecumenical celebration of the Augsburg Confession.

JUNE 23

1625 John Fell, Bishop of Oxford (1676-86) and chaplain to King Charles II, was born in Longworth, England; he was immortalized in the doggerel verse by Thomas Browne: "I do not love thee, Dr. Fell;/The reason why I cannot tell; But this alone I know full well,/I do not love thee, Dr. Fell" (died 1686).

1707 John Mill, English biblical scholar, died at 62; noted for his 30-year effort on a critical edition of the Greek New Testament, for which he collected 30,000 various readings.

1780 The British advance on Springfield, N.J. was checked by American troops, who had to use hymnal pages from the First Presbyterian Church for gun wadding.

1786 Nathaniel W. Taylor, Congregational clergyman and educator, was born in New Milford, Conn.; professor of didactic theology, Yale Divinity School (1822-58); developed elaborate system of theology, involving freedom of will (Taylorism), which created considerable controversy (died 1858).

1803 Jason Lee, Methodist missionary, was born in Stanstead, Vt. (now in Canada); missionary to Oregon and a founder of the Oregon territorial government and Oregon Institute, which later became Willamette U. (died 1845).

1854 James C. R. Ewing, Presbyterian missionary to India, was born in Rural Valley, Pa.; principal, Forman Christian College, Lahore (1888-1918); dean (1890-1907), vice chancellor (1910-17) of Punjab U. (died 1925).

1860 St. Joseph Cafasso, who worked with prisoners and convicts, died at 49; canonized 1947; also observed as his feast day.

1877 Religious instruction in Italian secondary schools was abolished in the elementary schools on July 15.

1956 The General Council of the Congregational Christian Churches voted to unite with the Evangelical and Reformed Church in 1957 to form the United Church of Christ.

1964 Pope Paul VI stated that the Catholic Church was giving "wide and profound" study to the problem of birth control.

1967 Pope Paul VI issued an encyclical, "Sacerdotalis Caelibatus," strongly reaffirming the traditional Catholic rule on clerical celibacy.

1973 Associate Justice M. A. Haywood of the Washington (D.C.) Superior Court was elected moderator of the ninth biennial general synod of the United Church of Christ, the first black woman to hold a position of top leadership in an American biracial denomination.

JUNE 24

Feast day in the Catholic Church of St. John the Baptist, forerunner of Jesus, whom he baptized; executed on order of Herodotus.

1386 St. John of Capistrano, one of the most prominent 15th Century ecclesiastics, was born in Italy; largely responsible for the rapid growth of the Observants, serving as the order's vicar general (1446-51); as papal inquisitor, he was severe against the Fraticelli* and the Jews (died 1456).

1485 Johannes Bugenhagen, Protestant religious and educational reformer, was born in Wollin, Germany; assisted Luther in preparing High German translation of the Bible, was a practical organizer of the Reformation, instrumental in promoting Protestant schools and churches; reorganized church in Denmark and northern Germany, and the U. of Copenhagen (died 1558).

1499 Johann Brenz, German reformer, was born near Stuttgart; a leader of the Reformation in Württemberg, proponent of the Ubiquitarian* theory (died 1570).

1519 Theodore Beze (or Beza), French theologian who aided John Calvin, was born in Vezelay; became one of the leading educators, theologians, and statesmen of the Reformation; wrote Greek and Latin translations of the New Testament, which were basic to Protestant students for two centuries; succeeded Calvin as leader of the movement (1564-1605) (died 1605).

1542 St. John of the Cross, Carmelite mystic and poet, was born in Spain; founder of the Discalced Carmelites; his "Obras espirituales," contains three great mystical poems; canonized 1726, made Doctor* of the Church 1926 (died 1591).

1546 Robert Parsons, English jurist, was born near Bristol; Jesuit missionary to England, who with Edmund Campion carried on intrigue designed to subject England to papal authority; founded seminaries for English Catholics in France and Spain; helped organize resistance to Elizabethan Protestant regime; rector, English College in Rome (1597-1610) (died 1610).

1579 Rev. Francis Fletcher, chaplain to Sir Francis Drake, read the first English church service in North America in what is now San Francisco.

1615 The first mass in Canada was celebrated by the Recollet Fathers at Riviere des Prairie (on the island of Montreal); first mass in Quebec was celebrated June 25.

1663 Jean Baptiste Massillon, Bishop of Clermont (1719-42), was born near Toulon; one of the greatest preachers of the court of Versailles; renowned for funeral orations (Prince de Conti, Louis XIV) (died 1742).

1687 Johann A. Bengel, German Lutheran theologian, was born near Stuttgart; produced the first critical edition of the Greek New Testament, marking the beginning of modern scientific work in the field; the first to classify the New Testament into Asiatic and African families (died 1752).

1729 Edward Taylor, Puritan clergyman and poet, died at 87; religious poems were not published until 1939; considered finest poet of colonial America.

1797 John J. Hughes, first Catholic Archbishop of New York (1851-64), was born in Tyrone County, Ireland; founded St. John's (now Fordham) College, began construction of St. Patrick's Cathedral (1858) (died 1864).

1803 George J. Webb, organist and composer, was born in Wiltshire, England; organist at Old South Church, Boston; a founder, Boston Academy of Music; remembered for hymn, "Stand up for Jesus" (died 1887).

1813 Henry Ward Beecher, influential Congregational clergyman, was born in Litchfield, Conn., the fourth son of Lyman Beecher; spokesman and symbol of Protestantism of his time; pastor, Plymouth Church, Brooklyn (1847-87); charged with adultery (1874), six month sensational trial ended in hung jury, but scandal overshadowed his last years (died 1887).

1844 Joseph and Hyrum Smith, Mormon leaders and brothers, were arrested in Carthage, Ill. for their part in the riot following destruction of the Nauvoo (Ill.) paper June 7.

1876 J. Leighton Stuart, Presbyterian missionary to China, was born in Hangchow, China; first president, Yenching U. (1919-46); ambassador to China (1946-47) (died 1962).

1965 The 100th anniversary of the founding of the Salvation Army was observed in ceremonies in Albert Hall, London.

1976 In a statement, 67 Episcopal bishops said they would sponsor church legislation to permit the ordination of women to priesthood.

1977 Bishop Josiah M. Kibiro, black activist bishop from Tanzania, was elected the first African and first black to head the Lutheran World Federation.

JUNE 25

Feast day in the Orthodox Church of the birth of St. John the Baptist.

1080 Clement III, born Wilbert of Ravenna, became anti-pope and took over Rome, which he held until the Pierleoni family deposed him in 1098.

1243 Innocent IV, born Sinisbaldo Fieschi, was elected pope, served until 1254; carried on continual struggle with Emperor Frederick II; his bull, "Ad extirpenda" (1252), permitted the use of torture in the Inquisition.

1438 Council of Basel, which had been feuding with Pope Eugenius IV since it opened in 1431, deposed the pope.

1530 The Augsburg Confession, Lutheran Reformation's basic particular creed, was presented at the Diet of Augsburg; chief author was Philip Melancthon, using earlier Lutheran statements of faith; divided into two parts - the first in 21 articles epitomized the essential Lutheran doctrines, the second reviewed abuses which required remedies; answered August 3 by a group of Catholic theologians in "Confutatio pontificia," the Confession influenced subsequent Anglican 39 Articles and John Wesley's 23 Articles.

1580 Book of Concord, the collected doctrinal standards of the Lutheran Church, was issued in German (Latin translation 1584); issuance culminated 30 years effort to heal breaches in Lutheranism after Luther's death; met with much opposition outside Germany; never possessed the authority of the Augsburg Confession.

1663 John Bramhall, English primate, died at 69; Protestant Archbishop of Armagh (1661-63); argued against Thomas Hobbes on freedom of the will.

1667 Johannes F. Buddeus, German theologian and philosopher, was born; considered the most universally accomplished German theologian of his time, a renowned church historian (died 1729).

1684 Robert Leighton, English prelate, died at 73; principal, divinity professor, Edinburgh U. (1653-61); persuaded by Charles II to become Bishop of Dunblane (near Perth, Scotland) (1661-70); later Archbishop of Glasgow (1670-74); tried unsuccessfully to keep best of Episcopal and Presbyterian faiths as basis for unity.

1692 Innocent XII issued the bull, "Romanum decet pontificem," which ended nepotism in the Vatican.

1744 The first Methodist conference was convened in London.

1773 Eliphalet Nott, Presbyterian clergyman and educator, was born in Ashford, Conn.; served First Church, Albany; president, Union College (1804-66); invented a base-burning anthracite coal stove (died 1866).

1834 Gregory XVI issued an encyclical, "Singulari nos," condemning a book by Felecite de Lamennais, French Catholic liberal.

1873 The Italian legislature enacted a law to expel the Jesuits.

1886 James F. McIntyre, Catholic prelate, was born in New York City; Archbishop of Los Angeles (1948-79), elevated to cardinal 1953 (died 1979).

1897 Louis Joseph Paul Bruchesi was named Catholic Archbishop of Montreal.

1957 The United Church of Christ was formed in the United States by the union of the Evangelical and Reformed Church and the Congregational Christian Church; officially in force July 4, 1961.

1962 The U. S. Supreme Court held 6-1 that the reading of an official prayer in New York public schools violated the First Amendment of the Constitution.

1977 Frederick W. Frantz was elected president of Jehovah's Witnesses on the death of Nathan H. Knorr June 11.

1977 The National Council of Churches Committee on Faith and Order declared the Unification Church of Rev. Sun Myung Moon is "not a Christian church" as it professes to be and that many of its teachings are "incompatible" with Christian belief.

1984 The 23rd General Assembly of the Unitarian Universalist Association opened in Columbus, Ohio; gave initial approval to new statement of "Principles and Purposes."

1986 V. Carney Hargroves, president of American Baptist churches (1954-55) and the Baptist World Alliance (1970-75) died at 85.

1844 A public meeting in Warsaw, Ill. decided that Mormon destruction of the Nauvoo newspaper office was revolutionary and tyrannical; that Mormons should be driven out.

1858 Federal troops established a post in Cedar Valley by arrangement with Brigham Young; rebellion by Mormons ended and Gov. Alfred Cumming assumed office in Salt Lake City June 30.

1934 The Evangelical & Reformed Church was formed in Cleveland by the union of the Evangelical Synod of North America and the Reformed Church in the United States.

1967 Pope Paul VI reaffirmed his call for an international status for Jerusalem.

1979 The United Church of Christ, the first church to ordain an avowed homosexual, voted overwhelmingly at its biennial meeting in Indianapolis, to continue its policy of leaving ordination decisions to local authorities.

JUNE 26

Feast day of St. Deodatus, pope from 672 to 676.

684 St. Benedict II was consecrated as pope, served until 685; won agreement with Constantine IV to abolish imperial confirmation of pope-elect.

1178 St. Anthelm died at 72; served as Bishop of Bellay and minister general of the Carthusian Order; also observed as his feast day.

1245 The first Council of Lyon (France) opened; Pope Innocent IV called for clerical reform, a crusade to retake Jerusalem, and a settlement of the dispute between the papacy and Emperor Frederick II; council ended July 17.

1701 Philip Doddridge, English Dissenting clergyman, was born in London; author of books which provided an incentive to faith (The Family Expositor, The Rise and Progress of Religion in the Soul); wrote several hymns (O God of Bethel (Jacob), by whose hand; Ye servants of the Lord) (died 1751).

1703 Thomas Clap, Congregational clergyman, was born in Scituate, Mass.; rector, later president, Yale College (1739-66) (died 1767).

JUNE 27

Feast day of St. Ladislaus (1040-95), king of Hungary; built many churches, promulgated a series of laws on religious and civil matters; canonized 1192.

444 St. Cyril, patriarch of Alexandria (412-444), died at about 68; expelled Jews from Alexandria, presided over Council of Ephesus (431) at which Nestorius was condemned as a heretic; a Doctor* of the Church; also observed as his feast day in the Catholic Church.

1818 James Lloyd Breck, theologian, was born near Philadelphia; founder of Nashota House in Wisconsin (1841) as a semi-monastic center for study, worship, evangelism; founder of Seabury Divinity School, Faribault, Minn. (1857) (died 1876).

1844 A mob of armed men with blackened faces stormed the jail in Carthage, Ill. and murdered Mormon Church founder, Joseph Smith, and his brother, Hyrum.

1924 Dermot Ryan, Catholic Archbishop of Dublin and primate of Ireland (1972-84), was born in Dublin; proprefect of Congregation for Evangelization (1984-85) (died 1985).

1946 Sally Priesand, first American woman to be ordained a rabbi (1972), was born in Cleveland.

1961 Arthur Michael Ramsey was enthroned as the 100th Archbishop of Canterbury and primate of All England.

1985 The General Synod of the United Church of Christ, meeting in Ames, Iowa, declared its ecumenical partnership with the Christian Church (Disciples of Christ).

1986 Leaders of 12 religious groups joined Pope John Paul II in a World Day of Prayer for Peace in Assisi.

JUNE 28

Feast day of St. Irenaeus, a Father*, Doctor,* and saint of the church (about 130-200); apostle of the Gauls and Bishop of Lyon (177-200); considered the first great Catholic theologian.

767 St. Paul I, pope from 757 to 767, died; brother of Pope Stephen II; reign dominated by relations with Frankish and Lombard kings; also observed as his feast day.

1476 Paul IV, pope from 1555 to 1559, was born as Giovanni Pietro Caraffa in Naples.

1490 Albert of Brandenburg, elector of Mainz and Archbishop of Magdeburg (1514-45), was born in Aschaffenburg, Germany; attacked by Martin Luther over sales of indulgences* for the building of the new St. Peter's in Rome, with part of the proceeds to be used for the archbishopric; a vigorous opponent of Reformation (died 1545).

1629 Peace of Alais was signed, ending the Huguenot war in France, with the Huguenots retaining their freedom of conscience, but losing their military advantages.

1703 John Wesley, co-founder of Methodism, was born in Epworth, England, son of Samuel Wesley and brother of Charles; bought deserted gun factory near London for preaching; rejected doctrine of election and caused later secession of Welsh Calvinistic Methodists; journeyed through British Isles, averaging 8000 miles a year to organize "societies" and visited American colonies; a man of great courage and persistence, with a vast capacity for leadership and organization; his personality was magnetic, his piety and charity incontestable; considered one of the greatest Christians of his age; wrote numerous educational works and edited, compiled Methodist hymnal and translated many German hymns (died 1791).

1793 The Synod of Upper and Lower Canada was formed, with Dr. Jacob Mountain as the first Anglican Bishop of Canada.

1847 Algernon S. Crapsey, liberal Episcopal clergyman, was born in Fairmount, Ohio; rector of St. Andrew's Church, Rochester, N.Y. (1879-1906); found guilty of heresy (1906), deposed; author (Religion and Politics, The Last of the Heretics) (died 1927).

1854 John Maclean (1800-86), Presbyterian clergyman, was installed as president of Princeton U., served until 1867.

1930 The Mexico City Cathedral was restored to the control of the Mexican Catholic Church by decree of the president.

1962 The Lutheran Church in America was formed by consolidation of the United Lutheran Church in America, the Angustana Evangelical Lutheran Church, and the Finnish Evangelical Lutheran Church.

JUNE 29

Feast of Sts. Peter and Paul, the "princes of the apostles," who according to legend were put to death by Emperor Nero on the same day (AD 64 or 65) in Rome.

1628 Miguel de Molinos, Spanish priest, was born in Muniesa, Spain; proponent of extreme Quietism;* imprisoned for heresy during the Inquisition (died 1696).

1721 John Ettwein, Moravian leader, was born in Freudenstadt, Germany; served as official correspondent for Moravian Church of North America and his letters are a historical treasure; consecrated bishop (1784) and presiding officer of the church (died 1802).

1737 Platon, metropolitan of Moscow, was born as Peter Levchin; became Archbishop of Moscow (1775), metropolitan (1787-1812); helped prepare foundation of Russian Bible Society (died 1812).

1797 Frederic Baraga, Catholic missionary, was born near Döbernig, Austria; served the Indians in Michigan and became the first Bishop of Upper Michigan (1853-68) (died 1868).

1810 The first foreign missionary society was formed in Boston by the General Association of Massachusetts.

1857 Charles D. Tenney, American missionary, was born in Boston; selected by the Chinese Government to be the first president of the Imperial Chinese University, Tientsin (1895-1906) (died 1930).

1872 Vanderbilt U. at Nashville, Tenn., including its seminary, was chartered by the Methodist Episcopal Church, South.

1896 Pope Leo XIII issued the encyclical, "Satis cognitum," which said reunion of all Christians is only possible if the pope is recognized as the center of unity.

1908 The American Catholic Church was removed from the jurisdiction of the Roman Congregation for the Propagation of Faith and placed under the Roman Curia.

1930 Seven North American martyrs were canonized - Jean de Brebeauf, Noël Chabanel, Anthony Daniel, Charles Garnier, Rene Goupil, Isaac Jogues and Gabriel Lalemont; all had served as Jesuit missionaries to the Indians and were murdered.

1943 Pope Pius XII issued the encyclical, "Mystici corporis Christi," emphasizing the units of the Church in the mystical body of Christ.

1958 Pope Pius XII issued the encyclical, "Ad apostolorum principis," excommunicating all Chinese bishops who had consecrated pro-government prelates without Vatican approval.

1982 The United Presbyterian Church voted to approve the merger with the Presbyterian Church in the United States.

1988 Archbishop Marcel Lefebvre ordained 16 Catholic priests in Econe, Switzerland in defiance of papal orders; the following day he consecrated four bishops which automatically resulted in his expulsion from the church.

JUNE 30

296 St. Marcellinus became pope, served until 304.

1139 St. Otto, Bishop of Bamberg (1102-39), died at 77; the "apostle of Pomerania" (region along southern shore of Baltic Sea); he took part in founding more than 20 monasteries; canonized 1189; also observed as his feast day.

1315 Raymond Lully, Catalan ecclesiastic and scholastic philosopher, died at about 83; known as "Doctor Illuminatus;" devoted to life as a missionary, dedicated to conversion of Mohammedans in Africa; stoned to death outside Bougie (North Africa).

1644 William Chillingworth, English theologian, died at 42; his book, "The Religion of Protestants, a Safe Way to Salvation," was a vindication of sole authority of the Bible in matters of salvation and the individual's right to interpret it.

1886 Bishop James Gibbons of Baltimore was consecrated as the second American cardinal.

1891 Bishop Frederic X. Katzer was consecrated as Archbishop of Milwaukee, served until 1903.

1963 Pope Paul VI was crowned as the 262nd pope of the Catholic Church.

1968 Pope Paul VI issued a 3000-word "Credo of the People of God," stressing acceptance of church dogma.

1980 Pope John Paul II began the first papal visit to Brazil, which lasted 12 days.

JULY 1

Feast of the Most Precious Blood.

Feast day in the Catholic Church of St. Pamphilus, priest and teacher of Caesaria (seaport of Roman Palestine) and a devout Christian teacher in Alexandria.

Feast day in the Orthodox Church of Sts. Cosmas and Damian, brothers and patron saints of physicians; reputedly they were doctors who refused fees for their work.

1381 St. Lawrence Justinian, first patriarch of Venice and spiritual writer, was born; founded about 35 religious houses; his writings exerted wide influence; general of Augustinian Order and drew up its constitution; canonized 1690 (died 1456).

1555 John Bradford, English Protestant martyr, was burned at the stake; imprisoned (1553) on a charge of sedition for about six weeks after Queen Mary's accession.

1574 Joseph Hall, Anglican prelate, was born in Ashby-de-la-Zouch, England; defended church against Catholic and Puritan attacks; Bishop of Exeter (1627-41) until imprisoned on charges of treason with 11 other bishops (1641-42); retired to the country (died 1656).

1633 Johann H. Heidegger, Reformed Church theologian, was born in Switzerland; chief author of the unsuccessful formula designed to unite all Swiss Reformed churches (1675) (died 1698).

1750 Jonathan Edwards preached his final sermon to the Northampton (Mass.) Church, which let him go after 21 years over differences on church admission.

1861 *L'Osservatore Romano*, Vatican newspaper, was published for the first time.

1899 The Christian Commercial Men's Association of America was formed by traveling salesmen at a meeting in Boscobel, Wisc.; better known as the Gideons, the organization places Bibles in hotel rooms; first Bible was placed in the Superior Hotel, Iron Mountain, Mont. in November 1908.

1932 The National Council of Congregational and Christian Churches was formed in Seattle by the union of the National Council of Congregational Churches and the General Convention of Christian Churches.

1959 Ground was broken in Dayton, Ohio for the new Evangelical United Brethren administration building.

1966 The Congregational Council for World Mission was formed in Great Britain, uniting the work of the former London Missionary Society and the Commonwealth Missionary Society.

1978 Worldwide Church of God founder, Herbert Armstrong, excommunicated his son, Garner Ted Armstrong, from the church for his actions in seeking to become the designated heir.

1982 Rev. James Parker became the first non-celibate priest to celebrate a Western rite mass; a former Episcopal priest, he was ordained June 29 with the Pope's approval.

1985 The U.S. Supreme Court ruled that public school teachers could not enter parochial school classrooms to provide remedial or enrichment instruction.

JULY 2

311 St. Miltiades became pope, served until 314; reign marked by the halt of persecution of Christians.

862 St. Swithin, English ecclesiastic, died at about 62; Bishop of Winchester (852-862); associated with legend that if it rains on July 15, it will rain for the next 40 days.

1489 Thomas Cranmer, first Archbishop of Canterbury of the reformed Church of England (1533-55), was born in Aslacton, England; helped Henry VIII strengthen his case for divorce from Catherine of Aragon; as archbishop he nullified several of Henry's marriages and maintained the divine right of kings; promoted translation of the Bible into the vernacular, produced "The English Book of Common Prayer"; sought through Philip Melancthon to promote a union of reformed churches; on accession of Queen Mary, he was condemned for treason for acquiescing in the plot to put Lady Jane Grey on the throne; burned at the stake (1556).

1505 Martin Luther, while returning from a visit to his parents, was overtaken by a thunderstorm and cried out, "Help, St. Anne, and I'll become a monk;" he did so two weeks later.

1524 The Custodia del Santo Evangelio was established by the Franciscans in Mexico City; by 1580 it had more than 50 convents.

1565 Francis of Borgia, duke of Gandia, became the third general of the Society of Jesus (Jesuits); served until 1572.

1724 Friedrich G. Klopstock, great German religious poet, was born near Magdeburg; wrote the religious epic, "The Messiah," and such other works as "David" and "Oden" (died 1803).

1813 Samuel Wolcott, Congregational clergyman, was born in South Windsor, Conn.; wrote hymn, "Christ for the world we sing" (died 1886).

1833 Henry M. Butler, educator and hymnist, was born in Gayton, England; headmaster, Harrow School (1859-86), master of Trinity College, Cambridge (1896-1918); known for Anglican hymn, "Lift up your hearts! We lift them, Lord" (died 1918).

1853 Frederick T. Gates, superintendent of missions, American Baptist Home Missionary Society (1877-85), was born in Maine, N.Y.; instrumental in raising funds for the University of Chicago and the involvement of John D. Rockefeller; chairman, General Educational Board and Rockefeller Institute of Medical Research; helped establish Rockefeller Foundation (died 1929).

1872 George W. Mundelein, Archbishop of Chicago (1915-39), was born in New York City; elevated to cardinal 1934, the "first cardinal of the West" (died 1939).

1883 Amendments to the German ecclesiastical laws were passed by the Diet and reconciliation with the Vatican was made closer.

1906 Catholic Bishop James H. Black was consecrated as Archbishop of New Orleans; served until 1917.

1959 Pope John XXIII, in his first encyclical - "Ad Petri Cathedrum" - appealed to world statesmen to try every approach that might lead to international unity and peace.

1972 Joseph Fielding Smith, president of the Mormon Church, died at 95.

1985 The foundation was laid for the extension of the William Booth Memorial Training College in South London.

JULY 3

Feast day in the Catholic and Syrian churches of St. Thomas the Apostle.

683 St. Leo II, pope from 681 to 683, died; also observed as his feast day.

1570 Aonio Paleario, Italian humanist and martyr, was burned at the stake in Rome; works in which he objected to the doctrine of purgatory were considered heretical; tried twice, then seized by the Inquisition and imprisoned, martyred.

1836 George Batchelor, Unitarian clergyman, was born in Southbury, Conn.; secretary, American Unitarian Association (1893-98); editor, *Christian Register* (1898-1911) (died 1923).

1894 Jaime de Barros Camara, Archbishop of Rio de Janeiro (1941-71), was born in Sao Jose, Brazil; elevated to cardinal 1946 (died 1971).

1926 The Mexican Government outlined offenses against religious provisions of the Constitution; all ministers were required to be of Mexican birth, churches administered by foreigners were to be closed July 31.

1956 President Eisenhower approved a bill authorizing the payment of $964,199.35 to the Vatican as damages for the accidental bombing by American planes of the summer residence of Pope Pius XII during World War II.

JULY 4

740 St. Andrew of Crete, regarded as one of the greatest hymn writers of the Orthodox Church, died at about 80; believed to have originated musical or Greek canon, wrote various hymns (Christians, dost thou see them); also observed as his feast day.

950 St. Odo the Good died; Archbishop of Canterbury (942- 950), active in restoring the Cathedral buildings, raising the morals and discipline of the clergy; also observed as his feast day.

965 Benedict V, born Grammaticus and pope in 964-965, died in Germany, where he was a prisoner of German Emperor Otto I, who had selected Leo VIII as pope.

973 St. Ulrich, Bishop of Augsburg (923-973), died at 83; he was the first person known to have been canonized by a pope (John XV in 993); also observed as his feast day.

1415 Pope Gregory XII resigned at the Council of Constance to help end the papal schism.

1533 John Frith, an English Protestant martyr, was burned at the stake; wrote "Articles," which denied the doctrines of purgatory and transubstantiation; helped Tyndale translate the New Testament.

1623 William Byrd, English composer and organist, died at 80; dominated the "golden age" of English music and composed much music for both the Catholic and Anglican liturgy.

1648 St. Anthony Daniel, French Jesuit missionary and martyr, died at 47; spent life among Huron Indians in the Georgian Bay area; canonized (1930) along with six other North American martyrs.

1794 George Duffield, Presbyterian clergyman, was born in Carlisle, Pa.; became center of doctrinal dispute with the publication of "Spiritual Life; or, Regeneration" (1832); charged with heresy and dismissed from pastorate at Carlisle, where he had been 19 years; pastor, First Presbyterian Church, Detroit (1836-68); moderator, New School general assembly (1862) (died 1868).

1797 John Breckenridge, Presbyterian clergyman and editor, was born in Lexington, Ky.; founder, editor, *The Western Luminary*; secretary and general agent, Presbyterian Board of Education (1831-36); secretary, Presbyterian Board of Foreign Missions (1838-41) (died 1841).

1804 Patrick E. Moriarity, American superior of Augustinian Order, was born in Dublin, Ireland; founder, Villanova College (1842), president (1854-75) (died 1875).

1812 Thomas March Clark, Episcopal prelate, was born in Newburyport, Mass.; Bishop of Rhode Island (1854-1903), presiding bishop (1899-1903) (died 1903).

1816 Richard Watson, English clergyman and chemist, died at 79; as chemist, he discovered the principle of the black bulb thermometer; as Bishop of Llandaff, he wrote a defense of Christianity against Edward Gibbon and a defense of the Bible against Thomas Paine.

1836 The first white women to cross the Rockies into Oregon Territory were Narcissa P. Whitman and Eliza H. Spalding, wives of missionaries in a party organized by the American Board of Commissioners for Foreign Missions.

1870 James Moffatt, Scottish theologian, was born in Glasgow; professor of church history, Union Theological Seminary (1927-39); made translation of the Bible, which bears his name (died 1944).

1873 John A. F. Gregg, primate of the Church of Ireland (Protestant) (1938-59), was born in Deptford, England (died 1961).

1880 Phillips Brooks, rector of Boston's Trinity (Episcopal) Church, preached in Westminster Abbey; the following Sunday, before the Queen in Windsor Chapel.

1885 Charles E. Raven, divinity professor and author, was born in Paddington, England; his works include "Christian Socialism 1848-54" and "Apollinarianism" (died 1964).

1887 Edward McGlynn, New York Catholic priest, was excommunicated for political activities, refusal to retract statements, and failure to appear in Rome; later investigation by the Church resulted in his reinstatement (1892).

1961 The constitution of the United Church of Christ was declared officially in force in the United States; resulted from the merger of the Evangelical and Reformed and the Congregational Christian churches.

1968 Protestant and Orthodox leaders from more than 80 countries opened the fourth assembly of the World Council of Churches in Upsala, Sweden.

1971 The Electoral College of the Bulgarian Orthodox Church, meeting in Sofia, elected Maxim, the metropolitan of Lovets, to become patriarch of the church.

1884 Enrico Dante, prefect of pontifical ceremonies at the Vatican (1947-67), was born in Rome; elevated to cardinal 1965 (died 1967).

1958 Serbian Patriarch Vikentije Prodanov died in Belgrade at about 68.

1959 The American Baptist Convention held services at Valley Forge, Pa., dedicating the 55-acre site of the convention's new $5-$6 million headquarters.

1977 The United Church of Christ, at its biennial general synod, voted to spend two years exploring the possibility of uniting with the Christian Church (Disciples of Christ).

1982 Reuben Mueller, Evangelical United Brethren prelate, died at 85; helped establish (1950), president, National Council of Churches; led movement to merge his church with the Methodist Church (1968).

1988 Church of England leaders voted in favor of proposals to admit women to the priesthood, despite the opposition of Archbishop of Canterbury Robert Runcie; the legislation now will be debated by the church's 44 dioceses, then go back to the General Synod for final approval and then must be approved by Parliament.

1988 The 69th general convention of the Episcopal Church meeting in Detroit unanimously approved an anti-discrimination resolution to protect AIDS sufferers.

JULY 5

Feast day of St. Athanasius the Athonite; established the first monastery on Mt. Athos in Greece; served as abbot general of the Mount communities.

767 Constantine II, pope from 767 to 768, was named through the military force of his brother, the Duke of Nepi.

1294 St. Celestine V, born Pietro di Murrone, a hermit, was elected pope at the age of 80; resigned in December; kept interned until his death in 1296; founder of the Order of Celestines.

1539 St. Antony Zaccaria died at 39; founder of the Clerks Regular of St. Paul (1533); canonized 1897; also observed as his feast day.

1559 Nicholas Heath, Archbishop of York and lord chancellor, was deprived of his see and imprisoned for refusing the oath of supremacy; released (1565) and allowed to live in retirement.

1818 Thomas T. Lynch, English Congregationalist, was born; wrote the hymn, "Gracious Spirit, dwell with me" (died 1871).

1843 Mandell Creighton, historian and Anglican clergyman, was born in England; Bishop of Peterborough (1891-97), of London (1897-1901); first editor, *English Historical Review*; author (History of the Papacy, Cardinal Wolsey) (died 1901).

1865 The first meeting was held of the Christian Mission in England, which was founded and led by William Booth; took name of Salvation Army in June 1878.

1877 Judah L. Magnes, American rabbi and educator, was born in San Francisco; served Temple Emanu-el (1906-10) and B'nai Jeshurun (1911-12), both in New York City; a founder, first chancellor (then president), Hebrew University, Jerusalem (1925-48) (died 1948).

JULY 6

1415 Jan Huss (Hus), Czech religious reformer, was burned at the stake as a heretic, following his conviction by the Council of Constance and his refusal to recant; his death resulted in his becoming a national hero; influenced by the writings of John Wycliffe and was excommunicated for preaching them; his work, which anticipated Luther by a century, was transitional between medieval thought and the Reformation; after his excommunication, he continued to preach until the Constance "trial;" q author of "De Ecclesia" (The Church).

1439 Pope Eugenius IV, as a result of the Council of Ferrara-Florence, issued the bull, "Laetentur coeli," proclaiming the reunion of the Greek and Roman churches, which turned out to be only temporary.

1535 Sir Thomas More, English statesman and martyr, was beheaded.

1583 Edmund Grindal, Archbishop of Canterbury (1575-83), died at about 64; suspended by Queen Elizabeth I for his laxity with the Quakers, for not suppressing prophesying; bears large share of the credit for the rise of standards of learning among the clergy; was a vigorous opponent of Catholicism.

1757 William McKendree, first American-born Methodist bishop (1808-35), was born in William City, Va.; associate of Francis Asbury, first Methodist superintendent, and his successor (died 1835).

1758 Clement XIII was named pope, served until 1769; reign marked by fierce attacks on Jesuits, who were suppressed in Portugal (1759), France (1764), and Spain (1767); issued bull opposing the suppressions.

1762 Ashbel Green, Presbyterian clergyman and educator, was born in Hanover, N.J.; president, College of New Jersey (later Princeton) (1812-22); editor, *Christian Advocate* (1822-34) (died 1848).

1768 Johann C. Beissel, German-born founder of the Dunkers, died at 78; founded the "Solitary Brethren of the Community of Seventh-Day Baptists" (Dunkers) in Ephrata, Pa. (1732); author of many hymns which influenced American hymnology.

1800 Alonzo Potter, Episcopal prelate, was born in Dutchess County, N.Y., brother of Horatio Potter; Bishop of Pennsylvania (1845-65), established Episcopal hospital (1860) and divinity school (1863) in Philadelphia (died 1865).

1852 Katherine Tingley, Theosophist leader, was born in Newburyport, Mass.; succeeded in merging Theosophical Society into a new organization, Universal Brotherhood, of which she was the head (died 1929).

1896 Otto J. Baab, American Methodist clergyman and educator, was born in Chicago; professor, Garrett Bible Institute and other schools; member, War Labor Board (1942-45) (died 1958).

1904 Leon J. Suenens, an outspoken Catholic cardinal and primate of Belgium, was born in Brussels; felt that the pope's primacy cannot be exercised in separation from the bishops.

1908 A pontifical decree was issued by the Vatican for the reform of the organization and operations of different congregations.

JULY 7

Feast day of St. Palladius the Deacon, allegedly the first missionary to Ireland (about the Fifth Century); sent to combat Pelagianism*.

Feast day of St. Prosper of Aquitaine (about 390-483), theologian and secretary to Pope Leo I; championed theology of St. Augustine and had considerable influence on Carolingian* theologians.

Feast day of St. Pantaenus (died about 190), the first known head of the Catechetical School of Alexandria, designed to spread Christianity among the more cultured classes.

Former feast day in the Catholic Church of Sts. Cyril and Methodius, two Greek brothers, who were the "apostles to the Slavs"; now observed Feb. 14.

786 St. Willibald, English missionary Bishop of Eichstädt (742-786), died; a nephew and associate of St. Boniface; founded double monastery in Würtemberg; also observed as his feast day.

1274 Gregory X issued the papal bull, "Ubi periculum," which established the conclave method of selecting the pope.

1304 Blessed Benedict XI, pope in 1303-04, died suddenly; it is believed he was poisoned; beatified 1773; also observed as his feast day.

1647 Thomas Hooker, one of the foremost colonial preachers, died at 61; sometimes called "the father of American democracy."

1713 Henry Compton, Anglican prelate, died at 81; Bishop of London and leader of the revolution of 1688; protested illegal acts of James II and voted to declare the throne vacant; crowned William and Mary, helped revise church liturgy.

1762 Alexander McDonnell, Canadian Catholic prelate, was born in Glen Urquhart, Scotland; first Catholic bishop of Upper Canada (1826-40) (died 1840).

1874 Henry Ward Beecher demanded an investigation by his church of the charges of scandal brought against him by Theodore Tilton, who later sued for alleged improper relations with his wife.

1910 Spain prohibited additional religious orders from entering the country, pending negotiations with the Vatican.

1959 The General Synod of the United Church of Christ issued its first major pronouncement, stressing the role of the church in ameliorating social, international, and political problems and urging an end to segregation.

1959 The American Lutheran Church was established by the merger of the Evangelical Lutheran and United Evangelical Lutheran churches.

1960 The General Synod of the United Church of Christ adopted a constitution for the newly-formed church in sessions in Cleveland.

1972 Athenagoras I, Archbishop of Constantinople (1948-72), died in Istanbul at 86; spiritual leader of 150 million Orthodox Church members; met with Pope Paul VI (1964) in Jerusalem, the first such meeting since 1439.

1972 Harold B. Lee was named the 11th prophet and president of the Mormon Church.

1982 The General Synod of the Anglican Church failed to approve closer bonds with other Protestant churches.

JULY 8

Feast day of St. Adrian III, pope from 884 to 885.

Feast day of St. Kilian (or Cilian), Irish missionary in Germany in the Seventh Century, and two co-workers who were put to death in 697.

1115 Peter the Hermit (also Peter of Amiens), French preacher of the First Crusade, died at 65; took part in capture of Jerusalem (1099); returned to France, founded and headed Abbey of Neufmoutier (Huy).

1153 Eugenius III, pope from 1145 to 1153, died; also observed as his feast day.

1547 A papal bull made Mexico an archdiocese.

1623 Gregory XV, pope from 1621 to 1623, died at 69.

1654 The first Jew to settle in North America, Jacob Barsimon, arrived in New York City, the first of 21 Jewish immigrants in that year; they founded Congregation Shearith Israel.

1850 James Strang's Mormon colony on Big Beaver Island in Lake Michigan was organized as the Kingdom of St. James; Strang was elected "king."

1850 Frederic de S. Mendes, rabbi and editor, was born in Montego Bay, Jamaica; assistant rabbi (1874-78), rabbi (1878-1920), Congregation Shaaray Tefila, New York City; a founder, editor, *American Hebrew* (1875-79); author (Outlines of Jewish History) (died 1927).

1886 Edward F. Paget, first Anglican Archbishop of Central Africa (1955-71), was born in Oxford, England (1955-71) (died 1971).

1959 Representatives of Congregational Christian Church and the Evangelical and Reformed Church, meeting in Oberlin, Ohio, adopted a statement of faith for the United Church of Christ into which they were merging.

1969 The Church of England convocation in London failed to ratify plans for a merger with the Methodist Church in what was described as "the most crucial day for English religion since the Reformation;" vote of 69% failed to reach the required 75%; Methodists, meeting in Birmingham, voted 77% for merger.

1984 A devastating fire, possibly caused by lightning, seriously damaged the York Minster Gothic cathedral in York, England; structure was built between 1220 and 1470; treasures of the church were saved; cathedral will be restored.

1985 Egypt banned religious bumper stickers in an effort to curb the spread of Islamic fundamentalism.

JULY 9

Feast day of St. John Fisher (1459-1535), English Catholic bishop and martyr.

Feast day of Sir Thomas More, English statesman and author; lord chancellor, who refused to accept Henry VIII as head of the church; author of "Utopia;" beheaded.

381 Nestorius, first patriarch of Constantinople (428-431), was born in what is now Maras, Turkey; preached the doctrine that in Jesus Christ a divine person and a human person were joined in perfect harmony of action but not in the unity of a single person; deposed for heresy by the Council of Ephesus (431), banished to the Libyan Desert; followers (Nestorians) flourished for several centuries (died 451).

1228 Stephen Langton, Archbishop of Canterbury (1207-28), died.

1572 Angry mob of Calvinists invaded the Dutch town of Gorkum, marched 19 Catholic priests and friars to the gallows.

1763 The Jesuits were expelled from Louisiana; embarked from New Orleans Nov. 24.

1838 Philip P. Bliss, singing evangelist, was born in Clearfield County, Pa.; wrote numerous favorite gospel hymns (Hold the fort; Only an armor bearer; Let the lower lights be burning; Pull for the shore) (died 1876).

1838 Sir Robert Grant, governor of Bombay, died at 51; wrote the Anglican hymn, "O worship the King, all glorious above."

1846 Merriman C. Harris, Methodist prelate, was born in Beallsville, Ohio; superintendent, Japanese mission of Methodist Church, San Francisco (1886-1904); Bishop of Japan and Korea (1904-16) (died 1921).

1847 Joseph Eugene Bruno Guiges was named the first Catholic Bishop of Ottawa.

1850 Bab, who laid down the foundations of the Bah-i faith, was publicly executed in Tabriz.

1855 James J. Strang, Mormon sect leader, died; his Mormon settlement on Big Beaver Island in Lake Michigan was destroyed and the inhabitants driven away.

1917 The Evangelical Seminary (Protestant) opened in Mexico City.

1962 Eighty-one countries sent 250 Protestant and Orthodox delegates to the third World Institute on Christian Education which opened in Belfast, Northern Ireland.

JULY 10

Feast day of Our Lady of Fatima, commemorating the appearance to three children of the Virgin Mary in Fatima, Portugal.

Feast day of St. Alexander and the six sons of St. Felicity, all of whom were martyred; St. Felicity's feast day is observed Nov. 23.

983 Benedict VII, pope from 974 to 983, died; reasserted position of the papacy, advanced monasticism, condemned simony* at a synod in March 981.

1073 St. Anthony of the Caves died at 90; founder of the Caves of Kiev; also observed as his feast day.

1509 John Calvin, theologian and reformer, was born in Picardy, France; sought to establish a theocratic government in Geneva, but was driven out by a popular revolt (April 23,1538), recalled (1541); succeeded in setting up such a government, which served as a focal point for the defense of Protestantism throughout Europe; his zeal and writings brought into one body of doctrine (Calvinism) the scattered and unsystematic reformed opinion of the period; his reputation and influence as an ecclesiastical statesman, as a religious controversialist, educator, and author was widespread; his knowledge of languages, his precision and his clear and pithy style made him the most influential writer among the reformers; founded an academy in Geneva, which became the intellectual center of international Calvinism; wrote "Institute of the Christian Religion" (died 1564).

1588 Edwin Sandys, Anglican prelate, died at 72; imprisoned in Tower of London for espousing cause of Lady Jane Grey (1553), escaped; on accession of Elizabeth I, he became Bishop of Worcester (1559), of London (1570), then Archbishop of York (1576-88); helped prepare Bishops' Bible.

1629 The first non-Separatist Congregational church in the United States was established in Salem, Mass. by Francis Higginson and Samuel Skelton, two newly-arrived ministers.

1762 Alexander Kilham, founder of the Methodist New Connection, was born in Epworth, England; New Connection was a church formed by those seceding from Wesleyan Methodism and completely separated from the Church of England (died 1798).

1773 Finis Ewing, Presbyterian leader, was born in Brevard County, Va.; principal founder of the Cumberland Presbyterian Church (1810) (died 1841).

1783 Bennet Tyler, Congregational theologian and educator, was born in Middlebury, Conn.; president, Dartmouth College (1822-28); became leader of a conservative clerical group; a founder, professor, and president, Theological Institute of Connecticut (now Hartford Theological Seminary) (1834-57) (died 1858).

1796 John Johns, Episcopal prelate and educator, was born in New Castle, Del.; Bishop of Virginia (1862-76); president, College of William & Mary (1849-54) (died 1876).

1858 Four Redemptorist priests, led by Isaac Thomas Hecker, were released from their obligations by Pope Pius IX and founded the Paulist Fathers (Missionary Society of St. Paul the Apostle) in New York City.

1888 Toyohiko Kagawa, Japanese reformer and evangelist, was born in Kobe; regarded as the leading Christian in Japan; influential in democratization of Japan; organized first labor union in Japan (1921); established Kingdom of God movement to promote conversions to Christianity (died 1960).

1902 Maurice N. Eisendrath, religious leader, was born in Chicago; president, Union of American Hebrew Congregations (1946-73) (died 1973).

1908 Phoebe P. Knapp, philanthropist and hymn writer, died at 69; wife of founder of Metropolitan Life Insurance Co., she was active in philanthropy and Methodist affairs; remembered for the hymn, "Blessed assurance."

1970 Catholic Bishop James Walsh arrived in Hong Kong after being imprisoned in China as a spy for 10 years.

1982 Catholic Archbishop of Cincinnati Joseph L. Bernardin was named Archbishop of Chicago; had been auxiliary bishop of Atlanta (1966-68), general secretary, Bishops' Conference (1968-72), Archbishop of Cincinnati (1972-82).

JULY 11

Feast day of St. Pius I, pope from 140 to 155; little is known of his life or reign.

Feast day of St. Olga, popular saint of the Russian Church; wife of Prince Igor of Kiev; she ruled Kiev (945-955) after Igor's death.

1276 Adrian V, born Ottobuono de Fieschi and a nephew of Pope Innocent IV, was named pope; served one month until his death Aug. 18; his one act was to suspend the rigid rules by which popes were elected.

1681 St. Oliver Plunkett, Archbishop of Armagh and primate of Ireland (1669-81), was martyred, the last Catholic to die for his faith in England and the first Irish martyr to be beatified; accused of involvement in the Popish plot and was found guilty of treason; canonized 1975; also observed as his feast day.

1713 Joseph Stennett, early English Baptist hymn writer, died at 50; among his hymns was "Another six days work is done."

1748 The cornerstone was laid for the Catholic cathedral in Santiago, Chile by Bishop Juan Gonzales Marmolejo.

1767 John Quincy Adams, Unitarian sixth president of the United States, was born in Braintree, Mass.; wrote entire "Version of the Psalms," 17 of which (including five hymns) were inserted in the Christian Psalmist (1841); three are still used (died 1848).

1780 Timothy Flint, Congregational clergyman and author (Francis Berrian, Shoshone Valley), was born in North Reading, Mass. (died 1840).

1847 John Henry Barrows, Congregational clergyman and educator, was born in Medina, Mich.; president, Oberlin College (1898-1902); organized Parliament of Religion at the Columbian Exposition, Chicago (1893) (died 1902).

1914 Donald S. Harrington, pastor, New York Community Church (1944-66) and leader of the New York Liberal Party, was born in Newton, Mass.

1951 The New York State Court of Appeals upheld the practice of released time for religious studies by school children in the state; upheld also by the U.S.Supreme Court in April 1952.

JULY 12

Feast day of St. Veronica, who according to legend wiped Jesus' brow while He was carrying the cross to Golgotha; the cloth miraculously retained the imprint of His countenance.

526 St. Felix IV was consecrated pope, served until 530; chosen through the influence of Theodoric, king of the East Goths; formed the church of Sts. Cosmas and Damian from two pagan shrines, restored the basilica of St. Saturninas.

1073 St. John Gaulbert, founder of the Vallombrosan Benedictines, died; canonized 1193; also observed as his feast day.

1153 Anastasius IV was crowned pope, served through 1154; settled controversy over candidacy of Frederick I for emperor; issued interdict* against Arnold of Brescia; restored the Pantheon at Rome.

1691 Innocent XII was named pope, served until 1700; reign marked by church reform; ended nepotism in the Vatican, restored peace by his handling of Jansenism, quietism*, and Gallicism controversies.

1730 Clement XII was named pope, served until 1740; vigorously supported missionary training colleges, condemned Freemasonry, took action against Jansenism.

1774 Freeholders and freemen issued a declaration of independence in the First Presbyterian Church in Carlisle, Pa.

1790 The French legislature adopted "Constitution Civile du Clergé" declaring the French church independent of the papacy, except in strict doctrinal matters; Louis XVI signed it against his will; condemned by Pope Pius VI in 1791.

1803 Thomas Guthrie, clergyman and philanthropist, was born in Brechin, Scotland; known as the "apostle of the ragged schools" (schools for destitute children); preached in Edinburgh (1837-64), mostly in Free St. John's Church (died 1873).

1843 Joseph Smith, Mormon leader, announced that a divine revelation had sanctioned the practice of polygamy; announcement in Nauvoo, Ill. caused bitter feelings among both Mormons and non-Mormons.

1850 Joseph Signay became the first Catholic Metropolitan Archbishop of Quebec.

1888 The Jesuit Estate Act was passed by the Quebec legislature, authorizing the payment of $400,000 for confiscated estates which reverted to the Crown when the Jesuit Order was suppressed in 1773.

JULY 13

Feast day in the Catholic Church of St. Silas, early (First Century) Christian prophet and missionary; accompanied St. Paul on first visit to Macedonia and Corinth.

574 John III, pope from 561 to 574, died.

939 Leo VII, pope from 936 to 939, died.

1024 St. Henry II, German King (1002-24) and Holy Roman Emperor (1014-24), died; assisted in removing Greek supremacy in Italy; legend ascribes to him outstanding piety and asceticism; also observed as his feast day.

1105 Rashi (Shelomo ben Yitzhak), French rabbinical scholar, died at 65; his commentaries on the Hebrew Bible and the Babylonian Talmud were the basis for their traditional study.

1205 Hubert Walter, Archbishop of Canterbury (1193-1205), died; accompanied Richard I on Third Crusade as Bishop of Salisbury; led army back to England as Archbishop of Canterbury (1193); governed kingdom and raised Richard's ransom; chancellor (1199-1205).

1298 Blessed James (Jacobus) of Voragine (1230-98), Dominican prelate and theologian, died; Archbishop of Genoa (1292-98), wrote "Golden

Legends or Lives of the Saints;" beatified 1816; also observed as his feast day.

1590 Clement X, pope from 1670 to 1676, was born as Emilio Altieri in Rome.

1635 Jacques Bruyas, French Jesuit missionary, was born in Lyon; served Iroquois Indians, was general superior of Jesuits in Canada (1693-98) (died 1712).

1769 Thomas Kelly, dissenting preacher and hymn writer, was born in Ireland; used own wealth to erect chapels for dissenters, where he preached; wrote many hymns (Look, ye saints, the sight is glorious; The head that once was crowned with thorns; Come, see the place where Jesus lay) (died 1855).

1771 Anthony Kohlmann, Jesuit priest, was born in Kaiserburg, Germany; administrator of the New York Diocese, won the law suit which sought to compel him to reveal source of information obtained in a confessional; led to later state legislation protecting confessions (died 1836).

1811 Sir George G. Scott, church architect of the Gothic revival, was born in Gawcott, England; restored such cathedrals as Ely, Salisbury, Litchfield, and Westminster Abbey (died 1878).

1814 Jose S. Alemany, Catholic prelate, was born in Vich, Spain; missionary bishop to the American West, first Archbishop of San Francisco (1853-84) (died 1888).

1886 Edward J. Flanagan, Catholic priest, was born in Roscommon, Ireland; founder, head (1922-48) of Boys Town near Omaha, Nebraska (died 1948).

1886 Clifford Bax, playwright and author, was born in England; wrote a number of hymns (Turn back, O man, forswear thy foolish ways) (died 1962).

JULY 14

Feast day of St. Bonaventure, Italian-born general of the Franciscan Order (1257-73) and influential spiritual writer; elevated to cardinal 1273; served as Bishop of Albano (southeast of Rome) (1273-74); was a key figure at the Council of Lyon; among his many works are "Commentaries" and "Sentences;" canonized 1482, declared a Doctor* of the Church 1588.

664 St. Deusdedit, first Anglo-Saxon Archbishop of Canterbury (655-664), died; also observed as his feast day.

939 Stephen VIII was elected pope, served until 942; owed election to Alberic II of Spoleto, who controlled Rome.

1575 Richard Taverner, English biblical scholar, died at 70; prepared a revision of Mathew's Bible, known as the Taverner's Bible (1539), and a commentary on epistles and gospels (1540).

1602 Jules Mazarin, French cardinal and statesman, was born in Pescina, Italy; papal nuncio to Paris and then became French leader on the death of Richelieu; worked successfully to save and strengthen France; elevated to cardinal 1641 (died 1661).

1614 St. Camillus of Lellis, patron of the sick and nurses, died at about 60; founder (1582) of Ministers of the Sick (Camillians); canonized 1746.

1634 Pasquier Quesnel, French theologian, was born in Paris; member of the Oratory (Fathers of the Oratorium), writings placed on the Index and his refusal to condemn Jansenism forced him to flee to Brussels and later to Amsterdam, where he founded a Jansenist Church (died 1719).

1773 The first annual conference of American Methodists convened in St. George's Church in Philadelphia.

1800 Matthew Bridges, Anglican Romanist hymn writer, was born in England; best remembered for "Crown Him with many crowns" (died 1894).

1829 Edward W. Benson, Archbishop of Canterbury (1883-96), was born in Birmingham; expanded missions and improved relations with other churches; prevented disestablishment of the Church of Wales; delivered the historically important judgment at the trial of Dr. Edward King, Bishop of Lincoln, charged with ritual offenses; intolerant of opposition and criticism, vigorously upheld the Establishment; developed Wellington College; author (Cyprian, The Apocalypse) (died 1896).

1833 John Keble, an Oxford don, gave a sermon at Oxford in which he attacked the Whig plan to eliminate ten of the established bishoprics of the Church of Ireland as an act of "national apostasy;*" the sermon marked the start of the Oxford Movement, which sought a revival of sacramental pilety and a return to the theology of the 17th Century High Church.

1883 The first class of American rabbis (four) was ordained in Cincinnati, after graduation from Hebrew Union College.

1912 Laurian Rugambwa, the first black cardinal, was born in Bukongo, Tanganyika; Bishop of Rutabo, elevated to cardinal 1960.

1961 Pope John XXIII appealed in an encyclical ("Mater et Magistra") for aid to underdeveloped areas without creation of a new form of colonialism or the spread of materialism.

JULY 15

Feast day of St. Swithin, Ninth Century English Bishop of Winchester; considered to have rain-making powers; legend has it that if it rained on this day, it would rain for the ensuing 40 days.

Feast day of Our Lady of Mt. Carmel, commemorating the Carmelite Order.

Feast day of St. James (Jacob) of Nisibis, Bishop of Nisibis (northeast Syria) and called the "Moses of Mesopotamia;" honored by both Syrians and Armenians as a theological doctor.

Former feast day of St. Henry II, German king (1002-1024) and Holy Roman Emperor (1014-24); now observed July 13.

885 Stephen V was elected pope, served to 891; reign was marked by a decline of the papacy.

1015 St. Vladimir, grand prince of Russia, where he launched Christianity, died at 59.

1099 Jerusalem fell to forces of Crusaders led by Godfrey of Bouillon and most residents were massacred; Crusaders set up a ruling government and the Holy Sepulchre was recovered.

1274 St. Bonaventure, general of the Franciscan Order, died suddenly during the Council of Lyon; canonized 1482.

1386 John Ball, a leader of the Peasants' Revolt (1381), was hanged for his part in the uprising; a priest at York and Colchester, he agitated for revolt for 20 years.

1631 Richard Cumberland, English Anglican divine and philosopher, was born in London; Bishop of Peterborough, best remembered for his "Laws of Nature," a reply to Hobbes, presenting principles of universal benevolence as opposed to Hobbes' egoism and setting up the greatest good of a universe of rational beings as the foundation of ethical theory; regarded as the founder of English utilitarianism (died 1718).

1704 August G. Spangenberg, Moravian leader, was born in Klettenburg, Germany; bishop (1744-62) of the Unitas Fratrum* and founder of the Moravian Church in North America; returned to Germany; a dominant figure in his church (1762-92) (died 1792).

1779 Clement C. Moore, Hebrew scholar, was born in New York City; donated land on which the General Theological Seminary was built in New York City; compiled "A Compendium of the Hebrew Language;" best known for his ballad, " 'Twas the night before Christmas" (1822) (died 1863).

1801 Napoleon Bonaparte, in a concordat concluded with Pope Pius VII, recognized that Catholicism was the faith of most Frenchmen and restored it and papal authority in France.

1802 Robert Aitken, Scottish-born printer, died at 68; his greatest accomplishment was the first complete English Bible printed in America (1782).

1808 Henry E. Manning, Archbishop of Westminster (1865-92), was born in Totteridge, England; founder, superior of the Oblates of St. Charles; elevated to cardinal 1875; one of the leaders of the Oxford Movement (died 1892).

1817 Thomas Bowman, Methodist prelate and educator, was born in Berwick, Pa.; founder, head, Dickinson Seminary, Williamsport, Pa. (1848-58); president, Indiana Asbury U. (later DePauw) (1858-72); Methodist bishop (1872-1914) (died 1914).

1845 The Buffalo Synod, Lutheran Church, was formed by Johannes A. A. Grabau; later (1930) merged into the Lutheran Church.

1848 William A. Leonard, Episcopal prelate, was born in Southport, Conn.; Bishop of Ohio (1889-1930), responsible for building cathedral in Cleveland; served as acting presiding bishop (1929-30) (died 1930).

1849 The Pope's authority over Rome was restored with the help of French troops.

1850 St. Francis Xavier Cabrini (Mother Cabrini) was born in Lodigiano, Italy; founder, Missionary Sisters of the Sacred Heart (1880); the first American citizen to be canonized (1946) (died 1917).

1851 Blessed Anne Mary Javouhey, French-born congregation founder, died at 72; founded Congregation of St. Joseph of Cluny; beatified 1950.

1884 Will W. Alexander, one-time Methodist clergyman who led in founding the Committee on Interracial Cooperation, was born in Morrisville, Mo.; committee director (1919-44); director, Farm Security Administration (1937-40) (died 1956).

1901 Truman B. Douglass, church leader, was born in Grinnell, Iowa; he was a moving spirit in the unification of the Congregational and Evangelical & Reformed denominations into the United Church of Christ (died 1969).

1904 The first Buddhist temple in the United States was organized in Los Angeles.

1961 Pope John XXIII issued the encyclical "Mater et Magistra" to commemorate 70th anniversary of "Rerum novarum," issued by Pope Leo XIII, which rejected Marxist and 18th Century liberalism teachings.

JULY 16

Feast day in the Catholic Church of St. Eustathius, Bishop of Antioch (324-330); strongly opposed Arians at Council of Nicaea; deposed (331) and banished, resulting in a schism which lasted until 413.

622 Traditional date of the beginning of "hegira," the flight of Mohammed from Mecca to Medina; the date is the starting point of the Mohammedan calendar.

1194 St. Clare was born as Clara Scefi in Assisi, becoming a co-founder of the Order of Poor Clares; abbess of the Order (1212-53), canonized 1255 (died 1253).

1216 Innocent III, pope from 1198 to 1216, died.

1546 Anne Askew, English Protestant martyr, was burned at the stake for refusing to recant her opinions on transubstantiation and the Eucharist.

1705 Pope Clement XI issued the bull, "Vineam domini sabaoth," condemning Jansenism.

1769 Junipero Serra, Spanish missionary, founded the first California mission at San Diego de Alcala.

1803 Johann Baptista Baltzer, theologian, was born in Germany; sought to reconcile Catholic teaching with newer German philosophy; became ardent promoter of Old Catholic movement (died 1871).

1821 Mary Baker Eddy, founder of the Christian Science Church, was born in Bow, N.H.; as an invalid she sought many types of healing, but it was not until she turned to the Bible that she founded the spiritual, metaphysical system called Christian Science; founded the *Christian Science Journal* (1883) and the Christian Science Publishing Society (1898) (died 1910).

1846 St. Mary-Magdalen Postal died at 90; founder, Sisters of the Christian Schools of Mercy (1807); canonized 1925; also observed as her feast day.

1859 William D. Mackenzie, Congregational theologian and educator, was born in Fauresmith, South Africa; professor, systematic theology, Chicago Theological Seminary (1895-1903); professor, president, Hartford (Conn.) Theological Seminary (1904-30) (died 1936).

1874 Henry S. Tucker, Episcopal presiding bishop (1937-46), was born in Warsaw, Va.; Bishop of Kyoto (1912-23), Bishop of Virginia (1927-46); president, Federal Council of the Churches of Christ (1942-46) (died 1959).

1903 Rev. James H. Griffiths, Vatican observer at the United Nations, was born in New York City; auxiliary bishop of the New York Diocese (1949-64) (died 1964).

1972 Metropolitan Dimitrios was elected to succeed Athenagoras I as Ecumenical Patriarch of the Eastern Orthodox Church; known as Dimitrios I.

JULY 17

521 St. Magnus Felix Ennodius, French-born ecclesiastical writer and Bishop of Pavia (south of Milan) (514-521), died at about 47; his work was probably the last serious attempt to combine pagan culture and Christianity; also observed as his feast day.

561 John III was named pope, served until 574; during his reign the Lombards frequently ravaged Italy; he was able to bring about a return of obedience to Rome.

855 St. Leo IV, pope from 847 to 855, died; also observed as his feast day.

1048 Damasus II, born Poppo, was consecrated as pope; died August 19; had served as Bishop of Brixen in Bavaria.

1048 Benedict IX, pope from 1032 to 1045, was driven from Rome after he sought to regain the papacy; a nephew of Benedict VIII and John XIX, he was put into the papacy by the Tusculan party; driven out 1045 by a Roman insurrection and replaced by Clement II; Benedict reappeared Nov 8, 1047 and sought unsuccessfully to retake the papacy.

1505 Martin Luther entered the Augustinian Hermits monastery at Erfurt to study.

1674 Isaac Watts, English Nonconformist clergyman and a leading hymn writer, was born in Southampton; regarded as the father of English hymns, creator of the modern hymn as opposed to the medieval office hymn and the Reformation metrical paraphrase of the Psalms; wrote about 600 hymns (When I survey the wondrous cross, There is a land of pure delight; Our God, our help in ages past; Come ye, that love the Lord; Joy to the world) (died 1748).

1766 Samuel Finley, Presbyterian clergyman and educator, died at 51; an active participant in the religious revival of the day; accused of "censoriousness" and enthusiasm; expelled from Connecticut where he went to preach; president, College of New Jersey (later Princeton) (1761-66).

1768 Stephen T. Badin, first Catholic priest ordained in the United States (1793), was born in Orleans, France (died 1853).

1794 Bethel African Methodist Episcopal Church, the first African Methodist Episcopal church, opened in Philadelphia; dedicated by Francis Asbury July 29.

1907 A decree was issued by the Vatican containing a syllabus of 65 modern errors against the faith.

1961 Mampre Calfayan, Archbishop of North America of the Armenian Church, died in Miami at about 65.

1980 Rev. Marjorie S. Matthews, 64, of Traverse City, Mich. became the first woman named to the ruling hierarchy of an American church when she was elected a bishop of the United Methodist Church.

JULY 18

Feast day of St. Camillus (Camillo) (1550-1614), founder of the Ministers of the Sick (Camillians).

641 St. Arnulf, Bishop of Metz (610-627), died at about 61; retired to live in the Vosges Mountains as a hermit; also observed as his feast day.

1216 Honorius III, born Cencio Savelli, was named pope, served until 1227; reign was marked by efforts to restore order to Europe, to gain control of the Holy Land, and to further Christian piety; confirmed the Dominican (1216) and Franciscan (1223) orders.

1270 Boniface of Savoy, Archbishop of Canterbury (1241-70), died enroute to a crusade.

1323 Thomas Aquinas (1225-74), was declared a saint by Pope John XXII.

1504 (Johann) Heinrich Bullinger, Swiss reformer, was born in Bremgarten, Switzerland; associate and successor of Huldreich Zwingli; primary interest was to establish a common evangelical front for all reformed churches; involved in preparing two Helvetic confessions with John Calvin, including the "Consensus Tigurinus" on the Lord's Supper (died 1575).

1534 Zacharias Ursinus, German Reformed clergyman, was born in Breslau; helped draw up the Heidelberg Catechism (died 1583).

1823 Archibald A. Hodge, Presbyterian educator, was born in Princeton, N.J., son of Charles Hodge; professor of systematic theology, Western Theological Seminary (1864-77), Princeton Theological Seminary (1877-86); author (Outlines of Theology, The Atonement); a founder of the Presbyterian Review (died 1886).

1827 Presbyterian clergymen, alarmed by the departure of Charles G. Finney's evangelism from strict Westminster standards, met for nine days in New Lebanon, N.Y.; resulted in heightened feeling and renewed rupture.

1852 Paul Carus, editor and author, was born in Ilsenburg, Germany; editor (1887-1919) of Open Court, a forum for discussion of religion and ethics; author (Religion and Science) (died 1919).

1870 The First Vatican Council, after considerable debate, agreed on "papal infallibility," promulgating the doctrinal constitution, "Pastor aeternus," by a vote of 533 to 2, which asserted that "the Roman Pontiff, when he speaks ex cathedra, that is, when in discharge of the office of pastor and teacher of all Christians, by virtue of his supreme apostolic authority he defines a doctrine regarding faith or morals to be held by the universal Church, by the divine assistance promised to him in blessed Peter, is possessed of that infallibility with which the divine Redeemer willed that his church should be endowed."

1896 Patrick A. O'Boyle, Catholic prelate, was born in Scranton, Pa.; Archbishop of Washington (1948-73), emeritus (1973-); elevated to cardinal 1967.

1976 The Museum of American Jewish History opened in Philadelphia.

JULY 19

Feast day of St. Vincent de Paul, founder of the Lazarists and the Confraternities of Charity.

514 St. Symmachus, pope from 498 to 514, died; also observed as his feast day.

1598 Gilbert Sheldon, English prelate, was born near Derby; Bishop of London (1660-63), Archbishop of Canterbury (1663-77); severe against Dissenters, built the Sheldonian Theater at Oxford (1669) (died 1677).

1759 St. Seraphim of Sarov, famed Russian Orthodox mystic, was born in Kursk; canonized 1903 (died 1833).

1814 Patrick H. Mell, president, Southern Baptist Convention and educator, was born in Walthourville, Ga.; vice chancellor, U. of Georgia (1860-78), chancellor (1878-88) (died 1888).

1876 Ignaz Seipel, Catholic priest and government official, was born; apostolic prothonotary*, became chancellor of Austria (1922-24,1926-29) (died 1932).

1876 Joseph Fielding Smith, president of Mormon Church (1970-72), was born in Salt Lake City; president of Council of 12 of the church (1951-69) (died 1972).

1904 Catholic Bishop Verhaeghen, his brother, and another Belgian missionary were murdered in Hu-pei, China.

1980 Msgr. Marcel Lefebvre, French traditionalist archbishop suspended by Pope Paul VI in 1976 from all priestly duties, announced he would open a university in Paris in October.

JULY 20

Feast day in the Orthodox Church of Elijah, considered the greatest of prophets.

Feast day of St. Aurelius, Bishop of Carthage (about 391-430); presided over a series of ecclesiastical councils.

Feast day of St. Jerome Emiliani (1481-1537), founder of the Somaschi Order (1532); canonized 1767, made patron saint of orphans and abandoned children 1928.

514 St. Hormisdas became pope, served until 523.

1519 Innocent IX, pope from October to December 1591, was born as Giovanni Antonio Faccinetti in Bologna, Italy.

1591 Anne Hutchinson, English-born religious liberal, was baptized in Alford, England; preached salvation by individual intuition of God without regard for church; banished from Massachusetts, settled in Rhode Island and then near what is New Pelham, N.Y., where she and her family were massacred by Indians (1643).

1629 Samuel Skelton was named pastor of the first church in Massachusetts.

1866 Charles R. Erdman, Presbyterian clergyman, was born in Fayetteville, N.Y.; a leader of conservatives in the Presbyterian Church; moderator, Presbyterian General Assembly (1925) (died 1960).

1888 Alwyn T. P. Williams, chairman of the committee which prepared the "New English Bible: New Testament" (1950-61), was born in Barrow-in-Furness, England; Anglican Bishop of Durham (1939-52), of Winchester (1952-61) (died 1968).

1892 Joseph E. Ritter, Archbishop of St. Louis (1946-67), was born in New Albany, Ind.; Archbishop of Indianapolis (1944-46); elevated to cardinal 1960 (died 1967).

1903 Pope Leo XIII died, had served since 1878.

1910 The Christian Endeavor Society of Missouri began a campaign for movies censorship, banning all movies depicting kissing between people not related.

JULY 21

230 Pontianus was named pope, served until he resigned in exile in 235.

810 al-Bukhari, Arab author, was born; greatest of the Traditionalists; recorded the sayings and acts of Mohammed; traveled throughout Moslem world collecting 600,000 traditions ("Hadiths"), he issued 7,275 in "Sahih" (Sincere Book); next to Koran in importance and influence on the Moslem mind (died 870).

1414 Sixtus IV, pope from 1471 to 1484, was born as Francesca Della Rovere in Cella Ligure, Italy.

1515 St. Philip Neri, congregation founder, was born in Florence, Italy; an outstanding figure of the Counter Reformation, known as the "second apostle of Rome;" founder (1564) of the Institute of Oratory (Oratorians) and co-founder (1548) of the Confraternity of the Most Holy Trinity to care for pilgrims and convalescents; canonized 1622 (died 1595).

1663 Claude Jean Allouez was appointed vicar general for all natives and traders of the American Northwest (upper Great Lakes).

1773 Pope Clement XIV issued a brief, "Dominus ac redemptornoster," which suppressed the Jesuits for the hostility they had incurred and the controversies in which they had been involved.

1801 Theron Baldwin, pioneer Western missionary, was born in Goshen, Conn.; headed Society for the Promotion of Collegiate and Theological Education in the West; founder, president, Monticello Seminary, Godfrey, Ill. (1838-43) (died 1870).

1847 Vanguard of westward-moving Mormons reached Salt Lake City, Utah; rest came two days later.

1860 Edward J. Hanna, Catholic prelate, was born in Rochester, N.Y.; named auxiliary bishop of San Francisco (1912), Archbishop (1915-35); first chairman, National Catholic Welfare Conference (1919-44) (died 1944).

1874 Catholic associations in Berlin were closed by the government.

1953 Methodist Bishop G. Bromley Oxnam of Washington, D.C. demanded that House Un-American Activities Committee clear its files of unsubstantiated charges against him; Committee acknowledged it had no evidence of Communist sympathy against him.

JULY 22

Feast day of St. Mary Magdalen, a disciple of Jesus and his most devoted female follower.

1376 Simon Langham, Archbishop of Canterbury (1366-76), died; expelled Wycliffe and secular clergy from Oxfordshire Hall; elevated to cardinal without approval of Edward III and was forced to resign the archbishopric (1368).

1559 St. Lawrence of Brindisi, a Doctor* of the Church, was born in Brindisi, Italy; polemicist of the Counter Reformation; canonized 1881 (died 1619).

1581 Richard Cox, Bishop of Ely (1559-80), died at about 80; an active promoter of the Reformation in England; helped compile the first English Book of Common Prayer; chancellor of Oxford U. (1547-52), eradicated books, manuscripts and statutes with Catholic leanings.

1620 Separatist Puritan congregation from Scrooby, England, which had taken refuge in Leyden, Netherlands, with its pastor, John Robinson, left for England to emigrate to America; became the Pilgrim Fathers.

1647 St. Margaret Mary Alacoque, Vistandine nun, was born in Lauthecour, France; initiated modern practice of devotion to the Sacred Heart of Jesus; canonized 1930 (died 1690).

1649 Clement XI, pope from 1700 to 1721, was born in Urbino, Italy as Giovanni Francesco Albani.

1676 Clement X, pope from 1670 to 1676, died at 86.

1680 Richard Cameron, Scottish Covenanter leader, was ambushed and killed; leader of Nonconformist Presbyterian sect (Cameronians) which had declared war against King Charles II; a powerful field preacher.

1732 John Ewing, Presbyterian minister, was born in East Nottingham, Md.; served church in Philadelphia (1759-1802); first provost, U. of Pennsylvania (1791-1802) (died 1802).

1763 Calvin Chapin, Congregational clergyman, was born in Chicopee Falls, Mass.; served Stepney Parish, now Rocky Hills, Conn. (1794-1851); a founder, Connecticut Bible Society, American Board of Foreign Missions (died 1851).

1822 Gregor J. Mendel, Augustinian abbot, was born in Heinzendorf, Austria; best known for his research into the fundamental laws of inheritance through breeding experiments with peas in the monastery garden (died 1884).

1847 The advance company of Mormons, led by Anson Pratt, erected a camp on the site of Salt Lake City; Brigham Young and the rest of the settlers arrived July 23, celebrated by Mormons as their day of deliverance.

1902 John C. Bennett, Congregational clergyman and theologian, was born in Kingston, Canada; professor of social ethics, Union Theological Seminary (1943-64), president (1964 on).

1960 A constituting convention began in Minneapolis where three major Lutheran churches were formally merged into the American Lutheran Church — the three were the American Lutheran Church, Evangelical Lutheran Church, and the United Evangelical Lutheran Church.

1969 The first worldwide youth congress of the Seventh-Day Adventist Church opened in Zurich, Switzerland.

1972 A revised high holy days prayer book for Conservative Judaism was published in the United States; sought to strike a balance between Orthodoxy's strict interpretation of Biblical themes and the liberal views of worship of Reformed Judaism.

JULY 23

Day of Deliverance in the Mormon Church, commemorating the arrival of settlers in Salt Lake City, Utah.

Feast day of St. Lawrence of Brindisi (1559-1619), a Doctor* of the Church; canonized 1881.

Feast day in the Catholic Church in Marseilles of St. John Cassian, founder of the monasteries in Marseilles and an ecclesiastical writer.

Feast day of St. Apollinaris, first Bishop of Ravenna, who reputedly was a martyr.

685 John V was consecrated as pope, served until 686; a Syrian, he was the first of several pontiffs of Eastern origin.

1373 St. Bridget (or Brigitta) of Sweden died at 70; founder (about 1346) of the Brigittine Order (or Order of the Savious) and a mystic; mother of St. Catherine of Sweden; author of "Revelations," a description of the visions she had; canonized 1391; also observed as her feast day.

1431 The Council of Basel opened, continued despite papal order to disband.

1793 Nathaniel L. Frothingham, Unitarian clergyman, was born in Boston; served First Church, Boston (1815-50); hymn writer (O God, whose presence glows in all; We meditate the day; O Lord of life and truth and grace) (died 1870).

1834 James Gibbons, Catholic prelate, was born in Baltimore; Bishop of Richmond, Va. (1872-77), Archbishop of Baltimore (1877-1921); a founder, first chancellor, Catholic U., Washington, D.C. (1889); second American cardinal; author (The Faith of Our Fathers) (died 1921).

1904 St. Patrick's Cathedral in Armagh, Ireland was consecrated.

1966 The World Council of Churches condemned the "growing American military presence in Vietnam."

1969 The seventh High Council of the Salvation Army elected Swedish Commissioner Erik Wickberg as general.

1978 Archbishop of Canterbury Donald Coggan opened the 11th Lambeth Conference in England, attended by bishops from 100 countries.

JULY 24

1725 John Newton, English clergyman and hymnist, was born in London; impressed on board a man-of-war, made midshipman; deserted, spent four years in the African slave trade; became curate of Olney, England and joint producer of the Olney Hymns, writing 281 of the 348 hymns, including "Glorious things of Thee are spoken," "One there is above all others," "How sweet the name of Jesus sounds," and "Amazing grace" (died 1807).

1858 Knox College, Presbyterian seminary in Toronto, was chartered.

1918 The cornerstone of Hebrew University was laid in Jerusalem by Dr. Chaim Weitzmann.

1974 Churchmen of 150 countries represented in the World Evangelization Congregation decided not to form a permanent organization in opposition to the World Council of Churches.

JULY 25

Feast day in the Catholic Church of St. James the Great, the apostle of Jesus and patron saint of Spain.

Feast day in the Orthodox Church of St. Anne, mother of Mary, and of her husband, St. Joachim.

Former feast day of St. Christopher, patron of wayfarers ; according to legend, he devoted himself to carrying wayfarers across a river which had no bridge; on one occasion, he carried a child who grew constantly heavier until Christopher almost failed to reach the other side; the child revealed himself to be Jesus; the observance was dropped in 1969.

1492 Innocent VIII, pope from 1484 to 1492, died.

1593 Henry IV of France became a Catholic.

1798 Albert Knapp, German spiritual song writer, was born in Tübingen; compiled various collections of religious poems, including many originals (died 1864).

1805 Thousands attended the first Methodist camp meeting in Smyrna, Del.

1823 Benjamin T. Roberts, religious leader, was born in Gowanda, N.Y.; expelled from Methodist Episcopal Church (1858) because of his criticism of church practices; a founder (1860) of the Free Methodist Church, general superintendent (1860-93) (died 1893).

1881 Sidney M. Berry, Congregational clergyman, was born in Southport, England; secretary, Congregational Union of England and Wales (1923-48); secretary, International Congregational Council (1949-61) (died 1961).

1889 John Walsh was named Archbishop of Toronto.

1893 Carlo Confalonieri, dean of the Sacred College of Cardinals, was born in Sevasso, Italy; private secretary to Pope Pius XI (1922-39), prefect of the Sacred Consistorial Congregation (1961-86); elevated to cardinal 1958 (died 1986).

1910 The Norwegian legislature passed a law providing for religious instruction in the secondary schools.

1926 The Mexican Catholic Church announced the suspension of all church rites on July 31 in protest against anti-church decrees.

1929 The Pope appeared outside the Vatican for the first time since 1870 to take formal possession of papal territory.

1959 Isaac H. Herzog, Israeli religious leader, died in Jerusalem at 71; chief rabbi, Irish Free State (1925-36); chief rabbi, Israel (1936-59).

1967 Pope Paul VI on a "peace pilgrimage" met with Athenagoras I, ecumenical patriarch of Istanbul, in what was considered a major step toward reconciliation of the Catholic and Eastern Orthodox churches.

1967 Joseph Cardijn, founder of the Young Christian Workers, died in Louvain, Belgium; elevated to cardinal 1965.

JULY 26

Feast day in the Orthodox Church of St. Simeon Stylites; originated the form of asceticism that required standing day and night on top of a column.

Feast day in the Catholic Church of St. Anne, mother of Mary.

1030 St. Stanislaw (or Stanislaus), Bishop of Cracow (1071-79), born; murdered while celebrating mass by King Boleslaw II (1079) for his denunciation of Boleslaw's excesses; first Pole to be canonized; patron saint of Poland.

1417 Benedict XIII was deposed by the Council of Constance, but he continued as anti-pope until 1423.

1429 Clement VIII, born Egidio Munoz, resigned his claims to the papacy; had been anti-pope since 1425; recognized only by Alfonso II of Aragon.

1471 Paul II, pope from 1464 to 1471, died.

1556 James Melville, Scottish reformer, was born near Montrose, Scotland, nephew of Andrew Melville; a church leader whose importance lies in his meticulous diaries and preservation of documents of the period (died 1614).

1833 St. Bartolomeo Capitaino, co-founder of the Sisters of Charity of Lovere, died; canonized 1950; also observed as her feast day.

1856 William Rainey Harper, Hebrew teacher and educator, was born in New Concord, Ohio; first president, U. of Chicago (1892-1906); teacher, Semitic languages, Baptist Union Theological Seminary, Chicago (1879-86), Yale (1886-91); author (Religion and the Higher Life, The Trend in Higher Education) (died 1906).

1869 The Irish Parliament passed a bill creating the Irish Catholic Church.

1984 The 25th triennial conference of the International Association of Religious Freedom opened in Tokyo.

JULY 27

Feast day of St. Pantaleon (died about 305), reputedly a Christian doctor martyred by Diocletian because of his faith; patron saint of physicians.

432 St. Celestine I, pope from 422 to 432, died; also observed as his feast day from 1922 until observance was dropped in 1969.

1534 John Allen, Archbishop of Dublin, was murdered during the rebellion of Lord Thomas Fitzgerald; served as archbishop from 1528; also chancellor of Ireland (1528-30).

1681 Donald Cargill, Scottish Covenanter leader, was beheaded; had been excommunicated with Richard Cameron after the insurrection against Charles II.

1837 Georg von Kopp, German prelate, was born near Göttingen; served under Bismarck as mediator between state and church to end the "Kulturkampf;" helped bring about social reform, built churches and other institutions; elevated to cardinal 1893 (died 1914).

1860 John Henry Bernard, English prelate, was born in India; dean, St. Patrick's Cathedral, Dublin (1902); Archbishop of Dublin (1915-19); provost, Trinity College (1919-27) (died 1927).

1865 The Chilean constitution provided for freedom of religious worship for non-Catholic sects and allowed them to establish private schools.

1870 Hilaire Belloc, British Catholic writer, was born in Paris; noted for biographies, political writing; his works on religion included "Europe and the Faith," "The Great Heresies," and a four-volume history of England, written to correct what he considered the overly Protestant view of history (died 1953).

1891 Douglas Horton, head of the Congregational Church (1938-55), was born in Brooklyn, N.Y.; negotiated merger of Congregational Christian churches and the Evangelical & Reformed Church (1957); dean, Harvard Divinity School (1955-59) (died 1968).

1959 The 18th general council of the World Presbyterian Alliance opened in Sao Paulo, Brazil, marking the 100th anniversary of Presbyterianism in Brazil.

JULY 28

Feast day of St. Victor I, pope from 189 to 198; disputed with bishops of Asia over Easter usage.

Feast day of St. Innocent I, pope from 401 to 417.

1057 Victor II, pope from 1055 to 1057, died.

1148 Forces of the Second Crusade besieged Damascus, but withdrew after five days; the Crusade collapsed.

1804 Ludwig A. Feuerbach, German philosopher, was born near Munich; pupil of Hegel, who abandoned Hegelian idealism for a naturalistic materialism; later attacked orthodox religion and immortality, arguing that God is the outward projection of man's inward nature (died 1872).

1824 Holland N. McTyeire, Methodist prelate and editor, was born in Barnwell District, S.C.; bishop, Methodist South Church (1866-89); editor, Christian Advocate (1858-62); instrumental in founding Vanderbilt U., with aid from Cornelius Vanderbilt (died 1889).

1856 James H. Blenk, Catholic prelate, was born in Edenkoben, Germany; first Bishop of Puerto Rico, then Archbishop of New Orleans (1906-17) (died 1917).

1859 Ballington Booth, second son of William Booth and active Salvation Army leader, was born in Brighouse, England; headed Army in Australia (1885-87), United States (1887-96); disagreed with father and founded, headed, Volunteers of America (1896-1940) (died 1940).

1871 Henry D. A. Major, theologian who was a leading apostle of modernism, was born in Plymouth, England; founder, editor, *Modern Churchman* (1911-56) (died 1961).

1881 John G. Machen, Presbyterian leader, was born in Baltimore; assailed Presbyterian Board of Foreign Missions' liberalism, tried on disciplinary charges, found guilty and suspended (1935); a founder (1936) of Presbyterian Church of America, later known as the Orthodox Presbyterian Church; a founder, Westminster Theological Seminary (1929) (died 1937).

JULY 29

Feast day in the Catholic Church of St. Martha, sister of Mary and Lazarus; patron saint of housewives.

Feast day of St. Olave (995-1030) (Olaf Haraldsson), patron saint of Norway and king of Norway (1016-29).

1099 Blessed Urban II, pope from 1088 to 1099, died.

1644 Urban VIII, born Maffeo Barberini and pope from 1623 to 1644, died at 76; issued bulls canonizing Filippo de Neri, Ignatius Loyola, and Francis Xavier; opened China and Japan to all religious orders, wrote many hymns and prayers; condemned Jansenism and founded the Collegium Urbanum (missionary training school), the Vatican Seminary, and the College of Propaganda.

1798 John Barclay, Scottish clergyman, died; founder of sect (Barclayites or Bereans), which was based solely on the Scriptures without reference to any human activity.

1830 John S. J. Gardiner, Welsh-born Episcopal clergyman, died; rector of Trinity Church, Boston (1805-30); a founder, Boston Athenaeum.

1968 Pope Paul VI issued an encyclical on the birth control question, "Humanae vitae," which reasserted the church's position against the use of artificial means of birth control.

1974 Eleven woman Episcopal priests were ordained in the Church of the Advocate, North Philadelphia, by four bishops; ordination was ruled invalid by the House of Bishops Aug 25 but on Oct 17, the House approved in principle the ordination of women as priests.

JULY 30

Feast day in the Orthodox Church of St. Silas, early Christian prophet and missionary; accompanied St. Paul on the first visit to Macedonia and Corinth.

Feast day of St. Peter Chrysologus; had been observed Dec. 4.

579 Benedict I, pope from 574 to 579, died while Lombards were besieging Rome.

657 St. Vitalian was consecrated pope, served until 672; sought unsuccessfully to end controversy over Monotheletism*.

1233 Konrad von Marburg, German priest, was assassinated; inquisitor for German monasteries (1227), censured for fanatical and limitless persecution.

1286 Gregorius Bar-Hebraeus, Syrian scholar and primate of the Jacobite Church (1264-86), died at 60; Jacobites were a Syrian Christian sect.

1540 Robert Barnes, English Protestant martyr, was burned as a heretic with two other Lutherans; a close friend of Martin Luther, he helped spread Lutheranism.

1630 The first church in Boston was constituted in Charlestown (transferred to Boston 1632); John Wilson was elected teacher.

1812 Osmon C. Baker, Methodist theologian, was born in Marlow, N.H.; organized Newbury (Vt.) Theological Seminary (later in Concord, N.H.); became first Methodist theological professor (1843-44); bishop (1852-71); wrote administrative guide for Methodist clergy (died 1871).

1831 Helena Petrovna Blavatsky, co-founder of the Theosophical movement, was born in Ekaterinaslav, Russia; began movement with Col. Henry Steele Olcott (1875) to counter materialism and agnosticism; moved from New York to India (1882) to establish international center; founded The Theosophist; many of her miracles were later demonstrated as fraudulent; at time of her death in 1891, she had 100,000 followers.

1872 Bishop James R. Bayley was named Archbishop of Baltimore; served until 1877.

1904 A running dispute between the French Government and the Vatican over teaching by religious teachers resulted in a break of diplomatic relations.

1915 Pope Benedict XV issued an appeal for peace to the heads of the warring governments; made second appeal in 1917, suggesting arbitration.

JULY 31

Feast day of Blessed Giovanni Colombini (about 1300-67), founder of the Gesuati (Congregation of the Gesuati).

Feast day in the Orthodox Church of St. Joseph of Arimathea, who buried Christ after the Crucifixion.

432 St. Sixtus III was consecrated pope, served until 440; restored various churches and the Basilica of Liberius.

448 St. Germain (Germanus), Bishop of Auxerre (418-448), died at about 68; established clerical schools and successfully controverted the Pelagian* heresy in England.

855 Ibn Hanbal, Islamic theologian, died; founder of one of four great schools of Islamic law (Hanbalite); punished and imprisoned (842) for his conservatism; freed (846); compiled the "Musnad," a collection of about 28,000 traditions.

1009 Sergius IV was named pope, served until 1012; Roman nobility dominated the reign.

1396 William Courtenay, English prelate, died at about 54; Bishop of London (1375-81), Archbishop of Canterbury (1381-96), chancellor of England (1381); strong supporter of papal authority, except when the national interest was involved; called Blackfriars' Council (1382), which condemned Wycliffe's doctrines.

1556 St. Ignatius of Loyola, Spanish co-founder, first general, Society of Jesus (Jesuits) (1541), died at 65; his major contributions were the reform of the church through education, more frequent use of the sacraments, and preaching the Gospel to the newly-discovered pagan world; canonized 1622; also observed as his feast day.

1566 Bartolomé de Las Casas, Spanish Dominican "apostle of the West Indies," died at 92; one of the first, most influential New World missionaries and foremost critic of the brutal treatment of the Indians.

1841 Robert S. MacArthur, Baptist leader, was born in Dalesville, Canada; pastor, Calvary Church, New York City (1870-1911); president, Baptist World Alliance (1911-23) (died 1923).

1859 Control of cemeteries in Mexico was taken from the clergy; religious tolerance was decreed.

1874 The first party of 1,532 Mennonites from Russia arrived to settle in Manitoba, Canada.

1892 Joseph Charbonneau, Catholic archbishop coadjutor of Montreal (1940-50), was born near Ottawa (died 1959).

1968 The National Conference of Catholic Bishops supported Pope Paul VI's encyclical on birth control, which reiterated the condemnation of artificial methods of control; however, some Catholic priests and laymen publicly disagreed with the pope's position.

1969 Pope Paul VI flew to Uganda and addressed the closing session of the All-Africa bishops' conference.

AUGUST 1

Feast of St. Peter's Chains, commemorating the miraculous release of St. Peter from prison.

Feast day of St. Alfonso Maria de Liguori, founder of the Redemptorists and a Doctor* of the Church.

Feast day of St. Ethelwold (about 908-984), English prelate who helped revive monasticism in England; served as abbot of Abingdon, Bishop of Winchester (963-984); built the cathedral at Winchester.

1057 Stephen IX, born Frederick of Lorraine, was elected pope, served until 1058; continued the reforms begun by Leo IX.

1098 Adhemar de Monteil, Bishop of LePuy, died of the plague; led the First Crusade as the papal legate.

1252 Joannes de Plano Carpini, Franciscan monk, died; one of the first European travelers in the Mongol Empire; companion and disciple of St. Francis of Assisi; sent by Pope Innocent IV to protest to the Khan of Tatary against the Mongol invasion of Christian lands; took 15 months to get there, received unsatisfactory reply.

1545 Andrew Melville, Presbyterian reformer, was born in Baldaire, Scotland; gave the Scottish church its Presbyterian character with a ruling passion to preserve church independence from state control; helped draw up the "Second Book of Discipline," shaping the Presbyterian Church; preached boldly against absolute spiritual authority of the King; principal, Glasgow U. (1574-80), of St. Mary's College, St. Andrews (1580-1606); imprisoned in Tower of London (1607-11) for preaching against popery and superstition (died 1622).

1557 Olaus Magnus, Swedish prelate, died at 67; Catholic Archbishop of Sweden (1554-57); author of an influential history of Scandinavia.

1635 Georg Weissel, German hymn writer, died at 45; an important early Prussian hymn writer (Lift up your heads, ye mighty gates).

1639 Ursuline Convent was founded in Quebec by Mme de la Petrie and three other Ursuline nuns who arrived from Dieppe; convent burned 1650.

1689 A Protestant rebellion in Maryland was ended by a peace treaty; began with rumors that Catholics were taking over the colony; Protestant Association was formed by John Coode, who led a force to St. Mary's to demand the resignation of Lord Baltimore's representative.

1743 James Blair, Episcopal clergyman who obtained the charter for the College of William & Mary, died at 86 in Williamsburg, Va.; first William & Mary president (1693-1743).

1806 Peter A. Kenrick, Catholic prelate, was born in Dublin, Ireland, brother of Francis Kenrick; Bishop of St. Louis (1843-47), Archbishop (1847-96); opposed dogma of papal infallibility at the Vatican Council, accepted it when it was promulgated (died 1896).

1841 Eduard Herzog, Swiss prelate, was born; first bishop of the Old Catholic Church in Switzerland (1876); professor, Catholic theological faculty, U. of Bern (died 1924).

1844 David J. Burrell, Dutch Reformed clergyman and theologian, was born in Mt. Pleasant, Pa.; pastor, Marble Collegiate Church, New York City (1891-1926); president, World Council of Reformed and Presbyterian Churches (died 1926).

1847 Thomas J. Conaty, Catholic prelate and educator, was born in Ireland; a founder, Catholic Summer School of America, president (1893-97); a founder, president, National Catholic Education Association (1899-1903); Bishop of Los Angeles (1903-15) (died 1915).

1897 Pope Leo XIII issued an encyclical denouncing Protestantism as the "Lutheran rebellion, whose evil virus goes wandering about in almost all nations."

1911 Pericle Felici, who was in charge of revising and updating canon law, was born near Rome (died 1982).

1917 Pope Benedict XV proposed a just peace in a note, "Dès le debut," which foreshadowed President Wilson's 14 points.

1920 Papal encyclical warned against dangers threatening modern society.

1926 Pope Pius XI called on Catholics everywhere to pray for the deliverance of the Catholics of Mexico from persecution.

1976 The 41st International Eucharistic Congress opened in Philadelphia, with an expectation of 1 million pilgrims.

1978 Anglican bishops at the Lambeth Conference in Canterbury, England approved the ordination of women priests in the United States, Canada, New Zealand, and Hong Kong.

AUGUST 2

Feast day of St. Eusebius of Vercelli, Italian bishop and patron of the Piedmont area; became the first Western bishop to unite monastic with clerical life; sought to end dissension between Arians and the orthodox.

Former feast day of St. Alfonso Maria de Liguori, founder of the Redemptorists; canonized 1839, made a Doctor* of the Church 1871; now observed August 1.

257 St. Stephen I, pope from 254 to 257, died; also observed as his feast day.

640 Severinus, pope from 638 to 640, died; unable to secure imperial confirmation for more than a year after his election.

686 John V, pope from 685 to 686, died.

1703 Lorenzo Ricci, Jesuit leader, was born in Florence; general of the Society of Jesus (Jesuits) (1758-73); after order was dissolved by papal bull, Ricci was confined in the Castle of St. Angelo for the rest of his life (died 1775).

1802 Nicholas P. S. Wiseman, English Catholic prelate, was born in Seville, Spain; first Archbishop of Westminster (1850-65), elevated to cardinal 1850; rector of English College, Rome (1828-40); had great influence on Oxford Movement (died 1865).

1832 Henry S. Olcott, theosophist, was born in Orange, N.J.; co-founder with Helena Blavatsky (1875) of the Theosophical Society, its first president; after Madame Blavatsky's frauds were exposed, Olcott sought to develop Society along legitimate lines (died 1907).

1862 Arthur C. Headlam, English bishop, was born in Yorkshire; divinity professor, Oxford and canon of Christ Church, Oxford (1918-23); Bishop of Gloucester (1923-45); a vigorous promoter of Christian reunion (died 1947).

1907 Pope Pius X issued a decree (effective April 19,1908), "Ne temera," which declared that no marriage between Catholics is valid unless celebrated before a parish priest or one delegated for the ceremony.

1914 Pope Pius X issued a lament over the outbreak of World War I and appealed for peace.

AUGUST 3

Feast day in the Catholic Church of St. Hippolytus, early Christian ecclesiastical writer and first antipope (217-235); wrote "Apostolic Tradition," which provides an insight into the Roman liturgy.

1667 Jeremy Taylor, English scholar and theologian, died at 54; an important figure among 17th Century Anglicans, known as the "Caroline Divines;" author (Liberty of Prophesying, Holy Living, Holy Dying, Worthy Communicant).

1785 The first Episcopal ordination in the United States was held in Middletown, Conn. for the Rev. Ashbel Baldwin.

1858 Maltbie R. Babcock, Presbyterian clergyman, was born in Syracuse, N.Y.; best known for the hymn, "This is my Father's world" (died 1901).

1868 St. Peter Julian Eymard died at 57; founder of the Priests of the Blessed Sacrament (1857); also observed as his feast day.

1878 William D. O'Brien, president of the Catholic Church Extension Society (1925-62), was born in Chicago; auxiliary Archbishop of Chicago (1953-62) (died 1962).

1901 Cardinal Stefan Wyzynski, Catholic prelate, was born; primate of Poland for 32 years (died 1981).

1902 Martin Noth, Old Testament scholar and archaeologist, was born in Dresden, Germany; his main work concerned the early history of Israel (died 1968).

AUGUST 4

Feast day of St. Jean Baptiste Vianney, French Catholic priest with supernatural powers; principal patron of parochial clergy; canonized 1925; formerly observed August 9.

Former feast day of St. Dominic, Spanish-born founder of the Order of Friar Preachers (Dominicans or Black Friars); now observed August 7.

1521 Urban VII, pope in 1590, was born in Rome as Giambattista Castagna; elected pope Sept 15, 1590, but served only 12 days before his death.

1707 Johann A. Ernesti, Lutheran theologian, was born in Germany; noted for biblical interpretation, tried to reconcile the theological tradition of his church with historical criticism of the Bible (died 1781).

1792 Edward Irving, Scottish theologian, was born in Annan, Scotland; regarded as the founder of the Holy Catholic Apostolic Church (also known as Irvingites); built church in Regent Square, London; acquired fame as a preacher; compelled to retire from his church because of his acceptance of pentecostal phenomena (1832), condemned as a heretic (1833) (died 1834).

1841 James Chalmers, Congregational missionary and explorer, was born in Ardrishaig, Scotland; served in the Cook Islands (1865-75), then New Guinea, where he was one of the first white men; explored South Sea islands; killed by cannibals 1901.

1874 The Chautauqua Organization was formed by the first Sunday School Teachers Assembly in Fair Point, N.Y.

1879 Pope Leo XIII issued the encyclical "Aeterni Patris," which provided a charter for the revival of Thomism (theological system based on the thoughts of Thomas Aquinas) as the official philosophical and theological system of the Church.

1884 Sigmund Olaf P. Mowinckel, Old Testament scholar, was born in Kjerringy, Norway; best known for his work on the Psalms; responsible for the greater part of the translation of the Old Testament into Norwegian (died 1965).

1899 Ezra Taft Benson, Mormon leader, was born in Whitney, Idaho; U.S. Secretary of Agriculture (1953-61); president, Mormon Church (1985-).

1903 St. Pius X was named pope, served until 1914; encouraged more active participation of the people in the liturgy of the church, inaugurated reform in church music by restoring the Gregorian chant in the liturgy; began revision of ecclesiastical laws (1904); called the pope of Catholic Action; condemned modernism; canonized 1954.

1958 Mario Zanin, Catholic archbishop, died in Buenos Aires at about 69.

AUGUST 5

642 St. Oswald (about 605-642), king of Northumbria (England, north of the Humber River) and martyr, died; began establishment of Christianity in England with St. Aidan; also observed as his feast day.

1370 The Brigittine Order was approved by Pope Urban V.

1572 Isaac ben Solomon Luria, Jewish mystic and founder of the "new Cabala" (Luriatic Cabala), died at 38; had profound influence on the development of Hasidism*.

1604 John Eliot, Congregational clergyman, was born in Widford, England; worked with the Pequot people in Massachusetts; his catechism was the first book printed in English in America, his translation of the Bible into Pequot was the first book printed in America; called the "apostle of the Indians" (died 1690).

1633 George Abbot, Archbishop of Canterbury (1611-27), died at 71.

1789 The first conference of the Protestant Episcopal Church was held in Quebec on orders of Bishop Inglis.

1835 Thomas McCrie, Scottish Presbyterian clergyman, died at 63; ejected from his pastorate for nonconformity; wrote biography of John Knox, a history of the Reformation in Italy.

1868 Henry H. Tweedy, Congregational clergyman and theologian, was born in Binghamton, N.Y.; professor of practical theology, Yale Divinity

School (1909-37); wrote the hymn, "Eternal God, whose power upholds" (died 1953).

AUGUST 6

Feast of the Transfiguration in the Catholic Church.

258 St. Sixtus II, pope from 257 to 258, died; he was beheaded while celebrating services in a cemetery; also observed as his feast day.

523 St. Hormisdas, pope from 514 to 523, died; effected union of Orthodox and Catholic churches; also observed as his feast day.

1221 St. Dominic, Spanish founder of the Order of Friar Preachers (or Dominicans), died at about 50; the order combines the contemplative life of the monk and the active work of the evangelist; a man of heroic sanctity; canonized 1234.

1458 Calixtus III, pope from 1455 to 1458, died.

1504 Matthew Parker, second Anglican Archbishop of Canterbury (1559-75), was born in Norwich; tried to set limits to reformers' doctrines, the beginnings of Puritanism, which he called "mutinous individualism;" supervised and published (1572) a revised translation of the Bishops' Bible; prepared a new psalter (died 1575).

1630 Francis Higginson, nonconformist Anglican clergyman, died at about 43; settled in Salem, Mass., where he drew up a church covenant and a confession of faith.

1651 Francois de S. Fenelon, Archbishop of Cambrai (1695-1715), was born in Perigord, France; mystical theologian and writer on education; work had strong impact on educational philosophy and literature; tutor to grandson of Louis XIV, wrote numerous instructional works, including "Maximes des Saints," which was condemned in part by the pope (died 1715).

1727 The first American convent was opened by the Ursulines in New Orleans.

1774 Ann Lee, founder of the American Shakers, arrived in New York City with eight followers.

1801 A week-long evangelical meeting in Cane Ridge, Ky., called by the Presbyterian evangelist, Barton W. Stone, attracted between 10,000 and 25,000 people; referred to as the greatest outpouring of the spirit since Pentecost.

1807 Thomas Atkinson, Episcopal prelate, was born in Dinwiddie County, Va.; Bishop of North Carolina (1853-81), instrumental in reuniting northern and southern churches after the Civil War (died 1881).

1809 Alfred Lord Tennyson, renowned poet, was born in Somersby, England; wrote a number of Anglican hymns (Ring out, wild bells, to the wild sky; Strong Son of God, immortal love; Sunset and evening star) (died 1892).

1821 Edward H. Plumptre, Anglican hymn writer, was born in London; among his hymns were "Rejoice, ye pure in heart" and "Thine arm, O Lord, in days of old" (died 1891).

1878 Charles K. Gilbert, Episcopal bishop, was born in Bainbridge, N.Y.; suffragan bishop of New York (1930-46), bishop (1947-50) (died 1958).

1908 Fergus Patrick McEvay was appointed Catholic Archbishop of Toronto.

1964 Pope Paul VI issued an encyclical, "Ecclesian suam," on the role of the church in the world.

1966 Pope Paul VI issued a document implementing actions of the Second Vatican Council's final session, which called on bishops to resign at 75.

1967 Pope Paul VI issued the apostolic constitution, "Regimini ecclesias universae," which outlined regulations for the Sacred Congregation of Propaganda, dividing the congregation's work into numerous secretariats and commissions.

1968 The Lambeth Conference of the Anglican communion unanimously reaffirmed its endorsement of contraceptive practices.

1978 Paul VI, pope from 1963 to 1978, died at 81.

1980 East Germany announced plans to restore the birthplace of Martin Luther in Eisleben to its original 15th Century appearance in time for the 500th anniversary of his birth in November 1983.

AUGUST 7

Feast day of St. Dominic, founder of the Dominican Order; previously observed August 4.

768 Stephen III was named pope, served until 772; controversy of earlier papal elections marred his reign.

1316 John XXII, born Jacques d'Euse in France, was elected pope, served until 1334 while residing in Avignon; reign filled with political and theological conflicts; a capable administrator, enlarged and reorganized the Curia, put papal finances on a sound basis and strengthened the hierarchy.

1547 St. Cajetan of Thiene died; co-founder of the Oratory of Divine Love, which became the Theatines; canonized 1671; formerly observed as his feast day; changed to August 8.

1814 Pope Pius VII restored Jesuits to full legal validity with his bull, "Solicitudo omnium ecclesiarum."

1823 Rufus C. Burleson, Baptist clergyman and educator, was born near Decatur, Ala.; president, Baylor U. (1851-61); founder, president, Waco U. (1861); the two merged (1886) into Baylor, with Burleson as president (1886-97) (died 1901).

1825 Edward G. Andrews, Methodist prelate, was born in New Hartford, N.Y.; director, Cazenovia (N.Y.) Seminary (1855-64); Bishop of Des Moines (1872-1904) (died 1907).

1873 Pope Pius IX complained to the Emperor of Germany about the persecution of bishops, asserted his authority over all baptized persons; Emperor on Sep 3 said there is no mediator between man and God other than Jesus Christ.

1890 Kirby Page, American author and social evangelist, was born in Tyler County, Texas (died 1957).

1960 The Catholic Church, in a pastoral letter read in all Cuban churches, voiced its concern over the increasing advance of Communism.

AUGUST 8

Feast day of St. Cajetan, co-founder of the Theatines; previously observed August 7.

1471 Thomas à Kempis, German theologian, died at 91; credited with writing "Imitation of Christ," one of the most influential Christian books; considered the pearl of all the writings of the mystical German-Dutch school, ranking with St. Augustine's Confessions and Bunyan's Pilgrim's Progress among useful devotional manuals.

1652 Jacques Basnage, French Reformed Church clergyman, was born in Rouen; remarkable historical and patristic* scholar; exiled in Holland after revocation of the Edict of Nantes; aided diplomatically in arranging Triple Alliance at The Hague (died 1723).

1794 Jean Henri Merle d'Aubigne, Swiss ecclesiastical historian, was born in Geneva; best known for his multi-volume histories of the Reformation (died 1880).

1810 Emmanuel M.J. d'Alzon, congregation founder, was born in LeVegan, France; founder of the Augustinians of the Assumption (Assumptionists) (1845) (died 1880).

1814 George E. Ellis, Unitarian clergyman and editor, was born in Boston; served Harvard Unitarian Society (1840-69); with Harvard Divinity School (1857-63); an editor, *Christian Register*, *Christian Examiner* (died 1894).

1852 Gustaf Palmquist, Swedish-born Baptist clergyman, baptized three persons from Rock Island, Ill. in the Mississippi River, marking the start of the Swedish Baptist General Conference of America.

1876 Metropolitan Leonty, primate of the Russian Orthodox Eastern Church of America and metropolitan of all America and Canada, was born in Kremenets, Russia; dean of first Russian Orthodox theological seminary in the United States (Minneapolis, later Tenafly, N.J. 1906-15) (died 1965).

1910 The Sacred Congregation of the Sacraments issued a decree, "Quam singulari," recommending that Catholic children receive communion as soon as they reach the "age of discretion" (which according to tests was 7).

AUGUST 9

Feast day in the Orthodox Church of St. Matthias, disciple chosen to fill the place vacated by Judas Iscariot.

Former feast day of St. Jean Baptiste Vianney, French Catholic priest with supernatural powers; now observed August 4.

1048 Damasus II, pope from July to August 1048, died.

1420 Pierre d'Ailly, Bishop of Cambrai (1397-1420), died at 70; one of the distinguished churchmen who sought to end papal schism at the Council of Constance; chancellor, U. of Paris (1389-97).

1471 Sixtus IV was named pope, served until 1484; fostered doctrine of the Immaculate Conception; condemned abuses of the Inquisition; launched an extensive building program in Rome (Sistine Chapel, Sistine Bridge); reorganized the Vatican Library and opened it to scholars; reign marked by heavy taxes for the building program and nepotism.

1603 Johannes Cocceius, Dutch theologian, was born in Bremen, Germany; based his theory of life on the Bible and recommended a life in and through the Scriptures rather than the church and orthodoxy (died 1669).

1788 Adoniram Judson, American Baptist missionary to Burma, was born in Malden, Mass.; served in Burma (1813-50), translated the Bible from Hebrew and Greek into Burmese, wrote a Burmese-English dictionary (died 1850).

1797 The Methodist New Connection was formed by Alexander Kilham and three other Methodist clergymen in Leeds, favoring complete separation from the Church of England.

1884 Sir Edwyn C. Hoskyns, Anglican theologian, was born in London; strongly influenced biblical study with his "Essays Catholic and Critical" (died 1937).

1973 About 500 delegates representing more than 200 Southern Presbyterian churches, meeting in Asheville, N.C., severed ties to Presbyterian Church in the U.S. because they believed it had become too liberal.

1984 American Catholic bishops urged church members to promote the church's position on public policy issues; clergy were asked to refrain from supporting candidates.

AUGUST 10

258 St. Laurence (Lawrence), one of the most famous Roman martyrs, died; a deacon of Pope Sixtus II, whom he followed to death; also observed as his feast day.

654 St. Eugenius I was consecrated pope, served to 657.

1556 Philipp Nicolai, Lutheran clergyman and hymn writer, was born in Germany; known for several spiritual Evangelical hymns (O morning star! how fair and bright; Wake, awake, for night is flying) (died 1608).

1674 William Vesey, Anglican clergyman in New York City (1697-1746), was born in Quincy, Mass.; Vesey St. in New York City is named for him (died 1746).

1794 Leopold Zunz, German Jewish scholar, was born near Hanover; founder of the science of Judaism, the application of modern scholarly research methods to the study of Jewish religion, history, ritual, and liturgy (died 1886).

1827 George P. Fisher, theologian and author, was born in Wrentham, Mass.; professor, Yale Divinity School (1854-1901), dean (1895-1901); author (The Christian Religion, Outlines of Universal History, The Colonial Era) (died 1909).

1841 Mary A. Lathbury, author of children's books and hymns, was born in Manchester, N.Y.; wrote many hymns (Day is dying in the West, Break thou the bread of life, Arise and shine) (died 1913).

1855 Frederick J. F. Jackson, Anglican theologian, was born in Ipswich, England; professor of Christian institutions, Union Theological Seminary (1916-34); author (History of the Christian Church, Rise of Gentile Christianity) (died 1941).

1873 William E. Hocking, philosopher and educator, was born in Cleveland; professor, Harvard (1914-66), emphasized religious aspects of philosophy; author (The Meaning of God in Human Experience, The Meaning of Immortality in Human Experience) (died 1966).

1890 Paul Hutchinson, religious writer and editor, was born in Madison, N.J.; editor, *China Christian Advocate* (1916-21); managing editor, *Christian Century* (1924-56) (died 1956).

1915 Pope Benedict XV issued the constitution, "Incruentum altaris," allowing priests to offer three masses of requiem on All Souls Day.

AUGUST 11

Feast day of St. Alexander, Bishop of Comena in Asia Minor; martyred about 250 in the persecution of Emperor Decius.

Feast day of St. Clare of Assisi (1194-1254), co-founder with St. Francis of Assisi of the Order of Poor Clares, abbess of the Order (1212-53); canonized 1255.

1492 Alexander VI became pope, served until 1503; initiated censorship of books, excommunicated Savonarola for heresy after the latter denounced him as corrupt; his most important act was the bull of demarcation (1493), setting the line separating Spanish and Portuguese lands in the New World.

1519 Johann Tetzel, German Dominican priest, died at 54; first public antagonist of Martin Luther because of his preaching of indulgences, which led Luther to publish his 95 themes at Wittenberg.

1760 Philip Embury (1789-1835), first Methodist clergyman in the United States, arrived in New York from Ireland; founded Wesley Chapel (first John St. church)(1768).

1817 William H. Odenheimer, Episcopal prelate, was born in Philadelphia; Bishop of New Jersey (1859-74), first Bishop of Newark (1874-89) (died 1889).

1823 Charlotte M. Yonge, novelist, was born in Otterbourne, England; her books (The Heir of Radclyffe, The Daisy Chain) spread the influence of the Oxford Movement (died 1901).

1833 Robert G. Ingersoll, successful lawyer and "the great agnostic," was born in Dresden, N.Y.; lectured for the Free Religious Association (died 1899).

1834 The Ursuline convent in Charlestown, Mass., which had a successful girls' school, was destroyed by fire as part of an anti-Catholic campaign.

1837 Charles H. Fowler, Methodist prelate and educator, was born in Ontario, Canada; Bishop of San Francisco (1884-92), of Minneapolis (1892-96), of Buffalo (1896-1904), of New York (1904-08); president, Northwestern U. (1873-76); editor, *Christian Advocate* (1876-80); renowned fund raiser (died 1908).

1865 The Marianists (Society of Mary), founded by William J. Chaminade, was approved by the pope.

1884 The national religion of Japan was disestablished and freedom was given to all other religions.

1926 The Mexican Government ordered the seizure of the property administered by Catholic clergy.

1930 The American Lutheran Church was formed in Toledo, Ohio by the merger of the synods of Buffalo, Iowa and Ohio.

1933 Jerry Falwell, founder and head of Moral Majority, was born in Lynchburg, Va.

AUGUST 12

Former feast day of St. Clare of Assisi, co-founder of the Poor Clares; now observed August 11.

670 St. Fiacre, Irish abbot, died; founded a hermitage in Kilkenny, a monastery in France; his life of severe denial attracted many; his name was adopted by a Parisian inn where small hackney coaches (fiacres) were offered for hire.

1484 Sixtus IV, pope from 1471 to 1484, died at 70.

1591 St. Louise de Marillac, co-founder with St. Vincent de Paul, of the Daughters of Charity (Sisters of Charity), was born in Paris; canonized 1934 (died 1660).

1689 Innocent XI, pope from 1676 to 1689, died.

1787 The first Anglican Bishop of Nova Scotia, Charles Inglis, was consecrated by the Archbishop of Canterbury at Lambeth; arrived in Halifax October 16.

1794 William Ellis, English missionary to South Sea islands, was born in London; acclimatized tropical fruits and plants, set up printing press in area (died 1872).

1838 Sir Joseph Barnby, English organist and composer, was born in York; wrote the popular song, "Sweet and low" and the music for 250 hymns (Now the day is over, When morning gilds the skies; O perfect love, for all the saints) (died 1896).

1852 Michael J. McGivney, Catholic priest, was born in Waterbury, Conn.; a principal founder of the Knights of Columbus (died 1890).

1881 Richard J. Fitzgerald, Irish Catholic prelate, was born in Middleton, Ireland; Bishop of Gibraltar (1927-56) (died 1956).

1934 The Marion Congress, under auspices of the Servite Fathers, opened in the Sanctuary of Our Sorrowful Mother in Portland, Ore.

1950 Pope Pius XII issued the encyclical, "Humani generis," condemning several modern intellectual movements and tendencies of the Catholic Church.

1958 Metropolitan Samuel David, Antiochian Orthodox archbishop, died in Toledo, Ohio.

1967 Pope Paul VI announced changes in the Curia, the central administrative agency of the Vatican, including the appointment of non-Italian bishops from all over the world.

AUGUST 13

523 St. John I was consecrated pope, served until 526; was the first pope to leave Italy, visiting Constantinople; imprisoned on his return by Theodoric, who considered him a Byzantine supporter.

662 St. Maximus the Confessor, Byzantine martyred monk and spiritual writer, died; vigorous opponent of Monothelite* doctrine; banished to Thrace; also observed as his feast day in the Catholic Church.

1099 Paschal II, born Ranierus, was elected pope, served until 1118; renewed papal decrees against investiture but the issue was still unresolved at his death; reign marked by constant struggle with Emperors Henry IV and Henry V.

1596 Jean (Jan) de Bolland, Flemish Jesuit writer, was born in Tiremont, Belgium; editor (1643-65) of "Lives of the Saints," which was continued by his colleagues (Bollandists) after his death in 1665.

1777 Martin Stephan, German Lutheran clergyman, was born in Stramberg; originator of the congregation which became the nucleus of the Lutheran Missouri Synod (died 1846).

1818 Cornelius V. Van Dyck, Reformed Dutch medical missionary, was born in Kinderhook, N.Y.; served as missionary to Arabia (1840-93), helped complete translation of the Bible into Arabic, influenced renaissance of Arabic literature (died 1895).

1821 Henry M. Dexter, Congregational clergyman and editor, was born in Plympton, Mass.; served Pine St. Church, Boston (1849-67); editor-in-chief, *The Congregationalist* (1856-90) (died 1890).

1834 Philip Phillips, evangelist and singer, was born in Cassadaga, N.Y.; visited England (1868), sang 200 nights for the Sunday School Union and prepared "The American Sacred Songster," which sold over 1 million copies; traveled with Dwight L. Moody (died 1895).

1839 Michael A. Corrigan, Catholic prelate, was born in Newark, N.J.; Bishop of Newark (1873-80), Archbishop of New York (1885-1902); expanded parochial school system, built a major seminary in Yonkers (died 1902).

1851 Felix Adler, founder of Ethical Culture Movement, was born in Alzey, Germany; taught Hebrew and Oriental literature, Cornell U.; founder, Society of Ethical Culture (1876), a non-religious association for ethical improvement (died 1933).

1861 Morris Jastrow, an educator, was born in Poland, the son of Marcus Jastrow; professor of Semitic literature, U. of Pennsylvania (1892-1921), also University librarian (1898-1921); author (The Study of Religion, The Book of Job) (died 1921).

1913 Makarios III of Cyprus was born near Paphos; Archbishop of Cyprus Orthodox Church, president of Cyprus (1959-77) (died 1977).

1963 The third world Anglican Congress opened 10-day meeting in Toronto; ended with agreement that Anglicans should not live in isolation from other Christians and that racial segregation and other forms of discrimination are sin.

AUGUST 14

1367 Gil Alvarez Carillo de Albornos, Spanish cardinal, died at 67; Archbishop of Toledo (1337-50), legate to Rome under Pope Clement VI; issued constitution of the Papal States (1357), which remained in force until 1816.

1552 Paolo Sarpi, Italian prelate and scientist, was born in Venice; as scientist, he is credited with discovering contractility of the iris; opposed temporal power of pope, advocated banishing Jesuits from Venice; wrote history of the Council of Trent (died 1623).

1742 Pius VII, pope from 1800 to 1823, was born in Cessna, Italy as Luigi Barnaba Chiaramonti.

1750 Charles Butler, English fighter for religious tolerance, was born in London; prominent in movement to have anti-Catholic laws repealed; became (1791) first Catholic to be admitted to the bar since 1688; writer on theological history (died 1832).

1796 Benjamin Abbott, evangelist, died at 64; reputedly "ploughed and seeded to Methodism much of southern New Jersey."

1810 Samuel Wesley, English composer, was born in London; one of the most distinguished English church musicians of his time; wrote numerous hymns, including "The church's one foundation" (died 1876).

1867 George H. Jones, Methodist Bishop of Korea, was born in Mohawk, N.Y.; helped translate the Bible into Korean; president, Bible Institute and Union Theological School, Korea (1907-11) (died 1919).

1891 G. Bromley Oxnam, Methodist bishop (1936-60), was born in Sonora, Cal.; an organizer of the National Council of Churches; president, World Council of Churches (1948-54) (died 1963).

1961 Amleto Cicognani, who had been apostolic delegate to the United States for 25 years, was appointed papal secretary of state by Pope John XXIII.

AUGUST 15

Feast of the Assumption in the Catholic and Orthodox churches, commemorating the death of the Virgin Mary.

1195 St. Anthony of Padua, a Doctor* of the Church, was born in Lisbon, Portugal; the first lector* in theology of the Franciscan Order; noted preacher, directing sermons against avarice and usury; patron of the poor; canonized 1232, named a Doctor* 1946 (died 1231).

1257 St. Hyacinth, a patron saint of Poland, died at 72; missionary and founder of Dominican houses in Cracow and Danzig; canonized 1594.

1464 Pius II, pope from 1458 to 1464, died at 56.

1534 Ignatius of Loyola, St. Francis Xavier, and some associates bound themselves by vows of poverty, chastity, and obedience in St. Mary's Church, Montmartre, Paris; a forerunner of the Society of Jesus (Jesuits).

1601 John Campanius, Swedish Lutheran clergyman, was born in Stockholm; accompanied first Swedish settlers to Ft. Christiana (now Wilmington, Del.), missionary to nearby Delaware Indians; translated Luther's Catechism into Delaware (died 1683).

1652 John Wise, Congregational clergyman, was baptized in Roxbury, Mass.; pastor in Ipswich, Mass. (1680-1725); zealous advocate of democratic rights and his ideas of democracy in church and state had considerable influence on the political theorists of the American Revolution (died 1725).

1666 Johann A. Schall (von Bell), German Jesuit missionary and astronomer, died at 75; served in China from 1622, directed mathematical-astronomical bureau, revised Chinese calendar, translated many mathematical works into Chinese.

1678 René de Bréhant de Galinée, French Catholic missionary to North America, died; with another missionary, he was probably the first foreigner to see Niagara Falls and explore the northern shores of Lakes Erie and Huron; took formal possession of the territory for France.

1696 Ebenezer Gay, liberal Congregational clergyman, was born in Dedham, Mass.; served First Parish in Hingham, Mass. 69 years; his liberal Congregationalism was considered a forerunner of Unitarianism (died 1787).

1790 John Carroll was consecrated as the first American Catholic bishop at Lulworth Castle, England; he held his first synod Nov. 7, 1791.

1802 John H. Gurney, Anglican clergyman, was born in London; prebendary at St. Paul's Cathedral and a hymn writer (Lord, as Thy dear cross we flee) (died 1862).

1817 Roswell D. Hitchcock, Congregational clergyman and educator, was born in East Machias, Me.; professor of church history, Union Theological Seminary (1855-87), president of the faculty (1880-87) (died 1887).

1832 Gregory XVI issued the encyclical, "Mirari vos," against the democratic ideas of the French Catholic liberal, Felicite de Lamennais.

1846 Abraham Lincoln made his only public statement on religious conviction, which appeared in an Illinois newspaper — "That I am not a member of any Christian Church, is true; but I have never denied the truth of the Scriptures; and I have never spoken with intentional disrespect of religion in general, of any denomination of Christians in particular."

1879 The Irish House of Commons passed a bill to abolish Queen's University and to create a new Catholic university.

1879 Jules B. Jeanmard, American Catholic prelate, was born in Breaux Bridge, La.; the first Bishop of Lafayette, La. (1918-56) (died 1957).

1890 A general synod of the Church of England in Canada was created at a conference in Winnipeg, uniting all provincial synods.

1930 The Cathedral of Mexico City was formally reopened; closed since July 31, 1926.

1954 The second assembly of the World Council of Churches was held in Evanston, Ill.

1957 The first worldwide Lutheran meeting on American soil opened in Minneapolis with 32 countries represented, elected an American as president for the first time - Rev. Franklin C. Fry, president of the United Lutheran Church in America.

1974 The Episcopal House of Bishops voted 128 to 9 that the ordination of 11 women as priests July 29 was invalid.

AUGUST 16

Feast day of St. Roch, French patron of all who suffer from contagion; Franciscan monk who devoted himself to tending the sick (1295-1327).

1661 Thomas Fuller, English cleric and historian, died at 53; author (History of the Holy War, Church History of Britain); strong advocate of peace between king and Parliament; "chaplain in extraordinary" to Charles II.

1733 Matthew Tindal, English deist, died at about 80; originally a Catholic, he changed to rationalism; created storm with two publications - "The Rights of the Christian Church Asserted," which disputed any independent power of priests and defended state control, and "Christianity as Old as the Creation," divesting religion of the miraculous element.

1773 The Jesuits were expelled from Rome.

1794 James Walker, an organizer of the American Unitarian Association (1825), was born in Burlington, Mass.; editor, *The Christian Examiner* (1831-39); religion professor, Harvard (1839-53), president (1853-60) (died 1874).

1815 St. John Bosco, educator and congregation founder, was born in Becchi, Italy as Giovanni Melchior Bosco; a pioneer in education of the poor in the Piedmont, promoting industrial schools and evening classes where young men could be apprenticed for secular vocations in a religious background; founder of the Salesian Fathers; canonized 1934 (died 1888).

1831 Hiram Bingham, missionary to the Gilbert Islands, was born in Honolulu; reduced Gilbert language to writing, as did his father in Hawaii (Oct 30 1789) (died 1908).

1852 Hermann Soden, German biblical scholar, was born in Cincinnati; went to Germany, where he held various pastorates, taught New Testament interpretation, U. of Berlin; author of a new theory of the textual history of the New Testament (died 1914).

1865 Dennis J. Dougherty, Catholic prelate, was born in Girardville, Pa.; Bishop of Buffalo (1915-18), Archbishop of Philadelphia (1918-51); named cardinal 1921 (died 1951).

1868 James Gibbons, Catholic prelate, was consecrated as titular Bishop of Adramyttium, the youngest (34) of all 1200 Catholic bishops; became Bishop of Richmond (1872), Archbishop of Baltimore (1877-1921).

1877 John P. Scott, American hymn composer, was born in Norwich, N.Y.; wrote many popular hymns (The Lord is my shepherd, The old road, The dearest place, Come ye blessed) (died 1932).

1885 Alexandre Vachon, Catholic prelate, was born in St. Raymond, Canada; Archbishop of Ottawa (1940-53) (died 1953).

1886 Ramakrishna, best known Hindu saint of modern times, died at 50; presented an ideal of holiness and compassion, trying to bring old truths to light.

AUGUST 17

Feast day of St. Hyacinth, a patron saint of Poland.

309 St. Eusebius, pope from April to August 309, died; banished by Emperor Maxentius; also observed as his feast day.

682 St. Leo II was consecrated as pope, served until 683; healed schism between Rome and Ravenna, confirmed actions of Sixth Ecumenical Council.

1635 Richard Mather, colonial Congregational leader, arrived in Boston from England; became teacher of the Dorchester church (1636), helped prepare the "Bay Psalm Book;" father of Increase Mather, grandfather of Cotton Mather.

1723 Joseph Bingham, English clergyman, died at 55; fame rests on his 8-volume "Origines Ecclesiastical or The Antiquities of the Christian Church."

1736 Blessed John Delanque, congregational founder, died at 70; founded Sisters of St. Anne of the Providence of Saumur (1698); beatified 1947.

1740 Benedict XIV was elected pope by a conclave which lasted six months and named him as a compromise candidate on the 255th ballot; served until 1758; governed church with wisdom and firmness, enjoyed widespread popularity; greatly encouraged education, literature, and science; among his many writings was "On the Beatification and Canonization of Saints," which has remained the classic work on the subject; also compiled an extensive work on diocesan synods.

1761 William Carey, Baptist theologian and missionary, was born in Paulerspury, England; taught himself Latin, Greek, Hebrew, Dutch and French; helped organize the Baptist Missionary Society (1792); served in India for 30 years as professor at Ft. William College, Calcutta; published dictionaries, grammars, and translations of the New Testament in Bengali and other languages; largely responsible for the abolition (1829) of suttee, the ancient custom of death for the widow at the funeral of her husband (died 1834).

1780 George Croly, Anglican author and hymn writer, was born in Dublin; a prolific author, best remembered for the hymn, "Spirit of God, descend upon my heart" (died 1860).

1791 Daniel Baker, Presbyterian missionary, was born in Liberty County, Ga.; evangelistic missionary to Texas, where he helped organize the first Texas presbytery; founder (1849), president (1853-57), Austin College (died 1857).

1804 Barbara Heck, "mother of American Methodism," died at 70; Irish-born co-founder with Philip Embury (1766) of the first Methodist society in New York City.

1809 The Disciples of Christ Church was organized in Washington, Pa.

1823 Daniel Bliss, Congregational missionary to Syria, was born in Georgia, Vt.; founder of Syrian Protestant College (now American U.) in Beirut, president (1866-1902) (died 1916).

1834 John F. Hurst, Methodist prelate and educator, was born in Salem, Md.; president, Drew Theological Seminary (1873-80); bishop (1880-1903); author (History of Rationalism, History of Methodism) (died 1903).

1837 Auburn (N.Y.) Convention opened; resulted in a declaration that played an important part in dividing the Presbyterian Church, later (1870) formed basis for its reunion.

1843 Mariano Rampolla, Italian prelate, was born in Polizzi, Sicily; secretary of state for Pope Leo XIII (1887-1903); elevated to cardinal 1887; championed temporal power of pope against restrictions of Italian Government (died 1913).

1847 Pope Pius IX re-established the Inquisition.

1851 Henry Drummond, evangelical writer and lecturer, was born near Stirling, Scotland; sought to reconcile evangelical Christianity with evolution; lecturer, theology professor, New Jerusalem Church; author (Natural Law in the Spiritual World)(died 1897).

1879 Vedanayakan S. Azariah, Anglican bishop, was born in India; first Indian bishop in the Anglican Church of India, serving as Bishop of Dornakal (1914-45) (died 1945.)

1887 Samuel A. Stritch, Catholic prelate, was born in Nashville, Tenn.; Bishop of Toledo (1921-30), Archbishop of Milwaukee (1930-39), of Chicago (1939-58); elevated to cardinal 1946; named pro-prefect of the Sacred Congregation for the Propagation of the Faith, the first American to become a member of the Roman Curia (died 1958).

1961 The quinquennial World Methodist Conference opened in Oslo with 2000 representatives from 17 autonomous Methodist bodies on hand.

1963 The world Anglican leadership issued a manifesto in Toronto warning that the church must revolutionize its basic structure and attitudes.

AUGUST 18

Feast day in the Catholic Church of St. Helena, reputed discoverer of Christ's cross and nails used in the Crucifixion, and her son, Constantine I the Great.

Feast day of Blessed Beatrice da Silva, founder of the Conceptionist Nuns.

440 St. Sixtus III, pope from 432 to 440, died; also observed as his feast day.

849 Walafrid Strabo, German theological writer, died at 40; wrote widely read commentary on the Scriptures, "Glossa ordinaria."

1276 Pope Adrian V died after serving only one month.

1503 Pope Alexander VI accidentally died from poison intended for a guest.

1559 Paul IV, pope from 1555 to 1559, died.

1564 Federigo Borromeo, Italian cardinal and writer, was born in Milan; elevated to cardinal 1587; Archbishop of Milan (1601), a post once held by his cousin, St. Charles Borromeo; founder, Ambrosian Library; wrote extensively on mystical theology.

1832 The Methodist Church of Canada, meeting in Hallowell, voted to merge with the British Wesleyans.

1871 Francis J. McConnell, Methodist prelate and industrial relations expert, was born in Trinway, Ohio; Bishop of Pittsburgh (1912-53), active in the study of industrial relations and helped bring an end to the 12-hour day and seven-day week in the steel industry (died 1953).

1971 Lutheran church leaders met with South African Prime Minister Vorster in an effort to end apartheid in the nation; the four-hour session ended in a deadlock with Vorster "disposed" to keep the door open for further discussion, the church leaders emphasizing that unity "should be of more consequence than differences of race and color."

AUGUST 19

1458 Pius II became pope, served until 1464; issued bull (1460) against belief that councils were superior to popes; sought to lead a crusade against the Turks but died of fever at Ancona; prolific poet and writer, including a history of his times and a geography that reputedly influenced Columbus.

1531 Thomas Bilney, one of the earliest Protestant martyrs, was burned at the stake as a heretic; leader of a group of Cambridge men who were the vanguard of the English Reformation; denounced invocation of the saints, relic worship.

1536 Kaspar Olevianus, German theologian, was born; a founder of the German Reformed Church; introduced Calvinist Reformation in parts of Germany (died 1597).

1646 Alexander Henderson, a leader in developing the Reformed Church of Scotland, died at about 63; drafted the Solemn League and Covenant, adopted by the Westminster Assembly (1643); rector of Edinburgh U. (1643-46).

1680 St. Jean Eudes, French Catholic missionary, died at 79; founder of the Order of Our Lady of Charity (1641) and the Congregation of Jesus and Mary (Eudist Fathers) (1643); also observed as his feast day.

1692 George Burroughs, colonial clergyman, died as the only clerical victim of the witchcraft trials; charged by former Salem parishioners and convicted; made address before crowd watching the execution and moved them to tears, leading Cotton Mather to remind them that the devil often appeared as an angel of light.

1768 Edward D. Fenwick, Catholic prelate, was born in St. Mary's County, Md.; first Bishop of Cincinnati (1822-32), provincial of Dominicans in the United States (1828-32); brother of Benedict J. Fenwick, Boston bishop (died 1832).

1813 Mrs. Jemima Luke, Congregational hymn writer, was born in Islington, England; best remembered for "I think when I read that sweet story of old" (died 1906).

1831 William C. Langdon, Episcopal clergyman who was a founder of the American Young Men's Christian Association (YMCA), was born in Burlington, Vt. (died 1896).

1886 Christian Union, which later became the Cleveland bodies of the Church of God, was formed in Monroe County, Tenn. by Richard G. Spurling.

AUGUST 20

570 Mohammed was born in Mecca (died 632).

984 John XIV, pope from November 983 to 984, died; was Bishop of Pavia and made pope by Otto II, after whose death Antipope Boniface VII returned from Constantinople and imprisoned John in the dungeon of the Castle of Sant'Angelo, where he died.

1153 St. Bernard of Clairvaux, one of the most prominent personalities in church history and a founder of the Cistercians, died at 63; exercised tremendous influence on the political, literary, and religious life of Western civilization through his saintliness and personality; founded monastery at Clairvaux (southeast of Paris), which became the principal center of the Cistercians; called French Christians to the Second Crusade (1147); canonized 1774, named a Doctor* of the Church 1830; extolled in 1953 as "doctor melifluus" by Pope Pius XII; also observed as his feast day.

1632 Louis Bourdaloue, French Jesuit, was born in Bourges; considered the greatest court preacher of the 17th Century (died 1704).

1745 Francis Asbury, early leader of American Methodism, was born near Birmingham, England; first general superintendent of American Methodists (1784), presiding bishop (1785-1816); personified the itinerant ministry, covering up to 300,000 miles under difficult conditions; preached an estimated 17,000 sermons (died 1816).

1823 Pius VII, pope from 1800 to 1823, died.

1825 John Hennessy, Catholic prelate, was born in Ireland; first Archbishop of Dubuque (Iowa) (1893-1900), had been bishop (1866-93) (died 1900).

1829 Henry P. Liddon, Anglican clergyman and theologian, was born near Winchester, England; perhaps the most powerful advocate of the Oxford Movement; canon, St. Paul's Cathedral (1870), chancellor (1886) (died 1890).

1834 Gerhard Groote, Dutch founder of the Brethren of the Common Life, died at 44; father of a spiritual movement of the 19th Century, opponent of scholastic theologians and an advocate of reading Scriptures.

1856 William Dwight P. Bliss, Episcopal organizer of the first Christian Socialist society in the United States (1889), was born in Constantinople; founder, pastor, Mission of the Carpenter, Boston (1890-94); president, National Social Reform League (1889); published "Encyclopedia of Social Reform" (died 1926).

1874 Theodore Tilton filed charges against Henry Ward Beecher, renowned Congregational clergyman, for alleged adultery with Mrs. Tilton; sensational trial ended after six months with a hung jury; Congregational Council exonerated Beecher (1876).

1884 Rudolf K. Bultmann, controversial theologian, was born in Wiefelstede, Germany; advocated demythologizing the New Testament, resulted in a tremendous theological controversy (died 1976).

1886 Paul J. Tillich, influential theologian and philosopher, was born in Starzeddel, Germany; sought to bind religion and culture together; with Union Theological Seminary (1933-55); author (Systematic Theology, The Protestant Era, The Courage to Be, Dynamics of Faith) (died 1965).

1912 William Booth, founder of the Salvation Army, died at 83.

1914 St. Pius X, pope from 1903 to 1914, died at 79; canonized 1954.

1965 A white Episcopal seminarian engaged in civil rights activities and a white Catholic priest were critically wounded by shotgun blasts fired by a white special deputy sheriff in Hayneville, Ala.

1980 The National Conference of Catholic Bishops announced a plan, approved by the Vatican, that would allow married Anglican priests to become Catholic priests.

AUGUST 21

Feast of the Immaculate Heart of Mary.

Feast day of St. Jane Frances de Chantal, French co-founder of the Visitation Order (1610); canonized 1767.

Feast day of St. Pius X, pope from 1903 to 1914.

1245 Alexander of Hales, English theologian, died; one of the first to attempt correlation of Augustinian theology with ideas of Aristotle and Arab commentators; known as "Doctor Irrefragabilis."

1567 St. Francis de Sales, co-founder of the Order of Visitation of Holy Mary, was born in Thorens-Gliere, France; Bishop of Geneva (1602-22); helped found the Order in 1610; a leader of the Counter-Reformation; most famous writings were "Introduction to the Devout Life" and "Treatise on the Love of God;" canonized 1665, named a Doctor* of the Church 1877 and heavenly patron of Catholic writers (died 1622).

1912 W. Bramwell Booth, son of founder William Booth, became head of the American Salvation Army; served until 1929.

1969 The Al Aqsa Mosque in the old city of Jerusalem was damaged by fire; the mosque is part of the Haram ash Sharif, generally considered the third holiest place for Muslims after Mecca and Medina.

AUGUST 22

1241 Gregory IX, pope from 1227 to 1241, died.

1280 Nicholas III, pope from 1277 to 1280, died at about 64.

1532 William Warham, Archbishop of Canterbury (1503-32), died at about 82; lord chancellor (1504-15), married and crowned Henry VIII and Catherine of Aragon (1509); a patron of the New Learning and a generous benefactor of scholars; when English clergy were bidden (1531) to acknowledge Henry VIII as supreme head of the church, Warham introduced an amendment - "so far as the law of Christ will allow."

1760 Leo XII, pope from 1823 to 1829, was born as Annibale Francisco della Genga near Spoleto, Italy.

1798 William G. Shauffler, Congregational missionary, was born in Stuttgart, Germany; missionary to Turkey and Armenia, translated Old Testament into Sephardi; New Testament into Turkish (died 1883).

1798 Ignatius A. Reynolds, Catholic Bishop of Charleston, S.C., was born in Nelson County, Ky.; president, Bardstown College (Ky.) (1827-34) (died 1855).

1800 Edward B. Pusey, English leader of the Oxford Movement, was born near Oxford; headed the Catholic revival in the Church of England; religious professor of Hebrew at Oxford and canon of Christ Church (1828-43); suspended as university preacher on the grounds of heresy; produced tracts on baptism, the Holy Eucharist; sought to unite the Anglican and Catholic churches (died 1882).

1821 The Colombian Congress abolished the 200-year old Inquisition.

1860 Samuel Holdheim, German Jewish rabbi, died at 54; a founder and leader of Reform Judaism in Germany.

1968 Pope Paul VI was the first reigning pontiff to visit Latin America, arriving in Bogota, Colombia for the 39th International Eucharistic Congress.

1972 The World Council of Churches voted overwhelmingly to liquidate its financial stake in all corporations doing business with white-ruled African countries.

1982 Rev. Athenagoras Aneste was installed as the 15th bishop of the Greek Orthodox Archdiocese of North and South America in the Cathedral of the Holy Trinity, New York City.

AUGUST 23

1285 St. Philip Benizi, leader of the Order of the Servants of Mary (Servites), died at 52; canonized 1671; also observed as his feast day.

1348 John Stratford, Archbishop of Canterbury (1333-48), died; chancellor (1330-34, 1335-37), chief advisor of Edward III (1330-40).

1549 Thomas Sternhold, English hymnist, died; versified many (about 40) of the Psalms.

1761 Jedidiah Morse, Congregational clergyman and America's leading geographer, was born in Woodstock, Conn.; launched the "Unitarian controversy," forcing Unitarian believers out of the Congregational Church; formed coalition which led to establishment of Andover Theological Seminary; pastor of Charlestown, Mass. church (1789-1819) (died 1826).

1814 James R. Bayley, Catholic prelate, was born in Rye, N.Y.; nephew of Elizabeth Ann Seton; first Bishop of Newark (1853-72), Archbishop of Baltimore (1872-77) (died 1877).

1857 Warren A. Candler, Methodist prelate and editor, was born in Carroll County, Ga.; editor, *Christian Advocate*, organ of Methodist Church South (1886-88); president, Emory College (1888-98); Methodist bishop (1898-1941) (died 1941).

1879 The Church of Christ, Scientist, was chartered by Mary Baker Eddy.

1948 The World Council of Churches was officially established in Amsterdam, Netherlands, with 144 member churches; located its headquarters in Geneva, Switzerland.

AUGUST 24

Feast day in the Catholic Church of St. Bartholomew, one of the apostles.

1560 The Scottish Parliament abolished the jurisdiction of the pope in Scotland.

1572 The massacre of St. Bartholomew's Day began in Paris during the night; Gaspard de Coligny (1519-72) and other Huguenot leaders and 5,000-10,000 Huguenots were killed; the massacre, instigated by Queen Mother Catherine de Medici, an ardent Catholic, went on for two days.

1572 Claude Goudimel, French church musician, was killed in Lyon during the St. Bartholomew's Day massacre; originally a Catholic, he founded a music school in Rome (1540) and his music helped develop the classical style of Catholic Church music; returned to France and became a Protestant.

1662 The return of Charles II to England resulted in the enforcement of 39 Articles of Uniformity in religion, use of the same form of worship and Book of Common Prayer, and the ejection of 1,909 nonconformist ministers from their livings; the day known as "Black Bartholomew Day," marked a turning point in English dissent.

1683 John Owen, English Puritan clergyman, died at 67; a leading advocate of freedom of conscience; served as chaplain for Oliver Cromwell, dean of Christ Church College at Oxford.

1747 John Dickins, a pioneer of American Methodism, was born in London; helped found Cokesbury College (near Baltimore), headed Methodist Book Concern (1789-98) (died 1798).

1759 William Wilberforce, English legislator and philanthropist, was born in Hull; worked against slavery and was responsible for British Emancipation bill, ending slavery in the British Empire (1807); leader of "Clapham sect" of evangelical Christians (died 1833).

1799 John D. Lang, Australian religious and political leader, was born in Greenock, Scotland; a founder of the Presbyterian Church in Australia (died 1878).

1810 Theodore Parker, Unitarian clergyman, was born in Lexington, Mass.; ultraliberal who denied the special authority of the Bible, the supernatural origin of Christ; active abolitionist who secretly aided John Brown in the Harpers Ferry raid; author (Discourse on Matters Pertaining to Religion) (died 1860).

1829 Oscar P. Fitzgerald, Methodist missionary in California, was born in Caswell County, N.C.; editor, *Pacific Methodist and the Christian Spectator*, and *Nashville Christian Advocate*; California superintendent of public instruction (1867-71); bishop (1890-91); president, Pacific Methodist College (died 1911).

1854 The German Lutheran Synod of Iowa was organized.

1856 St. Emily de Vialar died at 59; founder, Sisters of St. Joseph "of the Apparition" (1832); canonized 1951.

1895 Richard J. Cushing, Catholic prelate, was born in Boston; Archbishop of Boston (1944-70), becoming at 49 the youngest Catholic archbishop in the world; elevated to cardinal 1958 (died 1970).

1964 Rev. Frederick McManus of Catholic University celebrated in St. Louis the first full Catholic mass in English in the United States.

1981 The Salvation Army resigned from membership in the World Council of Churches, charging that the organization aided armed liberation movements.

1982 Joseph L. Bernardin was installed as Archbishop of Chicago at the Holy Name Cathedral with the Most Rev. Pio Laghi, apostolic delegate, present.

AUGUST 25

Feast day in the Orthodox Church of St. Titus, associate of the Apostle Paul.

Feast day of St. Joseph Calasanctius (1556-1648), founder of the Order of Piarists.

Feast day of St. Mary Michaela Desmaisieres (1809-65), founder of Handmaids of the Blessed Sacrament; canonized 1934.

608 Boniface IV became pope, served until 615; reign marked by dealings with Anglo-Saxon church; converted the Roman Pantheon into the Basilica of Sancta Maria and Martyrs.

776 St. Gregory of Utrecht, Frankish associate of St. Boniface in his missionary efforts, died; directed Frisian mission for 20 years after

Boniface's martyrdom; also observed as his feast day.

1270 St. Louis (Louis IX, king of France 1226-70), died; went on Sixth Crusade and was a captive for four years; started another Crusade (1266-70) and died enroute before Tunis; canonized 1297; also observed as his feast day.

1282 St. Thomas de Cantelupe (Cantilupe) died at about 64; Bishop of Hereford (1275-82) and known for his ascetic life and strict discipline; chancellor of England (1265) and chief advisor of Edward I; canonized 1320.

1556 Jan David Joris, Dutch Anabaptist*, died at about 55; founded new Anabaptist sect (Davidists or Jorists); assumed role of new Messiah; retired incognito in Switzerland (1544); identified after death, denounced for heresy and his remains were exhumed and burned (1559).

1662 John Leverett, colonial church leader and educator, was born in Boston; a founder of Brattle St. Church, Boston, along "broad and catholik" lines; president, Harvard (1707-24) (died 1724).

1824 The first conference of the Methodist Church in Canada was held.

1886 Ignatius Smith, Dominican priest and educator, was born in Newark, N.J.;dean, school of philosophy, Catholic University (1936-57) (died 1957).

1907 The German Catholic Congress opened in Würzburg.

1987 A federal appeals court overturned a lower court decision ordering Hawkins County, Tenn. schools to excuse fundamentalist children from reading class because their parents found the books offensive to their religious beliefs.

AUGUST 26

Feast day of St. Zephyrinus, pope from about 199 to 217; reign marked by many controversies over doctrine but little is known about him.

1349 Thomas Bradwardine, Archbishop of Canterbury (1349), died at 59 of the plague; called the "profound Doctor;" wrote "De Causa Dei," directed against Pelagianism*.

1792 A decree of the Revolutionary National Assembly resulted in the exile of 40,000 priests from France.

1827 Beal M. Schmucker, Lutheran leader and liturgical scholar, was born in Gettysburg, Pa., the son of Samuel S. Schmucker; collaborated with A.T. Geissenhainer in "A Liturgy for the Use of the Evangelical Lutheran Church" (died 1888).

1838 St. Elizabeth Bichier des Ages, co-founder of the Daughters of the Cross or Sisters of St. Andrew (1811), died at 65; canonized 1947; also observed as her feast day.

1857 James J. Keane, Catholic prelate, was born in Joliet, Ill.; Bishop of Cheyenne (Wyo.) (1902-11), Archbishop of Dubuque, Iowa (1911-29) (died 1929).

1877 Henry A. Atkinson, who helped establish and operate the Church Peace Union (1914-55), was born in Merced, Cal.; his work around the world led to the formation of the World Council of Churches (1948); secretary, Congregational Department of Church and Labor (1911-18); general secretary, Universal Christian Conference of Life and Work (1920-32) (died 1960).

1908 Rufino J. Santos, Archbishop of Manila (1853-76), was born in Guagua, Philippine Islands; elevated to cardinal 1960 (died 1976).

1908 Cynthia Clark Wedel, first woman elected president of the National Council of Churches (1969-72), was born in Dearborn, Mich.; president, World Council of Churches (1975-83) (died 1986).

1913 Julius Döpfner, Catholic Bishop of Berlin, was born in Hausen, Germany; elevated to cardinal 1958.

1930 Catholic Bishop Samuel A. Stritch was named Archbishop of Milwaukee; became Archbishop of Chicago in 1939, serving until 1946.

1961 Catholic Archbishop Gerard de Millville of Conakry was expelled from Guinea after criticizing a government plan to nationalize all schools.

1967 The largest youth meeting in the history of Christian Science ended in Boston; about 6000 college students from more than 1100 colleges and universities in 32 countries attended.

1978 John Paul I was elected pope; served until his sudden death September 29.

AUGUST 27

542 St. Caesarius, Archbishop of Arles, France (about 502-542) and celebrated preacher, died at about 71; apostolic vicar of Gaul and Spain; introduced many ecclesiastical reforms and founded several monasteries; also observed as his feast day.

827 Eugenius II, pope from 824 to 827, died; supported reforms and advanced the cause of learning.

1061 Nicholas II, pope from 1058 to 1061, died.

1255 St. Hugh of Lincoln, English child saint, died; often called "Little St. Hugh;" allegedly a victim of a ritual murder, he is credited with many miracles; also observed as his feast day.

1590 Sixtus V, pope from 1585 to 1590, died.

1640 Inhabitants of Providence, R.I., drew up an agreement in which they agreed, among other things, "To hould forth liberty of conscience."

1648 St. Joseph Calasanctius, founder of the Clerks Regular of the Religious Schools (Piarists), died; under his influence, the first free school was established in Rome (1597); canonized 1767.

1737 John Hutchinson, English theological writer, died at 63; his fundamental idea was that the Bible contains the key to all knowledge; wrote "Moses' Principia" and works of religious symbolism; taught that Hebrew scriptures contain a complete system of natural science and theology.

1749 James Madison, Episcopal prelate and educator, was born in Staunton, Va.; first Bishop of Virginia (1795-1812); president, College of William & Mary (1777-1812) (died 1812).

1772 Gideon Blackburn, Presbyterian clergyman and missionary to the Cherokee Indians, was born in Augusta County, Va. (died 1838).

1803 Edward Beecher, educator and editor, was born in East Hampton, N.Y., the second son of Lyman Beecher; first president, Illinois College, Jacksonville (1830-44); a founder, editor, *Congregationalist* (1849-53); active anti-slavery worker and defended Elijah Lovejoy in efforts to maintain press freedom (died 1895).

1841 Patrick W. Riordan, Catholic prelate, was born in New Brunswick, Canada; Archbishop of San Francisco (1884-1914) (died 1914).

1859 Adrian G. Morice, Canadian missionary, was born; missionary to the Indians of British Columbia (1880-1938); compiled several Indian dictionaries and grammars, made valuable maps of Canadian Northwest (died 1938).

1864 Catholic Bishop John McCloskey was installed as Archbishop of New York.

1870 A group of professors, led by Johann J. I. Döllinger, met in Nuremberg to voice opposition to a decree of papal infallibility, giving rise to the creation of the Old Catholic Church.

1870 Romolo Murri, Italian priest and social reformer, was born; founded a Christian Democratic movement, which was condemned (1901) by Pope Leo XIII; founded the National Democratic League (1905) for which he was excommunicated (1909); reconciled with church before his death in 1944.

1877 Lloyd C. Douglas, author and Congregational clergyman, was born in Columbia City, Ind.; pastor of several American and Canadian churches; chaplain, religious director, U. of Illinois; best known for his Christian novels (The Robe, The Magnificent Obsession, Disputed Passage) (died 1951).

1910 Mother Theresa, "saint of the gutters," was born; awarded 1979 Nobel Peace Prize.

1956 World Federation of Methodist Women began four-day meeting at Lake Junaluska, N.C.; voted to become a part of the World Methodist Council.

AUGUST 28

430 St. Augustine of Hippo, dominant personality of the Western church and the greatest thinker of Christian antiquity, died at 76; also observed as his feast day.

1764 Ambrose Marechal, Catholic prelate, was born; Archbishop of Baltimore (1817-28) (died 1828).

1771 Timothy Alden, Congregational clergyman and educator, was born in Yarmouth, Me.; founder, first president, Allegheny College, Meadville, Pa. (1817-39) (died 1839).

1774 Elizabeth Ann Seton, founder, superior of religious congregation, was born in New York City; a founder, Society for Relief of Poor Widows with Small Children (1797), first charitable organization in New York; founder, superior, American Sisters of Charity (1809-21); a founder, St. Joseph's College, Emmittsburg, Md.; canonized 1975 (died 1821).

1794 Pope Pius VI issued the bull, "Auctorum fidei," which condemned 85 articles of the Synod of Pistoia (1786).

1796 William H. Bathurst, English hymn writer, was born near Bristol; wrote various versions of the Psalms and more than 200 hymns (Hark, the distant isles proclaim; Holy Spirit from on high; Eternal Spirit, by whose power; O for a faith that will not shrink) (died 1877).

1840 Ira D. Sankey, evangelist, was born in Edinburg, Pa.; noted for hymn singing; associated with Dwight L. Moody (1870-99); compiled collections of popular hymns (Sacred Songs and Solos, Gospel Hymns) (died 1908).

1842 Placide L. Chapelle, Catholic prelate, was born in Runes, France; Archbishop of Santa Fe, N.M. (1894-98), Archbishop of New Orleans (1898-1905) (died 1905).

1973 Patriarch Dimitrios, titular head of Eastern Orthodox Christianity, reaffirmed his church's commitment to efforts for reunion of churches at a World Council of Churches meeting.

AUGUST 29

Feast of the Beheading of St. John the Baptist.

1261 Urban IV, born Jacques Pantaleon, was elected pope, served until 1264; named many French cardinals, later a cause of the Western schism; instituted the Feast of Corpus Christi.

1484 Innocent VIII, born Giovanni Battista Gibo, was elected pope, served until 1492; reign marked by sharp decline in spiritual leadership in the papacy; appointed (1487) Torquemada as grand inquisitor in Spain; the Moors were driven from Spain during his reign (1492) (died 1492).

1632 John Locke, philosopher and father of English empiricism, was born in Bristol; author of many works, including "Essay Concerning Human Understanding," which dealt with settling what questions human understanding was or was not fitted to deal with, and "An Essay Concerning Toleration," in which he expressed his views on religion (died 1704).

1769 (Rose) Philippine Duchesne, French founder of a convent, was born in Grenoble; founded first convent of the Sacred Heart in the United States; beatified 1940 (died 1852).

1792 Charles Grandison Finney, "father of modern revivalism" and a Presbyterian evangelist, was born in Warren, Conn.; conducted evangelistic meetings through Pennsylvania, in Wilmington, Del. and the Broadway Tabernacle (Congregational) in New York City, which was specially organized for him (1834-37); professor, Oberlin (Ohio) College (1837-75), president (1851-66) (died 1875).

1799 Pius VI, pope from 1775 to 1799, died.

1805 (John) Frederick D. Maurice, one of the greatest English theologians of the 19th Century, was born in Normanston, England; divinity professor, author (The Kingdom of Christ, Social Morality) (died 1872).

1809 Oliver Wendell Holmes, author and educator, was born in Cambridge, Mass.; best known for his writings (The Autocrat of the Breakfast Table); wrote several hymns (Lord of all being, throned afar) (died 1894).

1829 Patrick A. Feehan, Catholic prelate, was born in Tipperary County, Ireland; Bishop of Nashville (1865-80), first Archbishop of Chicago (1880-1902); created more than 100 new parishes (died 1902).

1847 Sebastian G. Messmer, Catholic prelate and educator, was born in Goldach, Switzerland;

professor of canon law, Catholic U.; Bishop of Green Bay, Wis. (1891-1902), Archbishop of Milwaukee (1902-30) (died 1930).

1854 Joseph Jacobs, Jewish historian, was born in Sydney, Australia; author of works on Jewish history, fables; served as revising editor of the Jewish Encyclopedia (1900-06) (died 1916).

1877 Brigham Young, Mormon leader, died in Salt Lake City; survived by 17 wives and 47 children.

1883 The first Canadian Salvation Army services were held in London, Ontario.

1957 Catholic scholars assembled at the Benedictine abbey of St. Procopius in Lisle, Ill. to search for ways of uniting 200 million Eastern Orthodox Christians with the Roman Catholic Church.

AUGUST 30

Feast day of St. Rose of Lima, the first native of the New World to be canonized; patron saint of South America.

Feast day of St. Fiacre, Irish abbot who founded a monastery in France.

257 Sixtus II became pope, served until Aug. 6, 258, when he was martyred in the Valerian persecution; reconciled churches of North Africa.

410 St. Pammachius, Roman Christian, died during the Gothic invasion; spent his possessions on works of piety, such as hospital at Portus; also observed as his feast day.

1181 Alexander III, pope from 1159 to 1181, died; constantly at odds with Emperor Frederick I Barbarossa, until reconciled in 1177; renowned legislator, during reign, Third Lateran Council (1179) confirmed the exclusive right of the College of Cardinals to elect the pope.

1464 Paul II was named pope, served until 1471; principal aim of reign was to create a Christian league in the face of a Turkish invasion; a patron of scholars; probably introduced printing into Rome; established (1470) ordinary jubilees at 25 year intervals; enjoyed life of splendor.

1817 John Williams, theologian and educator, was born in Deerfield, Mass.; Episcopal bishop (1865-99), presiding bishop (1887-99); president, Trinity College, Hartford (1848-53); a founder, professor and dean, Berkeley Divinity School, Middletown, Conn. (1854-99) (died 1899).

1900 Franklin C. Fry, Lutheran leader, was born in Bethlehem, Pa.; president, United Lutheran Church (1944-62); president, Lutheran World Federation (1957-63); president, American Lutheran Church (1962-68) (died 1968).

1982 Nahum Goldman, one of the world's foremost Zionists, died in West Germany at 87.

AUGUST 31

577 Johannes III Scholasticus, patriarch of Constantinople (565-577), died; prepared a collection of ecclesiastical laws or canons, now known as "Nomocanon in 50 Titles" or "Nomocanon of Johannes Scholasticus."

651 St. Aidan, first Bishop of Lindisfarne*, died; spread Christianity throughout Northumbria (northern England).

1740 Jean (Johann) Frederic Oberlin, French clergyman and industrialist, was born in Strasbourg; labored for his poor parishioners in every way, preaching three sermons a month in French, one in German; initiated orphan asylums and his social and educational methods won international recognition; principles of infant education were developed by Pestalozzi; Oberlin College (Ohio) named for him (died 1826).

1792 Wilbur Fisk, Methodist clergyman and educator, was born in Middletown, Conn.; a founder, first president, Wesleyan U. Middletown (1830-39) (died 1839).

1836 Alfred M. Randolph, Episcopal Bishop of Southern Virginia (1892-1918), was born in Winchester, Va. (died 1918).

1857 John G. Murray, Episcopal prelate, was born in Lonaconing, Md.; Bishop of Maryland (1911-

29); first elected presiding bishop of the church (1925-29) (died 1929).

1897 Gabriele Acacio Coussa, Syrian prelate of the Catholic Church, was born in Aleppo; prosecretary of the Congregation for the Oriental Church; elevated to cardinal 1962 (died 1962).

1958 A second meeting of Methodist and Catholic representatives, held in London, discussed the Eucharist and authority in the church.

1974 Bahai conference opened in St. Louis to initiate a five-year expansion program.

1976 The 13th World Methodist Congress in Dublin ended with a call for continued talks with the Catholic Church on world church unity and for similar discussions with Lutheran and Eastern Orthodox churches.

1981 Sacred Buddhist writings, it was announced, would be published by the Dharma Publishing Co. in a 120-volume collection.

SEPTEMBER 1

Feast day of St. Giles, Grecian-born patron of cripples, beggars, and blacksmiths; a hermit in a desert region near Arles, France; one of the most popular medieval saints.

Feast day in the Orthodox Church of St. Simeon Stylites (about 390-450), the first of the stylite or pillar ascetics, who spent all their time atop a pillar, occasionally preaching to crowds below.

1159 Adrian IV, pope from 1154 to 1159, died.

1181 Lucius III was named pope, served until 1185; stayed in Rome only briefly because he could not control the Romans; with Emperor Frederick I Barbarossa, he presided over the church-state assembly at Verona 1185.

1271 Blessed Gregory X, born Teobaldo Visconti, was named pope, served until 1276; worked out a short-lived truce with the Orthodox Church at the Council of Lyon, which he convoked in 1274.

1646 Congregational churches of Massachusetts began meetings in Boston which resulted in a platform formulating relations between church and state.

1727 Jean Baptiste Gobel, Archbishop of Paris (1791-93), was born; resigned to join the Hébertistes in the "worship of reason;" guillotined 1794.

1784 John Wesley, co-founder of Methodism, made a fateful decision for American Methodism — "Being now clear in my own mind, I took a step which I had long weighed...and appointed Mr. (Richard) Whatcoat and Mr. (Thomas) Vasey to go and serve the desolate sheep in America."

1785 Peter Cartwright, most famous Methodist circuit rider on the American frontier, was born in Amherst County, Va.; served as presiding elder of the West; served two terms in the Illinois state legislature, was defeated in a race for Congress (1846) by Abraham Lincoln (died 1872).

1836 Marcus Whitman and H.H. Spalding, missionaries, with their wives reached Fort Walla Walla on the Columbia River, established the first white settlement in northern Oregon.

1849 Charles B. Galloway, Methodist prelate, was born in Kosciusko, Miss.; served as bishop of the Methodist Church South (1886-1909); a prime mover in founding Millsaps College, Jackson, Miss. (died 1909).

1866 Frederick R. Tennant, English philosophical theologian, was born in Burslem; sought to harmonize science and religion; his chief work was "Philosophical Theology" (died 1957).

1871 (Joshua) Reuben Clark Jr., Mormon first counselor and apostle (1934-61), was born in Grantsville, Utah; Ambassador to Mexico (1930-33) (died 1961).

1904 Norman Gerstenfeld, American leader of Reformed Judaism, was born in Croydon, England; rabbi of Washington Hebrew Congregation (1939-68) (died 1968).

1910 Pope Pius X instituted the anti-modernism oath, a profession of faith in connection with the condemnation of modernism.

1935 Abraham Isaac Kook (Kuk), Latvian-born rabbi and talmudic scholar, died at 71; first chief rabbi of Palestine under the British mandate (1921-35).

1956 The ninth World Methodist Conference opened at Lake Junaluska, N.C. with representatives from 40 nations in attendance.

1957 Billy Graham closed a 16-week evangelical campaign in New York City with a giant rally in Times Square; meetings drew almost 2 million people and 56,767 made "decisions for Christ."

SEPTEMBER 2

595 St. John the Faster (John IV), patriarch of Constantinople, died; also observed as his feast day in the Orthodox Church.

1192 The Third Crusade was ended with the signing of a treaty, a peace which lasted five years; while Jerusalem was not retaken in the Crusade, other territory was gained in retaining a Christian kingdom in the area.

1750 St. Paul's Church in Halifax, the oldest Protestant church in Canada, was opened by the Rev. William Tutty.

1784 John Wesley appointed Thomas Coke superintendent of the American Methodist Church.

1790 Johann N. von Hontheim, German Catholic prelate, died at 89; an opponent of ultramontanism*; best known for a work published under the pseudonym, Justinus Febronius, advocating a philosophy known as Febronianism, describing the powers and abuses of the papacy and urging a return to the spirit of primitive Christianity.

1838 Erastus Blakelee, Congregational clergyman, was born in Plymouth, Conn.; organized the Bible Study Publishing Co., Boston (1892) and the Bible Study Union, which published about 170 volumes of Bible lessons (died 1908).

1858 Newton D. Hillis, Congregational clergyman, was born in Magnolia, Iowa; pastor, Plymouth Congregational Church, Brooklyn (1899-1924); president, Plymouth Institute (1914-29) (died 1929).

1921 The first general synod of the African Orthodox Church convened in New York, with George A. McGuire as the first bishop.

1988 PTL founder Jim Bakker submitted a $165 million plan to buy back the television evangelistic movement from which he had been ousted after a sex scandal; however, Bakker was unable to produce a $3 million letter of credit which would have secured the deal.

SEPTEMBER 3

590 St. Gregory I the Great was consecrated pope, served to 604; a Father* and Doctor* of the Church; regarded as one of the great saints and churchmen of Christian History; restored monastic discipline, enforced celibacy of the clergy, zealous in propagating Christianity; exerted great influence on doctrinal matters, introduced changes in the liturgy; supposed to have arranged the Gregorian chants and wrote several hymns; also observed as his feast day.

1680 Paul Raguemeau, French Jesuit missionary and explorer, died at 72; served among the Indians in Canada, headed Jesuit Canadian missions.

1782 Benedict J. Fenwick, Catholic prelate, was born in St. Mary's County, Md., brother of Edward D. Fenwick; second Bishop of Boston (1825-46), founder of one of the earliest Catholic newspapers in the United States (1829); president, Georgetown College (1822-25) (died 1846).

1795 Francois N. Blanchet, Catholic missionary to the Northwest, was born in Quebec; first Archbishop of Oregon City (moved to Portland 1862) (1840-83) (died 1883).

1847 James Hannington, missionary and Anglican prelate, was born near Brighton, England; named Bishop of Eastern Equatorial Africa (1884), killed by Ugandan soldiers Oct. 20, 1885.

1852 Charles C. Hall, Presbyterian clergyman and educator, was born in New York City; pastor, First Presbyterian Church, Brooklyn, (1877-97); president, Union Theological Seminary (1897-1908) (died 1908).

1864 Francis C. Burkitt, English theologian, was born in London; divinity professor, Cambridge (1905-35), author of books on early church history, the New Testament, and sources for the life of Jesus (died 1935).

1873 Pope Pius IX wrote to Emperor William I of Prussia complaining of ecclesiastical persecution, asserted his authority over all baptized persons; Emperor justified his actions by asserting there is no mediator between God and Man but Jesus Christ.

1894 Helmut Richard Niebuhr, theologian and author, was born in Wright City, Mo., brother of Reinhold Nieburh; professor, Yale Divinity School (1938-62); chief contribution was in philosophical areas of ethics and theology; author (The Kingdom of God in America, Christ and Culture) (died 1962).

1901 Ellen N. Stone, American missionary in Europe, was captured by Turkish brigands in the Salonika district of Bulgaria; held her for ransom, released Feb 23, 1902 on payment of $72,500 which had been raised by public subscription.

1914 Benedict XV was elected pope, served until 1922; spent considerable time and effort trying to end World War I.

1957 A North American study committee began meetings at Oberlin (Ohio) College to study the basic principles that should underline efforts to unite churches.

1959 Tom Cunningham, British-American priest known as the Catholic parish priest of the Arctic; died in Point Barrow, Alaska at about 53; supervised an area of 150,000 sq. mi. north of the Arctic Circle.

1965 Pope Paul VI issued the encyclical, "Mysterium fidei," restating the traditional eucharistic teachings, emphasizing the doctrines of the real presence and transubstantiation.

1978 The pontificate of Pope John Paul I was inaugurated with an outdoor mass celebrated by the Pope in St. Peter's Square.

1979 Tibetan Buddhist leader, Dalai Lama, arrived in New York City for 49-day tour of the United States to advance the cause of Tibetan independence.

1984 The Vatican repudiated certain forms of liberation theology, condemning the Marxist concept of violent class struggle to attain social justice.

SEPTEMBER 4

Feast day in the Orthodox Church of St. Babylas, Bishop of Antioch (about 240-250); once refused an emperor admission to church because of an unrepented crime.

422 St. Boniface I, pope from 418 to 422, died; also observed as his feast day.

454 Dioscorus, patriarch of Alexandria (444-454), died after three years in exile.

1417 Robert Hallam, Bishop of Salisbury (1407-17), died; represented England at the Council of Constance; nominated for Archbishop of York and a cardinal but nomination was opposed by the crown and not consummated.

1634 Robert South, English court preacher, was born in London; waged verbal war against Romanism and Puritanism, supported doctrine of passive obedience and divine right of kings; chaplain to Charles II; renowned for sermons (died 1716).

1645 The first American Lutheran church building was dedicated in Essington, Pa.

1802 Marcus Whitman, missionary to the Northwest, was born in Rushville, N.Y.; instrumental in helping get Oregon for the United States; killed with wife by Indians (1847).

1808 George E. Hare, Episcopal educator, was born in Philadelphia; principal, Philadelphia Episcopal Academy (1846-57); professor, Philadelphia Episcopal Divinity School (1857-92) (died 1892).

1809 Carlo M. Curci, Jesuit editor, was born in Naples; co- founder, editor, *Civilta Cattolica*, a Jesuit publication (1850-53,1856-63); expelled (1877) from Jesuits for opposition to Vatican political policy; reinstated shortly before death (1891).

1813 The first religious weekly in the United States, *Religious Remembrancer*, was founded by John W. Scott; through successive mergers, magazine became the *Christian Observer*.

1835 Edwin Hatch, English educator and theologian, was born in Derby, England; secretary, Board of Faculties at Oxford; remembered for Anglican hymn, "Breathe on me, breath of God" (died 1889).

1842 Thomas W. Goodspeed, Baptist clergyman and educator, was born in Glens Falls, N.Y.; worked with William Rainey Harper on plans for U. of Chicago; secretary, Board of Trustees, U. of Chicago (1890-1922); secretary, Board of Trustees, Baptist Union Theological Seminary (1894-1927) (died 1927).

1872 Pistro Fumasoni-Bondi, Italian prelate, was born in Rome; served as prefect of the Congregation for the Propagation of Faith for 27 years; elevated to cardinal 1933 (died 1960).

1880 Marshall B. Stewart, American theologian, was born in Galveston, Texas; professor, dogmatic history, General Theological Seminary (1928-56) (died 1956).

1886 Albert W. T. Orsborn, general of the Salvation Army (1946-54), was born in Maidstone, England (died 1967).

SEPTEMBER 5

Feast day in the Orthodox Church of St. Elizabeth, wife of the priest Zacharias (St. Zachary) and mother of St. John the Baptist.

Feast day of St. Lawrence Justinian (1381-1456), first patriarch of Venice; canonized 1690.

Feast day in the Orthodox Church of St. Zacharias, pope from 741 to 752.

1568 Tomaso Campanella, Dominican monk and writer, was born in Italy; known especially for "Civitas Solis" (City of the Sun), a story of a utopian state, similar Plato's Republic; jailed (1599-1626) on charges of conspiracy to free Naples from Spain (died 1639).

1569 Edmund Bonner, last Catholic Bishop of London (1539-49), died at about 69; chaplain to King Henry VIII (1532-40), imprisoned (1549-53) for insistence that royal supremacy was in abeyance during Edward VI's minority; restored at the ascendancy of Mary, becoming the principal agent in persecuting reformers; when Elizabeth I became queen, he refused (1559) to take the oath under the Act of Supremacy; spent the rest of his days in Marshalsea prison.

1823 Willibald Beyschlag, German Protestant leader, was born in Frankfurt; founder, leader of Evangelical Union (1886-1900); designed to protect German Protestant interests (died 1900).

1883 A conference resulted in the union of all Canadian Methodist churches.

1885 Antonio Bacci, the Vatican's ranking Latinist who wrote the Latin versions of the encyclicals of four popes, was born in Giugnola, Italy; elevated to cardinal 1960 (died 1971).

1981 Egyptian President Anwar el Sadat deposed Shemuda III, spiritual leader of 6 million Christian Coptics; gave his authority to a committee of five bishops.

SEPTEMBER 6

Feast day of St. Zachariah, noted for his tireless efforts to get the temple in Jerusalem rebuilt after the Babylonian captivity and his prophecies about Messiah.

972 John XIII, pope from 965 to 972, died.

1711 Henry M. Muhlenberg, "father of Lutheranism" in America, was born in Einbeck, Germany; missionary to America (1742), organized the United Lutheran Church (died 1787).

1748 Edmund Gibson, English prelate, died at 79; Bishop of London (1720-48); was offered archbishopric of Canterbury (1747) but declined because of his age.

1777 James H.M.N. Joubert de la Mursille, Catholic clergyman, was born in St. Jean d'Angely, France; founder, Oblate Sisters of Providence (1831) (died 1843).

1809 Bruno Bauer, German radical theologian, was born in Halle; lecturer on theology (1834-42), deprived of his license as a result of his destructive criticism of the Bible (died 1882).

1812 Samuel D. Burchard, Presbyterian clergyman, was born in Steuben, N.Y.; pastor, Hudson St. Church, New York City (1839-79); active in social, political affairs (died 1891).

1812 John D. Lee, Mormon elder, was born in Kaskaskia, Ill.; notorious for his role in the Mountain Meadows (Utah) massacre of federal troops (1857); long legal procedure ended in his being found guilty, executed in 1887.

1849 Archibald McLean, Disciples of Christ missionary, was born in Summerside, Prince Edward Island, Canada; corresponding secretary (1882-1900), president (1900-19), Foreign Christian Missionary Society (died 1920).

1908 The Russian Holy Synod appealed to all true believers to abstain from celebrating Count Leo Tolstoy's 80th birthday.

1910 The four-day Catholic Eucharistic Congress opened in Montreal.

SEPTEMBER 7

1159 Alexander III, born Orlando Bandinelli, became pope, served until 1181; because of schism and enmity of Frederick I Barbarossa, he lived mostly in France; presided over Third Lateran Council (1179), which adopted a rule requiring a two-thirds vote by the cardinals to elect a pope (died 1181).

1524 Thomas Erastus, German Swiss physician and religious controversialist, was born near Zurich; name is preserved in "Erastianism," a doctrine of the supremacy of the state in ecclesiastical affairs, for which he is erroneously credited; excommunicated on a charge of Socianism* (1570-75); taught medicine and ethics in Basel, where he established the Erastian Foundation to help poor medical students (died 1583).

1604 The Seminario de San Bartolome, the first Jesuit college in Colombia, opened in Bogota.

1697 Samuel Jones, a founder of Welsh nonconformity, died at 69; established the first nonconforming theological academy in Wales, to which present Carmarthen Presbyterian College traces its origin.

1785 The Society for the Support and Encouragement of Sunday Schools in England was formed; popularly known as the Sunday School Society.

1805 Samuel Wilberforce, English Anglican bishop, was born in London, son of William Wilberforce; Bishop of Winchester (1869-73), strengthened efficiency of Church of England administration; Bishop of London (1845-69); involved in numerous controversies (died 1873).

1837 Joseph Dwenger, Catholic prelate and seminary founder, was born in Minster, Ohio; founder, first president, Seminary of Congregation of Precious Blood, Carthagena, Ohio; secretary of Congregation (1867-72); Bishop of Ft. Wayne, Ind. (1872-93) (died 1893).

1875 Herbert C. Noonan, Jesuit educator, was born in Oconto, Wis.; president, Marquette U. (1915-22); philosophy professor, Creighton U. (1931-56) (died 1956).

1958 The National Council of Churches announced that church membership had increased 5% in 1958 to 109,557,741.

1960 A group of Protestant ministers and laymen, including Dr. Norman Vincent Peale, issued a statement expressing fear that a Catholic president would be under the control of the church hierarchy; Peale later denied participating in the statement.

1971 The International Commission of the Anglican and Roman Catholic Churches announced "substantial agreement" on the doctrine of the Eucharist.

1979 Robert Runcie was selected to become the 102nd Archbishop of Canterbury on Jan. 26, 1980, succeeding Donald Coggan.

SEPTEMBER 8

Feast of the Nativity of the Blessed Virgin Mary.

1100 Clement III, anti-pope from 1080 to 1098, died.

1276 John XXI, born Pedro Juliani in Lisbon, Portugal, was elected pope, served until 1277; sent legates to Tatary, wrote a popular treatise on logic (Sumulae Logicales).

1380 St. Bernardino of Siena, Franciscan reformer, was born in Massa Marittima, Italy; served as vicar general of the Italian Observants, a strict Franciscan order (1438-42); his chief aim was to regenerate the age in which he lived; responsible for moral reforms in many cities; perhaps the most influential religious force in Italy; canonized 1450 (died 1444).

1413 St. Catherine of Bologna, a founder and abbess of the convent of Poor Clares (1456-63), was born as Caterina Vigi in Bologna, Italy; writer of Italian and Latin verse and prose (Seven Spiritual Weapons); canonized 1712 (died 1463).

1565 The first American Catholic parish was founded by Father Don Martin Francisco Lopez de Mendozo Grajales in St. Augustine, Fla.

1624 Marco Antonio Dominis, Italian Catholic archbishop and theologian, died at 58; opposed monarchical constitution of the church and was charged as a heretic; imprisoned by the Inquisition; judged a heretic after his death.

1635 Catholic Archbishop Cristobal de Torres arrived in Bogota, Colombia.

1654 St. Peter Claver, Spanish Jesuit missionary, died at about 73; known as the Apostle of the Negroes; served as missionary to Colombia (1610-54); canonized 1888.

1713 Pope Clement XI issued the bull, "Unigenitus dei filius," condemning Jansenism.

1727 Naphtali Daggett, theologian, was born in Attleboro, Mass.; first professor of divinity at Yale College (1756); acting president (1766-77) (died 1780).

1783 Nikolai F.S. Grundtvig, Danish bishop and theologian, was born in Udby, Denmark; founder of a theological movement which revitalized the Danish church, advocating a system of church organization under which each congregation would be virtually an independent community; poet, wrote epic, "Decline of the Heroic Life in the North" (died 1872).

1817 John M. Brown, educator and editor, was born in Odessa, Del.; principal, Union Seminary, Columbus U. (1844-53), predecessor of Wilberforce U.; editor, Christian Recorder; bishop, African Methodist Episcopal Church (1868-93) (died 1893).

1871 Perry B. Fitzwater, instructor and dean, Moody Bible Institute (1913-57), was born in Hardy County, W. Va. (died 1957).

1873 David O. McKay, Mormon leader, was born in Huntsville, Utah; president, Mormon Church (1951-70) (died 1970).

1907 Pope Pius X issued the encyclical, "Pascendi dominici gregos," formally condemning modernism as "the resume of all the heresies."

1910 The encyclical, "Sacrorum Antistitum," was issued by Pope Pius X imposing an anti-modernist oath on all clergy.

1928 Pope Pius XI issued the encyclical, "Rerum orientalium," promoting the study of the history, doctrine, and liturgy of the Eastern Christian churches.

1957 Pope Pius XII, in his encyclical, "Miranda peorus...," urged bishops to keep a watchful eye on the manifestations of modern communications techniques.

1961 A Polish edict severely restricting the teaching of Catholicism to Polish children was announced.

SEPTEMBER 9

440 St. Isaac the Great, 10th Catholicos (patriarch) of the Armenian Church, died at about 90; also observed as his feast day in the Armenian Church.

701 St. Sergius I, pope from 687 to 701, died; also observed as his feast day.

1159 Victor IV, born Octavian, was elected antipope by Romans and supported by Emperor Frederick I; not recognized in England, France, or Germany; served until 1164.

1515 St. Joseph of Volokolamsk, Russian church leader and Orthodox saint, died at about 75; founded monastery in Volokolamsk; canonized 1578.

1530 First cathedral in Mexico City was founded by King Charles V and a bull of Pope Clement VII.

1598 A celebration was held on the completion of the first church in New Mexico at San Juan de los Caballeros.

1747 Thomas Coke, first Methodist superintendent in the United States, was born in Brecom, Wales; served as American superintendent along with Francis Asbury (1784-97); president, English Methodist Conference (1797-1805) (died 1814).

1828 Leo Tolstoy, noted author (War and Peace, Anna Karenina), was born in Yasnaya Polyana, Russia; renounced Russian Orthodox Church (1876), evolved new Christianity whose central creed was non-resistance to evil; Tolstoyism became an organized sect (1884) (died 1910).

1866 Owen R. Lovejoy, Congregational clergyman, was born in Jamestown, Mich.; assistant secretary, National Child Labor Committee (1904-26); secretary, Children's Aid Society of New York (1927-35) (died 1962).

1900 Sir Kenneth G. Grubb, president of Church Missionary Society (1944-69), was born in

Oxton, England; editor, World Christian Handbook, for 20 years (died 1980).

1982 Episcopal Church delegates at their New Orleans convention approved the first revision in the church's hymnal by adopting a book of 100 hymns.

SEPTEMBER 10

Feast day of St. Aubert of Avranches, who began the construction of Mont St. Michel off the Normandy coast.

422 St. Celestine I was elected pope, served until 432; convoked Council of Ephesus (431), which condemned Nestorian* heresy; reputedly sent St. Patrick and Palladius to Ireland as missionaries.

1224 Agnellus of Pisa (about 1194-1235) with eight other friars arrived in England to found the English Franciscan Province, with friars in Dover, Canterbury, and Oxford; English Franciscans observe his memory on this date.

1305 St. Nicholas of Tolentino died; patron of souls in purgatory; canonized 1446; also observed as his feast day.

1487 Julius III, pope from 1550 to 1555, was born as Giammarin Ciocchi de Monte in Rome.

1604 William Morgan, Welsh prelate, died at 59; Bishop of Llandaff (1595-1601), of St. Asaph (1601-04); translated Bible into Welsh.

1724 The "Black Code" was published by Sieur de Bienville in New Orleans, which regulated the governing of slaves, ordered all Jews to leave the colony.

1791 James Edmeston, English architect, was born; wrote nearly 2000 Anglican hymns (Saviour, breathe an evening blessing; Lead us, Heavenly Father, lead us) (died 1867).

1834 Sir John R. Seeley, English historian and writer, was born in London; caused storm of controversy with essays, "Ecce Homo" and "Natural Religion," arguing that supernaturalism is not essential to religion (died 1895).

1839 Isaac K. Funk, Lutheran clergyman and publisher, was born in Clifton, Ohio; prepared material for ministers, then became associated with Adam Wagnalls in publishing the *Literary Digest*; helped publish a 12-volume Jewish encyclopedia (1901-06), dictionary (died 1912).

1846 Nauvoo, Ill. was besieged until Sep 16, when the Mormons surrendered the city and their arms, agreed to leave Illinois.

1861 The first Anglican provincial synod met in Canada.

1867 Robert E. Speer, Presbyterian clergyman and author, was born in Huntingdon, Pa.; secretary, Presbyterian Board of Foreign Missions (1891-1937); author (The Man Christ Jesus, Missions and Modern History) (died 1947).

1960 The Democratic presidential candidate, John F. Kennedy, a Catholic, reaffirmed his belief in separation of church and state, speaking before the Houston Ministerial Association.

1965 Father Divine, black religious leader, died in Lower Merion Township, Pa. at about 85; born as George Baker, he founded the Peace Mission with about 200 centers in New York City and Philadelphia, and preached equality among races.

1982 The Episcopal Church convention approved a multi-million dollar program to aid the poor.

1985 Bishop Edmund L. Browning of Hawaii was elected presiding bishop of the Episcopal Church for a 12-year term.

SEPTEMBER 11

Feast of Our Lady of Coromoto, patron of Venezuela.

Feast day of St. Paphnutius (died about 360), Egyptian monk and Bishop of Thebes; opposed Arian heresy*; was severely mutilated in persecution by Emperor Maximinus Daia.

1069 Aldred, English prelate, died at about 69; served as Archbishop of York and Bishop of Worcester; first English bishop to make pilgrimage to Jerusalem.

1097 Lucius III, pope from 1181 to 1185, was born as Ubaldo Allucingoli, in Lucca, Italy.

1279 Robert Kilwardby, Archbishop of Canterbury (1273-78), died near Rome at 79.

1637 Jan Bogerman, Dutch theologian, died at 61; helped translate Bible into Dutch; presided at the Synod of Dort.

1838 John Ireland, Catholic prelate, was born in Burnchurch, Ireland; Archbishop of St. Paul (1888-1918), after having served as coadjutor bishop and bishop from 1875 (died 1918).

1857 Thomas J. Shahan, Catholic priest and editor, was born in Manchester, N.H.; domestic prelate of the pontifical court and rector of Catholic U. (1909-28); editor, Catholic Encyclopedia (1907-13) (died 1932).

1880 Luther A. Weigle, biblical scholar and translator, was born in Littlestown, Pa.; chairman of committee which produced the Revised Standard Version of the Bible (1930-57); with Yale Divinity School as professor of religious education (1916-49), dean (1928-49) (died 1976).

1893 The World Parliament of Religions opened in Chicago in conjunction with the Columbian Exposition.

1895 Acharya Vinoba Bhave, spiritual leader of India after Gandhi's death, was born in Gagode, India.

1901 Vincent J. Flynn, Catholic priest and educator, was born in Avoca, Minn.; president, College of St. Thomas (1944- 56) (died 1956).

1904 Jose Maria Bueno y Monreal, Catholic Archbishop of Seville, was born in Saragossa, Spain; elevated to cardinal 1958.

SEPTEMBER 12

Feast day of Blessed Victoria Fornari-Strata, founder of the Blue Nuns of Genoa (1604).

1362 Innocent VI, pope from 1352 to 1362, died.

1729 John William Fletcher, an associate of John and Charles Wesley, was born in Nyon, Switzerland; vicar at Madely (1760-85); author of various theological works, including a defense of his Arminian* beliefs (died 1785).

1788 Alexander Campbell, religious leader and educator, was born in Antrim County, Ireland; with his father, Thomas, organized (1809) a Baptist sect which became the Church of Christ (Disciples of Christ); a founder, president, Bethany College, W.Va. (1840-66) (died 1866).

1805 Johann J. Herzog, German Protestant theologian, was born; editor, 22-volume Encyclopedia for Protestant Theology and Churches, a standard reference (died 1882).

1818 George Duffield Jr., Presbyterian clergyman, was born in Carlisle, Pa., the son of George Duffield (7/4/1794); wrote many hymns (Stand up, stand up for Jesus) (died 1880).

1839 John J. Keene, Catholic prelate, was born in Ballyshannon, Ireland; Bishop of Richmond, Va. (1878-89); first rector, Catholic U. (1889-96); named titular bishop of Damascus, assigned to the Congregations of Propaganda and of Studies in Rome; Archbishop of Dubuque, Iowa (1900-11) (died 1918).

1851 Francis E. Clark, Congregational clergyman, was born in Quebec, Canada; founder of Christian Endeavor movement (1881) while pastor of the Williston Church, Portland, Me.; president, United Society of Christian Endeavor (1895-1927) and World Christian Endeavor Union; editor, *Golden Rule* (later *Christian Endeavor World*) (died 1927)

1904 John C. Murray, Jesuit priest, was born in New York City; principal architect of the Declaration on Religious Liberty at the Second Vatican Council (died 1967).

1922 The American Episcopal Church voted to delete the word "obey" from the marriage service.

1979 The Episcopal Church triennial convention in Denver approved a revision of the Book of Common Prayer.

SEPTEMBER 13

407 St. John Chrysostum, patriarch of Constantinople (398-403) and a Father* of the (Orthodox) Church, died; considered the greatest Christian expositor; driven from his see and died after being persecuted; also observed as his feast day in the Catholic Church.

604 Sabinian was consecrated as pope, served until 606; reign marked by fending off attacks from the Lombards.

608 St. Eulogius, patriarch of Alexandria (579-608), died; had been abbot of monastery in Antioch; also observed as his feast day.

1541 John Calvin returned to Geneva after three years absence; a few months later, he prepared the Ecclesiastical Ordinances, erecting a system of disciple, preaching worship, and instruction, with a ministry of pastors, teachers, elders and deacons.

1565 Guillaume Farel, French Reformation leader, died at 76; induced John Calvin to take up reform and work in Geneva; wrote "Sommaire," the first Reformed confession, the basis of later Calvinist confessions; pastor at Neufchatel (1538-65).

1814 Nikolaas Beets, author and clergyman, was born in Haarlem, Netherlands; held several pastorates, taught theology at U. of Utrecht (1874-84) (died 1903).

1843 Louis Marie O. Duchesne, early church history pioneer, was born in St. Servan, France; pioneer in applying archaeological, topographical, liturgical, theological and social studies to early church history (died 1922).

1863 Cyrus Adler, Jewish leader, was born in Van Buren, Ark.; president, Dropsie College, Philadelphia (1908-40); president, Jewish Theological Seminary (1924-40); founder (1892), president (1898-1922), American Jewish Historical Society; editor, American Jewish Yearbook (1899-1906); editor, *Jewish Quarterly Review* (1910-40) (died 1940).

1896 Pope Leo XIII issued the encyclical, "Apostolocae curae," declaring priestly ordinations of Anglican clergy invalid.

1983 Rev. Peter-Hans Kolvenbach, Dutch priest, was elected the 29th superior general of the Society of Jesus (Jesuits) in Rome; spent 15 years in Beirut; rector, Pontifical Oriental Institute in Rome (1981-83).

SEPTEMBER 14

Feast of the Exaltation of the Cross, commemorating the showing of the supposed true cross in Jerusalem (629) after its recovery from the Persians.

Feast day of St. Cornelius, pope from 251 to 252; opposed by antipope (Novatian); exiled to Civitavecchia; was a friend of St. Cyprian.

891 Stephen V, pope from 885 to 891, died.

1523 Adrian VI, pope from 1522 to 1523, died at 64.

1543 Claudio Aquaviva, fifth general of the Society of Jesus (Jesuits) (1581-1615), was born in Naples, Italy; considered the Jesuits' greatest general; during his reign the order developed considerably, especially in missionary work (died 1615).

1601 Meletios Pagos, patriarch of Alexandria (1590-1601), died at 52; a capable theologian and defender of orthodoxy.

1607 John Harvard, Congregational clergyman, was born in London; left 260 books and about 800 pounds to a proposed school, which was begun in 1638 and named for him in 1639 (died 1638).

1704 William Hubbard, English-born Congregational clergyman and historian, died at 83; Pastor at Ipswich, Mass. (1658-1703); author (General History of New England).

1735 Robert Raikes, English publisher and philanthropist, was born in Gloucester; a pioneer in the Sunday School movement (died 1811).

1740 George Whitefield, English founder of Calvinistic Methodism, arrived in Newport, R.I., where he preached the following week and then on to Boston, spending six weeks in the area, preaching with sensational impact.

1775 John H. Hobart, probably the greatest American Episcopal leader, was born in Philadelphia; rector, Trinity Church, New York City (1801-16); assistant bishop (1811-16), Bishop of New York (1816-30); established the Protestant Episcopal Theological Society (1806), which became the General Theological Seminary (died 1830).

1799 David O. Allen, Congregational missionary to India, was born in Barre, Mass.; translated Bible into Marathi.

1803 Orestes A. Brownson, writer and editor, was born in Stockbridge, Vt.; Unitarian clergyman, converted to Catholicism (1844); organized Society for Christian Union and Progress to reach workingmen untouched by other churches; editor, *Brownson's Quarterly Review*, which became one of the nation's most influential journals of Catholic opinion (died 1876).

1883 Martin Dibelius, German biblical scholar, was born in Dresden; professor of New Testament at Heidelberg; one of the originators of "form criticism" in New Testament studies (died 1947).

1887 Mervyn G. Haigh, Anglican Bishop of Coventry (1931-42) when the Cathedral was destroyed by German bombing, was born in London (died 1962).

1892 Barnett R. Brickner, rabbi in various synagogues including Fairmount Temple, Cleveland (1925-58), was born in New York City; founder, Young Judea movement (died 1958).

1964 The third session of Vatican Council II began; ended Nov. 21 with promulgation of the Dogmatic Constitution, which stressed the hidden spiritual reality of the church rather than its juridicial structures; the Decree on Ecumenism, which called for a surge of common effort toward unity, and the Decree on the Eastern Catholic Churches, restoring these churches to their esteemed place within the universal church.

1964 Pope Paul VI, opening the third session of Vatican Council II, called on Catholic bishops to define for themselves a new measure of authority without infringing on papal supremacy.

1965 The final session of Vatican Council II was opened in St. Peter's Basilica by Pope Paul VI, who announced his decision to establish a worldwide synod of bishops to help him govern the church.

1975 Elizabeth Ann Seton became the first native-born American to be canonized; she was beatified in 1962, declared a saint by Pope Paul VI.

SEPTEMBER 15

1500 John Morton, English prelate, died at about 80; Archbishop of Canterbury (1486-1500), elevated to cardinal 1493; chancellor of Oxford (1495).

1510 St. Catherine of Genoa, Italian mystic who served the sick, died at 63; converted her pleasure-loving husband to also serve the sick; "Treatise on Purgatory" and "Dialogue" attributed to her; patroness of hospitals in Italy; canonized 1737; also observed as her feast day.

1590 Urban VII was elected pope, served only 12 days until he died.

1644 Innocent X was elected pope, served until 1655; condemned Jansenism.

1648 Titus Oakes, renegade Anglican priest, was born in Oakham, England; with Israel Tonge, invented the "popish plot" of 1678, which told of a vast Jesuit conspiracy to assassinate Charles II and that Catholics would massacre Protestants; lies finally caught up with him in 1685, imprisoned until 1689 (died 1705).

1733 Samuel Horsley, English prelate and scientist, was born in London; Bishop of St. David's, Rochester, and St. Asaph; carried on long controversy with scientist Joseph Priestley on the incarnation (1783-90); edited the works of Isaac Newton (died 1806).

1813 James B. Mozley, English theologian, was born near Lincoln; attempted to reconcile Christian tradition of baptism with the theology of Calvinism (died 1878).

1824 Joseph Hergenröther, Catholic theologian and historian, was born in Germany; curator of the Vatican archives; author (Anti-Janus); elevated to cardinal 1879 (died 1890).

1838 Friedrich W. F. Nippold, German Protestant clergyman, was born near Münster; a founder of the Evangelical Union (died 1918).

1857 Brigham Young, Utah territorial governor, ordered his troops to repel the "invasion" of federal troops being sent in to help establish new territorial government; two trains carrying supplies for federal troops were burned (Oct 5).

1872 Germanos, Greek Archbishop of Thysteira, was born; a leader of the ecumenical movement; first president, World Council of Churches (1948) (died 1951).

1895 Gregory Agagianian, head of the Sacred Congregation for the Propagation of Faith (1958-70), was born in Akhaltsikhe, Russia; elevated to cardinal 1946 (died 1971).

1963 A Negro church in Birmingham, Ala. was bombed; four were killed, 20 injured; rioting followed the incident.

1976 The House of Bishops of the Episcopal Church voted 95 to 61 to permit the ordination of women to be priests and bishops; House of Deputies concurred on Sep. 16.

1981 Pope John Paul II issued the encyclical, "Laborem exerceus," calling for greater social justice and fuller participation of workers in management and the fruits of production.

SEPTEMBER 16

Feast day of St. Ninian, Scottish apostle of Christianity; first missionary and early monastic bishop of Northern Britain; first to preach Christianity to the southern Picts (early Scots) (died about 432).

Feast day of St. Cyprian, Bishop of Carthage, best known for repudiation of heretical baptism; also known for his writings on theology; beheaded 258.

655 St. Martin I, pope from 649 to 655, died in exile in the Crimea; deposed by Emperor Constance II (653); the last pope to be venerated as a martyr.

1087 Blessed Victor III, pope from 1085 to 1087, died; also observed as his feast day.

1226 Pandulf, Roman papal envoy to England, died; originally excommunicated King John (1211) for refusing to negotiate over archbishopric, later (1215) took his side over the Magna Carta; named papal legate (1218) and virtual ruler of England during the minority of Henry III (1219-21).

1386 Ambrose of Camaldoli, theologian and noted Greek scholar, was born in Portico, Italy as Ambrogio Traversari; general of the Camaldolese Order (1431-39) (died 1439).

1394 Clement VII, anti-pope from 1378 to 1394, died at 52; born Robert of Geneva, he was chosen antipope by a group of cardinals and supported by France, Scotland, the Spanish kingdoms, and part of Italy.

1498 Tomas de Torquemada, the grand inquisitor, died at 78; Spanish Dominican monk and inquisition general of Spain (later grand inquisitor); the worst aspects of religious fanaticism and cruelty are associated with him.

1519 John Colet, English educator and clergyman, died at 53; foremost of the Oxford reformers, he was dean of St. Paul's Cathedral (1504-10) and founder, with his inheritance, of the famed St. Paul's School.

1589 Michael Baius (Bajus), Flemish Catholic theologian, died at 76; based his teachings directly on the Bible and writings of church fathers, especially St. Augustine; teachings, often considered forerunner of Jansenism, were condemned by Pope Pius V; made formal recantation (1579).

1620 The Mayflower set sail from Plymouth, England with 101 passengers (56 adults, 14 servants, 31 children) and a crew of 48; voyage took 65 days, during which one passenger died and two children were born; formed first Puritan settlement in Massachusetts.

1796 William A. Muhlenberg, Episcopal clergyman, was born in Philadelphia, the great grandson of H. M. Muhlenberg (9/6/1711); with Flushing Institute, a Christian preparatory school, for 18 years; rector, Church of the Holy Communion, New York City; a founder, St. Luke's Hospital (1858); wrote several hymns (I would not live alway) (died 1877).

1828 Abraham Kuenen, Dutch theologian and biblical scholar, was born in Haarlem; leader of the modern critical school in the Netherlands (died 1891).

1830 Patrick F. Moran, Australian Catholic prelate, was born in Leighlinbridge, Ireland; Archbishop of Sydney (1884-1911); elevated to cardinal 1885 (died 1911).

1907 Pope Pius X issued an encyclical condemning modernism.

1976 The ordination of women was approved by the 65th triennial general convention of the Episcopal Church.

1977 Disaffected members of the Episcopal Church held a three-day meeting in St. Louis to form the Anglican Church of North America.

SEPTEMBER 17

1179 St. Hildegard, German abbess and mystic, died at 81; a pioneer in science and natural history; founder, abbess of convent at Rupertsburg; famed for visions and prophecies; also observed as her feast day.

1552 Paul V, pope from 1605 to 1621, was born as Camillo Borghese in Rome.

1656 Massachusetts enacted severe laws against Quakers, who were to be committed to the house of correction and kept at hard labor until transported.

1721 Samuel Hopkins, Congregational theologian, was born in Waterbury, Conn.; one of two most important disciples of Jonathan Edwards; introduced systematic theological doctrine with his book, "System of Doctrines Contained in Divine Revelation, Explained and Defended" (died 1803).

1792 Thomas J. Claggett was consecrated as Episcopal Bishop of Maryland, the first to be consecrated in the United States.

1829 Robert K. Hargrove, Methodist bishop (1882-1905) and educator, was born in Pickens County, Ga.; president, Centenary Institute (Ala.) (1865-67), Tennessee Femele College (1868-73); secretary, College of Bishops (1884); president, Epworth League Board of Management (1894-98) (died 1905).

1843 William E. Griffis, clergyman and educator who taught in Japan, was born in Philadelphia; author (Mikado's Empire, Religions of Japan) (died 1928).

1856 Thomas F. Gailor, Episcopal prelate, was born in Jackson, Miss.; coadjutor bishop of Tennessee (1893-98), bishop (1898-1908); chancellor, U. of the South (1908-35) (died 1935).

1926 Jean-Marie Lustiger, Archbishop of Paris (1983-), was born.

1983 Humberto S. Medeiros, Archbishop of Boston (1970-83), died at 67; elevated to cardinal 1973.

SEPTEMBER 18

1643 Gilbert Burnet, Bishop of Salisbury (1689-1715). was born in Edinburgh; author of a history of the English Reformation; fled to Holland on accession of James II; counseled William and Mary, accompanied them to England (1688), preached their coronation sermon (1689); influential at court during life of Queen Mary; tried to develop plan to incorporate nonconformists into Church of England; devised scheme to distribute vacant church livings, known as Queen Anne's Bounty (died 1715).

1765 Gregory XVI, pope from 1831 to 1846, was born in Belluno, Italy as Bartolomeo Alberto Cappelari (died 1846).

1841 Thomas K. Cheyne, English biblical scholar, was born in London; introduced German critical scholarship into England; on board of revisions of Old Testament (died 1915).

1858 Henry G. King, Congregational clergyman and educator, was born in Hillsdale, Mich.; with Oberlin College (1891-1927) as professor of philosophy (1891-97), of theology (1897-1925), president (1902-27) (died 1934).

1856 For the first time in 2000 years, Catholic cardinals, bishops and priests met in Assisi, Italy to study the practical problems of liturgy.

1976 Rev. Sun Myung Moon, head of the evangelical Unification Church, presided over a "God Bless America" rally in Washington, D.C. that drew 50,000 persons; Moon, who advocated American defense of South Korea, was denounced by established church leaders of perverting Christian doctrine.

1979 The House of Deputies of the Episcopal Church concurred with earlier action of the House of Bishops holding that homosexuals should be accepted into the church but not ordained if sexually active.

SEPTEMBER 19

Feast day in the Catholic Church of St. Januarius, Bishop of Benevento and patron saint of Naples; two phials believed to contain his blood are preserved and exhibited twice a year when the substance in the phials miraculously liquifies.

690 St. Theodore of Tarsus died at about 88; Archbishop of Canterbury (668-690) who unified the English church; also observed as his feast day.

1790 James Madison (1749-1812) was consecrated as the first Episcopal Bishop of Virginia.

1804 Elling Eielsen, Lutheran leader, was born in Voss, Norway; a lay preacher, he founded the Norwegian Evangelical Lutheran Church of North America (1846) (died 1883).

1841 Richard C. Morse, Presbyterian clergyman, was born in Hudson, N.Y.; general secretary, international committee, YMCA (1869-1915) (died 1926).

1852 St. Emily de Rodat, founder, Congregation of the Holy Family of Villefranche (1815), died; canonized 1950; also observed as her feast day.

1914 Reims Cathedral in France was bombarded by the Germans and severely damaged.

1966 Pope Paul VI issued an encyclical appealing to world leaders to end the war in Vietnam.

1970 Theodosius VI, patriarch of Antioch, died; he was succeeded by Elias IV, metropolitan of Aleppo, Syria.

1168 Paschal III, anti-pope from 1164 to 1168, died.

1274 Letter from Pope Gregory X, "Nuper in concilio," to the Blessed John Vercelli, master general of the Dominicans, launched a crusade in reverence which resulted in Holy Name societies.

1608 Jean Jacques Olier, founder (1641) of the Sulpicians, was born in Paris; founded church, seminary at St. Sulpice in Paris, which became the model for other dioceses to whom Olier loaned priests (died 1657).

1858 William R. Huntington, Episcopal clergyman and author, was born in Lowell, Mass.; rector, All Saints Church, Worcester, Mass. (1862-83), Grace Church, New York City (1883-1909); active in founding, building, Cathedral of St. John the Divine, New York City; author of a major ecumenical document, "The Church Idea" (died 1909).

1870 King Victor Emmanuel took Rome, making it the capital of a free and united Italy, and confined the pope to the Vatican and a purely ecclesiastical role.

1883 Albrecht G. Alt, biblical scholar, was born in Bavaria; one of the most important Old Testament scholars; decisively influenced such studies throughout the world (died 1956).

1900 Willem A. Visser't Hooft, Dutch Protestant leader, was born in Haarlem, Netherlands; general secretary, World Council of Churches (1938-66) (died 1985).

1976 The Episcopal House of Bishops approved the most extensive revision of the Book of Common Prayer in 400 years.

SEPTEMBER 20

Feast day in the Catholic Church of St. Agapetus I, pope in 535-536; a strong believer in orthodoxy.

Feast day in the Orthodox Church of St. Martin I, pope from 649 to 655.

Former feast day of St. Eustace, early Christian martyr and patron saint of Madrid; observance dropped in 1969.

SEPTEMBER 21

Feast day in the Catholic Church of St. Matthew, one of the 12 apostles.

1452 Girolama Savonarola, Florentine leader and reformer, was born in Florence; created a democratic government in Florence; Pope Alexander VI sought to reduce his influence by combining the Congregation of San Marco, of which Savonarola was vicar, with another; Savonarola continued to preach and was excommunicated; he preached against corruption in secular life, licentiousness of the ruling class, and the worldliness of the clergy; wrote the hymn, "Jesus, refuge of the weary;" was hanged and burned May 23, 1498.

1676 Blessed Innocent XI was elected pope, served until 1689; his piety and zeal inspired several church reforms and he encouraged daily communion; reign was marked by conflict with France over the exercise of royal rights to receive the revenues of vacant sees and to appoint bishops.

1695 John Glas (or Glass), independent Presbyterian clergyman, was born in Auchtermuchty, Scotland; believed that churches are gatherings of true believers rather than parochial congregations; deposed from Presbyterian church and formed Glassite Church, a sect of independent Presbyterians (died 1773).

1776 Trinity Church in New York City was destroyed by fire.

1823 Joseph Smith, founder of the Mormon Church, was reported to have had a vision showing the location of the golden plates on which the Book of Mormon was written; this is the documentary foundation of Mormonism; took possession of the plates Sep 22, 1827.

1840 Charles J. Little, theologian, was born in Philadelphia; professor of church history (1891-1911), president (1895-1911), Garrett Biblical Institute (died 1911).

1921 The Papal Legation was re-established in the Netherlands.

1966 A proposed amendment to the U.S. Constitution that would have permitted voluntary prayers in the public schools failed 49 to 37 to win the necessary two-thirds majority in the Senate.

1988 The Southern Baptist Convention stopped distributing the Surgeon General's report on AIDS to the 14.6 million denomination members because the government document failed to condemn all sex outside marriage.

SEPTEMBER 22

Feast day of St. Felix IV, pope from 526 to 530; was observed January 30 up to 1922.

530 Boniface II became pope, served until 532; many Roman clergy refused to accept him, but backed him after the death of Dioscorus of Alexandria (Oct 14).

687 Conon, pope from 686 to 687, died.

1158 Otto of Freising, German prelate and historian, died at about 45; Bishop of Freising in Bavaria (1137-58), wrote a remarkable medieval history (The Two Cities) and philosophical works; took part in disastrous crusade (1147-49).

1503 Pius III, born Francesco Todeschini de Piccolomini, was named pope; a nephew of Pope Pius II, he served until Oct 18, 1503, when he died.

1662 John Biddle, often called the father of English Unitarianism, died of fever in prison.

1725 Wilhelm Christoph Berkemeyer, Dutch Lutheran clergyman, arrived in New Netherlands and organized the "parish," which ran from Albany into New Jersey; parish consisted of 23 congregations; laid foundation for New York Ministerium.

1774 Clement XIV, pope from 1769 to 1774, died at 69.

1812 Samuel W. Williams, Congregational missionary, was born in Utica, N.Y.; devoted self to study of Chinese, Japanese; served as interpreter for Admiral Perry's expedition to Japan (1853-54); secretary, interpreter for American legation in China (1856-76) (died 1884).

1824 Gaspar Mermillod, Swiss Bishop of Lausanne and Geneva (1883-92), was born; a formulator of Catholic social doctrine; elevated to cardinal 1890 (died 1892).

1827 Joseph Smith related that he received the Book of Mormon from the Angel Moroni in the form of golden plates; contains a sacred history of the American continents, written in a language known as "reformed Egyptian."

1880 Dame Christabel Pankhurst, British suffragist and evangelist, was born in Manchester (died 1958).

1881 Walter R. Matthews, dean of St. Paul's Cathedral (1934-73), was born in London; chaplain to the King (1923-31) (died 1973).

1963 The Church Center for the United Nations was consecrated for ecumenical use.

SEPTEMBER 23

Feast day of St. Linus, reputed immediate successor to St. Peter as Bishop of Rome (about 67 or 69).

Former feast day in the Catholic Church of St. Thecla, one of the most celebrated saints in the Greek Church; reputedly a disciple of St. Paul; observance dropped in 1969.

704 St. Adamnan, Irish-born abbot of Iona, Scotland (679-704), died; his biography of St. Columba, founder of the Iona monastery, considered one of the best early religious biographies; one of Iona's greatest abbots; also observed as his feast day.

1152 Concordat of Worms restored peace temporarily in Christendom; acknowledged that the investiture of clergy was forever conceded to the church while the Emperor retained certain legal rights.

1650 Jeremy Collier, English bishop of the Nonjurors, was born in Stow-by-Quy, England; consecrated 1713 by the sole surviving Nonjuror bishop and became primus of the Nonjurors; a leader in the effort to unite with the Eastern Church (died 1726).

1786 John England, Catholic prelate, was born in Cork, Ireland; first bishop of Charleston, S.C. (1820-42); founder, *U.S. Catholic Miscellany*, the first Catholic newspaper in the United States (died 1842).

1858 William D. Hyde, Congregational clergyman and educator, was born in Winchendon, Mass.; president, Bowdoin College; hymn writer (Creation's Lord, we give Thee thanks) (died 1917).

1892 The Christian Science Church was organized in Boston by Mary Baker Eddy and and 12 followers.

1930 The sixth National Eucharistic Congress opened in Omaha, Neb.

1962 The cornerstone was laid for the $2 million 12-story Church Center at the United Nations.

1965 The Russian Orthodox Church in America elected a new primate, Metropolitan Ireney, to succeed Metropolitan Leonty.

SEPTEMBER 24

Feast day in the Orthodox Church of St. Thecla, one of the most celebrated saints in the Greek Church; reputedly a disciple of St. Paul.

366 Liberius, pope from 352 to 366, died; lived in exile 355-358.

366 Ursinus was elected anti-pope on the death of Liberius; reign marked by constant conflict with Damascus; died about 385.

787 The second Nicene Council opened with 350 bishops in attendance; continued until Oct 23; resulted in decisions on various disciplinary matters.

1143 Innocent II, pope from 1130 to 1143, died.

1757 Jonathan Edwards, noted colonial clergyman, became president of the College of New Jersey (later Princeton); served until his death in 1758.

1759 Charles Simeon, Anglican churchman, was born in Reading; curate of Trinity Church, Cambridge (1783-1836); a leader of the evangelical movement and left a mark on the religious life of Cambridge (died 1836).

1763 The Jesuits were expelled from Illinois; embarked from New Orleans Nov 24.

1827 Catherine McAuley founded the new Order of the Sisters of Mercy by opening a dwelling in Dublin to teach poor children and house homeless young women.

1843 Samuel A. W. Duffield, Presbyterian hymnologist, was born in Brooklyn, grandson of George Duffield (7/4/1794); author (English Hymns: Their Authors and History) (died 1887).

1850 A papal bull established a Catholic hierarchy in England.

1889 The Declaration of Utrecht was drawn up by an assembly of Old Catholic bishops setting a doctrinal basis for the Old Catholic Church, which repudiated decrees on papal infallibility, the dogma of the Immaculate Conception, and others.

1889 John W. E. Bowen, resident Methodist bishop of the Atlantic Coast area (1948-62), was born in Baltimore (died 1962).

1890 The president of the Mormon Church issued a manifesto ending polygamy, following years of contention with the government; the Mormons were advised to "refrain from contracting any marriage forbidden by the law of the land."

1919 The National Catholic Welfare Council was organized.

1961 The Pan-Orthodox Conference of the 12 largest Eastern Orthodox churches met for the first time since 1787 in Rhodes, Greece.

1961 Alfred Haatanen, president of the Finnish Lutheran Evangelical Church of America (1922-50), died in Houghton, Mich. at 85.

1988 The Episcopal Diocese of Massachusetts elected the first female bishop in the 450 year history of the Anglican Church; the election of Rev. Barbara C. Harris of Philadelphia.

SEPTEMBER 25

Feast day of St. Sergius of Redonezh (1315-92), Russian spiritual leader to whom the monastery of Troitse-Sergiyevo owed its lasting fame as the nation's religious and social center; considered the greatest Russian saint.

Feast day in Switzerland of St. Nicholas of Flüe, its patron saint; as ascetic whose sanctity led many to seek his advice; canonized 1947.

1534 Clement VII, pope from 1523 to 1534, died at 56.

1555 Religious Peace of Augsburg was promulgated; the first permanent legal basis for the existence of Lutheranism and Catholicism in Germany; promulgated as part of the final resolution of the Diet of the Holy Name Empire and marked the culmination of the German religious controversy and the half-century old movement for the political reconstitution of the Holy Roman Empire; while designed for peace, it paved the way for further trouble by excluding the Calvinists from the settlement.

1758 Christopher Sower, German-born religious printer, died at 65; published a religious and secular journal in Pennsylvania that exerted great influence on Germans; also published Bible in German, the first foreign language Bible printed in the United States.

1800 Philip W. Otterbein and Martin Boehm convened a conference of 13 clergymen near Frederick, Md. which resulted in the formal organization of the Church of the United Brethren in Christ.

1869 Rudolf Otto, theologian, was born in Peine, Germany; made important practical contributions to Lutheran Church devotions and its missionary work; author (The Idea of the Holy) (died 1937.)

1872 Joseph H. Hertz, British chief rabbi, was born in Rebreny, Hungary; rabbi in Johannesburg, South Africa (1898-1911); chief rabbi, British United Hebrew Congregations (1913-46); author (Book of Jewish Thoughts) (died 1946.)

1889 William Godfrey, seventh Archbishop of Westminster (1956-63), was born in Liverpool; rector, English College in Rome (1930), first apostolic delegate to Great Britain (1938-53) and domestic prelate to Pope Pius XI; Archbishop of Liverpool (1953-56); elevated to cardinal 1958 (died 1963).

1988 Rev. Junipero Serra, founder of California missions, was beatified by Pope John Paul II in the Vatican.

1988 Delegates to an unprecedented meeting called by the Catholic Archdiocese of New York strongly urged a greater voice for the laity in the church's organization and prayer life.

SEPTEMBER 26

Feast day of the North American martyrs, all French Jesuit missionaries to the American and Canadian Indians — Jean de Brebeuf, Noel Chabanel, Anthony Daniel, Charles Garnier, Rene Goupil, Isaac Jogues, and Gabriel Lalemant.

Feast day in the Catholic Church of Sts. Cosmas and Damian brothers and patron saints of physicians; reputedly they were doctors who refused to accept payment for their services.

Feast day in the Orthodox Church of St. John the Apostle.

1143 Celestine II, born Guido de Castellis, was elected pope; served until 1144; reign marked by settlement of the dispute between the papacy and the French king, Louis VII.

1626 Lancelot Andrewes, Bishop of Winchester (1619-26), died at 71; one of the translators of the Authorized Version of the Bible, a renowned preacher, and a great influence in forming a distinctive Anglican theology; wrote "Private Devotions" in Greek, Latin and Hebrew.

1729 Moses Mendelssohn, Jewish philosopher, was born in Desau, Germany; gave strong impetus to Jewish enlightenment movement and to 19th Century Reform Judaism; sometimes called the "German Socrates;" author (Jerusalem; A Treatise on Religious Power and Judaism); translated the Psalms and Pentateuch* into German, advancing the education and culture of the Jews (died 1786).

1737 Jonathan Odell, Anglican clergyman who was satirist for the loyalist cause, was born in Newark, N.J. (died 1818).

1794 Frederick A. Packard, religious editor, was born in Marlborough, Mass.; editorial secretary, American Sunday School Union, edited Sunday School publications (1828-58) (died 1867).

1833 Charles Bradlaugh, free thought lecturer and writer, was born near London; prosecuted (1876) along with Mrs. Annie Besant for republishing Malthusian "Fruits of Philosophy;" found guilty but decision was overturned and remaining restrictions on press freedom were removed; successfully fought for the right to affirm rather than swear on the Bible (died 1891).

1835 Pope Gregory XVI issued the bull, "Dum acerbissimas," condemning the writings of Georg Hermes (1775-1831), German Catholic theologian who tried to explain dogmatic theology rationally.

1860 Morrin College, Presbyterian theological seminary, was founded in Quebec.

1862 Roman Catholicism was made the sole religion of Ecuador by a concordat signed in Rome.

1897 Paul VI, pope from 1963 to 1978, was born as Giovanni Battista Montini.

1980 Pope John Paul II opened a month-long synod of Catholic bishops in Rome by reaffirming his strong opposition to divorce and called on Catholic families to preserve the Church's "fundamental values."

1982 The National Cathedral in Washington, D.C. observed its 75th anniversary by unveiling the west front; the edifice is now 90 percent completed with two planned towers yet to be built.

SEPTEMBER 27

Former feast day in the Catholic Church of Sts. Cosmas and Damian, the brothers who are patron saints of physicians; now observed Sep.26.

1540 Pope Paul III approved a formula for creation of the Society of Jesus (Jesuits), co-founded by Ignatius of Loyola, and issued his official sanction in the bull, "Regimini militantis ecclesiae."

1627 Jacques B. Bossuet, French prelate and author, was born near Paris; tutored the Dauphin (son of Louis XIV), brilliant author and considered one of the greatest preachers of all time; served as Bishop of Meaux (northeast of Paris) (1681-1704); author (Discourses on Universal History, the Art of Governing) (died 1704).

1660 St. Vincent de Paul, founder of the Lazarists and the Sisters of Charity, died at 79.

1696 St. Alfonso Maria de Liguori, Italian moral theologian, was born in Naples; founder (1732) of the Congregation of the Most Holy Redeemer

(Redemptorists); canonized 1839, made a Doctor* of the Church, named patron of moralists and confessors (1950) (died 1787).

1700 Innocent XII, pope from 1691 to 1700, died at 85.

1715 Thomas Burnet, English clergyman, died at 80; author of "The Sacred Theory of the Earth," used to reconcile biblical account of the creation, paradise, and the deluge with scientific principles.

1793 Dennis A. Affre, Archbishop of Paris, was born in St. Rome-de-Tarn, France; served as archbishop from 1840 until June 27, 1848, when he was killed while trying to quiet a mob during the revolution.

1810 Michael O'Connor, Catholic prelate, was born in Cork, Ireland; first Bishop of Pittsburgh (1843-72) (died 1872).

1837 Edward McGlynn, Catholic priest, was born in New York City; pastor, St. Stephen's parish, New York City (1866-87); suspended twice for political speeches, excommunicated (1887), reinstated (1892) (died 1900).

1846 Francis J. Chavasse, Anglican prelate, was born near Birmingham; Bishop of Liverpool (1900-23); Liverpool Cathedral begun during his episcopate (died 1928).

1857 Chicago Theological Seminary was organized by the Midwest Congregational churches; opened Oct 6,1858.

1875 Archbishop John McCloskey of New York was invested as the first American cardinal.

1886 Karl M. Block, Episcopal Bishop of California (1941-58), was born in Washington, D.C. (died 1958).

1894 President Grover Cleveland issued a general amnesty to Mormons convicted under the Anti-Polygamy (Edmunds) Act.

1907 Raul Silva Henriquez, Archbishop of Santiago, Chile (1961-), was born in Talca, Chile; elevated to cardinal 1962.

1965 The Ecumenical Council agreed that laymen must have a greater voice in church affairs and approved creation of a new secretariat for the laity at the Vatican.

1985 The General Synod of the United Church of Christ opened its conference in which it declared its ecumenical partnership with the Christian Church (Disciples of Christ).

1988 It was reported that laboratory carbon-dating tests show that the Shroud of Turin material was made in the 14th Century and could not be the burial cloth of Christ.

SEPTEMBER 28

Feast day of St. Julia Eustochium (370 to about 419), Roman virgin of noble descent, who with her mother built four monasteries in Bethlehem.

235 St. Pontianus, pope from 230 to 235, resigned after being exiled by Emperor Maximinus.

929 St. Wenceslaus died, patron of Czechoslovakia; crown of St. Wenceslaus came to be a symbol of Czech independence; also observed as his feast day.

1394 Benedict XIII, born Pedro de Luna, was elected anti-pope by cardinals of Avignon on the promise of ending the papal schism; refused changes and stayed on until 1423 despite ouster (1417) by the Council of Constance.

1808 Andover Theological Seminary was officially opened with 36 students at Andover, Mass.; later moved to Cambridge.

1823 Leo XII was named pope, served until 1828; reign marked by extremely reactionary policy.

1840 Henry M. MacCracken, Presbyterian clergyman and educator, was born in Oxford, Ohio; vice-chancellor (1885-91), chancellor (1891-1910), New York U. (died 1918).

1850 President Millard Fillmore appointed Brigham Young governor of the Utah Territory.

1872 Shirley J. Cass, Baptist theologian and educator, was born in Hatfield Point, New Brunswick, Canada; with U. of Chicago Divinity School - professor of New Testament (1908-17), early Christian history (1917-38), dean (1933-38); dean, School of Religion, Florida Southern College (1938-47) (died 1947).

1927 Thomas J. J. Altizer, theology professor at Emory U. and a leader of the "God is dead" movement, was born in Cambridge, Mass.; author of "Mircea Eliade and the Dialectic of the Sacred," in which he stated that although God as known in history no longer exists, "Christ, the Incarnate Word, lives."

1956 The Disciples of Christ international convention opened in Des Moines, Iowa; authorized exploration of the possibility of joining with the Congregational Christian and Evangelical and Reformed churches into the "United Church of Christ."

1956 Priests and scholars from around the world met in the Benedictine abbey of St. Procopius near Chicago to seek an acceptable path by which millions of separated eastern Christians might re-enter the Catholic Church.

1966 The International Convention of Christian Churches closed its largest session ever in Dallas; amended its bylaws to change the annual meeting from a mass assembly to a delegate assembly; distributed to all congregations a "provisional design" for a new structure that would be called the Christian Church (Disciples of Christ).

1971 Joszef Cardinal Mindszenty arrived at the Vatican after 15 years spent in the American embassy in Budapest.

SEPTEMBER 29

Feast day in the Catholic Church of three of seven archangels - Michael, Gabriel, and Raphael.

440 St. Leo I the Great was consecrated as pope, served until 461; one of the greatest popes of Christian antiquity, centralizing the church government; obtained from Emperor Valentinian III an edict which commanded all to obey the pope on the grounds the latter held the "primacy of St. Peter;" convened the Council of Chalcedon (451), convinced Attila to spare Rome (451); sought to drive out all heresy, active in disciplinary reforms; named a Doctor* of the Church.

855 Benedict III was consecrated as pope, served until 858; a model of virtue, he strove for sanctity of married life among the greatest men and women of his time.

1179 Innocent III, born Lando of Sezza, was elected anti-pope as the final act of opposition to Pope Alexander III; when his protector abandoned him, he was confined in an Italian monastery in January 1180.

1636 Thomas Tenison, English prelate, was born near Cambridge; championed Protestantism in reign of James II; Bishop of Lincoln (1691-94), Archbishop of Canterbury (1694-1715); a commissioner for union with Scotland; a founder, Society for Propagation of the Gospel (died 1715).

1642 St. René Goupil, French Jesuit missionary to Canadian Indians, was killed; canonized along with six other North American martyrs 1930.

1691 Richard Challoner, English Catholic bishop, was born near London; coadjutor in London (1741), vicar apostolic in London (1758); sought to revitalize the Catholic Church in England; revised the Reims-Douai translation of the Bible; author of "Gardens of the Soul," a popular manual of devotion (died 1781).

1747 Four ministers and 27 elders, representing 12 German Reformed churches, met in Philadelphia, the first organizational gathering; adopted the Heidelberg Catechism and the Canons of Dort.

1787 Catherine E. McAuley, religious congregation founder, was born near Dublin; founder of the House of Our Blessed Lady, which became the Sisters of Mercy; superior (1831-41) (died 1841).

1803 The first Catholic church in Boston was dedicated.

1907 Rev. Francis Hodur was consecrated by the bishops of the Old Catholic Church in the Netherlands as bishop of the Polish National Catholic Church, based in Scranton, Pa.

1929 Vassilious, patriarch of the Greek Orthodox Church, died at 79.

1963 The second session of the Second Vatican Council began and continued until Dec. 4; produced a Constitution on the Sacred Liturgy, designed to renew the church through a renewal of the liturgy.

1964 The Ecumenical Council meeting in the Vatican approved in principle the admission of married men of mature age to the order of deacons.

1967 The first synod of bishops, called in conformity with the Second Vatican Council, was convened by Pope Paul VI to advise on canon law, seminary organization, liturgy, doctrinal matters, and intermarriage.

1978 John Paul I, pope since Aug. 26, died suddenly at 65.

1979 More than 2 million people welcomed Pope John Paul II on his arrival in Ireland.

1987 Rev. M.G. "Pat" Robertson announced that he would resign his Southern Baptist ordination and leadership of his multi-million dollar religious broadcasting empire (CBN) to pursue his campaign for the presidency.

SEPTEMBER 30

Feast day of St. Otta (1062-1139), Bishop of Bomberg and "apostle of Pomerania."

Feast day in Armenian, Byzantine, and Syrian Christian churches of St. Gregory the Illuminator (about 257-337), founder and patron saint of the Armenian Church; known as the "apostle of Armenia."

420 St. Jerome, one of the four Doctors* of the Western Church and the most learned of the Latin fathers, died at about 78; went to Bethlehem, where he went into a monastery and devoted self to writing; translated the Bible into Latin (the Vulgate Bible), a large number of works of ecclesiastical history and biblical interpretations; also observed as his feast day.

653 St. Honorius of Canterbury died; served as the fifth Archbishop of Canterbury from 627 to 653; also observed as his feast day.

1770 George Whitefield, Methodist revivalist, died in Newburyport, Mass.

1801 Zacharias Frankel, German rabbi and theologian, was born in Prague; founder of the Breslau school of historical Judaism; chief rabbi, Dresden and Leipzig (1836-54); his beliefs resulted in Conservative Judaism in the United States (died 1875).

1850 A papal bull was issued creating Catholic bishops in England and Dr. Nicholas P.S. Wiseman as cardinal and Archbishop of Westminster; Parliament (July 1851) enacted the Ecclesiastical Titles Act, declaring the papal bull null and void but the act was never enforced, repealed in 1871.

1943 Pope Pius XII issued an encyclical, "Divino afflaute spiritu," stressing the need to follow the literal meaning of Scripture whenever possible, but opened the way for more liberal approach to biblical criticism by Catholic scholars.

1970 The New American Bible was published in its entirety for the first time; this was the first Catholic-sponsored translation in English created directly from original sources.

1972 Nichiren Soshu Buddhist sect dedicated its new main temple at the foot of Mt. Fuji, Japan.

OCTOBER 1

Feast day of St. Remy (Remi or Remigius), Bishop of Reims (459-530), "apostle of the Franks."

Feast day of St. Romanas, Byzantine hymnographer and greatest master of the kontakion (metrical sermon chanted to music).

Feast day in the Catholic Church of St. Gregory the Illuminator (about 257-337), the "apostle of Armenia."

366 St. Damasus I became pope, served until 384; during his reign, Latin became the principal liturgical language in Rome, replacing Greek; commissioned St. Jerome to revise existing versions of the Bible and it became known as the Latin Vulgate Bible.

965 John XIII the Good was elected pope, served until 972; became pope through the influence of Otto I and was kept in power by Otto II; the Poles and Hungarians were converted during his pontificate.

1404 Boniface IX, pope from 1389 to 1404, died.

1500 John Alcock, English prelate, died at 70; Bishop of Rochester, Worcester, and Ely; briefly lord chancellor, lord president of Wales; founded Jesus College at Cambridge.

1567 Pope Pius V issued the bull, "Ex omnibus affictionibus," condemning the views of Flemish Catholics Michael Baius and John Hessels.

1674 Pope Clement X created the bishopric of Quebec, with Francoise de Laval as the first bishop.

1723 Richard Mansfield, Episcopal clergyman, was born in Berlin; rector, St. James Church, New York City (1748-1820); first Episcopalian to receive doctor of divinity degree from Yale (1792) (died 1820).

1753 Thomas Olivers, Methodist pioneer, joined John Wesley as an evangelist; wrote an elegy on Wesley's death, many hymns (The God of Abraham praise).

1847 Annie (Wood) Besant, theosophist, was born in London; president, Theosophical Society (1907-33); founder, Central Hindu College, Benares (1898) (died 1933).

1862 Charles R. Brown, Congregational clergyman and educator, was born in Bethany, W. Va.; dean, Yale Divinity School (1911-28), dean emeritus (1928-50) (died 1950).

1883 The Missionary Training College opened in New York City, with four students; moved to South Nyack in 1897.

1891 The Evangelical Lutheran Theological Seminary opened in Chicago.

1892 The Baptist Theological Union became the Divinity School of the U. of Chicago with the opening of the University.

1899 Diomede Falconio, first permanent apostolic delegate, arrived in Quebec.

1904 Austin M. Farrer, theologian and biblical scholar (Oxford), was born in London; author (Finite and Infinite, The Freedom of the Will) (died 1968).

1966 The Orthodox Theological Society, grouping the faculties of Orthodox seminaries in America, was established.

1972 Thousands of Hasidic Jews from all over the world came to the Brooklyn center to receive guidance from Rabbi M. M. Schneerson, head of the worldwide Lubavitcher Movement.

1979 Pope John Paul II arrived in the United States for a week-long visit, including stops in Boston, New York, Washington, Philadelphia, Des Moines and Cumming, Iowa, and Chicago.

1983 Catholic and Lutheran theologians, conferring since 1978, reached agreement that faith in Jesus Christ, rather than human effort, is the prime requirement for salvation; agreement is expected to boost the nearly 20 years effort to overcome 500 years of animosity between Catholics and Protestants.

1987 A month long synod of Catholic bishops opened in Rome to examine the role of the laity in the church, especially the role of women; the synod includes 232 church leaders from more than 100 countries.

OCTOBER 2

1187 Jerusalem fell to the Moslems led by Saladin, ending the Second Crusade.

1264 Urban IV, pope from 1261 to 1264, died.

1538 St. Charles (Carlo) Borromeo, Archbishop of Milan (1560-84), was born in Arona, Italy; a nephew of Pope Pius IV, he was a leader in the Counter Reformation; in forefront of implementation of the reforms of the Council of Trent; founder of the Oblates of St. Ambrose (1578); canonized 1610 (died 1584).

1755 Hannah Adams, religious historian, was born in Medfield, Mass.; author (Truth and Excellence of the Christian Religion, History of the Jews) (died 1831).

1792 The Baptist Missionary Society was founded in England, with Andrew Fuller as the first secretary; now has about 200 missionaries working in India, China, Africa, and Jamaica.

1798 Anne-Therese Guerin (Mother Theodore), religious congregation founder, was born in Etables, France; founder of Sisters of Providence of St. Mary of the Woods, Ind. (died 1856).

1805 William Cunningham, Scottish theologian, was born near Glasgow; one of the founders of the Free Church immediately after the Disruption* (died 1861).

1828 The Methodist Church in Upper Canada, meeting in Ernestown, adopted resolutions separating from the American church; united with British Wesleyans Aug. 18, 1832.

1831 Oblate Sisters of Providence was founded by James H.M.N. Joubert de la Muraille.

1833 William Corby, Catholic prelate and educator, was born in Detroit; president, Notre Dame U. and local superior, Congregation of the Holy Cross (1866-72,1877-81); provincial general, Congregation of the Holy Cross (died 1897).

1848 Samuel N. Driver, English Semitic language scholar, was born in Southampton; regius professor of Hebrew, Oxford; co-editor of Hebrew-English lexicon of the Old Testament (died 1914).

1869 Mohandas Gandhi, Hindu revolutionary religious leader, was born in Porbandar, India; organized Satyagraha, a politico-religious movement of non-cooperation with the British Government in India (1919); assassinated Jan. 30, 1948.

1870 A plebiscite conducted in papal territories on the question of union with the Kingdom of Italy resulted in a vote of 133,681 for, 1,507 against; Rome was incorporated with Italy by royal decree Oct.9, named capital of Italy Dec.5.

1871 James DeW. Perry, Episcopal prelate, was born in Germantown, Pa.; Bishop of Rhode Island (1911-46), presiding bishop of the church (1930-37) (died 1947).

1921 Robert Runcie, Archbishop of Canterbury (1980-), was born; principal, Cuddesdon College (theological) (1960-69), Bishop of St. Albans (1970-79).

1929 The Church of Scotland and the United Free Church were reunited after a separation of 86 years.

1930 The International Lutheran Hour began on a network of 36 American radio stations, with Dr. Walter A. Maier as speaker until his death in 1950.

1964 The Assembly of the International Convention of Christian Churches (Disciples of Christ) opened in Detroit; voted to participate in the struggle for full moral and civil rights for all citizens and rejected proposals to allow prayer and Bible reading in public schools.

1979 Pope John Paul II addressed the United Nations General Assembly, warning against an arms race and calling for freer human conditions everywhere.

1988 The Catholic Archdiocese of Detroit recommended closing 43 of Detroit's 112 churches serving 10,000 parishioners because of low membership and high operating costs; closings are scheduled for June 1989.

OCTOBER 3

Feast day of St. Therese of Lisieux, known as the Little Flower of Jesus; canonized 1925.

Feast day of St. Thomas de Cantelupe (Cantilupe), French Bishop of Hereford and chancellor of England.

Feast day in the Orthodox Church of St. Denis, first Bishop of Paris and patron saint of France.

1226 St. Francis of Assisi, Italian founder of the Franciscan Order, died at 34; his generosity, simple and unaffected faith, passionate devotion to God and man, love of nature, and deep humility have made him one of the most cherished saints; wrote several hymns (All creatures of our God and King); canonized 1228.

1691 The Treaty of Limerick was enacted to provide among other things the freedom of the Catholic religion in Ireland; annulled by the Irish Parliament in 1695.

1802 George Ripley, Unitarian clergyman and a leading Transcendentalist, was born in Greenfield, Mass.; served Purchase St. Church, Boston (1826-41); helped organize the experimental Brook Farm community; author (Discourses on the Philosophy of Religion); literary critic, *New York Tribune* (1849-80) (died 1880).

1809 Robert Gray, first Anglican Bishop of Cape Town (1847-53), was born in Bristol, England; metropolitan of South Africa (1853-72) (died 1872).

1829 James T. Holly, Episcopal bishop, was born in Washington, D.C.; encouraged emigration of American blacks to Haiti; Bishop of Haiti (1874-1911) (died 1911).

1866 Public instruction in Spain was placed under the clergy.

1875 Hebrew Union College was opened in Cincinnati.

1901 More than half of France's 16,468 religious establishments completed applying for authorization under the new associations law; many (Jesuits, Passionists, Assumptionists, Benedictines) left the country.

1913 A constitutional amendment in Peru permitted the building of Protestant churches, missions, and schools.

1961 Jozsef Grosz, Archbishop of Kalocsa, Hungary, died in Vienna at about 74; chairman of the Catholic bishops of Hungary.

1963 The Vatican announced that the Czech Government had released from detention Archbishop Josef Beran of Prague and primate of Czechoslovakia.

1981 American bishops of the Roman and Eastern Orthodox Catholic churches completed their first round of talks aimed at helping clear the way for reunion of the two churches.

1982 Dr. Norman Vincent Peale marked his 50th anniversary with the Marble Collegiate Church in New York City.

OCTOBER 4

Feast day of St. Francis of Assisi, founder of the Franciscans and the principal patron of Italy.

1542 St. Robert Bellarmine, Italian cardinal and theologian, was born in Montepulciano, Italy, a nephew of Pope Marcellus II; professor of controversial theology, Collegium Romanum (1576-1602); known especially for his theological disputations with those denied the pope's temporal power; Archbishop of Capua (1602-05), elevated to cardinal 1598; canonized 1930, declared a Doctor* of the Church (1931) (died 1621).

1570 Peter Pazmany, Hungarian prelate, was born; Archbishop of Esztergom and primate of Hungary (1616-37); elevated to cardinal 1629; leader of Counter Reformation in Hungary (died 1637).

1829 The first provincial Council of the Baltimore Catholic Province was called by Archbishop James Whitfield, an epoch-making event in American Catholic history; attended by bishops from Baltimore, Boston, New York, Philadelphia, Charleston, and Cincinnati; developed uniform regulations and procedures.

1859 Francis J. Finn, Jesuit author, was born in St. Louis; created Catholic juvenile literature in English (Percy Wynn, Tom Playfair, Lucky Bob) (died 1928).

1861 Walter Rauschenbusch, theologian and author, was born in Rochester, N.Y.; professor, Rochester Theological Seminary (1897-1918); founder, Brotherhood of the Kingdom; considered foremost molder of American Christian thought of his time; author (Christianity and the Social Crisis, Social Principles of Jesus) (died 1918).

1864 The Pennsylvania Ministerium of the Lutheran General Council opened its own theological seminary in Philadelphia.

1893 Walter A. Maier, Lutheran editor and theologian, was born in Boston; editor, *Walther League Messenger* (1920-45); preacher, Lutheran Hour (1930-50) (died 1950).

1897 Pope Leo XIII issued the bull, "Felicitate quadam," which brought together all Observant branches of the Franciscans.

1965 Pope Paul VI visited the United States, speaking to the United Nations and pleading for peace and disarmament.

1979 Pope John Paul II reaffirmed the position that Catholic priesthood requires a lifelong commitment from men and is not a proper calling for women; his message was contained in an address in Philadelphia's Civic Center.

OCTOBER 5

869 The fourth Council of Constantinople opened with Emperor Basil attending; called to discuss iconoclasts, heresies; continued to Feb 28, 870.

1600 Thomas Goodwin, an outstanding Puritan, was born in Rollesby, England; helped draft the 1658 Savoy declaration of faith for Congregationalism; became one of Oliver Cromwell's principal advisors (died 1680).

1703 Jonathan Edwards, powerful colonial preacher and the greatest theologian of American Puritanism, was born in East Windsor, Conn.; accepted central Calvinistic doctrine of absolute divine sovereignty and the supreme right to bestow eternal salvation or damnation, and ardently opposed Arminianism*; led revival that spread and paved the way for the 1740-42 revival tour of George Whitefield; dismissed (1750) by his Northampton congregation, which he had served for 21 years, over terms of admission into full church membership; moved (1751) to Stockbridge, Mass., where he wrote his treatise on "Freedom of the Will;" president, College of New Jersey (later Princeton) (1757-58) (died 1758).

1748 Benjamin Moore, Episcopal prelate, was born in Newtown, N.Y.; Bishop of New York (1801-16); president, Columbia U. (1801-11); loyal to the British during the American Revolution (died 1816).

1781 Bernhard Bolzano, German Catholic theologian and mathematician, was born in Prague; a formulator of modern mathematical theory of functions (died 1848).

1784 The Dutch Reformed Church created the first American theological seminary in New York City; later moved to New Brunswick, N.J.

1840 John A. Symonds, English historian, was born in Bristol; best known for work on Italian Renaissance; also wrote Anglican hymn, "These things shall be! a loftier race" (died 1893).

1844 Joseph A. Carpenter, English Unitarian clergyman and scholar, was born near London; pioneer in the study of comparative religion; one of the first to introduce Old Testament study in theological college; lecturer, Manchester New College (1875-1906), president (1906-15) (died 1927).

1846 Francis A. Gasquet, Catholic historian, was born in London; superior, Benedictine monastery and the College of St. Gregory (1878-84); president of international commission to revise the Vulgate Bible; prefect of Vatican Archives (1918-29); elevated to cardinal 1914 (died 1929).

1910 St. Patrick's Cathedral in New York City was dedicated.

1957 Catholic delegates from 90 countries met in Rome for the Congress for Lay Apostolate.

1964 The Ecumenical Council gave overwhelming approval to the most liberal and conciliatory expressions of the Catholic Church's will to reunify Christianity since before the great Protestant schism of the 16th Century.

1980 Mormons from all over the world attended a conference in Salt Lake City, marking the 150th anniversary of the church.

OCTOBER 6

1101 St. Bruno, the founder of the Carthusians, died at about 71; founded a monastery at La Torre in Sicily.

1536 William Tyndale, New Testament translator and publisher, was executed for heresy; his influence was great on the English Reformation and biblical study because of use made of his renderings in the King James Version of the Bible.

1552 Matteo Ricci, Italian Jesuit missionary to China, was born near Florence; introduced Christianity to Chinese cities; founder of a mission in Peking (1601); author (On the Nature of God) (dated 1610).

1689 Alexander VIII (1610-91), born Pietro Ottoboni, became pope, served until 1691; reign marked by nepotism, but he did much to enrich Rome and the Vatican Library.

1798 Robert Baird, Presbyterian clergyman, was born near Uniontown, Pa.; general agent of the American Sunday School Union; author (Religion in America)(died 1863).

1816 William Bradbury, music editor and hymnist, was born in York, Pa.; wrote music for many hymns (He leadeth me; Savior, like a shepherd lead us; My hope is built; Sweet hour of prayer) (died 1868).

1856 George Hodges, Episcopal educator, was born in Rome, N.Y.; dean, Episcopal Theological School, Cambridge, Mass. (1894-1919) (died 1919).

1872 About 20,000 persons made a pilgrimage to the grotto at Lourdes, France, where the Virgin Mary reportedly made appearances to two girls (Feb 14, 1858).

1874 John E. Bode, Anglican clergyman, died at 58; delivered the Bampton lectures in 1855; hymn writer (O Jesus, I have promised).

1915 Humberto Medeiros, Archbishop of Boston (1970-83), was born in Arrifes, the Azores (died 1983).

1973 Rev. Sun Myung Moon, founder of the Unification Church, began his American tour in his One World Crusade.

1979 Pope John Paul II became the first pope ever to meet with an American president in the White House.

1984 Representatives from more than 4O countries attended the centennial observance in Three Rivers Stadium, Pittsburgh of chartering the Watch Tower Bible & Tract Society.

OCTOBER 7

336 St. Marcus, pope in 336, died; also observed as his feast day.

1518 Martin Luther held a personal interview with Cardinal Cajetan about his 95 theses fastened to the Church door; interview widened into a discussion of the relation between faith and sacramental grace, and finally broke down with Cajetan dismissing Luther and telling him to stay away unless he would recant unconditionally.

1573 William Laud, Archbishop of Canterbury (1633-45), was born in Reading; strong opponent of Calvinism and Presbyterianism and his antagonism was one of the main causes of the Puritan revolution; he was unable to understand the popularity of Puritanism and the hatred aroused by his violent measures; provoked a riot in St. Giles, Edinburgh, which led to the Bishops' War and the long Parliament, which impeached him for high treason (1640); imprisoned in the Tower of London (1641), beheaded (1645).

1746 William Billings, hymn composer and publisher, was born in Boston; published "The New England Psalm Singer" and other church music collections; composed hymns and the patriotic song, "Chester" (died 1800).

1810 Henry Alford, clergyman and scholar, was born in London, dean of Canterbury (1857-71); first editor, *Contemporary Review* (1866-70); wrote hymns (Come, ye thankful people, come; Ten thousand times ten thousand); best known for his edition of the New Testament in Greek (died 1871).

1815 Charles Beecher, Congregational clergyman, was born in Litchfield, Conn., the fifth son of Lyman Beecher; served pastorates in Ft. Wayne, Ind., Newark, and Georgetown, Mass.; convicted of heresy (1863) for believing in the pre-existence of souls; conviction was later rescinded (died 1900).

1832 Charles C. Converse, hymn composer, was born in Warren, Mass.; best known for "What a friend we have in Jesus" (died 1918).

1833 Margaret Fox, spiritualist, was born near Kingston, Canada; with sisters, Leah and Catherine, she claimed by means of spirit rappings to have established communications with the supernatural world; toured widely; confessed imposture (1888) but later withdrew the confession (died 1893).

1835 Folliott S. Pierpoint, Anglican hymn writer, was born in Bath; best known for the hymn, "For the beauty of the earth" (died 1917).

1866 The second Catholic plenary council convened in Baltimore making it then the largest formal conciliatory assembly in the Catholic Church since the Council of Trent; Council expressed its democratic faith and thankfulness for American institutions.

1931 Desmond M. Tutu, Episcopal Bishop of South Africa (1986-), was born in Klersdorp, South Africa; awarded the 1984 Nobel Peace Prize.

OCTOBER 8

Feast day in the Catholic Church of St. Demetrius, Bishop of Alexandria (189 to about 231).

Former feast day of St. Bridget of Sweden (1303-73), founder of the Brigittine Order; a mystic and patron saint of Sweden; now observed July 23.

451 Council of Chalcedon, the fourth ecumenical council, opened with more than 500 bishops (mostly from the Orthodox Church) on hand; drew up statement of faith (known as the Chalcedonian Definition) and issued regulations for pastoral discipline, most of which were accepted by the Catholic Church; ended Oct 31.

1609 John Clarke, Baptist clergyman and doctor, was born in Westhope, England; a founder of Rhode Island, obtaining a royal charter for the colony; with Roger Williams, responsible for maintaining the liberal democratic character of Rhode Island institutions (died 1676).

1662 Matthew Henry, English Nonconformist biblical scholar, was born in Broad Oak, Flintshire; author (Exposition of the Old and New Testaments) (died 1714).

1713 Ezekiel Landau, Polish rabbi, was born in Opatow; author of "responsa," decisions on questioned points of the law (died 1793).

1720 Jonathan Mayhew, colonial clergyman, was born in Chilmark, Mass.; his liberal preaching helped start Unitarian Congregationalism; pastor, West Church, Boston (1747-66) (died 1766).

1802 Petrus Hofstede de Groot, Dutch theologian, was born; a founder of Groningen school of theology, which paved the way for modern theology (died 1886).

1816 Robert T. S. Lowell, Episcopal clergyman and author, was born in Boston; author (The New Priest in Concepcion Bay, Antony Brade), poet (Relief of Lucknow)(died 1891).

1870 The Kingdom of Italy took over Rome from the pope, who was guaranteed his sovereign powers as head of the church.

1870 Daisetz T. Suzuki, chief exponent of Zen to the Western world, was born in Kanazawa, Japan; wrote scholarly works on Mahayana Buddhism (died 1966).

1882 Walter R. Bowie, Episcopal rector and theologian, was born in Richmond, Va.;rector, Grace Church, New York City (1923-39); professor, Union Theological Seminary (1939-50), Virginia Theological Seminary (1950-55); hymn writer (O Holy City, seen of John) (died 1969).

1910 Governmental decree in Portugal expelled religious orders and confiscated their properties.

OCTOBER 9

Feast day in the Catholic Church of St. Denis (died 258), first Bishop of Paris and patron saint of France.

Feast day of St. John Leonardi, founder (1580) of the Clerks Regular of the Mother of God; canonized 1938.

1047 Clement II, pope in 1046-47, died.

1253 Robert Grosseteste, English theologian and scholar, died at about 78; Bishop of Lincoln (1235-53); vigorously defended his rights, especially against the pope and Henry III; called a "harbinger of the Reformation."

1581 St. Louis Bertrand, patron saint of Colombia, died at 55; Spanish-born Dominican missionary; canonized 1671; also observed as his feast day.

1601 Nikolaus Crell, Saxon statesman and religious reformer, was beheaded; was chancellor of Saxony, he sought to supplant Lutheranism with his own faith, a form of Calvinism (1589); on death of Prince Christian (1591), Crell was imprisoned, later executed.

1623 Ferdinand Verbiest, Jesuit missionary, was born in Pitthem, Belgium; headed Chinese imperial astronomical bureau (1669-88) (died 1688).

1694 Johann L. von Mosheim, German Lutheran theologian, was born in Lübeck; founder of modern preaching and the pragmatic school of church history; a founder, U. of Göttingen, chancellor (1747-55) (died 1755).

1750 Sir George P. Tomline, English prelate, was born in Bury St. Edmunds; tutor and secretary to William Pitt the Younger, British prime minister, whose influence helped Tomline become dean of St. Paul's and Bishop of Lincoln (1787-1820) and Bishop of Winchester (1820-27); Pitt failed (1805) to persuade George III to name Tomline Archbishop of Canterbury (died 1827).

1755 Richard Furman, leading Baptist in the South, was born in Esopus, N.Y.; pastor, Charleston (S.C.) Baptist Church (1787-1822); Furman U. in Greenville, S.C., named for him (died 1825).

1798 Isaac Ferris, Reformed Dutch clergyman, was born in New York City; chancellor, U. of the City of New York (1852- 70) (died 1873).

1845 John Henry Newman, a leader of the Tractarian movement at Oxford was formally received into the Catholic Church.

1890 Aimee Semple McPhersen, popular evangelist, was born in Ingersoll, Canada; launched the "Foursquare Gospel" movement, opened her Angelus Temple in Los Angeles (1923) (died 1944).

1906 Anglican Bishop Arthur Sweatman of Toronto was made the primate of Canada.

1909 (Frederick) Donald Coggan, English prelate, was born in London; Archbishop of York (1961-74), of Canterbury (1974-80); a leading spokesman for the ecumenical movement in the Church of England.

1958 Pius XII, pope from 1939 to 1958, died.

1976 Delegates to the American Lutheran Church convention in Washington agreed to delete most references to gender in official church documents.

OCTOBER 10

Feast day of St. Francis Borgia, third general of the Jesuits (1565-72).

644 St. Paulinus, Catholic missionary to England, died at 77; Bishop of York (625-634), of Rochester (634-644); also observed as his feast day in some English churches.

1560 Jacobus Arminius, Dutch theologian, was born near Rotterdam; at first, he defended Calvinist doctrine of predestination, but later favored the doctrine of universal redemption and conditional predestination; founder of Arminianism*; preacher, Amsterdam (1588-1608), theology professor at Leiden (1603-09) (died 1609).

1610 St. Gabriel Lalemant, French Jesuit missionary, was born; along with St. Jean de Brebeuf, he was captured and killed by Iroquois Indians (1649); canonized with six other North American martyrs in 1930.

1710 The first Anglican service in Canada was held in Halifax, Nova Scotia.

1710 Alban Butler, English Catholic hagiographer, was born near London; compiled four-volume, "Lives of the Principal Saints" (died 1773).

1790 Theobald Mathew, temperance advocate, was born in Thomastown, Ireland; known as the "apostle of temperance;" Capuchin priest, he inaugurated total abstinence movement (1838), carried on crusades in Britain, United States (died 1856).

1800 Charles T. Beke, British biblical scholar and explorer, was born in London; first to determine the course of the Blue Nile, explored alleged location of Mt. Sinai; author (Researches in Primeval History) (died 1874).

1822 Samuel Johnson, preacher and author, was born in Salem, Mass.; co-author of two compilations of hymns; wrote several hymns (City of God, how broad and far; Life of ages, richly poured); author (The Worship of Jesus, Oriental Religions) (died 1882).

1823 Georg M. Grossman, Lutheran leader, was born in Grossbieberau, Germany; an organizer of the Synod of Iowa, president (1854-93); a founder, president, Wartburg Normal College (died 1897).

1847 Henry Ward Beecher became pastor of the newly-organized Plymouth Congregational Church, Brooklyn; served until 1887; led congregation out of the Congregational denomination (1882).

1847 Bernhard L. Duhm, Protestant theologian, was born in Bingum, Germany; author of commentaries on prophetic books of the Old Testament; proposed the Trito-Isaiah theory of authorship of portions of Isaiah (died 1928).

1865 Rafael Merry del Val, Spanish Catholic prelate, was born in London; papal secretary of state (1903-14), secretary of the Congregation of the Holy Office (1914-30), elevated to cardinal 1903 (died 1930).

1878 Thomas Galberry, Catholic prelate, died; superior of Augustinian missions in the United States (1866-70); president, Villa Nova College (1872-74); Bishop of Hartford, Conn. (1875-78).

1885 Edmund A. Walsh, Jesuit who was active in Catholic relief efforts, was born in Boston; dean at Georgetown U., Washington; director, Papal Relief Committee (1922); president, Catholic Near East Welfare Association (1926-31); Georgetown School of Foreign Service named for him (died 1956).

1897 Elijah Muhammad, Black Muslim leader, was born in Sandersville, Ga. as Elijah Poore; headed Muslims from 1934 to his death in 1975.

1982 Maximilian Kolbe, Polish-born Catholic priest, was declared a saint and martyr at canonization ceremonies by Pope John II; Kolbe volunteered to take the place of a man condemned to death by starvation in the Auschwitz concentration camp in 1944.

OCTOBER 11

Feast day in the Orthodox Church of Atticus, patriarch of Constantinople(404-425).

Feast day of St. Nectarius, Archbishop of Constantinople (281-297).

642 John IV, pope from 640 to 642, died.

965 St. Bruno I, German prelate, died at about 40; son of King Henry I, he was Archbishop of Cologne (953-965); harmonized rules of ecclesiastical and secular princes; also observed as his feast day.

1303 Boniface VIII, pope from 1294 to 1303, died.

1531 Huldreich Zwingli, Swiss reformer, was killed while serving as chaplain for a force defending Zurich; he was carrying the defenders' banner.

1643 Jean Dubergier de Hauranne, French theologian, died at 62; became known as Abbe de St. Cyran; associate of Cornelis Jansen and a co-founder of Jansenism; jailed by Cardinal Richelieu (1638-42).

1675 Samuel Clarke, metaphysician and theologian, was born in Norwich, England; one of the most learned clergymen of his age, served as chaplain to Queen Anne; opposed deists, materialists, empiricists and freethinkers; demonstrated existence and attributes of God in the Boyle Lectures (died 1729).

1792 Antoine Blanc, Catholic prelate, was born in Sury, France; Archbishop of New Orleans (1851-60); founder, Sisters of the Holy Family, first American black sisterhood (died 1860).

1836 Charles C. McCabe, Methodist educator, was born in Athens, Ohio; secretary, Methodist Missionary Society (1884-1902); chancellor, American U. (1902-06) (died 1906).

1882 John F. D'Alton, Catholic primate of Ireland (1946-63), was born in Claremorris, Ireland; elevated to cardinal 1953 (died 1963).

1896 Edward W. Benson, Archbishop of Canterbury (1883-96), died at 67.

1920 Anton T. Boisen, founder of the movement for clinical pastoral education, announced the discovery of a "process of regeneration which could be used to save other people."

1957 The International Convention of Disciples of Christ began its annual assembly in Cleveland; assembly changed the name of the organization to International Convention of Christian Churches (Disciples of Christ).

1962 The Second Vatican Council was opened by Pope John XXIII, explored the traditional causes of anti-clericalism.

1981 It was announced that an 18-member delegation from the National Council of Churches would visit China in November, the first group of American church leaders to be invited by China's two major Christian organizations.

1988 Rev. Ian Paisley, a militant Protestant leader from Northern Ireland, disrupted Pope John Paul II's unity speech to the European Parliament, shouting, "I renounce you as the anti-Christ!"

OCTOBER 12

Feast day of St. Wilfrid (or Wilfrith) (634-709), Anglo-Saxon Bishop of Ripon and York; built churches of architectural splendor.

633 King Edward of Northumbria (northern England,) a champion of Christianity, was killed in battle; converted to Christianity by Paulinus, whom he made Archbishop of York.

638 Honorius I, pope from 625 to 638, died.

1585 Johann Heerman, German hymn writer, was born in Silesia; his best known hymn is "Ah, Holy Jesus, how hast Thou offended" (died 1647).

1600 Luis de Molina, Spanish Jesuit theologian, died at 65; propounded controversial doctrine (Molinism) that divine grace is a free gift to all, but that its efficacy depends upon the will that accepts it.

1762 The Association of Philadelphia Baptists voted to establish a college in Rhode Island.

1775 Lyman Beecher, Presbyterian theologian, was born in New Haven, Conn.; served churches in East Hampton, N.Y., Litchfield, Conn., and Boston; first president, professor, Lane Theological Seminary, Cincinnati (1832-50); outstanding exponent of the revivalistic tradition of American Protestantism; accused (1835) by conservative Presbyterians of heresy, acquitted by synod (died 1863).

1841 The first Episcopal Bishop of Delaware, Alfred Lee, was consecrated.

1868 Jesuits and other orders were expelled from Spain and the law expelling Jews was abrogated; freedom of religious worship was decreed.

1925 Episcopal Bishop William M. Brown of Arkansas was deposed for heresy in writing "Communism and Christianity."

OCTOBER 13

Feast day of St. Edward the Confessor, king of England (1043- 66) and builder of Westminster Abbey; canonized 1161.

1525 Bishopric of Mexico was created.

1534 Paul III was named pope, served until 1549; called the Council of Trent (1545); patron of the arts, retaining Michelangelo to work on the Vatican; approved the founding of the Jesuits (1540); reorganized the Curia and the Sacred College; excommunicated Henry VIII of England (1538); introduced the Inquisition into Italy.

1720 Ferdinand Farmer, itinerant Jesuit missionary to the American colonies, was born in Swabia, Germany; organized the first Catholic congregation in New York City (died 1786).

1788 Thomas Erskine, Scottish theological writer, was born in Edinburgh; upheld Calvinism, interpreting its mystical side; developed unorthodox doctrine of universal atonement advanced by John M. Campbell (died 1870).

1843 B'nai Brith, Jewish fraternal society, was organized in New York City.

1862 Richard J. H. Gottheil, Semitic scholar and educator, was born in Manchester, England, the son of Gustav Gottheil (5/12/1827); professor of Semitic languages, Columbia U. (1892-1936); first president, American Federation of Zionists (1898-1904) (died 1936).

1886 Bernard I. Bell, Episcopal clergyman who in 20 books urged the church to lead in recovering permanent and universal moral values, was born in Dayton, Ohio (died 1958).

1908 The Church of the Nazarene was organized in Pilot Point, Texas by the union of several small religious bodies, including the Church of the Nazarene, the Association of Pentecostal Churches, and the Holiness Church of Christ.

1967 The first delegate assembly of the Disciples of Christ (Christian Churches) opened in St. Louis; agreed on a "provisional design" for restructuring the communion.

1968 The Reconstructionist Rabbinical College opened in Philadelphia.

1988 The Vatican officially announced that scientific carbon testing showed that the Shroud of Turin, revered for centuries as Jesus' burial cloth, could not be that because it is no more than 728 years old.

OCTOBER 14

Feast day of St. Calixtus I, pope from about 217 to 223; apparently originally a slave; built a cemetery famous as a shrine for martyrs in the Appian Way.

Feast day in the Orthodox Church of St. Cosmas Melodus, writer of Greek liturgical hymns.

530 Dioscorus, anti-pope in 530, died; accepted by most Roman priests instead of Boniface II; schism ended with Dioscorus' death.

1552 Oswald Myconius (born Geisshüsler), Swiss reformer, died at 64; co-worker and first biographer of Zwingli; helped draw up the first two Basel confessions.

1644 William Penn, founder of American Quakerism and Pennsylvania, was born in London; joined Society of Friends (Quakers) (1666), preached and wrote; made a trustee to manage the West Jersey Colony in the United States, had an important part in framing its charter (1677); inherited from his father a large financial claim against Charles II for which he received a grant of Pennsylvania (1681) as payment; prepared a Frame of Government, made treaties with the Indians, laid out Philadelphia; author of "No Cross, No Crown," a recognized Quaker classic (died 1718).

1656 Massachusetts enacted a fine of 40 shillings an hour for harboring Quakers; every Quaker coming into the Colony after punishment was to suffer the loss of one ear, for the second offense the loss of the other, and for the third offense to have their tongue "bored through with a hot iron."

1696 Samuel Johnson, leader of the Church of England movement in the colonies, was born in Guilford, Conn.; pastor, Stratford (Conn.) Anglican Church (1724-54); first president, Kings (later Columbia) College (1754-63) (died 1772).

1755 Thomas Charles, Welsh religious leader, was born; a founder of Calvinistic Methodism and the British and Foreign Bible Society, which printed a Welsh Bible (died 1814).

1814 Jean Baptiste Lamy, Catholic missionary in the Southwest, was born in Lempdes, France; bishop, Archbishop of Santa Fe, N.M. (1853-85); commemorated in Willa Cather's "Death Comes for the Archbishop" (died 1888).

1831 Ellison Capers, the first Episcopal bishop of South Carolina (1893-1908), was born in Charleston, S.C.; Confederate general (died 1908).

1835 William G. Fischer, bookbinder and composer, was born in Baltimore; wrote many hymns (I love to tell the story, I am coming to the cross) (died 1912).

1874 Emmaneul F. Poppen, president of the American Lutheran Church, was born in New Dundae, Canada (died 1961).

1876 Henry A. Ironside, evangelist, was born in Toronto; called the "archbishop of fundamentalism;" pastor, Moody Memorial Church, Chicago (1930-48) (died 1951).

1876 Joseph F. Rummel, Catholic Archbishop of New Orleans (1935-64), was born in Steinmaurer, Germany; a staunch defender of human rights (died 1964).

1893 Leslie D. Weatherhead, Methodist clergyman who served London's City Temple (1936-50), was born in London; president, Methodist Conference (1955-56, 1966-67) (died 1976).

1904 Archbishop William B. Bond (1815-1906) was named Anglican primate of Canada; a vigorous reformer, temperance advocate; Bishop of Montreal (1878-1901), archbishop and metropolitan (1901-06).

1956 Pope Pius XII deplored the employment of women in industry and heavy labor.

1960 John W. Keogh, American clergyman who founded the Newman Clubs, died at about 72.

1964 Rev. Martin Luther King Jr. of Atlanta, a civil rights leader, was awarded the Nobel Peace Prize.

1980 The recent rise of Christian fundamentalism was attacked by 61 prominent scholars and writers in a declaration that denounced absolutist morality, called for emphasis on science and reason rather than religion as a means of solving human problems.

1983 A new translation of Bible readings to eliminate references to God as solely male was announced by the National Council of Churches.

OCTOBER 15

Feast day of St. Theresa of Avila (1515-82), Spanish mystic and originator of Carmelite reform, founder of the Discalced Carmelites; canonized 1622.

Feast day in the Orthodox Church of St. Lucian of Antioch, famed theologian and martyr.

412 St. Theophilus, patriarch of Alexandria (385-412), died; also observed as his feast day in the Coptic Church.

1389 Urban VI, pope from 1378 to 1389, died.

1746 Leonard Neale, Catholic prelate and educator, was born in Port Tobacco, Md.; president, Georgetown College (1795-1815); coadjutor bishop of Baltimore (1795-1815), Archbishop of Baltimore (1815-17) (died 1817).

1757 Joseph McKeen, Congregational clergyman and educator, was born in Londonderry, N.H.; first president, Bowdoin College (1802-07); pastor, First Church, Beverly, Mass. (1785-1802) (died 1807).

1779 Joseph O. Wallin, Swedish poet and ecclesiastic, was born; Archbishop of Sweden (1837-39); compiled Swedish Psalm Book (1819), which included 130 hymns written by him (died 1839).

1784 Thomas Hastings, hymn writer, was born in Washington, Conn.; wrote numerous hymns (Hail to the brightness of Zion's glad morning; He that goes forth weeping; also music for Rock of ages, Retreat, Zion) (died 1872).

1851 George F. Moore, Orientalist and theologian, was born in West Chester, Pa.; taught at Andover Theological Seminary (1883-1902); professor of religious history, Harvard (1902-28); author (History of Religions) (died 1931).

1866 Max L. Margolis, Semitic philologist, was born in Merech, Russia; taught biblical philology in various colleges, including Dropsie (1909-32); author (Hebrew Scriptures in the Making, A History of the Jewish People); editor-in-chief of Bible translation, Jewish Publication Society of America (died 1932).

1873 Harry F. Ward, Methodist clergyman, was born in London; professor, Christian ethics, Union Theological Seminary (from 1918); chairman, American Civil Liberties Union (1920-40); chairman, American League for Peace and Democracy (1930-40) (died 1966).

1881 William Temple, Anglican prelate, was born in Exeter, England, the son of Frederick Temple; Archbishop of York (1929-42), Archbishop of Canterbury (1942-44); author (Christus Veritas; Nature, Man and God) (died 1944).

1960 Moshe Y. Toledano, Israeli minister of religious affairs (1958-60). died in Jerusalem at 79.

1962 Athenagoras, exarch of the Greek Orthodox Church in western and central Europe, died in London at 78.

1965 The Ecumenical Council voted 1,763 to 250 in favor of a decree offering friendship and respect to other world religions and denying collective Jewish guilt for the Crucifixion.

1967 The first official meeting of the Catholic Church and the World Methodist Conference took place in Ariccia, near Rome.

1981 Rev. Sun Myung Moon, head of the Unification Church, was indicted in New York City on charges that he filed false income tax returns omitting more than $150,000 of his income in 1973-75.

OCTOBER 16

Feast day of St. Gall, Seventh Century Irish monk; established monasteries in France, a hermitage at Steinach, Switzerland (present town of St. Gall).

Feast day in the Orthodox Church of St. Longinus, "the soldier with the spear" at the Crucifixion.

Feast day of St. Margaret Mary Alacoque, who initiated the practice of devotions to the Sacred Heart of Jesus.

1311 The first of three solemn sessions of the Council of Vienne (south of Lyon, France) was held; called by Pope Clement V at the demand of Philip IV of France, who wanted a posthumous trial of Pope Boniface VIII and the suppression of the Knights Templar; no trial was held but the Knights were suppressed; other sessions were held April 3 and May 6, 1312.

1333 Nicholas V, antipope (1328-30), died; died soon after being imprisoned.

1483 Gaspar Contarini, Italian cardinal, was born in Venice; tried to effect a reconciliation between Catholic and Protestant churches at the Diet of Ratisbon (1541) (died 1542).

1555 Nicholas Ridley and Hugh Latimer, English bishops active in the Reformation, were burned at the stake; Latimer's last words to Ridley were "...we shall this day light such a candle, by God's grace, in England as I trust shall never be put out;" Ridley, Bishop of London (155-53), helped Cranmer compile the English Prayer Book and the 39 Articles; denounced Queen Mary and Elizabeth as illegitimate and espoused the cause of Lady Jane Grey; on Mary's accession, he was declared a heretic and excommunicated; Latimer, Bishop of Worcester (1535-39), was one of Henry VIII's chief advisors (1534-39) and a popular court preacher (1548-53).

1588 Luke Wadding, British Franciscan author, was born near Cork, Ireland; historian of the Franciscan Order; published monumental (16 volumes) edition of life and writings of Dun Scotus (died 1657).

1591 Gregory XIV, pope from Dec 5,1590, died.

1594 William Allen, English cardinal, died at 62; noted for his efforts to preserve Catholicism in England; called on Catholics to rise against Elizabeth I; instrumental in organizing and heading college for English students in Douai, France (1568-88) and producing the Douai Bible; served as librarian at the Vatican.

1660 Hugh Peters, English Puritan clergyman, died at 62; arrived in New England in 1635, succeeding Roger Williams as pastor of Salem's First Church; active in building Harvard College; returned to England (1641), became involved in the civil war, was imprisoned and beheaded.

1688 Benjamin Griffith, Baptist historian, was born in County Cardigan, Scotland; was the first official historian of the Baptist Church (died 1768).

1701 Yale College was founded as the Collegiate School by Congregationalists dissatisfied with growing liberalism at Harvard.

1752 Johann G. Eichorn, biblical scholar and Orientalist, was born in Dörrenzimmern, Germany; one of the first to attempt scientific comparisons between biblical and other Semitic writings; did much to encourage Bible study and criticism (died 1827).

1808 Lars Paul Esbjörn, Lutheran leader, was born in Delsbo, Sweden; first Swedish Lutheran clergyman to come to America; organized independent Augustana Synod in Jefferson Prairie, Wis. (1860) (died 1870).

1836 John Clifford, English Nonconformist clergyman, was born in Sawley, England; headed National Free Church Council; first president, Baptist World Alliance (1905-11), World Brotherhood Federation (1919-23); his many writings were a great influence in directing church thought to social problems (died 1923).

1840 Frederick L. Hosmer, Unitarian hymn writer, was born in Framingham, Mass.; wrote numerous hymns (O Thou, in all my might so far; The kingdom comes on bended knee; Thy Kingdom come, O Lord) (died 1929).

1847 Sam (Samuel P.) Jones, evangelist, was born in Chambers County, Ala.; known as "the Moody of the South;" probably the foremost speaker of his generation (died 1906).

1948 The Hebrew Union School of Education and Sacred Music in New York City opened.

1978 John Paul II was named pope, the first non-Italian in more than 450 years.

1978 The U. S. Supreme Court refused to hear the appeal of the United Methodist Church to free itself of $360 million breach of contract suit stemming from the financial troubles of 14 apparently church-connected retirement homes and convalescent hospitals in California.

1988 Pope John Paul II celebrated his 10th anniversary as pope by beatifying three 19th Century priests — Rev. Wenceslaus Kozminiski, a founder of 20 religious orders and associations; Rev. Bernardo Silvestrelli, head of the Passionist Order, and Rev. Carlo Houbey, a Dutch missionary in England and Ireland.

OCTOBER 17

Feast day in the Syrian Church of St. Theophilus, patriarch of Alexandria (385-412).

Feast day of St. Etheldreda (about 630-679), Queen of Northumbria and founder of an abbey at Ely; consecrated as abbess of Ely in 673.

Feast day of St. Ignatius, Bishop of Antioch and a powerful theologian; martyred under Trajan (about 110), named a Father* of the Church.

Feast day of St. Nothelm, Archbishop of Canterbury (737-740).

Former feast day of St. Margaret Mary Alacoque, who initiated practice of devotions to the Sacred Heart of Jesus; now observed Oct 16.

532 St. Boniface II, pope from 530 to 532, died.

1404 Innocent VII, born Cosimo de Migliorati, was elected pope, served until 1406; sought vainly to heal schism in the church.

1582 Johann Gerhard, Lutheran orthodox theologian, was born in Quedlinburg, Germany; theology professor at Jena (1616-37); his theological system, set forth in nine volume "Loci theologici," was the most important dogmatic work of the Lutheran orthodoxy era (died 1637).

1792 Sir John Bowring, ardent Unitarian and editor, was born in Exeter, England; first editor, *Westminster Review* (1825); wrote many hymns (God is love, His mercy brightens; In the cross of Christ I glory; Watchman, tell us of the night) (died 1872).

1836 Matthew B. Riddle, Reformed Dutch clergyman, was born in Pittsburgh; member, American New Testament revision committee; an editor, American version; professor, New Testament, Hartford Theological Seminary (1871-87), Western Theological Seminary (Allegheny, Pa.) (1887-1916) (died 1916).

1851 The Catholic Defence Association was founded in Ireland.

1855 The first conference of rabbis in the United States was held in the Medical College, Cleveland, with Rabbi Isidore Kalisch as chairman.

1905 Alan Richardson, dean of York (1964-75), was born in Highfield, England; was one of two or three best known Anglican theologians of his time (died 1975).

1912 John Paul I, pope from Aug 26 to Sep 28, 1978, was born as Abino Luciano in Canale d'Agordo, Italy

1976 Pope Paul VI canonized the 17th Century Scottish Jesuit martyr John Ogilvie, who was hanged in 1615 for refusing to recognize King James' religious superiority.

1979 Mother Teresa of the Society of the Missionaries of Charity was awarded the 1979 Nobel Peace Prize.

1981 Pope John Paul II and Patriarch Abuna Tekle Haimanot of the Ethiopian Orthodox Union Church met, the first such meeting in modern times.

OCTOBER 18

Feast day of St. Luke, "the beloved physician," a companion of St. Paul and the most literary of the New Testament writers.

707 John VII, pope from 705 to 707, died.

1405 Pius II, pope from 1458 to 1464, was born as Eneas Silvio de Piccolomini in Pienza, Italy.

1417 Gregory XII, pope from 1406 to 1415, died.

1470 Santes Pagninus, Italian Dominican Hebrew scholar, was born in Lucca, Italy; his Latin version of the Bible from the original languages helped later translators (died 1536).

1503 Pius III, pope for only 27 days, died

1646 St. Isaac Jogues, French Jesuit missionary to North American Indians, was murdered by Mohawk Indians near present-day Auriesville, N.Y.; canonized with six other North American martyrs.

1685 Louis XIV of France revoked the 87-old Edict of Nantes, thereby depriving French Protestants of all religious and civil liberty.

1794 John Bede Polding, first Catholic Bishop of Australia, was born in Birmingham, England; went to Australia in 1835, became the first Archbishop of Sydney (1842-77) (died 1877).

1796 Hosea Ballou, Universalist clergyman, was born in Guilford, Vt., nephew of Hosea Ballou (4/30/1771); a founder, president, Tufts College (1854-61) (died 1861).

1815 Daniel P. Kidder, Methodist educator, was born in South Pembroke, N.Y.; served as denominational secretary, Sunday School Union; editor, Sunday School literature (1844-91) (died 1891).

1857 Caleb F. Gates, Congregationalist clergyman and educator, was born in Chicago; president, Euphrates College, Harput, Turkey (1894-1902), Robert College, Constantinople (1903-32) (died 1946).

1882 Robert F. Paine, Methodist bishop (1846-82) who was a leader in organizing the Methodist Church South, died at 83; president, LaGrange College (Ala.) (1830-46).

1883 Rev. Arthur W. Poole was consecrated as the Anglican Bishop of Japan.

1931 Rev. Herbert W. Chilstrom, first bishop of the Evangelical Lutheran Church, was born in Litchfield, Minn.; the church was formed by the merger of Lutheran denominations.

1950 Bishop Makarios of Kition was named Archbishop of Cyprus.

OCTOBER 19

Feast day of St. Frideswide, English abbess who founded a convent (about 727) in Oxford, which eventually became Christ Church College; patroness of Oxford U.

Feast day of St. Paul of the Cross, founder of the Passionists.

615 St. Deusdedit I was elected pope. served until 618; reign marked by his concern for the clergy and the troubles between the Holy Roman Empire and the Lombards.

1187 Urban III, pope from 1185 to 1187, died.

1512 Martin Luther received his Doctor of Theology degree from the University of Wittenberg.

1562 St. Peter of Alcantara, Spanish Franciscan mystic, died at 63; founder of the Spanish Discalced Franciscans; canonized 1669; also observed as his feast day.

1605 Sir Thomas Browne, renowned English physician, was born in London; author of "Religio Medici," which combined deep religious feeling and skepticism (died 1682).

1625 The Catholic cathedral in Lima, Peru was dedicated.

1673 Benjamin Colman, first pastor of the newly-formed Brattle St. Church, Boston (1699-1747), was born; a leader of the New England revival (died 1747).

1720 John Woolman, Quaker leader, was born in Rancocas, N.J.; his inspired appeal (1758) led the Philadelphia annual meeting of Friends to abandon and condemn slave holdings; his journal was recognized as one of the classics of inner life (died 1772).

1779 Thomas C. Brownell, Episcopal prelate, was born in Westport, Mass.; Bishop of Connecticut (1819-52), presiding bishop (1852-65); first president, Washington (now Trinity) College, Hartford, Conn. (1823-31) (died 1865).

1840 John W. Chadwick, Unitarian clergyman, was born in Marblehead, Mass.; wrote a number of hymns (Eternal ruler of the ceaseless round) (died 1904).

1856 Sir George A. Smith, Scottish biblical scholar and geographer, was born in Calcutta; his "Historical Geography of the Holy Land" went through 25 editions; author (The Early Poetry of Israel, The Twelve Prophets) (died 1942).

1884 Clarence E. Pickett, executive secretary of the American Friends Service Committee (1929-50), was born in Cissna Park, Ill. (died 1965).

1975 The six-day summit conference of world religions opened in the Cathedral Church of St. John the Divine in New York City, sponsored by the Temple of Understanding, a nonprofit organization promoting communications among world religions.

OCTOBER 20

1122 Ralph, Norman monk and Archbishop of Canterbury (1114-22), died.

1632 Christopher Wren, English church architect, was born in East Knoyle, England; designed and rebuilt St. Paul's Cathedral (1675-1716) in London; built 52 churches in London (died 1723).

1670 A religious hospital was established in Montreal.

1802 Ernst W. Hengstenberg, Lutheran theologian and editor, was born in Frödenberg, Germany; professor of theology in Berlin (1828-69); editor for more than 40 years of a journal which championed Lutheran orthodoxy, opposed Bible criticism, and rationalism (died 1869).

1822 Thomas Hughes, author and hymn writer, was born in Uffington, England; wrote several popular novels (Tom Brown's School Days) and Anglican hymns (O God of truth, whose living word) (died 1896).

1874 Joseph H. Oldham, active in international missionary cooperation, was born in Bombay; organized the first conference of missionary educators and colonial administrators; author (Christianity and the Race Problem) (died 1969).

1939 Pope Pius XII issued the encyclical, "Summi pontificatus," appealing to mankind to restore to God His due place in the life of the world and to unite in the defense of natural law.

1962 The first session began on the Second Vatican Council, ended Dec. 8; resulted in issuance of a "Message to Humanity."

OCTOBER 21

Feast day of St. Hilarion (about 291-371), father of the Christian eremitic (reclusive) life in Palestine; introduced monasticism to Palestine.

Former feast day of St. Ursula, legendary leader of 11,000 virgins on a pilgrimage to Rome; believed to have been slain by the Huns when their ships landed in the Rhine; observance dropped in 1969.

686 Conon, a Thracian priest, was consecrated as pope, served until 687.

1187 Gregory VIII, born Alberto di Mora, became pope; died suddenly Dec. 17, while trying to reconcile differences between Pisa and Geneva.

1633 Thomas Hooker (1586-1647), English-born colonial religious leader, was named pastor of Newtown (Conn.) Congregational Church (1633-36); helped found Hartford (1636); active in Framing and having adopted the "Fundamental Orders," which long served Connecticut as its constitution; author (Survey of the Summe of Church Discipline).

1672 Lodovico A. Muratori, Italian historian, was born near Florence; discovered the treatise on Bible canon, now called the Muratorian fragment (1740) (died 1750).

1749 Tadsusz Brzozowski, Jesuit leader, was born in Malbork, Poland; was the first general of the restored Society of Jesus (1814-20) (died 1820).

1808 Samuel F. Smith, Baptist clergyman and hymn writer, was born in Boston; editorial secretary, American Baptist Missionary Union (1854-95); wrote the hymn, "The morning light is breaking" and the lyrics for "America" (died 1895).

1812 Thomas H. Vail, Episcopal prelate, was born in Richmond, Va.; the first Bishop of Kansas (1864-89) (died 1889).

1855 Howard H. Russell, Congregational clergyman, was born in Stillwater, Minn.; a founder, first general superintendent, Anti-Saloon League of America (1895-1903) (died 1946).

OCTOBER 22

1303 Blessed Benedict XI, born Niccole Boccasini, was elected pope, served until 1304; had been master general of the Dominican Order (1296-1303) and served Pope Boniface VIII in various peacemaking efforts.

1735 James Manning, Baptist clergyman and educator, was born near Elizabethtown, N.J.; first president, Rhode Island College (later Brown) (1765-91) (died 1791).

1746 A charter was obtained for the College of New Jersey (later Princeton) by Jonathan Dickinson, leading Presbyterian of his time and the first president of the college (1746-47).

1839 (Louis) Auguste Sabatier, French Protestant theologian, was born near Marseilles; a representative of liberalism in theology, he influenced the Modernist movement and sought to reconcile faith and science (died 1901).

1844 Date set for the second coming of Christ by William Miller; his followers in Hannibal, Mo. climbed the 230-ft. high Lovers Leap to await the end of the world.

1910 The Portuguese Government prohibited the teaching of religion in primary schools.

1967 The United States Conference on Church and Society opened its meeting in Detroit "to plan strategies which can be used to help to direct economic and social development for full opportunity in a technological age."

1980 The Vatican announced it was reviewing the 347-year old heresy conviction of Galileo, 17th Century astronomer who was condemned for proving that the earth revolved around the sun.

1988 The Soviet Government turned over the Vilnius Cathedral and 20,000 Lithuanians celebrated a joyous pre-dawn mass, their first in 30 years; the 14th Century cathedral was a center of Christianity in the Middle Ages.

OCTOBER 23

877 St. Ignatius of Constantinople (797-877), patriarch of Constantinople, died; served as patriarch 846-58 and 867-877; also observed as his feast day.

1456 St. Giovanni Capistrano, Franciscan friar, died of the plague at 70; served as vicar general of the Order several times; canonized 1724.

1790 Chauncey A. Goodrich, theologian and editor, was born in New Haven, Conn.; professor of rhetoric, Yale (1817-38); of pastoral theology, Yale Divinity School (1839-60); editor-in-chief, Webster dictionaries (1829-60) (died 1860).

1853 Wallace Buttrick, Baptist clergyman, was born in Potsdam, N.Y.; secretary (1902-17), executive officer (1917-23) of the General Education Board established by John D. Rockefeller to promote education (died 1926).

1871 Edgar J. Goodspeed, biblical scholar, was born in Quincy, Ill.; head of the New Testament Department, U. of Chicago (1915-37); helped prepare "Revised Standard of the New Testament" (died 1962).

1981 Jarl Wahlstrom of Finland was elected the world head of the Salvation Army at a meeting in London.

OCTOBER 24

Feast day in the Catholic Church of St. Proclus, patriarch of Constantinople (434 to about 447).

Former feast day of St. Raphael the Archangel.

1669 William Prynne, English Puritan pamphleteer, died at 69; wrote controversial pamphlets assailing Arminianism* and ceremonialism, attacked popular amusements; imprisoned for alleged aspersion upon Charles I; released (1640), served in Parliament (1648-50), expelled for his vehement opposition to Oliver Cromwell; published valuable compilations of constitutional history.

1776 Presbytery of Hanover petitioned the Virginia House of Burgesses to provide religious liberty and eliminate the taxes collected for the support of the Anglican Church.

1781 A dispatch from Gen. George Washington reporting the victory at Yorktown was read to Congress and the members went in procession to the Dutch Lutheran Church to give thanks.

1830 Charles H. Payne, secretary, Methodist Board of Education (1888-99), was born in Taunton, Mass. (died 1899).

1870 St. Anthony Claret, Archbishop of Santiage de Cuba, died at 63; founder of the Missionary Sons of the Immaculate Heart of Mary; canonized 1950; also observed as his feast day.

1894 Pope Leo XIII met with Eastern Orthodox patriarchs to consider the reunion of the two churches; partial agreement was reached Nov. 8.

1956 Rev. Margaret Ellen Towner became the first woman ordained in the Presbyterian Church in ceremonies held in Syracuse, N.Y.

1965 The Vatican announced that the controversial worker-priest movement would be relaunched in France.

OCTOBER 25

Feast day of Sts. Crispin and Crispinian, brothers and patron saints of shoemakers; they made shoes for the poor without charge; beheaded about 287 during the persecution of Diocletian.

625 Pope Boniface V died; had served since 619.

1180 John of Salisbury, a colleague of Thomas à Becket and Bishop of Chartres (1176-80), died at 65; a prolific theological writer, biographer (St. Anselm, Becket); his letters shed important light on his time.

1241 Celestine IV, born Godfrey di Castigione, was elected pope, the first to be elected in a conclave; served less than one month.

1514 William Elphinstone, Scottish bishop and educator, died; founder of Aberdeen U. (1494); partially responsible for introduction of printing into Scotland (1507) and had the Aberdeen Breviary printed.

1727 Charles Chauncy (1705-87), liberal leader, was installed as pastor of the First (Congregational) Church, Boston, where he served for 60 years.

1800 Jacques P. Migne, French Catholic priest and publisher, was born near Marseilles; published "Patrology" (22 volumes in Latin, 81 in Greek, 166 in Hebrew/Latin), a 171-volume theological encyclopedia, a 100-volume collection of sacred orations (died 1875).

1811 Carl F. W. Walther, Lutheran leader, was born in Langenschursdorff, Germany; co-founder, president of Concordia Theological Seminary (1854-87); president, Missouri Synod (1847-50,1864-78); author (The Proper Distinction Between Law and Gospel) (died 1887).

1812 Frederic L. Godet, Swiss reformer, was born in Neufchatel; a founder of the Evangelical Church of Neufchatel, independent of the state; served as professor on its theological staff (died 1900).

1867 The first American rabbinical college, Maimonides College, opened in Philadelphia; closed for lack of support in 1873; a second Maimonides College opened in New York City in 1927.

1882 Andre Jullien, dean of the Sacred Roman Rota, was born in Pelussin, France; elevated to cardinal 1958 (died 1964).

1884 Elvind Berggrav, Norwegian bishop and theologian, was born in Stavanger, Norway (died 1959).

1891 Charles E. Coughlin, controversial Catholic radio priest, was born in Hamilton, Canada; published a magazine, *Social Justice*, attacking the financial community and President Franklin Roosevelt; silenced by superiors but allowed to continue his pastoral duties (died 1979).

1960 Rev. Martin Luther King Jr., arrested during an Atlanta sit-in demonstration, was given a one month sentence in Decatur, Ga. court for violating parole previously granted on a traffic charge.

1970 Cuthbert Mayne, first Catholic seminary priest executed in England (1577), was canonized among 40 martyrs of England and Wales.

1978 The new Anglican cathedral in Liverpool, under construction for 74 years, was dedicated by Queen Elizabeth.

OCTOBER 26

Feast day of St. Evaristus, pope from about 96 to 106.

Feast day in the Orthodox Church of St. Demetrius, Bishop of Alexandria (189-231).

Feast day of Alfred the Great (849-899), king of Wessex; promoted ecclesiastical reform and the revival of learning; remembered as a Christian king who saved the country for Christianity.

664 St. Cedd (or Cedda), Bishop of the East Saxons, died of the plague; founded many churches and monasteries; sometimes considered the second Bishop of London; brother of St. Chad.

1818 Elizabeth P. Prentiss, author, was born in Portland, Me.; wrote a number of Presbyterian hymns (More love to Thee, O Christ) (died 1878).

1833 Edward Fitzgerald, Catholic prelate, was born in Limerick, Ireland; Bishop of Little Rock, Ark. (1866- 1907); one of two bishops who voted against the doctrine of papal infallibility at the 1870 Vatican Council (died 1907).

1905 George Flahiff, Canadian Catholic prelate, was born in Paris, Ontario; superior general, Congregation of Priests of St. Basil (Basilian Fathers) (1954-61); Archbishop of Winnipeg (1961-69), emeritus (1969-), elevated to cardinal 1969.

1910 John J. Krol, Archbishop of Philadelphia (1961-88), was born in Cleveland.

1966 The first World Congress on Evangelism opened in West Berlin with approximately 600 delegates from about 100 countries.

OCTOBER 27

Feast day in the Catholic Church of St. Frumentius, founder and first bishop of the Ethiopian Church (Fourth Century).

625 Honorius I was elected pope, served until 638; took great interest in church affairs of England; favored Monothelete* doctrine, condemned for this by the Council of Constantinople as a heretic, confirmed by Pope Leo II.

1489 Desidarius Erasmus, Catholic reformer and most renowned scholar of his age, was born in the Netherlands; translated the New Testament from Greek to Latin; author (Adages, Praise of Folly, biographies of various church fathers); paved the way for the Reformation, but his scholarly character prevented him from joining the Protestants, threw him back on church tradition as the safeguard of stability (died 1536).

1556 Michael Servetus, Spanish theologian and physician, was burned at the stake as a heretic for his anti-trinitarian views; renowned as the reputed discoverer of pulmonary circulation; arrested and tried by the Inquisition in Vienna; escaped, but apprehended, imprisoned at the request of Calvin.

1795 Samuel R. Hall, Congregational clergyman, was born in Croydon, N.H.; set up teachers' training school (1823), the first American normal school, at Concord, Vt.; author of numerous textbooks (died 1877).

1809 Lewis Edwards, Calvinistic Methodist clergyman, was born in Penllwynn, Wales; responsible for uniting North and South Wales Calvinistic Methodist associations; one of the outstanding educators of modern Wales (died 1887).

1814 John McClintock, Methodist theologian, educator, and editor, was born in Philadelphia;

probably did more to raise the intellectual level of American Methodism than anyone else; first president, Drew Theological Seminary (1867-70); co-editor, "Cyclopedia of Biblical, Theological and Ecclesiastical Literature" (died 1870).

1874 Sam Higginbottom, American Presbyterian missionary to India (1903-45), was born in Manchester, England (died 1958).

1877 Aleksei, patriarch of Russia and the Russian Orthodox Church, was born in Moscow (died 1970).

1882 Mary Josephine Rogers, founder of the Maryknoll Sisters, was born in Roxbury, Mass. (died 1955).

1889 The first Lithuanian church in America (St. Casimir's) was organized in Plymouth, Pa.

1902 The Independent Catholic Church in the Philippine Islands was formed.

OCTOBER 28

Feast day in the Orthodox Church of St. Firmilian, Bishop of Caesaria (about 230-268); president of first Antioch synod; ranked as one of the most eminent churchmen of his time in the East.

Feast day in the Catholic Church of St. Simon, one of the 12 apostles, and St. Jude, referred to in Scripture as "Judas, not Iscariot."

1061 Bishop Cadalus of Parma was elected antipope (Honorius II) by a group of German and Lombard bishops; his limited recognition was withdrawn May 31, 1064 by a council at Mantua.

1510 St. Francis Borgia, general of the Jesuits, was born in Gandia, Spain; third general of the Society of Jesus (1565-72), established many schools and colleges, helped found "Collegium Romanum;" canonized 1671 (died 1572).

1582 Gregory Martin, English translator of the Bible, died; leading member of a team translating the Bible from Latin Vulgate into English (the Douai) (1578-82).

1646 The first Protestant service for Indians was held by Rev. John East in Nonantum, Mass.

1659 Nicholas Brady, Anglican clergyman, was born in Bandon, Ireland; chaplain to William III, Mary, and Queen Anne; translated Virgil's "Aeneid" into blank verse; with Nahum Tate, he prepared a metrical version of the Psalms (died 1726).

1810 The first Catholic Bishop of Philadelphia, Michael Egan (1761-1814), was consecrated.

1817 Henry Harbaugh, German Reformed clergyman and hymn writer, was born near Waynesborough, Pa.; did more than anyone else to popularize the Mercersburg theology; among his hymns is "Jesus, I live to Thee" (died 1867)

1885 Charles F. Potter, Unitarian modernist clergyman, was born in Marlboro, Mass.; resigned from ministry to found the First Humanist Society of New York; founded the Euthanasia Society of America (1938) (died 1962).

1890 Thomas Tien, Archbishop of Peking, was born in Chang-tsui, China; first Oriental to be elevated to cardinal (died 1967).

1892 Antonio Maria Barbieri, first Uruguayan Catholic cardinal (1958), was born in Montevideo; founded the first major seminary in Uruguay, Archbishop of Uruguay (1940).

1956 Stefan Wyszynski, Catholic primate of Poland, was released by the Polish Government.

1958 John XXIII was elected pope, served until 1963; increased the College of Cardinals from 70 to 75, created 23 new cardinals, convoked the Second Vatican Council (died 1963).

1965 Pope Paul VI formally promulgated as Catholic teaching five documents embodying significant changes in the church's policies and structure.

1966 Iakov I. Zhidkov, president of the All Soviet Union of Evangelical Christian Baptists, died in Moscow at about 82.

1969 A Catholic synod of bishops ended after taking steps to decentralize the church's governing authority.

OCTOBER 29

1038 Aethelnoth, Archbishop of Canterbury (1020-1038), died.

1562 George Abbot, Archbishop of Canterbury (1611-27), was born in Guilford; one of the translators of the New Testament in the King James Version; a persistent advocate of Protestant causes in foreign policy, encouraged Puritan elements in the House of Commons (died 1633).

1591 Innocent IX was elected pope, served only until Dec. 30; in short reign, he initiated reforms in the Vatican Secretariat and restored the German congregation.

1650 David Calderwood, Scottish Presbyterian clergyman and historian of the Church of Scotland, died at 75; he was banished for refusing to surrender signatures to a remonstrance; defended Presbyterianism in "The Altar of Damascus."

1662 William Pynchon, English colonist and religious writer, died at 72; a founder of Springfield, Mass.; returned to England (1652) after church leaders denounced him as a heretic for his tract, "The Meritorious Price of Our Redemption."

1666 Edmund Calamy, English Presbyterian leader, died at 66; one of the principal authors of "Smectymnuus," which became the platform for Presbyterians; opposed execution of Charles I.

1768 Joseph Grigg, Presbyterian clergyman, died at about 48; wrote numerous hymns (Jesus, and can it ever be; Behold a stranger at the door).

1837 Abraham Kuyper, Dutch theologian, was born near Rotterdam; foremost publicist of Protestant orthodoxy in the Netherlands; formed Free Reformed Church (1886); active in national government and championed social reform (died 1920).

1841 Catholic Bishop John J. Hughes urged New York State to support parochial schools; urged Catholics to use their votes to achieve this; move led to creation of independent Catholic schools, arousing anger and fear which led to some riots and an attack on Bishop Hughes' home in 1842.

1884 Several hundred clergymen met with James G. Blaine, offering their support in his presidential race with Grover Cleveland; Rev. Samuel D. Burchard, spokesman for the group, said: "We are Republicans and don't propose to leave our party and identify ourselves with the party whose antecedents are rum, Romanism, and rebellion;" phrase later attributed to Blaine and said to have cost him the election.

1894 The Hungarian legislature passed bills granting freedom of religious worship and recognizing the Jewish religion; approved by the Emperor.

1966 Pope Paul VI reaffirmed the traditional Catholic teaching on birth control and postponed a ruling on maintenance or modification of the ban on artificial contraception.

1972 Pope Paul VI beatified the late M. Rua, head of the Salesian Order (1888-1910).

OCTOBER 30

701 John VI, a Greek, was named pope, served until 705; decided a long standing dispute between St. Wilfrid of York and the See of Canterbury in the latter's favor.

1706 Samuel Mather, Congregational clergyman, was born in Boston, son of Cotton Mather; pastor of Second Church, Boston (1732-41), dismissed; formed new congregation, which he served from 1741 until his death in 1785.

1738 The Gray Nunnery (Gray Nuns of Montreal) was founded by Marie M. d'Youville (1701-71).

1768 Philip Embury, pioneer American Methodist, preached the dedicatory sermon to the first American Methodist congregation on the site of the present John St. Church, New York City; Embury helped build the 42 x 60 ft. stone structure.

1789 Hiram Bingham, missionary to Hawaii, was born in Bennington, Vt.; reduced Hawaiian language to writing; helped translate Bible into Hawaiian (died 1869).

1795 Charles Brooks, Unitarian clergyman, was born in Medford, Mass.; publisher of the Family Prayer Book, which went through 18 editions (died 1872).

1807 Christopher Wordsworth, Anglican prelate, was born in London; Bishop of Lincoln (1869-85); hymn writer (Gracious Spirit, Holy Ghost; O day of rest and gladness; O lord of heaven and earth and sea) (died 1885).

1825 Adelaide A. Procter, English hymn writer, was born in London; wrote numerous hymns (My God, I thank Thee, who has made; The shadows of the evening hour) (died 1864).

1832 Charles P. McIlvaine (1799-1873) was consecrated as Episcopal Bishop of Ohio; served until 1873.

1853 James R. Bayley was consecrated as the first Catholic Bishop of Newark; served until 1872.

1883 Bob (Robert R.) Jones, American evangelist, was born in Dale County, Ala.; founder, Bob Jones College in Lynn Haven, Fla. (1927), later moved to Cleveland, Tenn., then Greenville, S.C. (died 1968).

1909 Franciscan Friars of the Atonement, founded in the Anglican Church in 1899 by Paul J. Francis, were received into the Catholic Church.

OCTOBER 31

1439 Council of Basel, which had deposed Pope Eugene IV in June 1438, elected Felix V, but he was not generally recognized and resigned in 1449.

1517 Martin Luther, according to legend, fastened on the door of All Saints Church in Wittenberg the 95 Theses "for the purpose of eliciting truth" about indulgences — payments for absolution of sins; the act is considered the start of the Reformation; as a fact, he did send them to his archbishop, Albrecht of Mainz.

1538 Caesar Baronius, Italian historian and cardinal, was born near Rome; called the "father of ecclesiastical history;" superior of the Oratory (1593-97), librarian of the Vatican (1597-1607); elevated to cardinal 1596 (died 1607).

1556 Johannes Sleidanus, German historian, died at 50; Protestant chronicler of the Reformation; his work remained basic until the archives were opened in 19th Century.

1705 Clement XIV, pope from 1769 to 1774, was born as Giovanni Vincenzo Ganganelli near Rimini, Italy.

1801 Theodore D. Woolsey, Congregational theologian and educator, was born in New York City; with Yale U. (1831-71) - professor of Greek (1831-46), president (1846-71); chairman, New Testament group, American Bible Revision Committee (1871-81) (died 1889).

1809 George Burgess, Episcopal prelate, was born in Providence, R.I., brother of Alexander (see below); first Bishop of Maine (1847-66) (died 1866).

1819 Alexander Burgess, Episcopal prelate, was born in Providence, R.I., brother of George (see above); first Bishop of Quincy, Ill. (1878-1901) (died 1901).

1825 Charles M. A. Lavigerie, French Catholic prelate, was born in Bayonne; Archbishop of Algiers (1867-92), primate of Africa (1885-92); founder (1874) of the Order of White Fathers (Peres Blancs); opposed African slave trade and founded (1888) the Anti-Slavery Society (died 1892).

1829 John of Kronstadt (Ivan Ilyich Sergeev), "the great shepherd of Russia," was born near Archangel; founded (1874) brotherhood for social welfare work; revered by some Orthodox Christians as a saint, but not canonized (died 1909).

1864 Cosmo Gordon Lang, Archbishop of Canterbury (1928-42), was born in Aberdeen, Scotland; Archbishop of York (1908- 28); active in social work in industrial areas (died 1945).

1869 Phillips Brooks was ordained as minister of Trinity (Episcopal) Church, Boston; original building was destroyed by fire in 1872, replaced by Copley Square edifice in 1877; served until 1891.

1879 Wesleyan Theological College of Montreal was chartered.

1904 Henry Moeller, coadjutor bishop, was consecrated as Archbishop of Cincinnati, served until 1925.

1917 Tikhon (1865-1925), born Vasili Ivanovich Bolyavin, was named patriarch of the revived Church of Russia, the first patriarch since 1700; had served as metropolitan of Moscow; took determined stand against Bolsheviks, denouncing their cruelty, suppression of liberty, blasphemy, and sacrilege; imprisoned (1917-23), released after worldwide protests; retired to a monastery.

1956 Joseph Mindszenty, primate of Hungary, was freed from his prison by regular troops of the national Hungarian army.

1960 Percy Crawford, American evangelist who founded the Young People's Church of the Air, died at about 58.

1971 The Coptic Church of Egypt selected Bishop Shemuda to become patriarch of the church.

1980 Participants in the world synod of bishops gave Pope John Paul II a 14-point proposal on the rights of families and suggested it be submitted to the United Nations as a basis for an international charter of such rights.

1982 Pope John Paul II proclaimed the French settler of colonial Montreal, Marguerite Bourgeoys, and a 17th Century woman, Jeanne Delanoue, saints.

NOVEMBER 1

Festival of All Saints, commemorating all saints of the church, known and unknown, observed in the Catholic and Anglican churches.

1503 Julius II, born Giuliano Rovere, was elected pope, served until 1513; sought to extend papal authority and territory; convened Fifth Lateran Council; began rebuilding St. Peter's Basilica; issued a bull to reform pontifical elections; patronized arts and aided Raphael, Michelangelo, etc.; created the Swiss Guard; reign considered on of the most brilliant of the Renaissance era.

1678 William Coddington, a founder of Newport, R.I. (1639) and a governor of Rhode Island, died; left Massachusetts in protest to the religious persecution of Anne Hutchinson.

1757 (Johann) Georg Rapp, founder of the Harmonites sect and Harmony communities, was born near Stuttgart, Germany; the communities in Pennsylvania and Indiana were successful as religious communities; all property was held in common but the rule of celibacy finally led to their extinction (died 1847).

1788 The Religious and Literary Institution was opened in Windsor, Nova Scotia; eventually became King's College.

1793 Dr. Jacob Mountain, the first Anglican Bishop of Canada, arrived in Quebec.

1808 John Taylor, Mormon leader, was born in Milnthorpe, England; one of the original 12 Mormon apostles, president of the Mormon Church (1880-87) (died 1887).

1820 Erastus O. Haven, Methodist prelate and educator, was born in Boston; editor, *Zion's Herald*, a Methodist weekly (1856-63); president, U. of Michigan (1863-69), Northwestern U. (1869-72); chancellor, Syracuse U. (1874-80); bishop (1880-81) (died 1881).

1825 William Whiting, Anglican hymn writer, was born in London; among his hymns was "Eternal Father, strong to save" (died 1878).

1827 Morgan Dix, Episcopal clergyman, was born in New York City; rector of Trinity Church, New York City (1862-1908) (died 1908).

1833 Sisters of the Blessed Virgin Mary were founded by Mary Francis Clarke in Philadelphia.

1880 Sholem Asch, Jewish novelist, was born in Kutno, Poland; many of his works sought to bring together Judaism and Christianity through emphasis on their historical and theological connections (The Apostle, The Nazarene, The Prophet, Mary) (died 1957).

1885 Pope Leo XIII issued the encyclical, "Immortale Dei," on the Christian constitution of states; asserted both the legitimate mutual autonomy of church and state and the right of the church to freedom of action unhampered by the state.

1903 Fire in the Vatican damaged some rooms above the library.

1908 A papal decree recognized the Roman Curia.

1925 Monsignor Miron Cristea was enthroned as the first patriarch of the Orthodox Church in Rumania.

1948 Athenagoras I was elected the 268th patriarch of the Greek Orthodox Church.

1950 Pope Pius XII issued the apostolic constitution, "Munificetissimus deus," defining the doctrine of the Assumption of the Blessed Virgin Mary.

1970 The Church of Pakistan was formed by the union of Anglican, Methodist, Presbyterian, and Lutheran bodies and headed by a moderator.

1978 Wesley's Chapel in England, after a $2 million restoration, was reopened with festive services attended by Queen Elizabeth.

NOVEMBER 2

All Souls Day, the Catholic commemoration of all the faithful departed; observed Nov. 3 if Nov. 2 is on Sunday.

676 Donus (or Domnus), a Roman native, was consecrated as pope, served until 678.

1389 Boniface IX, born Pietro Tomacelli, was named pope, served until 1404; regained control of the Papal States and Rome.

1600 Richard Hooker, Anglican theologian, died at 46; was the greatest exponent of the Anglican Church's appeal to reason, Scripture, and tradition; author (The Laws of Ecclesiastical Polity).

1610 Richard Bancroft, Archbishop of Canterbury (1604-10), died at 66; chief overseer of the translation into English of the King James Version of the Bible; a stern opponent, persecutor of Puritans; assisted in re-establishing the episcopacy in Scotland.

1773 Stephen Grellet, Quaker missionary and philanthropist, was born in Limoges, France; traveled through Europe, the United States, and Canada at his own expense to report on conditions in prisons and poorhouses; led to many reforms (died 1855).

1789 All property of the French clergy was confiscated by Revolution leaders.

1790 Jacob R. Hardenburgh, Dutch Reformed clergyman, died at 64; a founder, Queens (now Rutgers) College (1766), first president (1786-90).

1809 A communion plate, a gift of the King, for the Cathedral (Metropolitan Church) in Quebec, was received.

1827 Paul Anton de La Garde, German Orientalist, was born in Göttingen; author of numerous books on the Bible and church fathers, and editor and translator of Greek, Chaldean, Arabic, Syriac*, and Coptic texts (died 1891).

1830 The Methodist Protestant Church was formed in Baltimore by 114 delegates who were unable to work out reforms within the Methodist Episcopal Church; the protestants insisted on the right of a layman to vote on any question in any church meeting and the administration of the church without bishops.

1848 Alfred G. Edwards, first Archbishop of Wales (1920-34), was born in Llanymawddy, Wales; Bishop of St. Asaph (1889-1934); wrote on Welsh church history (died 1937).

1877 Aga Khan III, spiritual head of the Ismailis and a direct descendant of the prophet Mohammed, was born in Karachi, India (died 1957).

1883 Jean Marie R. Villeneuve, Canadian Catholic prelate, was born in Montreal; Archbishop of Quebec (1931-47), elevated to cardinal 1933 (died 1947).

1965 Norman R. Morrison, a Friend from Baltimore, burned himself to death near the Pentagon in Washington, D.C. "to express his concern over the great loss of life and human suffering caused by the (Vietnam) war."

1979 The United Methodist Church Judicial Council ruled that Rev. Paul Abels, an avowed homosexual, could remain as pastor of the Washington Square Church, New York City; decision did not deal with the question of whether avowed homosexuals should be permitted to become ministers.

NOVEMBER 3

Feast day of St. Hubert, bishop and patron saint of Belgium.

Feast day of St. Winifred, Welsh martyr (about 650); according to legend, she was beheaded and her head lodged at the foot of a hill, where a spring gushed forth, the famous holy well in Flintshire.

1148 St. Malachy, Archbishop of Armagh (1132-36), died; papal legate in Ireland; one of the foremost Irish figures in the Middle Ages; canonized 1199; also observed as his feast day.

1585 Cornelis Otto Jansen, leader of a religious movement, was born in Acquoi, Netherlands; head of the Dutch theological college of St. Pulcheria, Louvain (1617-36); Bishop of Ypres (1636-38) and one of the fathers of Jansenism, a Catholic religious movement which maintained that the teachings of St. Augustine on grace, free will, and predestination was opposed to the teaching of the Jesuits; condemned by Pope Urban VIII (1642) (died 1638).

1631 Rev. John Eliot, the first American Protestant clergyman dedicated to the religious conversion of Indians, arrived in Boston from England; started as a teacher in Roxbury, began preaching to the Indians in 1646.

1639 St. Martin de Porres, Peruvian patron of social justice, died; canonized 1962.

1723 Samuel Davies, famed colonial preacher and religious leader, was born in New Castle

County, Del.; a founder of the Hanover Presbytery, the first in Virginia (1755); president, College of New Jersey (later Princeton) (1759-61), after he had gone to England to raise funds for the school (died 1761).

1784 Thomas Coke was named superintendent of American Methodists by John Wesley; arrived in New York from England accompanied by Richard Whatcoat and Thomas Vasey to organize the church.

1946 Archbishop of Canterbury Geoffrey F. Fisher in a sermon at Cambridge pleaded for free, unfettered exchange of life and worship and sacraments between the churches.

1962 Mother Mary Agnes, founder of the Order of Franciscan Nuns of the Most Blessed Sacrament and the St. Paul Shrine of Perpetual Adoration, died at 92.

NOVEMBER 4

Feast of St. Charles Borromeo, Archbishop of Milan (1560-84), led in implementing reforms of the Council of Trent; founder, Order of Oblates of St. Ambrose (1578); canonized 1610.

1184 Pope Lucius III ordered all archbishops and bishops to inspect suspected parishes once or twice a year, force members to reveal under oath secret or open heresy; accused were required to purge themselves under oath or face appropriate secular punishment.

1577 Father Joseph (Francois le Clerc du Tremblay), Capuchin mystic and religious reformer, was born in France; served as Richelieu's foreign minister (died 1638).

1646 A severe heresy law enacted in Massachusetts made death the punishment for anyone persisting in denying that the Holy Scriptures were the word of God "or not to be attended to by illuminated Christians."

1680 Joseph Glanvill, English clergyman, died at 44; attacked Scholastic philosophy in "The Vanity of Dogmatizing" and defended the preexistence of souls and belief in witchcraft.

1740 Augustus M. Toplady, English Calvinist and hymnist, was born in Farnham; champion of doctrinal Calvinism and a bitter foe of Wesley and Methodism; wrote many hymns (Rock of ages; Deathless principle, arise; If on a quieter sea) (died 1778).

1771 James Montgomery, British poet and journalist, was born in Irvine, England; best known for several popular hymns (Hail to the Lord's anointed; Forever with the Lord; Prayer is the soul's sincere desire) (died 1854).

1784 Isaac V. Brown, Presbyterian clergyman and educator, was born in Duckemin, N.J.; founder, principal, Lawrenceville (N.J.) Academy (1810-33); a founder, American Colonization Society; an original member, American Bible Society (died 1861).

1814 Stuart Robinson, Presbyterian clergyman who was a leader in the Southern Presbyterian church, was born in Tyrone County, Ireland; expelled from 1866 general conference in St. Louis for protesting political deliverances; in 1869, he induced the Kentucky Synod to united with the Southern Presbyterians (died 1881).

1891 The New York Presbytery dismissed charge of heresy against Dr. Charles A. Briggs; the case was referred Nov. 16 to the church's General Assembly.

1956 The Hungarian cardinal, Joszef Mindszenty, was given asylum in the American legation in Budapest.

1957 Shoghi Effendi, Bahai religious leader, died in Jordan at 61.

1958 John XXIII was crowned as the 262nd pope in ceremonies at St. Peter's in Rome.

1978 Rev. M. William Howard Jr., 32, was elected president of the National Council of Churches; the youngest person ever elected to the post.

NOVEMBER 5

Feast day of St. Martin de Torres, Peruvian national patron of social justice; canonized 1962.

Feast day in the Catholic Church of St. Elizabeth, wife of the priest Zacharias, and the mother of St. John the Baptist.

1359 Gregorius Palamas, Greek mystic and prelate, died at 63; Archbishop of Thessalonike (1347-59); incorporated mysticism into Greek theology.

1414 The Council of Constance began in Baden, Germany; designed to eliminate the great schism of the West, to reform the church, to study the teachings of John Wycliffe and Jan Hus; the schism was healed by deposing the three claimants - John XXIII (deposed 5/29/1415), Gregory XII (abdicated 7/4/1415), and Benedict XIII (deposed 7/26/1417)- and electing Odo Colonna, who became Martin V as the new pope, bound to reform the church; condemned the teachings of Wycliffe and Hus, declaring them obstinate heretics (7/6/1415).

1549 Philippe de Mornay (Duplessis-Mornay), Huguenot leader, was born in Buhy, France; escaped St. Bartholomew Day Massacre, fled to England; became known as the "Huguenot Pope" because of his influence with Henry of Navarre; secured enactment of the Edict of Nantes (1598) (died 1623).

1604 Thomas Shepard, Puritan clergyman, was born in Towcaster, England; came to America (1635), becoming pastor in Cambridge; his diary is a vivid record of colonial life (died 1649).

1727 Gideon Hawley, missionary to the Indians, was born in Stratfield, Conn.; ran a mission in Mashpee, Mass. (1758-1807) (died 1807).

1970 The Vatican issued instructions ending experimentation with the Catholic liturgy.

1982 A Carnegie Corporation study found that churches are the largest suppliers of day-care for American families, primarily poor families.

NOVEMBER 6

1003 John XVII, pope from June 13, died.

1032 John XIX, a brother of Pope Benedict VIII and pope from 1024 to 1032, died.

1406 Innocent VII, pope from 1404 to 1406, died.

1789 The first American Catholic diocese was created in Baltimore by Pope Pius VI.

1832 Joseph Smith, Mormon leader, was born in Kirtland, Ohio, son of Joseph Smith, Mormon Church founder; president, Reorganized Latter Day Saints Church, a non-polygamous offshoot of the original Mormon Church (1860-1914) (died 1914).

1836 Francis E. Abbott, Unitarian clergyman, was born in Boston; founder of Free Religious Association, which he said must replace "God in Christ" with "God in Humanity;" also founded the weekly, *Index* (died 1903).

1846 Caspar R. Gregory, German biblical scholar, was born in Philadelphia; taught in Leipzig (1889-1914); German officer in World War I, killed in Allied bombing in 1917.

1890 Henry K. Sherrill, Episcopal prelate, was born in Brooklyn, N.Y.; Bishop of Massachusetts (1930-47), presiding bishop (1947-50); president, National Council of Churches (1950-53) (died 1980).

NOVEMBER 7

680 Third Council of Constantinople opened with Pope Agatho presiding; continued until Sep 16, 681; accepted a document of faith which taught that two wills and two energies in Christ, while inseparable, are distinct.

739 St. Willibrod, English missionary to Friesland and Denmark and the "apostle of the Frisians" died at 81; also observed as his feast day.

1225 St. Engelbert I, Archbishop of Cologne (1216-25), was martyred; re-established law and order, improve the life of his people; also observed as his feast day.

1472 Lorenzo Compeggio, Italian cardinal, was born in Milan; papal legate to Germany, sent to reform the abuse of indulgences, but failed because of Luther and the Peasants' War; sent to England to judge the validity of Henry VIII's marriage to Catherine of Aragon, diplomatically referred matter to Rome; elevated to cardinal 1517 (died 1539).

1637 Anne Hutchinson was sentenced to banishment by the General Court of Massachusetts for her religious beliefs; allowed to remain until March.

1763 Benedict J. Flaget, Catholic prelate, was born in Contournant, France; first bishop of old Northwest (Kentucky to the Great Lakes, Alleghenies to the Mississippi) (1810-50); called the "Bishop of the Wilderness;" founder, Sisters of Loretto and the Sisters of Charity of Nazareth (died 1850).

1819 Robert Payne Smith, English Orientalist and theologian, was born near Gloucester; published Syriac* dictionary; dean of Canterbury (1870-95); member of the Old Testament revision committee (1870-85) (died 1895).

1832 Thomas D. Talmage, Dutch Reformed clergyman, was born in Bound Brook, N.J.; served in Brooklyn (1869-94) and Washington, D.C. (1894-99); editor, *Christian Herald* (1890-1902) (died 1902).

1862 Herbert Welch, senior bishop of United Methodist Church (1916-68), was born in New York City; president, Ohio Wesleyan (1905-16); resident bishop, Japan and Korea (1916-28), Pittsburgh (1928-32), Shanghai and Boston; overseas chairman, Methodist Committee for Overseas Relief (1941-49) (died 1968).

1883 Valerio Valeri, prefect of the Vatican's Sacred Congregation of the Religious, was born in Santa Fiora, Italy; elevated to cardinal 1953 (died 1963).

1906 Eugene Carson Blake, Presbyterian clergyman, was born in St. Louis; stated clerk, General Assembly of Presbyterian Churches (1951-58); president, National Council of Churches (1954-57); clerk, United Presbyterian Church of the USA (1951-66); general secretary, World Council of Churches (1966-72) (died 1985).

1918 Billy (William F.) Graham, evangelist, was born in Charlotte, N.C.; touring worldwide since 1949.

NOVEMBER 8

Feast day in the Orthodox Church of St. Michael the Archangel.

618 St. Deusdedit I (sometimes Adeodatus I), pope from 615 to 618, died; also observed as his feast day.

1308 John Duns Scotus, called Doctor Subtilis, the greatest medieval British theologian and philosopher, died at about 43; considered the leader of the Franciscan school of philosophy and theology; upholder of the separability and independence of the rational soul from the body; provoked long controversy between Scotists (which he founded) and the Thomists (followers of St. Thomas Aquinas); he argued that faith upon which theology rests is not speculative but an act of will; his system, accepted by the Franciscans as their doctrinal basis, exercised a profound influence during the Middle Ages.

1517 Francisco Jimenez de Cisneros, Spanish cardinal and theologian, died at 81; Archbishop of Toledo, he worked to convert the Moors to Catholicism, using many methods including the burning of Arabic books; founded the U. of Alcala (1500), first major Spanish intellectual center; oversaw the first critical edition of the Bible, the Complutensian Polyglot Bible.

1526 Hieronymus Emser, most indefatigable literary opponent of Martin Luther, died at 49; controversy became one-sided when Luther stopped answering attacks.

1541 Paul Eber, German theologian and reformer, was born; a disciple and secretary of Philipp Melancthon, then became a follower of Luther; wrote a revision of the Old Testament in the Wittenberg-German-Latin edition of the Bible (died 1569).

1675 Andreas Hammerschmidt, Bohemian composer, died at 63; made important contributions to Lutheran music; most of the chorale tunes in the Lutheran service are taken from his works.

1844 Knox College in Toronto, a Presbyterian theological seminary, opened.

1846 William R. Smith, Scottish Semitic scholar and encyclopedist, was born near Aberdeen; controversial ideas on biblical scholarship cost him his professorship at Free Church College, Aberdeen; studies on marriage and religion in the Middle East were influential in the fields of sociology and comparative religion; co-editor, Encyclopedia Brittanica (1880-87), editor-in-chief (1887-88) (died 1894).

1869 The First Vatican Council began, more than 300 years following the last previous council

(Trent); called by Pope Pius IX to discover the necessary remedies against the many evils which oppress the church;" Council issued some dogmatic decrees, a definition of papal primacy and jurisdiction, and a decree on the pope's gift of infallibility, limiting it to occasions when the pope spoke as pastor of the universal church.

1869 Joseph F. Rutherford, religious leader, was born in Booneville, Mo.; president, Jehovah's Witnesses (1916-42) (called Russellites until 1925); imprisoned (1917-19) for counseling people to be conscientious objectors rather than soldiers (died 1942).

1897 Dorothy Day, American Catholic social activist, was born in Brooklyn, N.Y.; co-founder, *Catholic Worker*, a monthly publicizing Catholic social programs (1933), opened houses of hospitality for the hungry and homeless (died 1980).

1978 The Church of England voted 272-246 not to carry through with its decision in principle made three years earlier to allow women to become priests and members of the church hierarchy.

1981 A Vatican commission completed 18 years work on new canon laws, replacing those published in 1917.

NOVEMBER 9

1522 Martin Chemnitz, German Lutheran theologian, was born near Berlin; one of the main influences in consolidating Lutheran doctrine and practice following Luther's death (died 1586).

1606 Hermann Conring, German scientist and physician, was born; devoted much time and writing to prove that the Protestant Church was entitled to existence as part of the universal church (died 1681).

1732 Redemptorists (Congregation of the Most Holy Redeemer) was founded by St. Alfonso Maria de Liguori in Scala, Italy; congregation was approved 1749.

1799 Asa Mahan, Congregational clergyman and educator, was born in Verona, N.Y.; first president, Oberlin (Ohio) College (1835-50); president, Adrian (Mich.) College (1860-71) (died 1889).

1868 Alfred Bertholet, noted Swiss biblical scholar, was born in Basel; wrote commentaries on various Old Testament books, a dictionary of religions (died 1951).

1884 Christopher M. Chavasse, Anglican Bishop of Rochester, England (1940-62), was born in Oxford; chairman of the commission which prepared the evangelistic report, "Towards the Conversion of England" (died 1962).

1966 The Vatican announced that the pope had authorized the Secretariat for Promoting Christian Unity to work with all other Christians in a common Bible project.

1978 Pope John Paul II upheld the mandatory celibacy of priests.

1982 Pope John Paul II concluded his visit to Spain, the first papal visit to that country.

NOVEMBER 10

461 St. Leo I (the Great), pope from 440 to 461, died.

627 St. Justus, fourth Archbishop of Canterbury (624-627), died; was sent to England with Mellitus (Apr. 24, 624) and others in 601; also observed as his feast day.

1241 Pope Celestine IV died after serving only one month.

1483 Martin Luther, a leading figure of the Protestant Reformation, was born in Eisleben, Germany; he led the fight against the current practices in the church and refused direction of the church to recant; therefore, he was excommunicated; also wrote several well-known hymns (A mighty fortress is our God; Out of the depths I cry to Thee) (died 1546).

1549 Paul III, pope from 1534 to 1549, died at 81.

1755 Aaron Bancroft, Massachusetts church leader, was born in Reading, Mass.; a leader of central Massachusetts churches from Puritanism to Unitarianism; a founder, first president,

American Unitarian Association (1825-36) (died 1839).

1809 David Einhorn, a Reform Judaism leader, was born in Bavaria; rabbi, Congregation Adath Jeshurem (which became Beth-El), New York City (1866-79) (died 1879).

1823 William G. McCloskey, Catholic prelate, was born in Brooklyn, N.Y.; first rector, American College in Rome (1859-68); Bishop of Louisville, Ky. (1868-1909) (died 1909).

1828 Lott Cary, Baptist missionary, died in an explosion in Liberia; an African Baptist preacher, he organized the Richmond African Missionary Society; organized first Baptist church in Liberia (1821).

1852 Henry Van Dyke, Presbyterian author and poet, was born in Germantown, Pa.; remembered for hymns, "Joyful, joyful, we adore Thee" and "Jesus, Thou divine companion" (died 1933).

1854 Walter R. Lambuth (Lambutti), Methodist South bishop and missionary, was born in Shanghai; served with father in China and Japan, founded mission on the Congo; general secretary, Board of Missions; bishop (1910-21) (died 1921).

1857 Walter S. Pratt, Congregational musician and educator, was born in Philadelphia; professor of music and hymnology, Hartford Theological Seminary (1882-1917), professor of public worship (1917-25); edited various hymn collections (died 1939).

1859 Isidore Singer, editor, was born in Weisskirchen, Austria; came to the United States (1895); managing editor of Jewish Encyclopedia (1901-05); author (La Question Juive, Christ or God) (died 1939).

1870 A decree was issued in France for melting some church bells to make cannon needed in Franco-Prussian War.

1891 Harry T. Stock, Congregational Christian Church official, was born in Springfield, Ill.; general secretary, Division of Education, Board of Home Missions (1938-58) (died 1958).

1979 The Church of England modernized its 300-year old Book of Common Prayer.

NOVEMBER 11

397 St. Martin, Bishop of Tours (372-397), died; missionary and father of monasticism in Gaul; founder of Abbey of Marmoutier; regarded as patron of publicans or innkeepers and a patron saint of France; also observed as his feast day in the Catholic Church.

537 St. Silverius, pope from 536 to 537, was exiled, forced to resign; died a short time later.

1215 Pope Innocent III convoked the Fourth Lateran Council; different from its predecessors in that the 1400 attendants were selected and the composition was broadened; various doctrinal and reforming decrees were enacted and the Council is considered as one of the most important held; ended Nov. 30.

1417 Martin V, born Otonne Colonna, was unanimously elected pope at the Council of Constance; served until 1431; elected at the Council after the deposition of Benedict XIII, Gregory XII, and John XXIII; three years after his election, he entered Rome and restored its churches and public buildings; greatly strengthened papal power, brought peace to the papacy, ending the Western schism.

1491 Martin Ducer, Protestant reformer, was born in Germany; best known for his peacemaking efforts between conflicting reform groups (died 1551).

1561 Hans Tausen, protagonist of the Danish Reformation, died at 67; called the "Danish Luther;" Protestant bishop in Ribe (1542-61); translated the Pentateuch* into Danish.

1571 The Inquisition was established in Mexico; the first great auto da fé took place in Mexico City (Feb 28, 1574) with 63 persons punished, five of them burned.

1647 Johann W. Baier, Lutheran theologian, was born in Nuremberg; left name in theology by his dogmatic compendium, which still preserves the early Protestant traditions among High Lutherans.

1679 Firmin Abauzit, Reformed scholar, was born in Uzer, France; one of the most learned men of his time; Isaac Newton acknowledged debt to him for some of his mathematical work; translated New Testament into French.

1764 Baroness Barbara J. von Krüdener, Russian mystic and author, was born in Riga; led active social life throughout Europe as ambassador, then (1804) was converted to the teachings of Moravians and was influenced by chiliasts* and Pietists; devoted self to preaching and prophesying, helped found the Holy Alliance* (died 1824).

1778 Anne Steele, Baptist hymn writer, died at 62; remembered for "Father of mercies, in Thy word."

1789 William Meade, Episcopal Bishop of Virginia (1841-62), was born in Millwood, Va. (died 1862).

1889 The first congress of American Catholic laity was held in Baltimore, Md.

1891 Walter W. Van Kirk, Methodist clergyman and radio commentator, was born in Cleveland; secretary, Department of international Justice and Goodwill, Federal Council of Churches of Christ (1925-50); executive director, Department of International Affairs, Federal Council (1950-56) (died 1956).

1898 Charles T. Leber, Presbyterian executive, was born in Baltimore; general secretary, Commission on Ecumenical Mission and Relations, United Presbyterian Church of the USA (died 1959).

1966 A merger vote was approved to join in 1968 the Methodist Church with its 10 million members and the Evangelical United Brethren Church with 750,000 members to form the United Methodist Church, the largest American Protestant church.

1977 The Church of England approved a new version of the Lord's Prayer that puts it in modern English.

1979 Rev. Archimendrite Mark Fosberg was consecrated bishop of the Albanian Archdiocese in America at services in St. George Cathedral, Boston.

1984 A committee of Catholic bishops in a pastoral letter called for sweeping economic changes to aid the poor, stating that the level of inequality between the wealthy and the poor was "morally unacceptable."

1985 The Mormon Church elected Ezra Taft Benson, 80, as president, succeeding Spencer Kimball.

1987 The Virginia Baptist General Association turned back a fundamentalist effort to take over the organization by electing Rev. Neal T. Jones as president, reaffirming its belief in separation of church and state and the independence of congregations within the denomination.

NOVEMBER 12

Feast day in the Orthodox Church of St. Martin, a patron saint of France; a missionary and father of monasticism in France.

Former feast day in Catholic Church of St. Martin I, pope from 649 to 655; now observed April 13.

607 Pope Boniface III died after serving only 11 months.

1555 Stephen Gardiner, English Bishop of Winchester (1531-51) and lord chancellor, died at 60; represented Henry VIII at papal court trying to get approval of the divorce from Catherine of Aragon; out of favor during Edward VI's reign, imprisoned in the Tower of London (1548-53); named lord chancellor to Queen Mary in 1553; regarded as the chief opponent in England of the Reformation and actively supported persecution of Protestants.

1808 Ray Palmer, Congregational clergyman, was born in Little Compton, R.I.; wrote many hymns (My faith looks up to Thee; Away from earth, my spirit turns; Take me, O my Father, take me; Jesus, these eyes have never seen) (died 1887).

1817 Bahau'llah, Persian founder and leader of the Bahai faith (1863), was born in Teheran; became follower of the Baba (1850), exiled several times (died 1892).

1876 James M. Gillis, Catholic writer and editor, was born in Boston; editor, *Catholic World*, Paulist monthly (1922-48); columnist ("Sursum Corda") for 50 diocesan papers around the country; featured speaker on the "Catholic Hour" (1930-41) (died 1957).

1879 Ralph S. Cushman, Methodist prelate and a temperance leader, was born in Poultney, Vt.; Methodist bishop (Denver, St. Paul-Minneapolis) (1932-52); president, Anti-Saloon League and Temperance League (1939-48) (died 1960).

1914 Edward Schillebeeckx, Catholic theologian who contributed to a renewal and democratization within the Catholic Church, was born in Antwerp, Belgium; author (An Experiment in Christology).

1915 The Peruvian congress granted freedom to all religious denominations.

1977 A major study and translation of the most recently discovered Dead Sea scroll contained insights into ancient Judaism and early Christianity that appear certain to create controversy among theologians and biblical students.

1980 The National Conference of Catholic Bishops, in response to complaints that Catholic liturgy reflects bias against women, petitioned the Vatican for permission to drop the word "men" from the eucharistic blessing of wine and to eliminate several other male-only references.

NOVEMBER 13

Feast day of St. Francis Xavier Cabrini, "saint of the immigrants;" first American citizen to bs canonized.

Feast day in the Orthodox Church of St. John Chrysostum, orator, patriarch of Constantinople (398-403), Father* of both the Catholic and Orthodox churches.

354 St. Augustine, greatest thinker of Christian antiquity, was born in North Africa; fused New Testament religion with Platonic tradition of Greek philosophy; the greatest Doctor* of the Church and one of the greatest and most influential figures in the history of thought; served as Bishop of Hippo (modern Annaba, Algeria) (396-430); his most famous works are "The City of God" and "Confessions" (died 430).

867 St. Nicholas I (the Great), pope from 858 to 867, died; also observed as his feast day.

1004 St. Abbon (Abbo) of Fleury (about 945-1004) died at about 60; in charge of studies (985-987) at the monastery school of Ramsey; helped Oswald, Archbishop of York, in restoring monasticism in England; abbot of Fleury (southeast of Orleans) (988-1004); ardent defender of papal authority and freedom of monasteries from all interference; also observed as his feast day.

1020 Aethelnoth was consecrated as Archbishop of Canterbury; served until 1038.

1486 Johann Eck, German theologian, was born in Egg, Germany; principal Catholic opponent of Martin Luther and the Reformation; helped Pope Leo X prepare condemnation of Luther's early writings and his excommunication (died 1543).

1564 Pope Pius IV issued the bull, "Injunctum nobis," setting forth the creed for the principal ecclesiastical offices of the church.

1615 Richard Baxter, one of the greatest English theologians, was born near Shrewsbury; sought to liberalize the Church of England enough to keep Puritans in the church; imprisoned (1685-86) for libeling church in his "Paraphrase on the New Testament;" his nearly 200 works reflect a deep piety and moderation; wrote several hymns (O Lord, it belongs not to my care; Ye holy angels bright) (died 1691).

1618 Synod of Dort opened in Dordrecht to settle the theological dispute between the supporters of Jacobus Arminius and the supporters of the Bezan form of Calvinism, led by Franciscus Gomarus; resulted in canons which were the basis of the Reformed Church of the Netherlands for 200 years; synod ended May 9, 1619.

1838 Joseph Fielding Smith, Mormon leader, was born in Far West, Mo., nephew of Joseph Smith, Mormon Church founder; president of Mormon Church (1901-18); did much during his administration to strengthen the church organization and to foster friendly relations with non-Mormons (died 1918).

1864 James Cannon Jr., Methodist prelate and prohibitionist, was born in Salisbury, Md.; called the "dry Messiah;" headed World League against Alcoholism; president, Blackstone College for Girls (1894-1918); bishop, supervisor of missions (from 1918) in Cuba, Mexico, Africa, and Brazil; leader of Southern Democrats opposed to Alfred E. Smith's presidential candidacy because of his anti-prohibition stand (died 1944).

1889 The School of Theology opened in Catholic University, Washington, D.C.

1929 Charles P. Anderson of Chicago (1864-1930) was named presiding bishop of the Episcopal Church of the United States; served until 1930.

1938 Mother Francis Xavier Cabrini was beatified in Rome, the first American to be so honored.

1986 The National Conference of Catholic Bishops issued a 115-page statement on the American economy, which declared that the level of American poverty was "a social and moral scandal;" called for less military spending, an increase in the minimum wage, and expansion of federal welfare programs.

NOVEMBER 14

Feast day in the Orthodox Church of St. Gregorius (Gregory) Palamas, Archbishop of Thessalonika and chief defender of hesychasm, which affirms that true spiritual life leads to the visions of the divine uncrested light.

Feast day in the Orthodox Church of St. Philip the Apostle.

Feast day of St. Dubricius, Bishop of Llandaff (cathedral city of Wales, near Cardiff) and founder of monasteries in the Sixth Century.

1180 St. Lawrence O'Toole, first Irish Archbishop of Dublin (1161-80), died at about 58; canonized 1226, the first Irish native so honored.

1263 St. Alexander Nevski, leader of Russia against the Swedes and the papacy, died at 45; refused to submit to Rome; canonized by the Orthodox Church.

1601 St. Jean Eudes, Catholic missionary and congregation founder, was born in Rinear, France; founder of the Order of Our Lady of Charity, the Congregation of Jesus and Mary (the Eudist Fathers), and the Society of the Admirable Heart of Mary; canonized 1925 (died 1680).

1623 St. Joseph Kuncewicz, Polish martyr, died at 43; Archbishop of Polotsk (1617-23), who worked for the union of churches; murdered by opponents of unification; also observed as his feast day.

1633 William Ames, English Puritan theologian, died at 57; prolific author whose works were of great influence ("Medulla theologiae" was the standard theology text at Harvard and Yale until the mid-1700s); died just before leaving for the American colonies to join his family which had left earlier.

1784 Samuel Seabury was consecrated by nonjuring Jacobite bishops of the Episcopal Church in Aberdeen Scotland as the first Episcopal bishop in America; English bishops refused his application.

1784 The first quarterly meeting of Methodists in Delaware was held in Barratt's Chapel in Frederica; Thomas Coke administered communion to about 500 persons, the first time communion had been given by an authorized Methodist minister in America.

1803 Jacob Abbott, Congregational clergyman and author, was born in Hallowell, Me., father of Lyman Abbott; taught theology at Amherst College and founded the Mt. Vernon School for Girls; author of the "Rollo" series of juvenile books (died 1879).

1838 Catholic missionaries Francois N. Blanchet and Modeste Demers arrived in Ft. Vancouver after a trans-Canada overland trip; Father Blanchet established a mission on the site of present St. Paul, Ore.; later became archbishop.

1843 Jenkin Lloyd Jones, Unitarian leader, was born in Cardiganshire, Wales; served various Midwest churches, including All Souls Church, Chicago, which he organized in 1882; a founder, editor, *Unity* (1880-1918) (died 1918).

1904 Arthur M. Ramsey, Archbishop of Canterbury (1961-80), was born in Cambridge, England; served as Archbishop of York (1956-61); met with Pope Paul VI (1966), an important step in ecumenical advancement (died 1988).

1918 The United Lutheran Church was formed by the union of three branches of the denomination.

1921 The shrine of the patron saint of Mexico, the Virgin of Guadelupe, was wrecked by a bomb.

1966 The National Conference of Catholic Bishops was established.

1976 The Plains (Ga.) Baptist Church, of which President (then a candidate) Carter is a member, voted to drop the ban on church attendance by blacks.

1977 A group of leading businessmen and professionals began planning a worldwide evangelistic campaign to be underwritten by a $1 billion five-year fund drive.

NOVEMBER 15

Feast day of St. Malo (Machutus), early Breton bishop (about 340).

1280 St. Albertus Magnus, German scholastic philosopher, scientist, and theologian, died at about 87; regarded as one of the most noted Christian scholars; one of his pupils was Thomas Aquinas; served as provincial for Dominicans in Germany (1254-59), Bishop of Regensburg (1260-62); his chief contributions were his influence on scholastic and Protestant theology and his efforts to unite theology and Aristotelianism; canonized and proclaimed a Doctor* of the Church 1931; also observed as his feast day.

1731 William Cowper, noted poet, was born in Great Barkhamstead, England; wrote several well-known hymns among the Olney hymns (God moves in a mysterious way; There is a fountain filled with blood; O for a close walk with God) (died 1800).

1769 Nicholas Snethen, Methodist clergyman, was born in Glen Cove, N.Y.; left Methodist Episcopal Church to help found (1828) the Methodist Protestant Church (died 1845).

1879 Francesco Bracci, secretary of the Sacred Congregation of the Sacraments, was born in Vignanello, Italy; elevated to cardinal 1958 (died 1967).

1980 Pope John Paul II arrived in West Germany for a five-day visit, the first by a pope since 1782.

NOVEMBER 16

Feast day in the Orthodox Church of St. Matthew, one of the apostles.

Feast day of St. Agnes of Assisi, who worked 40 years with the Poor Clares.

Feast day of St. Gertrude (1256-1302), German mystic who wrote a five-volume classic on mystical theology.

1093 St. Margaret, Queen of Scotland, who did much to bring Roman usages into the Scottish Church, died.

1200 St. Hugh of Lincoln, French-born Bishop of Lincoln (1186-1200) and the king's counselor, died at about 65; fearlessly protected the rights of the underprivileged; excommunicated King John (1194); canonized 1220.

1240 St. Edmund of Abingdon, Archbishop of Canterbury (1233-40), died at about 60; a distinguished scholar; canonized 1247; also observed as his feast day.

1603 Pierre Charon, French Catholic philosopher, died at 62; wrote on skeptical philosophy (Treatise on Wisdom); renowned pulpit orator.

1803 Heinrich G. A. von Ewald, a foremost German orientalist and theologian, was born in Göttingen; made important contributions as a biblical critic, grammarian; his Hebrew grammar marked new progress in biblical philology (died 1875).

1828 Timothy Dwight, Congregational clergyman, was born in Norwich, Conn., grandson of Timothy Dwight (1752-1817); renowned New Testament scholar, serving on the American revision committees for the St. James Bible; president, Yale (1886-98)(died 1916).

1837 Franz C. Overbeck, German church historian, was born in Russia; a renowned New Testament scholar, regarded as the forerunner of dialectical theology (died 1905).

1887 Philip H. Frohman, church architect, was born in New York City; an architect of the National Cathedral, Washington, D.C. and the Baltimore Episcopal Cathedral (died 1972).

1908 Pope Pius X celebrated pontifical mass in St. Peter's attended by missions from all the principal Catholic countries, 36 cardinals, 400 archbishops and bishops, and 50,000 people.

1946 The Evangelical United Brethren Church was formed in Johnstown, Pa. by the union of the

Church of the United Brethren in Christ and the Evangelical Church.

1959 Pope John XXIII named eight new cardinals, including two Americans - Archbishop Aloisius Muench of Fargo, N. D. and Archbishop Albert Meyer of Chicago.

1988 The National Conference of Catholic Bishops voted 205 to 59 to ask the Vatican to rewrite a draft document which questioned the authority of episcopal conferences such as the bishop's conference.

NOVEMBER 17

Feast day of Philippine Duchesne, French founder of the first American convent of the Society of the Sacred Heart.

Feast day of St. Gregory Thaumaturgus (about 213-270), Greek church Father* and missionary; an important ecclesiastical writer of the Eastern church; also known as St. Gregory of Neocaesarea (present day Niksar, Turkey), where he served as bishop (about 240-270).

Feast day of St. Hugh of Lincoln, French-born Bishop of Lincoln (1186-1200); canonized 1220.

461 St. Hilary was elected pope, served until 468; also observed as his feast day.

594 St. Gregory of Tours, Bishop of Tours (573-594), died; he was historian of the Franks; also observed as his feast day.

680 St. Hilda, founder and abbess of Whitby (657-680) and the foremost Anglo-Saxon abbess of her time, died at 66; was host to Synod of Whitby (664) that rejected Celtic ecclesiastical custom in favor of Roman reforms; also observed as her feast day.

1231 St. Elizabeth of Hungary, patroness of Catholic charities, died at 24; widow of Louis IV of Thuringia, she joined the Third Order of St. Francis, donating her dowry to build a hospital for the poor; also considered patroness of Franciscan tertiaries*, nursing, and bakers; canonized 1235; also observed as her feast day.

1558 Accession of Elizabeth I to the English throne led to the re-establishment of the Church of England.

1558 Reginald Pole, Archbishop of Canterbury (1556-58), died; as an English cardinal, he brought England back into the Catholic fold.

1624 Jacob Boehme (Bohme), German mystic, died at 49; works declared heretical; philosophy rested on the thesis of dualism of God, explained evil as necessary because of existence in divine nature of a principle complementary and antithetical to goodness.

1681 Pierre Francois le Courayer, French Catholic theologian, was born in Rouen; received doctorate from Oxford (1723) for his dissertation demonstrating the apostolic succession of English clergy; excommunicated (1728), spent rest of life in England (died 1776).

1753 Gotthilf H. E. Muhlenberg, Lutheran clergyman, was born in Trappe, Pa.; pastor, Holy Trinity Church, Lancaster, Pa. (1780-1815); first president, Franklin College (1787) (died 1815).

1790 Solyman Brown, Congregational clergyman and dentist, was born in Litchfield, Conn.; Swedenborgian clergyman after 1822; considered the founder of dentistry as an organized profession (died 1876).

1845 Frederick W. Faber (1814-63), English oratorian and hymn writer, was received into the Catholic Church; later became a priest, formed Brothers of the Will of God (1845); joined the Oratory of St. Philip Neri in London, became head of the congregation (1849-63); author (All for Jesus, Growth in Holiness, The Blessed Sacrament); hymn writer (Hark, hark, my soul; My God, how wonderful Thou art; The Pilgrims of the night; Faith of our fathers; The land beyond the sea).

1874 Burnett H. Streeter, English theologian and biblical scholar, was born in Croydon, England; made original contributions to knowledge of the origins of the Gospel (died 1937).

1875 The Theosophical Society of America was founded in New York City by Helena P. Blavatsky.

1924 Evangelical Patriarch Gregory VII of Greece died; Constantine was elected as his successor.

1956 The National Conference of Catholic Bishops repeated the pleas of Pope Pius XII for peace in a statement, "Peace, Unity - the Hope of Mankind."

1958 Pope John XXIII named 23 new cardinals, including two Americans - Archbishop Richard J. Cushing of Boston and Archbishop John F. O'Hara of Philadelphia.

NOVEMBER 18

942 St. Odo, Abbot of Cluny (northwest of Macon, France), died at 63; responsible for raising abbey to its prominent position; also observed as his feast day.

1095 Council of Claremont, convoked by Pope Urban II to plan the First Crusade, adopted a canon that granted plenary indulgence (remission of all penance for sin) to those who undertook to aid Christians in the East; also that no king or prince should grant investiture of ecclesiastical honors, that no meat be eaten between Ash Wednesday and Easter.

1105 Sylvester IV, born Maginulf, was elected antipope; Emperor Henry V gave him some recognition; when Henry and Pope Paschal II came to terms, Sylvester's "reign" ended April 1111.

1302 Pope Boniface VIII issued the bull, "Unam sanctam," declaring there was "One Holy Catholic and Apostolic Church" outside of which there was "neither salvation nor remission of sins."

1559 Cuthbert Tunstal, English Bishop of Durham (1530-52,1553-59), died at 85; a leading conservative in the English Reformation; employed by Henry VIII and Cardinal Woolsey on various diplomatic missions; Bishop of London (1522-30); adhered to Catholic dogma but acquiesced in royal supremacy, publicly defending Henry VIII's leadership of the church.

1575 Johannes Aurifaber of Weimar, German Lutheran divine, died at 54; best known as a collector and editor of the writings of Luther.

1626 St. Peter's Basilica at the Vatican was consecrated.

1647 Pierre Bayle, Protestant philosopher and critic, was born in Carla-Bayle, France; professor at Rotterdam (1681-93); removed because of his skeptical beliefs; regarded as founder of 18th Century rationalism; defender of liberty and religious tolerance; author (Dictionaire historique et critique) (died 1706).

1787 James Freeman, an Episcopal lay reader, was ordained as a Unitarian pastor; while lay reader at King's Chapel, he made numerous revisions in the Book of Common Prayer; when ordained, the first New England Episcopal church became the first American Unitarian church.

1800 John Nelson Darby, English reformer, was born in London; chief founder of the Plymouth Brethren (Darbyites); created the Darbyites when he left the church because of doubts as to the Scriptural authority for church establishments (died 1882).

1882 Jacques Maritain, French philosopher, was born in Paris; had tremendous influence on the Catholic Church and Pope Paul VI considered himself a disciple of Maritain; professor, Catholic Institute, Paris (1913-40), Columbia U. (1940-44), Princeton (1948-53); French ambassador to the Vatican (1945-48); author (Degrees of Knowledge, Prayer and Intelligence, Religion and Culture) (died 1973).

1893 Pope Leo XIII, in answer to interest in biblical studies based on science and archaeology, issued the encyclical, "Providentissimus Deus," which outlined the norms and attitudes Catholics should adopt in biblical criticism.

1965 The Second Vatican Council voted for promulgation of the Decree of the Apostolate of the Laity, which outlined a developing theology of the laity and offered guidelines to lay leadership.

1965 Pope Paul VI announced the initiation of the long process of beatification, the first step to sainthood, of his immediate predecessors, John XXIII and Pius XII.

1966 The National Conference of Catholic Bishops ruled that effective Dec. 2,1966, Catholics would no longer be required to abstain from meat except on Ash Wednesday and on Fridays during Lent.

1981 The National Theological Seminary reopened, a reflection of the new relative tolerance of religion in China.

NOVEMBER 19

Feast day of St. Pontianus, pope from 230 to 235.

Feast day in the Catholic Church of St. Mesrob, patriarch of Antioch (440) and inventor of the Armenian alphabet.

Feast day of St. Nerses (died about 373), Sixth Century Catholicos (patriarch) of the Armenian Church (about 363-373), who was reportedly poisoned by King Pap, whom he had censured for immorality.

Former feast day of St. Elizabeth, daughter of King Andrew II of Hungary; famed for her charity and love of the poor; canonized 1235; now observed Nov. 17.

766 Egbert of York, first Archbishop of York (735-766), died; established a school attached to the cathedral.

1190 Baldwin, Archbishop of Canterbury (1184-1190), died.

1472 Johannes Bessarion, Catholic prelate and translator, died at 79; cardinal, Archbishop of Nicaea (present Iznik, Turkey); translated Aristotle's Metaphysics and Xenophon's Memorabilia; collected a library of Greek manuscripts.

1802 Barnas Sears, Baptist theologian and educator, was born in Sandisfield, Mass.; with Newton Theological Institute as professor of Christian theology (1836-48), president (1839-48); president, Brown U. (1855-67); general agent for administration, Peabody Education Fund (1867-80) (died 1880).

1862 Billy (William A.) Sunday, Fundamentalist evangelist, was born in Ames, Iowa; a professional baseball player (1883-90); worked with J. Wilbur Chapman and then on his own as an evangelist; drew 1.4 million in ten weeks in New York City campaign, made 98,624 converts (died 1935).

1918 Joseph Fielding Smith, Mormon Church president, died at 80 in Salt Lake City.

1961 The World Council of Churches opened its third assembly in New Delhi, the first time the organization met in Asia.

1965 The Ecumenical Council voted 1945 to 249 to adopt a declaration affirming freedom of conscience as a church doctrine.

NOVEMBER 20

Feast day of St. Felix of Valois, a founder of the Order of the Most Holy Trinity (Trinitarians); observance dropped in 1969.

Feast day in the Orthodox Church of St. Proclus, patriarch of Constantinople (434 to about 447).

Ambrose of Camaldoli (Ambrogio Traversari), Italian humanist, commemorated this day, although never formally canonized.

869 St. Edmund the Martyr, king of East Anglia (865-869), was killed by the Danes; buried in a Benedictine settlement named for him - Bury St. Edmunds; also observed as his feast day.

1022 St. Bernward, German cleric and artist, died; Bishop of Hildesheim (993-1022); credited with designing the bronze doors of the Hildesheim Cathedral, the Bernward Cross, the Bernward Column; canonized 1193; also observed as his feast day.

1657 Manassah Ben Israel, Jewish theologian, died; born in Holland, went to England (1655) to petition Oliver Cromwell and the Parliament to abolish legislation forbidding Jews from coming to England; considered father of the modern Jewish community in England.

1660 Daniel E. Jablonski, German Reformed theologian, was born near Danzig; Bishop of the Moravian Church (1699-1741), worked for union of Lutherans and Reformed Protestants (died 1741).

1741 Samuel Kirkland, missionary to the Oneida Indians, was born in Norwich, Conn.; influential in keeping Six Nations neutral in the American Revolution; founder, Hamilton Oneida Academy (1793), which later became Hamilton College (died 1808).

1761 Pius VIII, pope from 1829 to 1830, was born as Francesco Saverio Castiglioni in Cingoli, Italy.

1855 Josiah Royce, philosopher and metaphysician, was born in Grass Valley, Cal.; developed philosophy of idealism, emphasizing individuality and will rather than intellect; author (The Religious Aspect of Philosophy, The Conception of God, Sources of Religious Insight) (died 1916).

1867 Patrick J. Hayes, Catholic prelate, was born in New York City; Archbishop of New York (1919-38); organized Catholic Charities; elevated to cardinal 1924 (died 1938).

1877 William E. Orchard, English clergyman, was born in Buckinghamshire, England; first a Free Church preacher and later a Catholic priest; sought a closer understanding between Protestants and Catholics (died 1955).

1903 The French Senate amended the Education Bill to forbid members of religious bodies from teaching.

1926 Pope Pius XI, in an encyclical, condemned the persecution of the Mexican Catholic Church and the "arbitrary character" of the Mexican Constitution.

1964 The Ecumenical Council approved an offer of friendship and respect to non-Christian people and specifically denied any special Jewish guilt in the crucifixion of Jesus.

1988 Mother Katherine Drexel, a Philadelphia nun, was beatified by Pope John Paul II; born to wealth, she took a vow of poverty and founded (1891) the Sisters of the Blessed Sacrament for Indians and Colored People.

NOVEMBER 21

235 St. Anterus was named pope, served until Jan. 3, 236.

496 St. Gelasius I, pope from 492 to 496, died.

1136 William of Corbeil died; Archbishop of Canterbury (1123-36); finished the Canterbury Cathedral 1130.

1495 John Bale, religious playwright and clergyman, was born in Cove, England; wrote religious plays, best known for "King John," one of the first English historical plays (died 1563).

1620 Pilgrims (Puritans), while aboard the "Mayflower," signed the Mayflower Compact, a typical "church covenant" of the times for forming religious congregations.

1768 Friedrich E. D. Schleiermacher, German theologian and philosopher, was born in Breslau; generally acknowledged as the most influential Protestant theologian between the Reformation and the 20th Century; placed strong emphasis on feeling as the basis of religion; author (On Religion, The Christian Faith) (died 1834).

1815 Henry B. Smith, Presbyterian clergyman and educator, was born in Portland, Me.; with Union Theological Seminary as professor of church history (1850-54) and theology (1854-74); editor, *American Theological Review* (1859-74) (died 1877).

1851 Désiré Joseph Mercier, Catholic philosopher and primate, was born in Braine-l'Alleud, Belgium; Archbishop of Malines and primate of Belgium (1906-26); elevated to cardinal 1907; spiritual leader of and spokesman for Belgians during World War I (died 1926).

1854 Benedict XV, pope from 1914 to 1922, was born in Regli, Italy as Giacomo della Chiesa.

1921 Pope Benedict XV declared himself ready to treat with foreign powers for the solution of problems concerning both church and state.

1963 The Ecumenical Council authorized the use of vernacular languages (English in the United States) in administering certain sacraments.

1964 Pope Paul VI closed the third session of the Ecumenical Council; conferred the title of "Mother of the Church" on the Virgin Mary.

1980 The Vatican reaffirmed the view that baptism must be administered soon after birth and not be deferred until people reach the age of reason.

NOVEMBER 22

Feast day of St. Cecelia, one of the most famous and most discussed Roman martyrs of the early church; despite vow of celibacy, she was forced to marry a young nobleman; converted him to Christianity and with him suffered martyrdom; patron saint of church music.

365 Felix II, anti-pope from 355 to 358, died; clergy accepted him as pope, but the people remained loyal to Liberius, who had been exiled from 355 to 358; Felix was driven out on the return of Liberius.

498 St. Symmachus was elected pope, served until 514; part of his reign (498-506) was marked by a schism, with some following Laurentius, who was deposed in 501.

1694 John Tillotson, Archbishop of Canterbury (1691-94), died at 64.

1856 Heber J. Grant, president of the Mormon Church (1918-45), was born in Salt Lake City (died 1945).

1987 Pope John Paul II beatified 85 British martyrs who were tortured and executed during the Reformation in the reign of Queen Elizabeth I; included were 63 Catholic priests and 22 lay members of the Catholic Church.

NOVEMBER 23

Feast day in the Orthodox Church of St. Alexander Nevski, Russian leader and hero.

Feast day of St. Clement I, pope from about 92 to 101 — probably the third bishop of Rome after St. Peter; author of the Epistle to the Corinthians, one of the most valuable works of the early church.

Feast day of St. Felicity, Second Century Roman who was martyred with her seven children.

615 St. Columbanus, Irish missionary and monastic founder, died at about 65; founded abbeys in France and gave new direction to Gallic monasticism by sending monks outside the cloister to do pastoral work.

1470 Guru Nanak, first Sikh guru, was born near Lahore, India; originally a Hindu, he made pilgrimage to Mecca and Medina, founded Sikhism; compiled part of the Sikh scriptures, later known as Grauth or Adigrauth (died 1538).

1585 Thomas Tallis, English composer and organist, died at 80; often referred to as "the father of English church music;" one of the first to compose settings for Anglican services.

1632 Jean Mabillon, Benedictine monk and scholar of the Congregation of St. Maur, was born near Reims, France; pioneered in the study of ancient handwriting (died 1707).

1700 Clement XI was elected pope, served until 1721; issued bulls against Jansenism in 1705 and 1713.

1726 Edward Bass, Episcopal prelate, was born in Dorchester, Mass.; first Bishop of Massachusetts (which then included Rhode Island and New Hampshire (1797-1803); rector of Newbury, Mass. church (1753-1803) (died 1803).

1970 Pope Paul VI issued a decree barring cardinals over the age of 80 from voting for a new pope.

NOVEMBER 24

Former feast day of St. John of the Cross, a 16th Century Spanish priest; named a Doctor* of the Church 1926; now observed Dec. 14.

Former feast day of St. Chrysogonus, martyred in Fifth Century during Diocletian persecution; observance dropped in Catholic Church; observed Dec. 22 in the Orthodox Church.

496 Anastasius II was consecrated pope, served until 498; condemned traducianism, the theory that human souls are regenerated by the souls of one's parents; sought to restore communion with the Eastern Church.

642 Theodore I was named pope, served until 649; reign was concerned primarily with the heresy of Monotheletism*.

1531 Johannes Oecolampadius (born Hausagen), German theological leader, died at 49; a leader in the Swiss Reformation, took position of Huldreich Zwingli in disputing Martin Luther and Philipp Melancthon on the Lord's Supper; helped Erasmus edit the New Testament in Greek.

1572 John Knox, leader and historian of the Scottish Reformation, died at about 59; fled on Mary Tudor's succession to the throne (1553), met Calvin and returned to Scotland (1559); published and preached throughout Scotland against the Catholic priesthood, image worship, mass, and against Mary, whom he called Jezebel; responsible for the creation of the Reformed Church, which held its first general assembly on Dec. 20,1560.

1713 Laurence Sterne, Anglican clergyman and noted author, was born in Clonmel, Ireland; served numerous pastorates; remembered for his novels, "Tristram Shandy" and "A Sentimental Journey" (died 1768).

1713 Junipero Serra, Franciscan missionary, was born in Petra, Majorca; set up the first mission in San Diego (1769) and eight others subsequently and the first European settlement in California; called the "apostle of California" (died 1784).

1771 Francis Asbury, who arrived in Philadelphia Oct. 27, began his preaching career as an English Wesleyan missionary, traveling through Westchester County (N.Y.) on a borrowed horse.

1781 James Caldwell, clergyman and patriot, was.during the American Revolution; in the British attack on Springfield, N.J., he used hymn book pages as wadding for guns.

1848 James G. K. McClure, Presbyterian theologian, was born in Albany, N.Y.; president, Presbyterian Theological Seminary (1905-28); author (Possibilities, Living for the Best) (died 1932).

1888 Bernard R. Hubbard, Jesuit priest who explored and photographed much of Alaska, was born in San Francisco (died 1962).

1901 The University of Athens was held by students in riots opposing the translation of the Gospel into modern Greek.

1960 Archbishop Francois Poirier, Catholic primate of Haiti, was expelled from the country on charges of aiding persons seeking the overthrow of the government.

1985 An extraordinary synod of bishops opened in St. Peter's Basilica in Rome to evaluate the results of the Second Vatican Council.

NOVEMBER 25

1185 Lucius III, pope from 1181 to 1185, died.

1185 Urban III, born Uberto Crivelli, was elected pope, served until 1187; spent reign in exile because of his opposition to attempts of the Roman Senate to govern the Papal States.

1277 Nicholas III, born Giovanni Gaetano Orsini, became pope, served until 1280; provided new constitution for Rome (July 18, 1278), freeing city from foreign influence; made Vatican the permanent residence of the pope, enlarged it, beautified the gardens.

1535 St. Angela Merici (1474-1540) and 27 companions consecrated themselves to God and the Company of St. Ursula; head of Ursulines (1537-40); canonized 1807.

1556 Jacques Davy DuPerron, French cardinal, was born in Paris; had major part in the conversion of Henry IV to Catholicism; elevated to cardinal 1604; Archbishop of Sens (1606-18) (died 1618).

1697 Garhard Torsteegen, German mystic and hymn writer, was born; one of three most important hymn writers in the German Reformed Church; among his hymns is "Lo, God is here, let us adore" (died 1769).

1742 Henry Melchior Muhlenberg, virtual "founder" of the Lutheran Church in America, arrived in Philadelphia from England, via Charleston, S.C.

1758 Noah Worcester, Congregational and later Unitarian clergyman, was born in Hollis, N.H.; first editor, *Christian Disciple* (1813-18) (died 1837).

1778 William Jenks, Congregational clergyman, was born in Newton, Mass.; pioneer in religious work among seamen; founded several New England chapels and churches; author (Composite Commentary on the Holy Bible) (died 1866).

1787 Franz Gruber, German organist and composer, was born; wrote music for "Silent Night" (died 1863).

1817 Samuel C. Bartlett, theologian and educator, was born in Salisbury, N.H.; a founder, professor, Chicago Theological Seminary (1858-77);

president, Dartmouth College (1877-92) (died 1898).

1858 Paul Haupt, philosopher and theologian, was born in Görlitz, Germany; professor of Semitic languages, Johns Hopkins U.; major achievement was editing the Polychrome Bible (died 1926).

1880 John Flynn, Presbyterian missionary, was born in Australia; served inland Australia (1712-39); founder of Flying Doctor Service to the area; moderator of the Presbyterian Church in Australia (1939-42) (died 1951).

1881 John XXIII, pope from 1958 to 1963, was born as Angelo Giuseppe Roncolli in Sotto il Monte, Italy.

1908 The first edition of the *Christian Science Monitor* was published, replacing the *Christian Science Weekly* (later *Sentinel*), which began in 1898.

NOVEMBER 26

399 St. Siricius, pope from 384 to 399, died; convened Council of Capua (391); much occupied with doctrines of heretics; also observed as his feast day.

579 Pelagius II was consecrated pope, served until 590; named without usual imperial confirmation because of invading Lombards; failed to end schism with Western bishops.

1267 St. Silvester Gozzolini, founder of Silvestrian Benedictines (1231), died at 90; also observed as his feast day.

1621 St. John Berchmans died at 22; prominent Jesuit student, defender of the faith; canonized 1888; also observed as his feast day.

1639 John Spottiswoode, Scottish prelate, died at 74; Archbishop of Glasgow (1603-15), St. Andrew's (1615-35); chancellor of Scotland (1635-38); compliant agent of James I, securing passage of Five Articles of Perth (1618) in the interests of confirming episcopal government; deposed, excommunicated by Glasgow Assembly.

1785 Nathan S. S. Beman, Presbyterian clergyman and educator, was born in New Lebanon, N.Y.; pastor, First Church, Troy, N.Y. (1823-65); president, Rensselaer Polytechnic Institute, Troy (1845-65); headed New School movement in church and was largely responsible for disruption of 1838 (died 1871).

1822 Octavius B. Frothingham, Unitarian clergyman, was born in Boston, the son of Nathaniel L.; pastor, North Church, Salem, Mass. (1847-55); broke with church over slavery; pastor, Independent Liberal Church, New York City (1867-95); a founder, president, Free Religious Association (1867-78) (died 1895).

1827 Ellen G. White, most influential leader of Seventh Day Adventists in her lifetime, was born in Gorham, Me. (died 1915).

1858 Israel Abrahams, Judaic scholar, was born in London; a leader of liberal Judaism in Great Britain; co-editor, *Jewish Quarterly Review* (1889-1907) (died 1925).

1858 Katherine Drexel, philanthropist, was born in Philadelphia; founder (1891) of Sisters of the Blessed Sacrament for Indians and Colored People; founder, Xavier U., New Orleans (1915) (died 1955). Beatified 1988.

1881 Gaetano Cicognani, prefect of the Sacred Congregation of Rite, was born in Brisighella, Italy; elevated to cardinal 1953 (died 1962).

1894 James C. McGuigan, Catholic prelate, was born; Archbishop of Regina, Saskatchewan (1930-34), Archbishop of Toronto (1934-74); elevated to cardinal 1946 (died 1974).

NOVEMBER 27

399 St. Anastasius I was elected pope, served until 401; renowned for the holiness of his life.

784 St. Virgil (Virgilius) of Salzburg died; known as the "apostle of Corinthia;" canonized 1233; also observed as his feast day.

1787 Andrew Reed, Congregational hymn writer, was born in London; among his hymns is "Spirit Divine, attend our prayers" (died 1862).

1820 Nathaniel A. Hewit, Catholic clergyman, was born in Fairfield, Conn.; took name Augustine Francis when ordained; joined Redemptorists;

helped Isaac Hecker organize the Congregation of the Missionary Priests of St. Paul the Apostle (Paulist Fathers) (1858); superior of the Order (1888-97) (died 1897).

1874 Chaim Weizmann, Zionist leader, was born in Motol, Russia; a successful research chemist, he became a Zionist leader in England, was largely responsible for the Balfour Declaration, which paved the way for a Jewish homeland; for many years, he headed the World Zionist Organization; was first president of Israel (1948-52) (died 1952).

1964 Mother M. Rose Elizabeth, superior general of the Sisters of the Holy Cross (1943-55), died at 71; founder (1935) and president, Dunbarton College of Holy Cross, Washington, D.C.

1982 The Vatican gave Opus Dei, an organization composed of priests and laymen, status equal to that of a religious order and set strict rules governing the organization.

NOVEMBER 28

741 St. Gregory III, pope from 731 to 741, died; also observed as his feast day.

1607 Sforza Pallavicino, Italian prelate, was born in Rome; noted for a history of the Council of Trent (died 1667).

1771 John H. Rice, Presbyterian clergyman who founded Union Theological Seminary {Virginia}, was born in Bedford County, Va.; served as first president (died 1831).

1851 Neil McNeil, Catholic Archbishop of Toronto (1912-34), was born in Mabou, Nova Scotia (died 1934).

1880 Patrick A. Feehan was consecrated as the first Archbishop of Chicago; served until 1902.

1964 The 58th international Eucharistic Congress was opened in Bombay by Gregory Cardinal Agagianian, special representative of Pope Paul VI.

NOVEMBER 29

1268 Clement IV, pope from 1265 to 1268, died.

1530 Thomas Wolsey, English prelate and lord chancellor, died at about 59; the last great ecclesiastic to dominate the affairs of state; fell from grace when he failed to get papal approval of Henry VIII's divorce from Catherine of Aragon; privy councilor under Henry VIII (1511-15); Archbishop of York (1514-30), elevated to cardinal 1515; lord chancellor (1515-29); affected extravagant pomp, arrogated royal privilege to himself; arrested on charges of high treason (1530), died enroute to London.

1577 Cuthbert Mayne was executed; first seminary priest to die for Catholicism in England; canonized 1970; also observed as his feast day.

1661 Brian Walton, English biblical scholar, died at about 60; with the help of scholars, he issued the London (or Walton's) Polyglot Bible; Bishop of Chester (1660-61).

1727 Ezra Stiles, Congregational clergyman and educator, was born in North Haven, Conn.; president, Yale (1778-95); considered most learned man of his time; pastor, Second Church, Newport, R.I. (1755-76) (died 1795).

1752 Jemima Wilkinson, religious zealot who inspired a short-lived movement in Rhode Island, Connecticut, and New York, was born in Cumberland, R.I. (died 1819).

1847 Marcus Whitman, missionary to Indians in Oregon, was massacred by Indians, along with his wife and 12 other persons.

1879 John H. Holmes, Unitarian clergyman and champion of pacifism and civil liberties, was born in Philadelphia; changed his Unitarian congregation New York City to The Community Church, intended to "apply democracy to the field of religion;" a founder, leader, NAACP and the American Civil Liberties Union (died 1964).

1950 The National Council of the Churches of Christ in the United States was formed in Cleveland; included 27 Protestant and seven Eastern Orthodox communities.

1962 Rabbi Aaron Kotler, founder (1943) and dean of Beth Medrash Gohova, postgraduate school for rabbinical study in Lakewood, N.J., died in New York City at 71.

1964 Revolutionary changes in the Catholic liturgy, including the use of English in many prayers and responses, became effective in the United States.

NOVEMBER 30

Feast day in the Orthodox Church of St. Frumentius, founder and first bishop of the Ethiopian Church (Fourth Century).

Feast day of St. Andrew, one of the 12 apostles; patron saint of Scotland, Russia, and golfers.

538 St. Gregory of Tours, Gallic historian and Bishop of Tours, was born in Clermont-Ferrand, France; wrote "History of the Franks," a main source of knowledge of the Merovingians* to 591, and "Books of Miracles" (died 594).

1406 Gregory XII, born Angelo Carrario, was elected pope, served until July 4, 1415, when he renounced the papacy; elected by Roman cardinals in opposition to Benedict XIII, anti-pope at Avignon; Council of Pisa deposed both in 1409, but Gregory refused to yield until the Council of Constance, when the schism was ended.

1433 Council of Basel successfully negotiated the Compact of Prague, which granted Bohemians certain doctrinal concessions.

1594 John Cosin, Anglican prelate, was born in Norwich, England; Bishop of Durham (1660-72); a reviser of the Book of Common Prayer (1661); used militia to coerce nonconformists into church attendance, repressed both Puritans and Catholic recusancy*; executed levies to pay for his two castles, Durham Cathedral (died 1672).

1628 John Bunyan, English religious author and clergyman, was christened in Elstow; spent much time in jail for preaching without a license; his books (The Pilgrim's Progress) related religion to life as man lives it and were a deep influence on English social history; also a hymn writer (He who would valiant be) (died 1688).

1670 John Toland, Irish philosopher and deist, was born near Londonderry; author of "Christianity Not Mysterious," a classic exposition of deism (died 1722).

1725 Martin Boehm, co-founder of the United Brethren Church was born in Lancaster County, Pa.; a Mennonite bishop, he was excluded from the Mennonite communion because of his liberal views and association with persons of other sects; he joined with Philip W. Otterbein and others to found the United Brethren in Christ Church (1789); Otterbein and Boehm were chosen as bishops (died 1812).

1729 Samuel Seabury, Episcopal prelate, was born in Groton, Conn.; first Protestant Episcopal bishop in the United States (1784-96) (died 1796).

1821 Frederick Temple, Archbishop of Canterbury (1896-1902), was born in Levkas, Greece; Bishop of Exeter (1869-85), of London (1885-96) (died 1902).

1830 Pius VIII, pope from 1829 to 1830, died.

1852 Sir Hermann Gollancz, British rabbi and Semitic scholar, was born in Germany; rabbi at Bayswater Synagogue (1892-1923); Hebrew professor, University College, London (1902-23); knighted 1923, the first British rabbi so honored (died 1930).

1884 Daniel A. Poling, Protestant clergyman who conducted nationwide weekly radio program in the 1920s, was born in Portland, Ore.; editor, *Christian Herald* (1925-65) (died 1968).

1916 Pope Benedict XV appealed to the German Government on behalf of the nearly 100,000 Belgians who were deported to Germany.

1928 Peter Hans Kolvenbach, superior general of the Jesuit Order (1983-), was born in Nijmegen, Netherlands.

1979 Pope John Paul II and Dimitrios I pledged in a joint declaration in Istanbul to hasten the day of full communion between the Catholic and Orthodox churches; they announced the formation of a joint commission to discuss the remaining differences.

1984 The basis for merging nine Protestant denominations was reached by the Consultation of Church Union after 22 years effort; the denominations are the African Methodist Episcopal, African Methodist Episcopal Zion, Christian Church (Disciples of Christ), Christian Methodist, Episcopal, International Council of Community Churches, Presbyterian (USA), United Methodist, and United Church of Christ.

DECEMBER 1

Feast day of St. Simon of Cyrene, a passerby who was pressed into service to carry the cross for the Crucifixion.

660 St. Eligius (or Eloi) died at about 71; French ecclesiastic who gained royal favor by his expert goldsmithing in making a throne; Bishop of Noyon (639-660), founded monasteries and churches; patron saint of goldsmiths; also observed as his feast day.

1145 Pope Eugenius III issued the encyclical, "Quantum praede cessorer," calling on the French people to join the Second Crusade; among those joining were French King Louis VII.

1521 Leo X, pope from 1513 to 1521, died.

1581 St. Edmund Campion, English Catholic martyr, was hanged on charges of treason; also observed as his feast day.

1763 Patrick Henry spoke against the "parson's cause," a lawsuit brought by ministers against the Virginia laws of 1755 and 1758 which set the price of tobacco, in which ministers were paid; Henry opposed the right of the King, who supported the clergy, to interfere in the colony's internal affairs.

1798 Albert Barnes, Presbyterian clergyman, was born in Rome, N.Y.; served in Philadelphia (1830-67); his sermon, "The Way in Salvation," which led to several heresy trials, triggered a schism in the church (died 1870).

1838 Joseph Smith and other Mormon leaders began a four-months jail term in Liberty, Mo.

1867 Philaret, born Vasily M. Drozdov, Russian prelate, died at 85; metropolitan of Moscow (1825-67), wrote standard catechism (1829), adopted by the Holy Synod of the Church of Russia.

1893 The German Parliament repealed the 1872 expulsion of Jesuits by a vote of 173-136.

1955 Rev. Martin Luther King Jr. led a boycott of the Montgomery, Ala. bus system after Rosa Parks refused to give her seat to a white man on a bus.

1983 The Vatican issued a major document stressing the need for "positive" sex education, calling for understanding of "particular problems" such as homosexuality, and maintaining the church's traditional view of sex and marriage.

DECEMBER 2

Feast day of St. Chromatius, Bishop of Aquileia (northern Italy) (about 388-407); a learned scholar, wrote many homilies, including a popular one on beatitudes.

537 St. Silverius, pope from 536 to 537, died in exile.

1381 Jan van Ruysbroeck, Dutch mystic of considerable influence, died at 88; called the "Ecstatic Doctor;" founded Augustinian abbey at Groenendaal; helped found the Brothers of the Common Life; beatified 1908; also observed as his feast day.

1670 Johann A. Freyllinghausen, German hymn writer and editor, was born; edited, published two collections with 1500 hymns, the first appearance of many Pietist hymns; wrote more than 40 hymns (died 1739).

1697 The new St. Paul's Cathedral in London was dedicated.

1818 John C. Burroughs, Baptist clergyman and educator, was born in Stamford, N.Y.; president of the old U. of Chicago (1857-73), chancellor (1873-77) (died 1892).

1831 Francis N. Peloubet, Congregational clergyman, was born in New York City; author of numerous religious works (Select Notes on the International Sunday School Lessons - 44 annual volumes (1875-1918); three grades of Sunday School Quarterlies for the Scholars (1880-1919) (died 1920).

1841 William Newton Clarke, theologian and author, was born in Cazenovia, N.Y.; influential professor at Colgate Seminary; author of "An Outline of Christian Theology," most widely-used liberal text in systematic theology (died 1912).

1873 The Reformed Episcopal Church was formed in New York City, with George D. Cummins, former Episcopal assistant bishop of Kentucky, as the presiding officer, and the Rev. Charles E. Cheney as the first bishop.

1908 The Federal Council of the Churches of Christ in America was formed in Philadelphia.

1964 Pope Paul VI was greeted by a crowd of more than 1 million on his arrival in Bombay for the Eucharistic Congress.

1967 A meeting of 150 Methodists and 150 Catholics in Westminster Cathedral was given over to informal dialogue and an agreement to meet again.

1980 Pope John Paul II issued an encyclical, "Dives in Misercordia," calling on nations to let mercy and justice guide their relationships rather than the Old Testament philosophy of "an eye for an eye and a tooth for a tooth."

1982 Pope John Paul II demanded that Catholic priests resign from posts in the Nicaraguan government as a condition for his visit.

DECEMBER 3

1154 Anastasius IV, pope in 1153-1154, died.

1483 Nikolaus von Amsdorf, one of Luther's most determined and active supporters, was born near Leipzig; Bishop of Naumburg (1542-46), supervised the Jena edition of Luther's works; his one-sided interpretation of Luther caused a split among the Lutherans; his teaching on the harmfulness of good works was criticized in the Formula of Concord (died 1565).

1552 St. Francis Xavier, one of the greatest missionaries and a founder of the Society of Jesus (Jesuits), died at 46; also observed as his feast day.

1586 Pope Sixtus V issued the bull, "Postquam versus," which set the number of cardinals at 70 and imposed new regulations on them.

1731 Stefano Borgia, Catholic prelate and collector of books and manuscripts, died at 73; his vast collection was given to various Italian museums; elevated to cardinal and prefect of the Congregation of the Index (1789), prefect of the Congregation of the Propaganda of the Faith (1802) (died 1804).

1796 Francis P. Kenrick, Catholic prelate, was born in Dublin, Ireland, brother of Peter R. Kenrick; Bishop of Philadelphia (1830-51), Archbishop of Baltimore (1851-63) (died 1863).

1799 Hugh Stowell, Anglican clergyman and hymn writer, was born on the Isle of Man; his hymns include "From every stormy wind that blows" and "Gracious God, look down in kindness" (died 1865).

1809 Samuel Adler, a leader of Reformed Judaism, was born in Worms, Germany; rabbi, Temple Emanu-el, New York City (1857-91); helped revise prayer book and to lay the foundation for Reformed Judaism (died 1891).

1839 Pope Gregory XVI issued an apostolic letter, "In supremo," condemning the slave trade.

1850 Frank M. North, Methodist clergyman, was born in New York City; corresponding secretary, New York City Society of Methodist Churches (1892-1912) and Methodist Board of Foreign Missions (1912-20); remembered for hymn, "Where cross the crowded ways of life" (died 1935).

1856 Arthur J. Brown, secretary of the Presbyterian Board of Foreign Missions (1895-1929), was born in Halliston, Mass.; a leader in the founding of the World Council of Churches (died 1963).

1882 Archibald C. Tait, Archbishop of Canterbury (1869-1882), died.

1910 Mary Baker Eddy, founder of the Christian Science Church, died at 89 in Newton, Mass.

1963 Pope Paul VI strengthened the pastoral authority of Catholic bishops by adding to their permanent powers and privileges.

DECEMBER 4

Feast day of St. John of Damascus, eminent theologian and Doctor of the Church; author of Orthodox Church standard textbook of dogmatic theology (Fount of Knowledge); canonized by both the Catholic and Orthodox churches.

Former feast day of St. Peter Chrysologus, famed Latin orator and writer; Archbishop of Ravenna (433-450); named Doctor* of the Church 1729; now observed July 30.

963 Leo VIII was elected pope, served until 965; the choice of Otto I, he had been chief archivist of the papal chancery.

1075 St. Anno (or Hanno), Archbishop of Cologne (1056-75), died at about 65; prominent in the political struggles of the Holy Roman Empire; canonized 1183; also observed as his feast day.

1093 St. Anselm was consecrated as Archbishop of Canterbury, served to 1109.

1099 St. Osmund died; Bishop of Salisbury (1078-99); noted chiefly for formation of Sarum use*; canonized 1457; also observed as his feast day.

1154 Adrian IV, born Nicholas Breakspear (about 1100-1159), was unanimously elected pope, the only Englishman named pope; served until 1159; a strong supporter of the clergy, strove to establish universal domination for the papacy (died 1159).

1334 John XXII, pope from 1316 to 1334, died at 85.

1584 John Cotton, Puritan clergyman, was born in Derbyshire, England; called the "patriarch of New England;" produced some of the clearest statements of Puritan theology; a leader in requiring experience of regenerating grace for adult church membership, a requirement which led to later problems in New England; opposed democratic institutions; a prime agent in publication of The Bay Psalm Book (died 1652).

1674 Father Jacques Marquette reached the site of Chicago and established a mission.

1786 A mission was founded at Santa Barbara, Cal.

1820 Charles F. Deems, Methodist clergyman, was born in Baltimore; founder, pastor of the non-denominational Church of the Strangers, New York City (1868-93); author (Life of Jesus, A Scotch Verdict in Evolution (died 1893).

1825 Catholic Bishop Panet was elevated to Archbishop of Quebec.

1859 A government decree in Mexico provided for full religious liberty.

1861 The Presbyterian Church in the Confederate States of America (later Presbyterian Church US) organized with 75,000 members.

1874 Mexico forbade religious instruction and exercises in all federal, state, and municipal schools.

1880 Pedro Segura y Saenz, Spanish cardinal, was born in Burgos; served as Archbishop of Burgos and became primate of Spain in 1926 (died 1957).

1928 Dr. Cosmo Gordon Lang was enthroned as Archbishop of Canterbury.

1963 The use of English in the United States in place of Latin for parts of the Catholic mass and for the sacraments was approved by the Ecumenical Council.

1966 The seventh triennial general assembly of the National Council of Churches opened in Miami Beach, Fla.; passed a resolution stating that national expenditures for defense and space "must not be allowed to impede the achievement of social justice."

1969 The National Council of Churches elected its first woman president, Cynthia Clark Wedel.

1976 Lutherans established the Association of Evangelical Lutheran Churches, an umbrella grouping of about 75,000 theological moderates in 150 congregations who left the Lutheran Church, Missouri Synod.

DECEMBER 5

532 St. Saba, founder and first abbot of the monastery of Mar Saba and other monasteries, died at 93; Mar Saba was in the desert halfway between Jerusalem and the Dead Sea; also observed as his feast day.

650 St. Birinus, first Bishop of Dorchester (near Oxford) and apostle to the West Saxons, died; also observed as his feast day.

1046 Clement II, a Saxon born as Suidger, was enthroned as pope, served until 1047; initiated several reforms, including condemnation of simony.*

1301 Pope Boniface VIII issued the bull, "Ausculata fili," in which he enunciated the doctrine of papal supremacy over princes and kingdoms.

1484 Pope Innocent VIII issued the bull, "Summis desiderantes," giving the church's sanction to witchcraft trials.

1590 Gregory XIV was elected pope, served until 1591.

1802 Andrew Byrne, first Catholic Bishop of Little Rock, Ark. (1844-62), was born in Navan, Ireland (died 1862).

1809 James C. Furman, Baptist clergyman and educator, was born in Charleston, S.C.; first president, Furman U., Greenville, S.C. (1852-79), which was named for his father, Richard Furman (10/9/1755) (died 1891).

1824 Walter C. Smith, Scottish Free Church clergyman, was born in Aberdeen; served churches in Glasgow and Edinburgh; wrote hymn, "Immortal, invisible, God only wise" (died 1908).

1847 Brigham Young was elected to succeed Joseph Smith as head of the Mormon Church.

1960 The National Council of Churches endorsed a plan which would unite within 10 years the Methodist, Episcopal, Presbyterian, and United Church of Christ churches in the United States.

1973 Conservatives in the Presbyterian Church of the US, meeting in Birmingham, Ala., established a new denomination, the National Presbyterian Church; conservatives were made up of 75,000 worshipers from 275 churches in 14 Southern and Border states.

1975 The World Council of Churches, meeting in Nairobi, Kenya, approved a plan to support liberation efforts around the world and to fight sex discrimination and racism.

1981 Rev. Elizabeth Canham of Great Britain was ordained in Holy Trinity Cathedral, Newark, N.J.; the Church of England would not ordain her.

1988 Former PTL President Jim Bakker was indicated on 24 counts of fraud and conspiracy by a federal grand jury in Charlotte, N.C.; three of his associates also were indicted; Bakker resigned from his television ministry in 1987 amid a sex and hush money scandal.

DECEMBER 6

Feast day of St. Nicholas, Fourth Century Archbishop of Myra (in Lycia, Asia Minor), who later became Santa Claus to millions and patron saint of Russia; according to legend, ha saved three dowerless maidens from being forced into shameful means of earning a living by throwing purses of gold into their windows on three successive nights, thus providing them with a dowry; thus came the custom of Christmas giving.

1352 Clement VI, pope from 1342 to 1352, died at 61.

1362 Urban V, born Guillaume de Grimoard, was named pope, served until 1370; tried to return papacy to Rome (1367-70), but unsuccessful because of unsettled conditions; founded or aided several universities and aided indigent scholars.

1640 Claude Fleury, French church historian, was born in Paris; his 20-volume "Histoire Ecclesiastique," was the first major church history (died 1723).

1678 Father Louis Hennepin visited Niagara Falls, drew the first known picture of the Falls.

1787 The first American Methodist college (Cokesbury) opened in Abingdon, Md.

1788 Richard H. Barham, English clergyman, was born in Canterbury; best known for his humorous poetry, "Ingoldsby Legends" (died 1845).

1835 John Atkinson, Methodist clergyman and author, was born in Deerfield, N.Y.; wrote "The Centennial History of American Methodism" and the hymn, "We shall meet beyond the river" (died 1897).

1846 (Johann) Wilhelm Herrmann, a leading German theologian, was born in Melkow; had profound influence on his students by the "unforgettable seriousness" of his teaching and his writing (The Communion of the Christian With God) (died 1922).

1848 Bertram Orth, Canadian Catholic prelate, was born in Rhine Province, Germany; missionary to Canada, first bishop of Vancouver, later archbishop (1903-08) (died 1931).

1860 Howard S. Bliss, educator, was born in Mt. Lebanon, Syria; succeeded his father, Daniel, as president of Syrian Protestant College (later American U.) in Beirut (1903-19) (died 1920).

1902 Robert C. Mortimer, Anglican Bishop of Exeter (1949-73), was born in Bristol, England (died 1976).

1932 Paul A. Reeves, Anglican archbishop and primate of New Zealand (1980-), was born in Wellington, N.Z.

1950 The eighth All-American Synod of the Russian Orthodox Church unanimously elected New York Archbishop Leonty as the new metropolitan of the United States and Canada.

1965 Pope Paul VI, after meeting with Patriarch Athenagoras I, issued a common declaration removing the mutual sentences of excommunication made in 1054, constituting an act of reconciliation between their two churches.

1965 The last public session of the Second Vatican Council was held, promulgating the Declaration of Religious Liberty, which asserted that every man has the right not to be coerced, either by individuals or society, into acting against his conscience or into not following his conscience in religious matters, and the Pastoral Constitution on the Church in the Modern World, which touched on the pressing problem of contemporary civilization and the church's basic principles for a Christian view of human life and destiny.

1972 Rev. W. Sterling Cary became the first black to be elected president of the National Conference of Churches.

1987 Pope John Paul II and Patriarch Dimitrios of Constantinople declared they would work toward unity between their churches, which have been divided for 900 years by a dispute over whether the pope outranks the patriarch.

1987 The beatification of Father Junipero Serra, the Franciscan friar known as the "Apostle of California," moved nearer as it was endorsed by a Vatican commission.

DECEMBER 7

Feast day of St. Ambrose, a Father* of the Catholic Church.

283 St. Eutychianus, pope from 275 to 283, died; also observed as his feast day.

1254 Innocent IV, pope from 1243 to 1254, died.

1649 St. Charles Garnier, French Jesuit missionary to Canada, was martyred during an Iroquois attack, canonized with six other North American martyrs (1930).

1835 Dom Joseph Pothier, monk and scholar, was born in Bouzemont, France; helped reconstitute the Gregorian chant (died 1923).

1847 Solomon Schechter, leader of Conservative Judaism, was born in Focsani, Rumania; discovered 50,000 manuscripts in an old Cairo synagogue (the Genizah of Fostat) (1896), which he donated to Cambridge U.; president, Jewish Theological Seminary (1902-15); founder, United Synagogue of America (1913) (died 1915).

1866 Edwin H. Hughes, Methodist prelate, was born in Moundsville, W. Va.; bishop (1908-50), senior bishop (1932-50) (died 1950).

1880 St. Josepha Rossello died at 69; founder, Daughters of Our Lady of Pity (1837); canonized 1949; also observed as her feast day.

1930 Judge Ben Lindsay of Denver was ejected from the Cathedral of St. John the Divine, New York City, on a charge of disturbing the public worship when he challenged Bishop William Manning's denunciation of the Lindsay book on companionate marriage; set free by court Dec. 17.

DECEMBER 8

Feast of the Immaculate Conception in the Catholic Church and parts of the Anglican Church.

1658 Francois de Laval was ordained Bishop of Petres and vicar apostolic of Canada; arrived in Canada June 16,1659.

1810 Elihu Burritt, "the learned blacksmith," was born in New Britain, Conn.; international peace advocate; founder, League of Universal Brotherhood; organized the Brussels Peace Congress (1848) (died 1879).

1823 Robert Collyer, Unitarian clergyman, was born in Keighly, England; originally a Methodist lay preacher, he then served Unity Church, Chicago (1859-79), Church of the Messiah, New York City (1879-1903) (died 1912).

1852 The former Seminary of Quebec, founded by Bishop Francois de Laval, received a royal charter as Laval University.

1854 Pope Pius IX published the doctrine of the Immaculate Conception of the Blessed Virgin Mary.

1854 Missionaries of the Sacred Heart (Society of the Missionaries of the Sacred Heart of Jesus) was founded by Jules Chevalier at Issoudon, France.

1859 William H. O'Connell, Catholic prelate, was born in Lowell, Mass.; Bishop of Portland, Me. (1901-06), Archbishop of Boston (1907-44); elevated to cardinal 1911 (died 1944).

1864 Pope Pius IX issued the encyclical, "Quanta Cura," condemning rationalism, Gallicanism, socialism, and those teachings that claim human progress is best achieved independently of religious sanctions.

1869 The first Vatican Council opened with 803 present; eventually resulted in the decision that the pope's infallibility is confined to those occasions when he makes pronouncements "ex cathedra."

1880 Clement Emile Roques, Archbishop of Rennes (1940-64), was born in Graulhet, France; elevated to cardinal 1946 (died 1964).

1888 The new Catholic cathedral in Peking was consecrated.

1892 Jacob Tarshish, American rabbi who was known as "The Lamplighter" on radio, was born in Lithuania (died 1960).

1906 Pope Pius X forbade French Catholics from complying with provisions of the act separating church and state (effective December 1907) and governing public meetings.

1962 The first black bishop to serve a predominantly white diocese of the Episcopal Church in the United States, the Rt. Rev. John M. Burgess, was consecrated as suffragan bishop of Massachusetts.

1981 The U. S. Supreme Court upheld 8 to 1 the constitutionality of religious services in campus buildings by student organizations at public colleges and universities.

DECEMBER 9

Feast of the Immaculate Conception in the Orthodox Church.

1565 Pius IV, pope from 1559 to 1565, died.

1575 Augustine Baker, Benedictine monk, was born in Abergavenny, England; an important writer on ascetic, mystical, theology (Santa Sophia, or Holy Wisdom) (died 1641).

1608 John Milton, famed poet and Puritan leader, was born in London; best known for "Paradise Lost" and "Paradise Regained;" also wrote series of pamphlets against episcopacy and a number of hymns (Let us with gladsome mind; The Lord will come and not be slow) (died 1674).

1618 Yamazaki Ansai, Japanese founder of Suiga Shinto, was born; the sect combined Neo-Confucian philosophy of Chu Hsi with the religious doctrines of Shinto (died 1682).

1640 St. Peter (Pierre) Fourier died at 75; co-founder of the Augustine Canonesses Regular of Our Lady; canonized 1897; also observed as his feast day.

1667 William Whiston, English mathematician and clergyman, was born near Leicester; initiated a revival of Arianism* in the 18th Century; dismissed from Cambridge for his views; author (Primitive Christianity Revived) (died 1752).

1669 Clement IX, pope from 1667 to 1669, died at 69.

1915 Catholic Bishop George W. Mundelein was named Archbishop of Chicago, served until 1939; hosted the 28th International Eucharistic Congress (1926).

DECEMBER 10

Feast day in the Catholic Church of St. Leo I the Great, pope from 440 to 461.

1520 Wittenberg University students lit a bonfire and fed the work of canonists into the flames, with Martin Luther adding the papal bull, "Exurge domine," issued against him, with the words, "Because you have corrupted God's truth, may God destroy you in this fire."

1561 Kaspar Schwenckfeld, German reformer, died at 72; a leader of the Protestant Reformation in Silesia; founded a widespread movement (Reformation by the Middle Way); spiritual ancestor of the Schwenckfeld Church, a small American denomination.

1664 John Williams, Puritan clergyman (Deerfield 1688-1729), was born in Roxbury, Mass.; he was one of the captives taken in a French-Indian raid (1704), released two years later (died 1729).

1741 John Murray, "father of American Universalism," was born in Alton, England; came to the United States (1770) as an itinerant preacher on universal salvation; organized the first church in Gloucester, Mass., the Independent Church of Christ (1779-93), then pastor of the Universalist Society, Boston (1793-1809) (died 1815).

1787 Thomas H. Gallaudet, Congregational clergyman and teacher of deaf, was born in Philadelphia; founded first free American school for the deaf, Hartford (later American) Asylum (1817), principal (1817-30); married one of his first pupils; Gallaudet College, Washington, D.C., was named for him (died 1851).

1791 Jacob Frank, Polish Jewish mystic, died at about 71; founded semi-Christian Frankist, or Zoharist, sect among Jews; led it through various affiliations, then set self up as Messiah; succeeded by daughter and sect eventually became Catholic.

1815 Henry Behrens, Jesuit superior and educator, was born in Munstadt, Germany; superior, Buffalo Mission (1872-78, 1886-92); founder, St. Ignatius (now John Carroll) College, Cleveland (1886) (died 1895).

1816 Oren B. Cheney, Baptist clergyman and educator, was born in New Hampshire; organized, headed, Maine State Seminary (which became Bates College 1863), president (1857-94) (died 1903).

1948 The United Nations General Assembly adopted a "Universal Declaration of Human Rights," which included the article: "Everyone has the right to freedom of thought, conscience, and religion...and freedom...to manifest his religion or belief in teaching, practice, worship, and observance."

1960 Pesach Zwi Frank, chief rabbi of Jerusalem (1936-60), died at 86.

DECEMBER 11

Feast day of St. Miltiades, pope from 311 to 314.

Feast day of St. Daniel, a stylite who lived atop his pillar outside Constantinople for 33 years; he was the most famous disciple of St. Simeon Stylites.

384 St. Damasus I, pope from 366 to 384, died; also observed as his feast day.

1475 Leo X, pope from 1513 to 1521, was born in Florence, Italy as Giovanni de Medici, the second son of Lorenzo the Magnificent.

1792 Jacob Mohr, Austrian Catholic clergyman, was born; as parish priest in Obendorf, he wrote the poem, "Silent Night;" he asked the village schoolmaster and organist, Franz Xavier Gruber, "to set to suitable music, for two solo voices, chorus, and guitar accompaniment;" sung for the first time Dec. 24, 1818 (died 1848).

1822 George D. Cummins, first bishop of the Reformed Episcopal Church, was born near Smyrna, Del.; consecrated assistant bishop, Episcopal Diocese of Kentucky (1866); resigned (1873) to help form the Reformed Church (1876) (died 1876).

1849 Henry Moeller, Catholic prelate, was born in Cincinnati; Bishop of Columbus, Ohio (1900-04), Archbishop of Cincinnati (1904-25) (died 1925).

1855 Fernand Cabrol, Benedictine monk, was born in Marseilles, France; abbot of Benedictine monastery at Farnsborough, England (1903-37); noted writer on history of Christian worship (died 1937).

1979 Synagogue Organization of Reform Judaism vowed to challenge the policy of the Israeli Government that recognizes Orthodox practices as the only official religion and prohibits non-Orthodox rabbis from performing legitimate ceremonies.

1982 The seven largest black denominations, representing 65,000 churches and 20 million members, established the Congregation of National Black Churches.

1808 The first American bible society was organized in Philadelphia, with Rev. William White as president; later became the Philadelphia Bible Society.

1866 Charles S. Macfarland, general secretary, Congregational Church (1912-31), was born in Boston (died 1956).

1881 Harold P. Sloan, Methodist clergyman who was the principal leader of the fundamentalist defense of the faith, which he called "historic Christianity," was born in Westfield, N.J.; president, Methodist League for Faith and Life (1925-31) (died 1961).

1885 Philip T. B. Clayton, founder in England of the Toc H movement (1920), was born in Maryborough, Australia; the movement was dedicated to fellowship, service, fair-mindedness, and the Kingdom of God; operated ordination school (1917-20) (died 1972).

1973 Capt. L. Potter was ordained an American Baptist minister and the first woman chaplain in the American Air Force.

1973 The 21-member Anglican-Roman Catholic International Commission announced it had reached "basic agreement" on the nature of priesthood and ministry of the laymen.

1975 Metropolitan Meliton of the Eastern Orthodox Church announced that a joint commission will be established to prepare for unification talks with the Catholic Church.

DECEMBER 12

Fiesta of Our Lady of Guadelupe, Mexico's major religious festival; commemorates the appearance of the Virgin Mary to an Indian named Juan Diego in 1531.

1154 St. Vicelin, "apostle of Holstein," died at about 64; founded a number of churches and monasteries; also observed as his feast day.

1254 Alexander IV, born Rinaldo Conti, became pope, served until 1261.

1527 Juan de Zumarraga, Franciscan priest, was made Bishop of Mexico; later became its first archbishop; during his reign, collections of Aztec manuscripts were burned as heretical books; championed the rights of Indians.

1718 John Cennick, Moravian clergyman and hymn writer, was born in Reading, England; originally worked with John Wesley, then George Whitefield; hymns include "Children of the Heavely King" (died 1755).

1779 St. Madeleine Sophie Barat, congregation founder, was born in Joiny, France; founded Society of the Sacred Heart of Jesus (1800) (died 1865).

1800 John R. Wreford, Unitarian clergyman, was born in England; wrote the hymn, "Lord, while for all mankind we pray" (died 1881).

1805 Frederic H. Hedge, Unitarian clergyman and transcendentalist, was born in Cambridge, Mass.; professor of ecclesiastical history, Harvard Divinity School (1857-76); president, American Unitarian Association (1859-62); translated many German authors; best known for his translation of Martin Luther's hymn, "A mighty fortress is our God" (died 1890).

1806 Isaac Leeser, rabbi and editor, was born in Westphalia, Germany; rabbi, Mikvah Israel Congregation (1829-50), Beth-el Emeth (1857-68), both in Philadelphia; founder, editor, *The Occident* and *American Jewish Advocate* (1834-68); founder, Maimonides College (1868) (died 1868).

DECEMBER 13

Feast day of St. Odila (died about 720), the patroness of Alsace; founder, head of large nunnery in a castle in the Vosges Mountains, which became the center for pilgrimages.

1124 Calixtus II, pope from 1119 to 1124, died.

1294 St. Celestine V, pope from July 5, resigned after issuing a bull declaring the pope's right to resign; kept in custody by his successor, Boniface VIII, until his death May 19, 1296.

1520 Sixtus V, pope from 1585 to 1590, was born near Ancona, Italy as Felice Peretti.

1545 Council of Trent began at the call of Pope Paul III and resulted in restoring church morale and overhauling and tightening doctrines and disciplines after the challenge of the Reformation; effective reforms restored pastoral efficiency of the church; council ended Dec. 3, 1563.

1778 Felix de Andreis, Vincentian priest, was born in Demonte, Italy; pioneer missionary to the American West, serving as vicar general (1817-20) (died 1820).

1802 Thomas J. Conant, biblical scholar, was born in Brandon, Vt.; a member of the American revision committee which helped produce the 1881 Revised Version of the Bible (died 1891).

1823 William H. How, Anglican prelate, was born in Shrewsbury, England; first Bishop of Wakefield; wrote many hymns (We gave Thee but Thine own; For all the saints who from their labors rest; O word of God Incarnate; O Jesus, Thou art standing (died 1897).

1824 Abram N. Littlejohn, Episcopal prelate, was born in Florida, N.Y.; Bishop of Long Island (1869-1901); built Cathedral Church of the Incarnate in Garden City (died 1901).

1831 William E. McLaren, Episcopal prelate and educator, was born in Geneva, N.Y.; Bishop of Illinois (1875-1905); founder, Western Theological Seminary, Chicago (1881) (died 1905).

1835 Phillips Brooks, Episcopal prelate, was born in Boston; rector, Trinity Church, Boston (1869-91); Bishop of Massachusetts (1891-93); considered one of the great preachers of his generation; wrote hymn, "O little town of Bethlehem" (died 1893).

1835 Samuel Fallows, Episcopal prelate and educator, was born near Manchester, England; president, Illinois Wesleyan U. (1874-75); rector, St. Paul's Reformed Episcopal Church, Chicago (1875-76), bishop (1876-1922) (died 1922).

1937 Aga Khan IV, Muslim leader, was born in Geneva, Switzerland; spiritual leader of the Shiite Muslims since 1957.

1959 Archbishop Makarios III was elected as the first president of Cyprus, served until 1977.

1961 Metropolitan Nikolai of the Hussian Orthodox Church (1941-59) died in Moscow at 69.

1978 The National Conference of Catholic Bishops announced that American Catholics will be allowed to take both bread and wine at ordinary masses at the option of the diocese's bishop.

1988 A Toronto real estate developer, Stephen Mernick, purchased the assets of the PTL television ministry for $65 million; the Bankruptcy Court approved the sale which includes the Heritage USA theme park in Charlotte, N.C. and a television satellite operation.

DECEMBER 14

872 Adrian II, pope from 867 to 872, died; refused papacy in 855 and 858, accepted reluctantly in 867; suffered much at the hands of Roman nobles, who murdered his wife and daughter; among his achievements was approval of the Slavonic liturgy of Sts. Cyril and Mathodius, convening of Second Council of Constantinople.

872 John VIII was named pope, served until 882; strove to keep the Saracens out of Italy; tried unsuccessfully to unite the Eastern and Western churches.

1272 Berthold of Regensburg, Franciscan friar and itinerant preacher, died at about 52; regarded as the most popular itinerant preacher in Germany in the Middle Ages, with churches overflowing at his presence.

1363 Jean Chartier de Gerson, French theologian, was born in Gerson, France; worked 39 years to eliminate the schism in the papacy, finally coming up with a solution, "Conciliarism," for the Council of Constance (1415), giving the Council the right to depose a pope; his views and mystical teachings had a deep, lasting influence (died 1429).

1586 George Calixtus, German Protestant theologian, was born near Hamburg; tried to develop a theological system which would reunite Lutherans, Calvinists, and Catholics; theology professor at Helmstadt (1614-56) (died 1656).

1591 St. John of the Cross, lyrical Spanish poet and mystic, died; one of the greatest mystics of all time; canonized 1726, proclaimed a Doctor* of the Church 1926; also observed as his feast day.

1775 Philander Chase, Episcopal prelate, was born in Cornish, N.H.; Bishop of Ohio (1819-31), of Illinois (1835-52), presiding bishop (1843-52); founder, Kenyon College, Ohio, and Jubilee College, Illinois, a theological school (died 1852).

1811 Noah Porter, Congregational clergyman and educator, was born in Farmington, Conn.; held various pastorates; served Yale U. as professor of metaphysics and moral philosophy (1846-71), president (1871-86) (died 1892).

1817 Catholic Bishop Ambrose Marechal (1764-1828) was consecrated as Archbishop of Baltimore; reduced European intervention in American Catholic churches; served until 1828.

1831 Griffith John, Welsh clergyman and missionary, was born in Swansea; the first Christian missionary to penetrate Central China (died 1912).

1836 Frances R. Havergal, Anglican hymn writer, was born in Astley, England; among her hymns are "Lord, speak to me that I may speak" and "Take my life and let it be" (died 1878).

1856 Louis Marshall, lawyer and Jewish leader, was born in Syracuse, N.Y.; best known for his efforts to extend religious and political freedom; helped develop many religious and philanthropic Jewish organizations (died 1929).

1873 Charles E. Cheney, a founder of the Reformed Episcopal Church, was named missionary bishop of the Northwest; later (1878) Bishop of Chicago, serving until 1916.

1877 Andrew J. Brennan, Catholic Bishop of Richmond, Va. (1926-45), was born in Towanda, Pa. (died 1956).

1927 The new Church of England Prayer Book was accepted by the House of Lords (241-88) but turned down by the House of Commons (238-205).

1979 Federal District Judge William R. Collinson ruled that the University of Missouri (Kansas City) is not required to furnish campus buildings for worship by student evangelical Christian organization, Cornerstone.

DECEMBER 15

Feast day of St. Mary di Rosa, founder of the Handmaids of Charity of Brescia; canonized 1954.

687 St. Sergius I was consecrated as pope, served until 701; made various liturgical innovations, notably the singing of the "Agnus Dei" in the mass; did much for the restoration of the Roman basilicas; supported English missions.

1756 Bartolomeo Pacca, Italian prelate and diplomat, was born; secretary of state, Papal States; imprisoned with Pope Pius VII by Napoleon (1809-13) for anti-French policies; both restored 1814; elevated to cardinal 1801; his memories provide source material for the period (died 1826).

1820 John Caird, Scottish Presbyterian clergyman and educator, was born near Glasgow; expounder of Hegel; theology professor, principal of Glasgow U. (1837-98); author (An Introduction to the Philosophy of Religion) (died 1898).

1823 Bernard J. McQuaid, Catholic prelate and educator, was born in New York City; first Bishop of Rochester, N.Y. (1868-1909); founder (1857), head of Seton Hall College and Seminary (died 1909).

1877 John T. McNichols, Catholic prelate, was born in County Mayo, Ireland; Archbishop of Cincinnati (1925-50) (died 1950).

1900 Count Leo Tolstoy, author, wrote to the Czar appealing for an end to religious persecution.

1982 Dr. Charles H. Buttimer, superior general of the Christian Brothers (1966-76), died at 76; the first non-French leader of the 200-year old order.

DECEMBER 16

882 John VIII, pope from 872 to 882, died.

955 John XII was named pope, served until 964; sometimes called the "Boy Pope," because he was about 17 when elected; was the first pontiff to change his name on ascending the throne; was Octavius when elected.

1826 John Ellerton, Anglican hymn writer, was born in London; wrote many hymns (Saviour, again to Thy dear name we raise; The day Thou gavest, Lord, is ended; This is the day of light; Now the laborer's task is o'er) (died 1893).

1830 Cornelis P. Tiele, Dutch theologian and scholar, was born in Leiden; exerted great influence on the study of comparative religion; author (Outlines of the History of Religion, Elements of the Science of Religion) (died 1902).

1836 James M. Buckley, Methodist clergyman and editor, was born in Rahway, N.J.; editor, *The Christian Advocate* (1880-1912); author (Oats or Wild Oats?) (died 1920).

1869 Bernard P. Grenfell, English papyrologist, was born in Birmingham; co-discoverer, editor and publisher of numerous papyri, including the famous "Logia Jesu" (died 1926).

1870 The Colored Methodist Episcopal Church of America was established in Jackson, Miss. by Bishop Robert Paine.

1896 Edward C. Ratcliff, British theologian, was born in Cambridge, England; an expert on liturgiology; author (The English Coronation Service, The Book of Common Prayer of the Churches of England) (died 1967).

1903 A decree of the Catholic Holy Office condemned the work by French biblical scholar, Alfred Loisy (The Gospel and the Church).

1960 Pope John XXIII named four new cardinals, including Joseph E. Ritter, Archbishop of St. Louis.

DECEMBER 17

1187 Gregory VIII, pope since Oct. 21, died.

1213 St. John of Matha (Jean de Matha), French congregation founder, died at 53; consecrated self to redemption of Christian captives of Turkey; co-founder of the Trinitarians; canonized 1679.

1662 Samuel Wesley, English clergyman and poet, was born near Southampton, father of Charles and John Wesley; rector at Epworth (1695-1735); active writer of pamphlets and zealous advocate of High Church against Dissenters; chief fame rests on his role, as he put it, of being "the grandfather of the Methodists" (died 1735).

1807 John Greenleaf Whittier, author and poet, was born near Haverhill, Mass.; best remembered for "Snowbound;" wrote many Quaker hymns (O brother man! fold to thy heart thy brother; Immortal love, forever full; Dear Lord and Father of mankind; All things are Thine, no gift have we) (died 1892).

1815 John Bapst, Jesuit missionary to Maine Indians, was born in LaRoche, Switzerland; ran Jesuit training school in Boston (1860-63), which became Boston College; served as its first rector (1863-69) (died 1887).

1824 Thomas Starr King, Unitarian clergyman, was born in New York City; pastor in Boston (1848-60), San Francisco (1860-64); helped save California for the Union in the Civil War (died 1864).

1877 Titus Lowe, Methodist prelate, was born in Bilston, England; Bishop of Singapore (1924-28), Portland, Ore. (1928-39), Indianapolis (1939-48); headed "Crusade for Christ" campaign which raised $25 million to repair war-damaged Methodist churches (died 1959).

1904 Rev. Bernard J. F. Lonergan, Jesuit who was the leading proponent of one of the strongest Catholic theological movements (transcendental Thomism), was born (died 1984).

1906 The Archbishop of Paris was expelled from his official residence under the separation bill.

1917 The Russian Government announced that the property of the Russian Church would be confiscated, religious instruction in the schools would be abolished.

DECEMBER 18

Feast day in the Coptic Church of St. Frumentius, Christian bishop and apostle to the Ethiopians in the Fourth Century.

1133 Hildebert of Lavardin, French prelate and humanist, died at 78; served as Bishop of LeMans (1096-1125), Archbishop of Tours (1125-1133); his letters became models of Latin style.

1352 Innocent VI, born Etienne Aubert, was elected pope, served until 1362 at Avignon; reign was marked by religious decline, but Innocent was instrumental in arranging the Peace of Bretigny between France and England.

1431 Pope Eugenius IV issued a bull dissolving the Council of Basel, but participants ignored it; two years later, he revoked the bull, recognized the Council.

1422 Pierre Cauchon, French prelate, died; Bishop of Beauvais (1420-29), selected and headed the panel of judges which tried Joan of Arc (1431).

1707 Charles Wesley, a co-founder of Methodism with his brother, John, was born in Epworth, England; called "methodist" by fellow students for his methodical study habits; gathered together at Oxford (1729) a group including his brother, James Harvey, and George Whitefield, who shared a fanatical religious zeal for regularity of living and strict observance of weekly sacraments; opposed separation from the Anglican Church; disagreed with brother's advocacy of doctrine of perfection and his ordination of presbyters; considered the "poet of Methodism," writing more than 6500 hymns which were a textbook of Methodist theology (Love divine, all love excelling; Hark, the herald angels sing; Christ the Lord is ris'n today; Soldiers of Christ arise; Jesus, lover of my soul) (died 1788).

1725 Johann S. Semler, German Lutheran theologian, was born near Leipzig; developed principles of textual criticism of the Bible; sometimes called the "father of German rationalism" (died 1791).

1819 Isaac T. Hecker, Catholic missionary and congregation founder, was born in New York City; originally a Methodist, converted to Catholicism; served as a Redemptorist missionary (1851-57); with four other Redemptorists, organized the Missionary Priests of St. Paul the Apostle (the Paulists) (1858), first superior (1858-88); founder, *Catholic World* (1865), *Young Catholic* (1870); author (Questions of the Soul, Aspirations of Nature) (died 1888).

1828 Abraham V. Rydberg, Swedish author and educator, was born near Gothenburg; wrote controversial "The Teachings of the Bible About Christ" and other works (died 1895).

1835 Lyman Abbott, Congregational clergyman and editor, was born in Roxbury, Mass.; originally a lawyer but was so impressed by Henry Ward Beecher that he entered the ministry; succeeded Beecher at Brooklyn's Plymouth Congregational Church (1887-99); main role was religious journalism, editor of *Illustrated Christian Weekly* (1870-76), *Christian Union* (1876-93), *The Outlook* (1893-1922); a leader in presenting social gospel, interpreting Christianity as it applied to social and industrial problems (died 1922).

1859 Francis Thompson, poet, was born in Preston, England; wrote "The Hound of Heaven," which described the crisis of a man pursued by God's love (died 1907).

1861 Catholic Archbishop Bialobzeski of Warsaw, who was arrested Nov.19 for closing the churches, was tried and sentenced to death; died before his execution.

1864 Samuel P. Cadman, Congregational clergyman and the first radio preacher, was born in Wellington, England; pastor, Metropolitan Temple, New York City (1895-1901), Central Church, Brooklyn (1901-36); president (1924-28), radio minister for the Federal Council of Churches of Christ in America, the first American radio minister (1928-36) (died 1936).

1893 Archbishop Robert Machray of Ruperts Land was elected the first Anglican primate of Canada.

1902 The Education Act transferred control of most education in Great Britain to local authorities; localities were not to insist that any form of religious belief shall or shall not be taught; denominational schools were to receive Public support.

1979 Hans Kung, Swiss Catholic theologian, was censured by the Vatican for his writings, including "Infallible? An Inquiry."

1985 The Supreme Court of Canada ruled unanimously that an employer must take reasonable steps to accommodate the religious practices of a Seventh-Day Adventist whose religious beliefs prevented her from working on her chosen day of worship.

DECEMBER 19

Feast day of St. Anastasius I, pope from 399 to 401; renowned for the holiness of his life.

1187 Clement III, born in Rome as Paolo Scolari, was elected pope, served until 1191; organized the Third Crusade, gave papal protection to Jews and other persecuted people.

1370 Urban V, pope from 1362 to 1370, died at 60.

1498 Andrew Osiander, German theologian, was born in Gunzenhausen, Germany; a brilliant, original, and erratic Lutheran reformer; the first Evangelical preacher at Nuremberg and first theology professor, U. of Königsberg (1549-52); carried on theological disputes with Martin Chemnitz and Philipp Melancthon (died 1552).

1808 Horatius Bonar, Scottish clergyman and hymnist, was born in Edinburgh; greatest Scottish hymn writer, he wrote three series of "Hymns of Faith and Hope," including such favorites as "What a friend we have in Jesus" and "I heard the voice of Jesus say" (died 1889).

1876 Enrique Pla y Deniel, Archbishop of Toledo, Spain, was born in Barcelona; restored the Pontifical Ecclesiastic University in Salamanca; elevated to cardinal 1946 (died 1968).

1891 The Mormon Church pledged obedience to laws and asked for amnesty from past offenses.

1913 Juan Landazuri Ricketts, Archbishop of Lima (1955-), was born in Arequipa, Peru; elevated to cardinal 1962.

DECEMBER 20

Feast day in the Orthodox Church of St. Ignatius, Bishop of Antioch and a martyr.

1334 Benedict XII, born Jacques Fournier, was elected pope, served until 1342; initiated a number of reforms, fought nepotism and avarice of clergy, improved the training of novices; began building the palace of the popes at Avignon.

1560 The Scottish Reformed Church, organized by John Knox, held its first general assembly.

1815 James Legge, Scottish missionary and Sinologist, was born near Aberdeen; missionary to Malacca and Hong Kong (1839-73); first professor of Chinese at Oxford U. (1876-97); published monumental edition (27 volumes) of Chinese classics (died 1897).

1863 Charles C. Torrey, Semitic scholar, was born in East Hardwicke, Vt.; offered a fresh critical appraisal and rearrangement of the books of Ezra and Nehemiah, held that the four Gospels were translations into Greek from Aramaic originals, and that the Revelation was a translation of an Aramaic original; professor of Semitic languages and literature (Yale 1901-32) (died 1956).

1876 Lorenzo Perosi, Italian composer of religious music, was born in Tortona, Italy; music director, St. Mark's in Venice and the Vatican's Sistine Chapel (1897-1915) (died 1956).

1979 The conservative wing of Judaism tabled consideration of the ordination of women when the faculty senate of the Jewish Theological Seminary voted 25-19 to set aside the issue.

1982 Daniel Pilarczyk, 48-year old Catholic auxiliary bishop, was installed as the Archbishop of Cincinnati.

DECEMBER 21

Former feast day in the Catholic Church of St. Thomas, one of the 12 apostles; now observed July 3; feast still celebrated this day in the Anglican Church.

882 Hincmar, Archbishop of Reims (845-882), died at about 76; an active, influential force in political and religious issues of his time.

1118 Thomas a Becket, royal chancellor and Archbishop of Canterbury, was born in London; served as lord chancellor (1155-62), archbishop (1162-70); one time close friend of Henry II as chancellor, opposed him strongly as archbishop over the matter of taxes; fled England (1164), returning six years later; refused to absolve disobedient bishops (who crowned Prince Henry in his absence) unless they swore obedience to the pope; Henry was outraged and four knights went to Canterbury, where they assassinated Becket Dec. 29, 1170; canonized 1172.

1124 Honorius II, born Lamberto Scannabecchi, was consecrated as pope, served until 1130; reign dedicated to enforcing the terms of the Concordat of Worms; confirmed the Order of Knights Templar.

1672 Benjamin Schmolk, Lutheran hymn writer, was born in Brauchitzehdorf, Germany; most popular hymn writer of his time (My Jesus as Thou wilt; A faithful friend is waiting yonder) (died 1737).

1811 Archibald C. Tait, Archbishop of Canterbury (1869-82), was born in Edinburgh; made archbishop by Disraeli to quiet strife over Irish disestablishment; withdrew opposition to Irish Church bill, aided settlement; aroused resentment by trying to solve the problem of ritualism by the Public Worship Regulation Act, providing for deprivation of recalcitrant clergy (1874) (died 1882).

DECEMBER 22

Feast day in the Orthodox Church of St. Alexander (died 251), Bishop of Cappadocia (present central Turkey) and first bishop coadjutor of Jerusalem; built a theological library in Jerusalem.

Feast day in the Orthodox Church of St. Chrysogonus, Fifth Century martyr.

401 St. Innocent I became pope, served until 417; exercised papal authority as head of both the Eastern and Western churches; established the anointing of the sick as a sacrament and recommended clerical celibacy; Rome was sacked (410) while he was away.

1667 The Cathedral of Mexico City was dedicated; begun in 1573.

1770 Demetrius A. Gallitzin, Catholic missionary, was born in The Hague; first priest to receive full theological training in the United States; served American frontier, known as the "apostle of the Alleghenies;" founded Loretto, Pa. (1799); Gallitzin, Pa. named for him (died 1840).

1821 Josiah B. Grinnell, Congregational clergyman and legislator, was born in New Haven, Vt.; began First Church, Washington, D.C., but was forced to leave because of his abolitionist views; founded Grinnell, Iowa and helped plan Grinnell College; member, House of Representatives (1863-67) (died 1891).

1823 Thomas W. Higginson, Unitarian clergyman, was born in Cambridge, Mass.; active anti-slavery worker; Colonel of first Negro regiment in Union Army (1862-64); author of biographies of Longfellow and Whittier (died 1911).

1889 Very Rev. Jean Baptiste Janssens, president general, Society of Jesus (Jesuits) (1946-64), was born in Malines, Belgium (died 1964).

1892 Peter Tatsui Doi, Archbishop of Tokyo (1937-), was born in Sendai, Japan; elevated to cardinal 1960, becoming the first Japanese cardinal

1903 Negotiations for the purchase of friars' land (about 400,000 acres) in the Phillipines concluded with an offer of $7,250,000; most land was transferred to the Phillipines Government; four religious orders withdrew voluntarily.

DECEMBER 23

619 Boniface V became pope, served until 625; organized missions in England.

1116 St. Yves (Ivo) of Chartres died at about 76; Bishop of Chartres (1090-1116).

1569 St. Philip of Moscow, primate of the Russian Church, was martyred by Ivan the Terrible.

1648 Robert Barclay, Scottish apologist for the Quakers, was born near Aberdeen; considered the most weighty and remarkable of all Quaker theologians; wrote important statement of Quaker doctrine (An Apology for the True Christian Divinity); a grantee of the province of East New Jersey, governor (1682-88) (died 1690).

1783 Gershon M. Seixas, Philadelphia rabbi, won case modifying the test clause in the Pennsylvania constitution banning Jews from holding public office.

1805 Joseph Smith, founder of the Mormon Church, was born in Sharon, Vt.; began having visions (1820), telling him to restore the church; received (1827) a book on golden plates which, after his translation, became "The Book of Mormon;" began westward movement which eventually ended in Utah; murdered by a mob in Nauvook, Ill. in 1844.

1817 Warren Felt Evans, publicist, was born in Rockingham, Vt.; first effective publicist of the New Thought Movement (The Mental Cure, Mental Medicine) (died 1889).

1889 Emil Brunner, Swiss theologian, was born in Zurich; one of the leaders of the movement to reaffirm central themes of the Protestant Reformation against the liberal theologies; one of the founders of the dialectical* school of theology; his major work was "Dogmatics" (died 1966).

1939 President Franklin Roosevelt appointed Myron C. Taylor, industrialist, as his personal representative to Pope Pius XII; this did not inaugurate formal diplomatic relations with the Vatican.

1968 Pope Paul VI called the first extraordinary session of the Synod of Bishops to meet in Rome in October 1969.

1970 A Catholic-Jewish conference Rome ended with an agreement to join forces against all forms of discrimination.

DECEMBER 24

640 John IV was elected pope, served until 642; noted for his zeal and orthodoxy, condemned the Monothelitic* statement of faith.

1256 St. Peter Nolasco, French-born knight who distributed his wealth to help the poor, died at 67; founder of the Order of Our Lady of Mercy (Mercedarians); canonized 1628.

1294 Boniface VIII, born Benedetto Caetani, was named pope, served until 1303; reign was generally considered the climax of papal attempts to claim jurisdiction over the political order of Europe; was imprisoned at Anagni (1303) as the result of a quarrel with Philip IV of France, died within a month.

1541 Andreas R.B. von Carlstadt, German Protestant Reformer, died; originally (1517) joined Luther's cause but later opposed Luther's policy of compromise; championed radical reforms and beliefs; joined Zwingli in Zurich.

1652 The British Parliament, still under Quaker control, passed a law reminding the public that "no observance shall be had on the five-and-twentieth of December, commonly called Christmas Day; nor any solemnity used or exercised in churches in respect thereof."

1698 William Warburton, English prelate, was born near Nottingham; Bishop of Gloucester (1760-69); prolific writer (The Alliance Between Church and State, Divine Legation of Moses, Essays on Man); preached against slavery as early as 1766 (died 1779).

1763 Abiel Holmes, Congregational clergyman and historian, was born in Woodstock, Conn.; pastor, First Church, Cambridge (1792-1829); author (American Annals, or a Chronological History of America (died 1837).

1772 Barton W. Stone, evangelist and church founder, was born near Port Tobacco, Md.; a founder of the Disciples of Christ Church (1832) (died 1844).

1818 According to legend, the first performance of "Silent Night" occurred; written by the parish priest of Obendorf, Austria, with music by Franz Gruber.

1873 The temperance movement in the United States began when Eliza Trimble Thompson of Hillsboro, Ohio, led 70 women from a prayer meeting to the outside of a saloon and sang and pleaded with the owner to close the saloon; visited 12 others in succeeding days; movement spread throughout the area and elsewhere.

1899 The holy year 1900 was inaugurated by the opening of the "holy door" of St. Peter's by Pope Leo XIII.

1907 John P. Cody, Catholic prelate, was born in St. Louis; Archbishop of New Orleans (1964-65), of Chicago (1965-82); elevated to cardinal 1967 (died 1982).

1951 "Amahl and the Night Visitors," an opera by Gian-Carlo Menotti, was shown for the first time on television; the story of a crippled boy and the Three Wise Men became an annual Christmas Eve feature.

DECEMBER 25

795 Adrian I, pope from 772 to 795, died.

1559 Pius IV was named pope, served until 1565; reconvened the suspended Council of Trent (1562); issued a bull confirming its decisions (1564); a patron of artists and commissioned new buildings in Rome.

1650 The first mass was celebrated in the Church of Notre Dame de la Paix in Montreal.

1709 John Peter Miller, Reformed clergyman, was born in Zweikirchen, Germany; head of the Ephrata Community (1768-96); engaged by the Continental Congress to translate the Declaration of Independence into several European languages (died 1796).

1717 Pius VI, pope from 1775 to 1799, was born near Florence as Giovanni Angelo Braschi.

1724 The first Church of England building in the American colonies was opened in Stratford, Conn. by Rev. Samuel Johnson.

1752 Philip Embury (1728-1773), Irish-born German Protestant was converted to Methodism by John Wesley and later became one of the founders of American Methodism; organized first Methodist Society in New York City.

1757 Richard Brothers, a religious fanatic, was born in Newfoundland; believed himself a descendent of David, "the nephew of the Almighty, the prince of Hebrew" (died 1824).

1784 Sixty ministers convened in Baltimore to form the American Methodist Church, with Francis Asbury and Thomas Coke unanimously elected as joint superintendents; adopted the disciplines of English Methodism, the liturgy, prayer book, and hymns, as well as the 24 Articles of Religion prepared by John Wesley.

1789 Elihu Baldwin, Presbyterian clergyman and educator, was born in Durham, N.Y.; first pastor of Seventh Church, New York City (1820-34); first president, Wabash College, Crawfordsville, Ind. (1834-40) (died 1840).

1793 Edward T. Taylor, seamen's chaplain, was born in Richmond, Va.; known as "Father Taylor," he was chaplain of the Seamen's Bethel, Boston (1829-71) (died 1871).

1811 Wilhelm E. Ketteler, German Catholic social reformer, was born in Münster; sometimes considered the outstanding German bishop of the 19th Century; Bishop of Mainz (1850), became Catholic leader of Germany, championed Christian socialism and social and economic reforms (died 1877).

1831 Christian D. Ginsburg, British biblical scholar, was born in Warsaw; an original member of the Old Testament revision group; published an edition of "The Massorah" (died 1914).

1835 Benjamin T. Tanner, African Methodist Episcopal bishop, was born in Pittsburgh; a licensed Methodist preacher, he advocated black separatism; served as AME Bishop of Philadelphia (1881-1923) (died 1923).

1865 Evangeline C. Booth, Salvation Army leader, was born in London, the seventh child of William Booth, the founder; she headed Army in the United States (1904-34); general of entire Salvation Army (1934-39) (died 1950).

1904 Pope Pius X issued the constitution, "Vacante sede apostolica," setting forth the rules governing the election of the pope by the College of Cardinals; modified in 1922 and 1925.

1961 Pope John XXIII issued a papal bull convening the Catholic Church's 21st Ecumenical Council to be held in 1962.

DECEMBER 26

Feast day in the Catholic Church of St. Stephen, the first Christian martyr commemorated by the church; accused of blasphemy, stoned to death.

Feast day of Blessed Vincentia Lopez of Vicuna; founder, Daughters of Mary Immaculate (1888); beatified 1950.

418 St. Zosimus, pope from 417 to 418 died; also observed as his feast day.

795 St. Leo III was unanimously elected pope, served until 816; crowned Charlemagne (800), emperor of the West; canonized 1673.

1490 Friedrich Myconius (Mecom), German reformer, was born in Lichtenfels; friend and co-worker of Martin Luther, preached the Lutheran doctrine at Gotha and Leipzig; sent to England to discuss articles of Augsburg Confession; wrote a history of the Reformation (died 1546).

1727 Francois Duplessis de Mornay was named Bishop of Quebec, succeeding Bishop de St. Vallier, who died.

1751 St. Clement Hofbauer, Catholic priest, was born in Tasswitz, Austria; known as the "apostle of Vienna;" early leader of the Redemptorists; canonized 1909 (died 1820).

1839 Charles J. Seghers, Catholic prelate, was born in Ghent, Belgium; twice Bishop of Vancouver Island; Archbishop of Oregon City (1878-85) (died 1886).

1849 Francis Brown, Semitic scholar, was born in Chester, N.H.; with Union Theological Seminary (1879-1916), president (1908-16); editor of "Hebrew and English Lexicon of the Old Testament" (died 1916).

1965 The World Muslim Conference in Somalia concluded its week-long sessions with a call for world peace and an end to colonialism.

DECEMBER 27

Feast day of St. Fabiola (died about 399), Christian noblewoman of Rome; credited with founding the first public hospital in western Europe.

Feast day in the Catholic Church of St. John the Apostle; Jesus' "beloved disciple."

Feast day in the Orthodox Church of St. Stephen, the first martyr commemorated by the church.

1555 Johann Arndt, German Lutheran theologian and mystic, was born near Magdeburg; devoted follower of Philipp Melancthon; author (True Christianity) (died 1621).

1603 Thomas Cartwright, English reformer, died; lectured against constitution of the Church of England; imprisoned for nonconformity; clergyman to English residents in Holland, returning later to promote Puritanism.

1797 Charles Hodge, Presbyterian theologian, was born in Philadelphia; at Princeton Theological Seminary (1822, 1840-78); the major figure in the "Princeton School" of the Reformed (Calvinistic) orthodoxy; exerted major influence with his writings (Systematic Theology); founder, editor, *Biblical Repository and Princeton Review* (1825-65) (died 1878).

1814 Joanna Southcott, English religious fanatic, died at 64; declared herself the woman in Revelation xii, announced that she was to be delivered of Shiloh, a second Messiah, on Oct 19, 1814; had about 100,000 followers.

1843 Benjamin H. Carroll, Baptist clergyman and theologian, was born in Carrollton, Miss.; dean of theology department, Baylor U. (1902-08); president, Southwest Baptist Theological Seminary (1908-13) (died 1913).

1844 Edward Judson, Baptist clergyman, was born in Maulmain, Burma, the son of Adoniram (8/9/1788); a pioneer of the institutional church, designed to help city dwellers adjust to social, economic,and spiritual environment; founder, pastor (1890-1914), Judson Memorial Church, New York City (died 1914).

1861 John A. Marquis, Presbyterian missionary and educator, was born in Dinsmore, Pa.; president, Coe College (1909-17); secretary, Presbyterian Board of Home (later National) Missions (1917-28) (died 1931).

1892 Cornerstone laid for the Cathedral of St. John the Divine, New York City; it was to be the largest American church (601 ft. long, 146 ft. wide at the nave and 320 ft. at the transept) and was to be of Romanesque architecture; construction stopped and started many times because of cost; still incomplete but construction has been resumed.

DECEMBER 28

Innocents' Day in the Catholic Church (Childermas or Feast of the Holy Innocents) celebrated in memory of the children massacred by Herod in an effort to destroy the infant Jesus.

418 St. Boniface I became pope but did not take office until April 10, 419, served until 422; a noted organizer, he did much to restore the authority of the papacy; encouraged St. Augustine to write against the Pelagian* heresy.

1065 Westminster Abbey was dedicated.

1622 St. Francis de Sales, French bishop and Doctor* of the Church, died at 55.

1714 George Whitefield, pioneer Methodist and evangelist, was born in Gloucester, England; founder of Calvinistic Methodism and responsible for the founding of many colleges, universities; succeeded Wesley as leader of the Methodists at Oxford; began open-air preaching in Bristol (1739), winning audiences of all classes; made evangelistic tours in the United States (1740, 1744-48, 1769); broke with Wesley over predestination, became leader of the rigid Calvinists (about 1741) (died 1770).

1868 Pope Leo XIII issued the encyclical letter, "Quod Apostolic Muneris," outlining the church's attitude toward "Socialists, Communists, and Nihilists...(who) strive to carry out the purpose long resolved upon, of uprooting the foundations of civilized society at large."

1879 Manuel Arteaga y Betancourt, Archbishop of Havana (1941-63), was born in Camaguey, Cuba; elevated to cardinal 1946 (died 1963).

1981 The Union of American Hebrew Congregations announced the creation of a $25 million "TV Library of Judaism" in New York City, the first such library.

DECEMBER 29

Innocents' Day in the Orthodox Church (Childermas or Feast of the Holy Innocents); celebrated in memory of the children massacred by Herod in an effort to destroy the infant Jesus.

Feast day of St. Peter the Venerable, born Maurice de Montboissier, abbot of Cluny (near Macon, France); first to have the Koran translated into Latin; honored as a saint though never canonized; reputedly placed Innocent II on the papal throne.

1170 Thomas à Becket, Archbishop of Canterbury (1162-70), was martyred in his cathedral by Henry II's knights; canonized 1772; his martyrdom is depicted in T.S. Eliot's "The Murder in the Cathedral;" also observed as his feast day.

1563 Sebastianus Castellio, French Reformer, died; one of the most fervent champions of religious liberty in the 16th Century; translated the Bible into French and Latin.

1799 A royal proclamation approved Canadian laws making valid marriages performed by ministers other than those of the Church of England.

1808 Edwards A. Park, Congregational clergyman, was born in Providence, R.I.; one of the last champions of old New England theology; editor-in-chief, Bibliotheca Sacra (1852-84) (died 1900).

1832 Francis Pott, Anglican hymn writer, was born in England; translated Latin hymn, "The strife is o'er, the battle done;" wrote numerous hymns (Angel voices, ever singing) (died 1909).

1836 Caldwell County, Missouri was established as a Mormon refuge; friction developed with settlers and Mormons departed.

1843 Auguste H. Gosselin, Canadian priest and historian, was born; wrote six-volume history of Canadian Catholicism (died 1918).

1878 Pope Leo XIII restricted the use of the papal bull "to conferring, erecting, and dividing the major benefices, and to solemn acts of the Holy See;" also that it be written in common, rather than stylized, Latin.

1888 Josef Beran, Archbishop of Prague and primate of Czechoslovakia, was born in Pilsen; spent 17 years in Nazi and Communist prisons; freed in 1965 and went to Rome where he was elevated to cardinal (died 1968).

DECEMBER 30

268 St. Dionysius I, pope from 260 to 268, died; reorganized the church after the Decian persecutions (250-251); also observed as his feast day.

274 St. Felix I, pope from 269 to 274, died.

1370 Gregory XI, born Pierre Roger de Beaufort, was named pope, served until 1378; a nephew of Pope Clement VI, he became a cardinal at 17; the last French pope, he returned the papacy to Rome from Avignon (1377); issued bulls against John Wycliffe's doctrines.

1591 Innocent IX, pope from October 29, died.

1637 William Cave, patristic* scholar, was born in Pickwell, England; author of "Apostolici," a history of the apostles and fathers of the first three centuries (died 1713).

1794 Christian Metz, religious leader, was born in Neuwied, Germany; led 800 members of the Community of True Inspiration to a settlement in Ebenezer, N.Y. (near Buffalo) (1842-54); then to Iowa, where he created the Amana community (died 1867).

1865 Rudyard Kipling, British author (Treasure Island), was born in Bombay; wrote several Anglican hymns (God of our fathers, known of old; Father in heaven, who lovest all) (died 1936).

1890 Francis P. Keough, Archbishop of Baltimore (1947-61), was born in New Britain, Conn. (died 1961).

1894 The first services were held in the Mother Church of the Christian Science Church in Boston, with Septimus J. Hanna as the First Reader; dedication services were held the following Sunday (Jan. 6,1895).

1966 Pietro Ciriaci, prefect of the Congregation of the Council and a Vatican diplomat for 25 years, died in Rome at 81; elevated to cardinal 1953.

DECEMBER 31

Feast day of St. Sylvester I, pope from 314 to 335; long reign overshadowed by Emperor Constantine, who dominated the world of that time.

1384 John Wycliffe, English religious reformer, died at about 64; rector of Lutterworth (1374-84), sought to bring the church back to apostolic purity; urged state to intervene in handling church property in the interest of the poor; opposed by the clergy, denounced by the pope and Archbishop of Canterbury; called the "morning star of the Reformation;" influenced John Hus, Luther, and Calvin; expounded the doctrine of "dominion as founded in grace," by which all authority, ecclesiastical and secular, is derived from God and is forfeited when its possessor falls into mortal sin; tried twice but not sentenced; retired; initiated first complete translation of the Bible into English; after his death, he was condemned at the Council of Constance (1415) and his body was disinterred and burned.

1588 Luis de Granada, Spanish Dominican spiritual writer, died at about 84; made important contributions to teaching on Christian perfection; his works enjoyed lasting popularity.

1712 Peter Boehler, Moravian bishop, was born in Frankfurt, Germany; bishop of Unitas Fratrum* (1748-75); led group on move from Georgia to Bethlehem, Pa. (died 1775).

1770 The first New Year's Eve "watch night" service was held in St. George's Methodist Church in Philadelphia.

1786 Andrew Norton, the "pope of Unitarianism," was born in Hingham, Mass.; professor of sacred literature, Harvard Divinity School (1819-30); among the most eminent exponents of Unitarianism; author (The Evidences of the Genuineness of the Gospels); translated Dante's Divine Comedy into English (died 1853).

1891 Samuel Crowther, Nigerian Anglican bishop, died at about 82; an Anglican missionary to Nigeria, he was consecrated an Anglican bishop (1864), the first black African to receive that office.

GLOSSARY

agnosticism a theory that does not deny God but denies the possibility of knowing Him; a term usually attributed to Thomas H. Huxley.

Anabaptist a member of one of the radical movements of the 16th Century Reformation which wanted more radical reforms than the Protestant movement and insisted that only adult baptism was valid and held that Christians should not bear arms, use force, or hold government office.

antinomianism a term used to mean lawlessness in general; specifically, a doctrine that holds that faith alone is necessary for salvation.

apologist a person who argues in defense or justification of another person or cause; originally, Christian writers who defended their faith.

apostasy an abandonment of one's religious faith, political party, or cause.

Arianism doctrines of Arius (c 265-356), denying that Jesus was of the same substance as God and holding instead that he was only the highest of created beings.

Arminianism doctrine developed by Jacobus Arminius, which favored conditional predestination and opposed absolute predestination; espoused universal redemption.

asceticism the belief that the ascetic life releases the soul from bondage to the body and permits union with the divine.

Belgic confession drawn up by Guido de Brés in an attempt to conciliate the Netherlands government by repudiation of Anabaptists; adopted by the Synod at Antwerp in May 1566 and again by the Synod of Dort in 1619.

benefices revenue-producing endowment that is permanently attached to a church office; originally, a grant of land for life in return for services.

Carolingian dynasty that governed France (754-987), Germany (754-911), and Italy (774-901).

Catharist heretical sect, taking name from the Greek word, "cathari" (pure), flourished in Western Europe in the 12th and 13th centuries; protested corruption in religion.

Catholicos at one time used by bishops of metropolitan rank, now restricted to the two patriarchs of the Nestorian and Armenian churches.

chiliasts those who believe Christ will reign on earth 1000 years.

Coenobite a religious in vows who lives in a community.

concordance a reference book indicating and usually quoting in part all the passages of the Scripture in which a given word is found.

Covenanter Presbyterians, who in the 16th and 17th centuries, bound themselves by religious and political oaths to maintain their religion.

dialectical distinction from dogmatic method of ecclesiastical orthodoxy, seeking to preserve absolute of faith.

Disruption great split in the established Church of Scotland, when the Free Church was formed in 1843; split healed in 1929.

Doctor of the Church Church title given since the Middle Ages to certain Christian theologians of outstanding merit and acknowledged saintliness; originally four, but now expanded to about 30.

Donatism a schism in the African Church which split from Christianity by refusing to accept Caecilian as bishop of Carthage (311) on the grounds that his consecrator, Felix of Aptunga, had been a traditor (one who surrendered his Scriptures in the Diocletian persecution).

ecstatic one who loses his or her senses by the violence of divine action on the soul.

empiricism view that experience, especially of the senses, is the only source of knowledge.

exegete a person skilled in interpretation of the Scriptures.

Father of Church an ecclesiastical author whose authority on doctrinal matters carried special weight.

Fraticelli an anti-ecclesiastical sect which developed in the late 1200s from the Observantine Franciscans; later applied to all dangerous heretics.

Hasidism Jewish mystical movement founded in Poland in the mid-1700s, based on doctrine of the Cabala, which states that the forms of creation broke into shells when God poured His light into them.

Hermesian heresy named for Georg Hermes, who sought to adjust Roman Catholic theology to the philosophy of Kant.

Holy Alliance originally Russia, Austria, and Prussia (1815); later all powers except the Papal States, England, and the Sultan; became synonymous with the interests of the Great Powers.

iconoclasm action or doctrine of destroying sacred images, or venerated institutions, practices, or attitudes.

indulgences remission of punishment for sins; now confined to the Pope, but previously granted by metropolitans and bishops.

interdict an ecclesiastical punishment in the Roman Catholic Church excluding the faithful from participation in spiritual things, but without the loss of the communion of the church.

Kulturkampf repressive political movement in Germany in the 1870s against the Catholic Church, inspired by Bismarck, who feared Catholicism would endanger the unity of the German Empire.

lector a cleric of the second lowest of the four minor orders in the early Christian church, having the office of reading the sacred books in church.

Manichean from Manes (or Manichaeus) (c. 216-276), who taught that religion was to release the light which Satan had stolen; called for severe asceticism.

Melitian schism there were two such schisms: (1) based on objections of Melitius, bishop of Lycopolis, Egypt, to the return of the church (about 306) during a lull in the Diocletian persecution, and (2) rivalry between two orthodox groups in Antioch, one led by St. Meletius, bishop of Antioch (360).

Merovingian the Frankish dynasty reckoned as the "first race" of the kings of France, deriving its name from Merovech, the father of Childeric I.

Mishnah first section of the Talmud, the early oral interpretations of Scriptures.

Monotheletism 7th Century heresy, confession of only one will in the God-man; a heresy of political rather than religious origin.

mystic one who attains immediate knowledge of God in this present life through personal religious experience.

Nestorianism doctrines of Nestorius, 5th Century patriarch of Constantinople, asserting that Christ had two distinct natures, divine and human, and that the Virgin Mary should not be called the Mother of God.

Nicene creed a formal statement of the tents of the Christian faith and chiefly the doctrine of the Trinity, set forth by the Council of Nicaea (325).

nonjurors term originally applied to Anglican clergy who refused to take the oath of allegiance to William and Mary on the grounds they were bound by their oaths to James II.

nuncio (papal) permanent diplomatic representative of the Holy See, accredited to a civil government.

ontological a branch of metaphysics dealing with being in general.

patristic of or relating to the fathers of the very early Christian church or to their writings.

Pelagianism doctrine of Pelagius, British monk, which denied original sin and affirmed man's ability

	to be righteous by the exercise of free will; condemned as heresy in 417.
Pentateuch	the five books of Moses (Genesis, Exodus, Leviticus, Numbers, and Deuteronomy).
Pietism	a 17th Century movement stressing the "practice of godliness," begun by P. J. Spener with the purpose of infusing new life into Protestantism.
plurality	in the Anglican church, the holding of more than one ecclesiastical benefice without the special permission of the archbishop of Canterbury.
procurator	agent with power of attorney; in Roman Empire, a financial agent; bursar of a monastary.
prothonotary	one of a college of 12 ecclesiastics charged with the registry of important pontifical proceedings.
quietism	a form of mysticism which holds that man, to be perfect, must attain complete passivity and annihilation of the will, abandoning himself to God to such an extent that he cares neither for heaven nor hell, nor for his own salvation.
recusancy	refusal by Roman Catholics to attend Church of England services between the reigns of Henry VIII and George II.
sarum use	or Salisbury use; local medieval modification of the Roman rite used in the Salisbury Cathedral and elsewhere, which laid the foundation for the first Book of Common Prayer.
scholasticism	method of philosophical and theological speculation which aims at a better understanding of revealed truths.
Sephardic	one of the main divisions of Jews, a Spanish or Portuguese Jew.
Septuagint	oldest and most influential Greek version of the Hebrew Old Testament (according to legend, it was done by 72 translators - hence septuagint - for the library at Alexandria).
simony	buying or selling of ecclesiastical pardons, offices, or emoluments.
Socinianism	pertaining to the doctrine which includes the denial of the divinity of Jesus; founded by Laelius and Faustus Socinus, 16th Century theologians.
stake	Mormon territory consisting of a group of wards under the jurisdiction of a bishop.
Syriac	ancient Aramaic language spoken in Syria from the 3rd to 13th centuries.
tertiaries	according to Catholic law, secular tertiaries strive for perfection; religious organizations usually affiliated with one of the mendicant orders.
Tetrapolitan confession	a Protestant confession drawn up by M. Bucer and W. Capito at the Diet of Augsburg (1530), based on the Augsburg confession.
theosophy	a belief which purports to derive from the sacred books of India.
Thomistic	theological and philosophical system of St. Thomas Aquinas, which became the basis of scholasticism.
Torah	scroll containing the Pentateuch and the entire body of Jewish teachings.
transubstantiation	conversion of the whole substance of the bread and wine used in the Roman Catholic Mass into the whole substance of the body and blood of Christ.
Ubiquitarian (theory)	belief that Christ in His human nature is present everywhere.
ultramontanism	policy that absolute authority in Catholic Church lies with the pope.
Unitas Fratrum	"society of brethren," the named assumed by Bohemian Brethren.
Vedanta	one of the six schools of thought to which Indian philosophers adhered; attracted a number of Western thinkers in the 20th Century.
Vulgate (Bible)	Latin version of the Bible most widely used in the West.

BIBLIOGRAPHY

Almanac of American History, edited by Arthur M. Schlesinger Jr.; G.P. Putnam's Sons, New York 1983

Butler's Lives of the Saints, edited by Herbert Thurston and Donald Attwater; P.J. Kennedy and Sons, New York 1956

Catholic Encyclopedia

(The) Cross and the Crown by Norman Beasley; Duell, Sloan and Pearce Inc., New York 1963

Current Biography yearbooks (1960 on); H.W.Wilson Co., New York

Days and Customs of All Faiths by Rev. Howard V. Harper; Fleet Publishing Co., New York 1957

Dictionary of American Biography; Charles Scribner's Sons, New York (26 vols)

Dictionary of American History; Charles Scribner's Sons, New York 1976

Dictionary of Dates by Helen Rex Keller; Macmillan Co. 1936 (2 vols)

(A) Dictionary of Hymnology, edited by John Julian; Dover Publications, New York 1967 (2 vols)

Documents of American History, edited by Henry Steele Commager; Appleton-Century-Crofts, New York 1963 (7th edition)

Encyclopedia Americana

Encyclopaedia Britannica

Encyclopedia of American Facts and Dates, edited by Gordon Caruth; Harper & Row, New York 1987

Famous First Facts by Joseph N. Kane; H.W. Wilson Co., New York City 1964

Foxe's Book of Martyrs, edited by William B. Forbush; Universal Book and Bible House, Philadelphia 1926

(The) Gospel in Hymns by Albert E. Bailey; Charles Scribner's Sons, New York 1950

Handbook of Christian Feasts and Customs by Francis L. Weiser; Harcourt Brace & World Inc., New York 1952

Handbook of Denominations in the United States by Frank S. Mead; Abingdon Press, New York 1951 (4th edition)

Luther by Richard Marius; Lippincott Co., Philadelphia 1974

(The) Mormon Experience by Leonard J. Arrington and Davis Bitton; Alfred A. Knopf, New York 1979

Oxford Dictionary of the Christian Church, edited by F. L. Cross and E. A. Livingstone; Oxford University Press, Cambridge 1978

(A) Religious History of the American People by Sydney E. Ahlstrom; Yale University Press, New Haven 1972

(The New) Schaff-Herzog Encyclopedia of Religious Knowledge; Baker Book House, Grand Rapids, Mich. 1966 (22 vols)

Westminster Dictionary of Church History, edited by Jerald C. Brauer; Westminster Press, Philadelphia 1971

Who Was Who in America, Marquis Who's Who, Chicago (8 vols)

INDEX

B

Buddeus, Johannes F. ..... June 25, 1667
Buddha ..... Jan 9, 1978
Buddhism ..... July 15, 1904, May 24, 1956, Aug 31, 1981
Bufalo, St. Caspar del ..... Jan 2, 1836
Buffalo Synod, Lutheran Church ..... July 15, 1845
Bugenhagen, Johannes ..... June 24, 1485
Bukhari, al ..... July 21, 810
Bulgakov, Sergey N. ..... June 16, 1871
Bulgarian Orthodox Church ..... July 4, 1971
Bulkeley, Peter ..... Jan 31, 1583
Bull, George ..... Mar 25, 1634
Bullinger, (Johann) Heinrich ..... July 18, 1504
Bultman, Rudolph K. ..... Aug 20, 1884
Bunting, Jacob ..... May 13, 1779
Bunyan, John ..... Nov 30, 1628
Burchard, Samuel D. ..... Sep 6, 1812, Oct 29, 1884
Burgess, Alexander ..... Oct 31, 1819
Burgess, George ..... Oct 31, 1809
Burgess, John M. ..... Dec 8, 1962
Burkitt, Francis C. ..... Sep 3, 1864
Burleigh, William H. ..... Feb 12, 1812
Burleson, Rufus C. ..... Aug 7, 1823
Burnet, Gilbert ..... Sep 18, 1643
Burnet, Thomas ..... Sep 27, 1715
Burr, Aaron ..... Jan 4, 1716
Burrell, David J. ..... Aug 1, 1844
Burritt, Elihu ..... Dec 8, 1810
Burroughs, George ..... Aug 19, 1692
Burroughs, John C. ..... Dec 2, 1818
Burrows, Eva ..... May 2, 1986
Burton, Ernest D. ..... Feb 4, 1856
Burton, Robert ..... Feb 8, 1577
Busenbaum, Herman ..... Jan 31, 1668
Bushnell, Horace ..... Apr 14, 1802
Butchkaivitch, Monsignor ..... Mar 31, 1923
Butler, Alban ..... Oct 10, 1710
Butler, Charles ..... Aug 14, 1750
Butler, Henry M. ..... July 2, 1833
Butler, Joseph ..... May 18, 1692
Buttimer, Charles H. ..... Dec 15, 1982
Buttrick, Wallace ..... Oct 23, 1853
Buttz, Henry A. ..... Apr 18, 1835
Butzer, Martin ..... see Bucer, Martin
Buxtenhude, Dietrich ..... May 9, 1707
Byrd, William ..... July 4, 1623
Byrne, Andrew ..... Dec 5, 1802
Byrom, John ..... Feb 29, 1692

C

Cabrini, St. Francis Xavier ..... Nov 13, July 15, 1850, Nov 13, 1938
Cabrol, Fernand ..... Dec 11, 1855
Cadalus of Parma ..... Oct 28, 1061
Cadman, Samuel P. ..... Dec 18, 1864
Caedmon ..... Feb 11
Caesarius, St. ..... Aug 27, 542
Cafasso, St. Joseph ..... June 23, 1860
Caggiano, Antonio ..... Jan 30, 1889
Caird, John ..... Dec 15, 1820
Caius, St. ..... see Gaius, St.
Cajetan of Thiene, St. ..... Aug 8, Aug 7, 1547
Cajetan ..... Feb 20, 1469
Calamy, Edmund ..... Oct 29, 1666
Calasanctius, St. Joseph ..... Aug 25, Aug 27, 1648
Calderwood, David ..... Oct 29, 1650
Caldwell, James ..... Nov 24, 1781
Calfayan, Mampre ..... July 17, 1961
California ..... Dec 4, 1786
Calixtus I, St. ..... Oct 14
Calixtus II ..... Feb 9, 1119, Dec 13, 1124
Calixtus III ..... Jan 13, 1378, Apr 8, 1455, Aug 6, 1458
Calixtus, George ..... Dec 14, 1586
Calov(ius), Abraham ..... Apr 16, 1612
Calvin, John ..... July 10, 1509, Apr 23, 1538; *1541* Jan 20, Sep 13; May 25, 1564
Calvinists ..... July 9, 1572
Camara, Jaime de Barros ..... July 3, 1894
Cambridge Synod ..... June 8, 1647
Camerarius, Joachim ..... Apr 12, 1500
Cameron, Richard ..... July 22, 1680
Camillus of Lellis, St. ..... July 18, July 14, 1614
Campanella, Tomaso ..... Sep 5, 1568
Campanius, John ..... Aug 15, 1601
Campbell, Alexander ..... Sep 12, 1788
Campbell, John McL. ..... May 4, 1800
Campbell, Thomas ..... Feb 1, 1763
Campion, St. Edmund ..... Jan 25, 1540, Dec 1, 1581
Canada ..... June 24, 1615, June 5, 1640, Dec 25, 1650, Oct 20, 1670, Oct 10, 1710, Sep 2, 1750, June 22, 1774, Mar 12, 1786, Aug 5, 1789, June 28, 1793, Dec 29, 1799, Nov 2, 1809, Aug 25, 1824, Oct 2, 1828, Aug 18, 1832, June 7, 1870; *1875* Jan 1, June 15; Mar 4, 1881, Sep 5, 1883, June 10, 1886; *1889* Feb 5, Mar 20; Aug 15, 1890, Jan 1, 1968, Dec 18, 1985, Jan 1, 1986
Canadian Unitarian Council ..... May 24, 1962
Canali, Nicola ..... June 6, 1874

E

L

M

S

X

Y

Z